Global Teacher, Global Learner

Graham Pike & David Selby

Hodder & Stoughton
A MEMBER OF THE HODDER HEADLINE GROUP

To Rosie, Rowena, Ben and Jan
who have so much to learn
and, in their freshness of vision, so much to teach.

ISBN 0 340 40261 X

First published 1988
Impression number   17 16 15 14 13 12 11 10 9
Year   1999 1998 1997 1996 1995

Typeset by Tradespools Ltd, Frome, Somerset.
Printed in Great Britain for Hodder & Stoughton Educational,
a division of Hodder Headline Plc, 338 Euston Road,
London NW1 3BH by Redwood Books, Trowbridge, Wiltshire.

Contents

Acknowledgments

This book has arisen out of the World Studies Teacher Training Project undertaken by the Centre for Global Education (formerly called the World Studies Teacher Training Centre) at the University of York. The Project, which ran from September 1982 until August 1985, was funded by Christian Aid, the European Community, Oxfam and the Joseph Rowntree Charitable Trust.

The authors would like to thank the hundreds of teachers who participated in the Project through involvement in in-service courses and workshops and through trying out new ideas and activities in the classroom. Particular thanks are due to those who have contributed their own activities and who have written accounts of their classroom experience for inclusion in the book; due acknowledgments are given at appropriate points in the text. The authors are also indebted to the following for allowing the photographer into their classrooms: Elaine Hicks and her students at Cabot Primary School, St Paul's, Bristol; Richard Hedge and his students at Southway School, Plymouth; Susan Fountain and her students at Les Marroniers Primary School, International School of Geneva; Patrick Hazlewood and his students at Queen's School, Wisbech.

Special thanks are owed to Shirley Brewer, Secretary to the Project, to Sue Coward, Karen Freakley and Caroline MacRae who typed the manuscript, and to the authors' other colleagues at the Centre. Their response to the many pressures of both project and book preparation was admirable throughout.

Bärbel Selby and Kate Mosse also gave much to both the Project and book in their unfailing love, advice and support.

The publishers would like to thank the following for permission to reproduce copyright material: Prentice-Hall Inc., New Jersey; Harper & Row Inc., New York; ERIC Clearinghouse for Social Studies/Social Science Education, Indiana University; Century Hutchinson Limited; extracts from *Playfair: Everybody's Guide to Noncompetitive Play* © 1980 by Matt Weinstein and Joel Goodman, reproduced for Centre for Global Education by permission of Impact Publishers Inc., PO Box 1094, San Luis Obispo, California 93406, USA; National Education Association, Washington DC; Scott, Foresman & Co., Illinois; National Council for the Social Studies, Washington DC; One World Trust, London; Oxford University Press; The Woburn Press, London; Avery Publishing Group Inc., New Jersey; Religious Society of Friends, Philadelphia; Social Science Education Consortium, Boulder, Colorado; extracts from *Intercom 79: Teaching Towards Global Perspectives II*, copyright by Global Perspectives in Education, Inc., 45 John Street, Suite 1200, New York, NY 10038, USA, adapted with permission; Excel Inc., Illinois; Richard Boston/*Guardian*; Robin Richardson; Holt, Rinehart & Winston, New York; extract from *Voluntary Simplicity* by Duane Elgin © 1981, reprinted by permission of the author and John Brockman Associates Inc., New York; Hippo Books/Scholastic Publications Ltd; 'A Parable' by Jon Rye Kinghorn from *A Step-by Step Guide for Conducting a Consensus and Diversity Workshop in Global Education*, a program of the Commission of Schools, North Central Association and the Charles F. Kettering Foundation; extracts from *Open Minds to Equality* by Nancy Schniedewind/ Ellen Davidson © 1983, pp. 23–4, 25, 125, adapted by permission of Prentice-Hall, Inc., Englewood Cliffs, New Jersey; Collins Publishers; Professor Magnus Haavelsrud, Universitetet I Tromso; New Society Publishers, Philadelphia; The Southern Examining Group; Longman Group; Frankie Armstrong; UNICEF; Unesco, Paris; World Council of Churches, Geneva; Noel Gough, Victoria College, Australia; Simon & Schuster Inc., for the diagram from *Teaching for the Two-Sided Mind* © 1983 by Linda Verlee Williams.

The authors and publishers would also like to thank the following for permission to reproduce photographs and illustrations in this book: Michael Freeman, p. 204; Maidenhead Teachers' Centre, p. 265; Vic Fowler, pp. 101, 103, 105, 142, 179; Patrick Hazlewood, pp. 254, 255; Elaine Hicks and children from Cabot

Primary School, Bristol, p. 147; Susan Fountain, pp. 168–9; Helen Tann, pp. 44, 45, 99, 128, 152, 189; Ian Condon, pp. 276, 277; Ann and Bury Peerless Slide Resources and Picture Library, p. 247; Format Photographers/Margaret Murray, p. 143; Oxfam, p. 229; The Commonwealth Institute, p. 263; Lego UK Limited, p. 226; Tim Furniss, p. 32; Sally and Richard Greenhill, pp. 5, 73, 85.

Every effort has been made to trace and acknowledge ownership of copyright. The publishers will be glad to make suitable arrangements with any copyright holders whom it has not been possible to contact.

A note on terminology

The deliberate use of *she* and *her* throughout the text is an indication of the authors' desire to stimulate reflection upon the role of language in maintaining dominant patriarchal values.

The term *student* is preferred at all levels of schooling in that 'pupil' has come to be too closely associated with an outdated paradigm of schooling which this book seeks to challenge.

Photocopying

Teachers should note that the symbol means that the material on that page can be photocopied without restriction.

Part One

THE GLOBAL LEARNER

1 The four dimensions of globality

1. The spatial dimension

Emily

Emily is just fourteen.[1] She has lived all her life in a small, fairly isolated village on the North Yorkshire Moors. From the front door of the stone-built house where she lives, she looks out on a rugged skyline of heather-covered hills, stone walls and farm buildings broken only by

the plantations of the Forestry Commission where her father works. Emily rarely travels very far from home. Most of her friends and relatives live in the towns and villages scattered along the edges of the Moors. The family drives once a fortnight to York to buy food from a large supermarket; most other provisions are purchased at the small village grocery store. On warm summer weekends, the family takes day trips to beaches or towns on the nearby North Yorkshire coast. The longest journey of the year is usually the August camping holiday in Devon or Cornwall. Two weeks ago, as a birthday treat, Emily and her two best friends went with her family to see a popular film showing at a cinema in York. Afterwards, they went to a hamburger bar. Emily spends her leisure time listening to pop music on her new radio cassette recorder (a birthday present from her parents), watching television, reading and sometimes going walking with friends on the Moors. She also enjoys going to Girl Guides, dancing and new clothes. Her favourite jeans, pullover and blouse top she bought herself out of her birthday money. Emily goes to a comprehensive school in a nearby market town. School buses collect students from the villages in the morning and return them in the afternoon. In snowy weather, the buses often do not run. At the moment, Emily's thoughts are very much on which subjects to choose as fourth and fifth-year options. The options literature from school stresses how important it is to bear in mind possible job preference in deciding which subjects to take. Emily – who would like to be a social worker – is all too aware that jobs are scarce in North Yorkshire and that she may well have to leave the area eventually in search of job opportunities.

On first impression, Emily's world may seem small, enclosed and, save for its beauty and relative remoteness, unexceptional. If we dig a little deeper, however, we discover a personal world rich in connections with the wider world. Take Emily's birthday present and recent purchases. Her radio cassette recorder was made by a Japanese transnational corporation at one of its South American plants; her pullover was made in Mauritius, her jeans in Czechoslovakia at a factory under contract to the United Kingdom's largest jeans manufacturer; her blouse was made in the Philippines by women working in factories directly contravening Article 23 of the UN Declaration of Human Rights, the right to just and favourable conditions of work and

pay. Or, take the boxes of shopping in the boot of the family car as it is driven home from a typical supermarket expedition. The oranges are from Israel; the tea from Sri Lanka; the jars of jam from Belgium and Poland; the peanut butter from nuts grown in USA; the coffee blended at the UK branch of a US transnational company from beans grown in Brazil and Kenya. The family car, incidentally, is 'British' but contains 40% foreign-made parts and is made up of raw materials from over seventy different countries. The school bus is, similarly, a global cocktail of manufactured parts and raw materials.

The meal at the hamburger bar also connects Emily to the global. The bar in question is but one of a rapidly growing American fast-food chain springing up all over the world. The hamburgers are produced from South American beef cattle shipped to the UK in Greek-owned refrigeration ships.

Not only is Emily a participant in the web of global economic life; she is also caught up in the global communications system and an emerging global culture. Watching her family's Japanese television set, she often learns of news events on the other side of the world within minutes of their happening. She watches US and British drama series that are also screened, with voice-overs where necessary, to millions of people around the world. She is tempted by adverts to buy products that are being similarly promoted in every continent save, perhaps, Antarctica. At the cinema, she watches a film enjoying international box office success. At home she listens and dances to pop releases that are being sold in virtually every country in the world, grossing the transnational record companies millions of pounds in sales. Her Mauritian pullover contains internationally-standardised washing instruction signs; the school bus driver responds to internationally-standardised road signs.

Emily and her family are also inescapably enmeshed in global issues, trends and developments. Her father recalls how long and often he had to queue to buy petrol at the time of the Arab-Israeli war of 1973 and his alarm at the prospect of life without a car. Steep rises in oil prices or the recurrence of an oil supply crisis, as predicted by some, are worries that remain somewhere at the back of his mind. On clear days, Emily's mother is sometimes made uneasy by the sight across the Moors of the Fylingdales early warning station, an important component part of the Western defence system. Could such a lonely local spot, a tourist attraction in summer, become in one horrific instant both a principal agent and object in a global nuclear war, she wonders? Emily sees the Moors as beautiful and unchanging, not as yet recognising the first signs of the environmental impact of acid rain dispersed on air currents by industry to the south and west; the same acid rain which is slowly poisoning the lakes and forests of Scandinavia and East and West Germany. Nor does Emily recognise that her employment prospects are inextricably bound up with the well-being or otherwise of the global economy or that she may find herself as an adult living and earning her livelihood in a multi-ethnic community, a possible future for which school has manifestly failed to prepare her.

Spatial globality

Like Emily, almost all of us are caught up in a network of links, interactions and relationships that encircle the planet like a giant and intricate spider's web so that the wider world is a pervasive and ubiquitous element in the routines of everyday life. The term 'global interdependence' is often used to describe this modern reality. It would be both ecologically false and historically parochial, however, to think of global interdependence as a purely contemporary phenomenon. Environmental interdependence, the connections that link all life forms into a mutually-sustaining web, pre-dates human society at all levels, local to global. It is also the case that evidence of global interdependence of lands and peoples can be found over the last five hundred years dating from the age of Western European exploration. The decimation of the native American population through war and the importation of new diseases in the century after Columbus, the presence in Georgian London of a black population numbering about 20,000 and the decline of the Indian cotton industry in the eighteenth and early nineteenth centuries are but three early manifestations of the impact of the trend towards globalisation.[2] What sets contemporary global interdependence apart as markedly different in character is its *degree of frequency*, its *depth* and its *scope*.

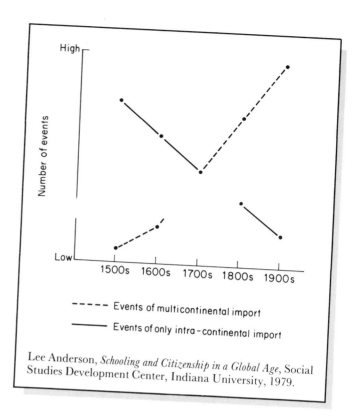

Lee Anderson, *Schooling and Citizenship in a Global Age*, Social Studies Development Center, Indiana University, 1979.

If we listed for each of the last five centuries the major events that have shaped history in the six inhabited continents of the world and classified those events into either events of intra-continental significance or events carrying significance for more than one continent, we would find that the latter overtake and then increasingly outstrip the former the closer we come to the present day. The *degree of frequency* of events involving global interdependencies has risen – and continues to rise – dramatically, whilst there has been a corresponding falling away in the number of events of consequence for only one continent.[3] The same findings would result were we to repeat the exercise a second time, analysing a range of national as opposed to continental histories over the past five centuries.

The *depth* and *scope* of global interdependence (i.e. the range and number of people and the range and number of human activities and concerns affected by interactions of a global nature) has also mushroomed dramatically in the contemporary world. Whereas in the past the impact of global interdependence was relatively limited, there are now almost no people and very few activities not affected in some part at least by the interdependent nature of the world. Emily is no exception singled out for sake of effect. Global interdependencies have become 'operationally immediate' for nearly all of us.[4] They affect the purity of the air we breathe and the water we drink, the levels of employment and inflation, the price of tea, the level of taxation, fuel costs, the survival prospects of wildlife, the availability and subject matter of the books and magazines we read, the changing respective roles of women and men in society, our relative peacefulness or unpeacefulness of mind and our image of the future.

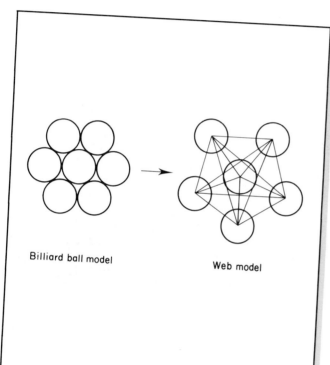

Billiard ball model

Web model

The transformation of the world from a *collection* to a *system* of lands and peoples can be represented symbolically as a transformation from a 'billiard ball' to a 'web' global model. On the billiard table, only the outer surface of the balls (states) are in contact. There is surface interaction, even occasional collision, but the structure/relationships within each ball (state) are not significantly affected. In the modern world, the 'billiard ball' model has given way to a far more complex and tangled web of global relationships so that states are closely interwoven.

As we gallop towards the twenty-first century, we are witnessing a relatively advanced stage in the continuing and quickening transformation of the world from a *collection* of many lands and peoples to a *system* of many lands and peoples. What, briefly, are some of the principal factors behind this 'profound change in the human condition'?[5]

In the first place, the isolating effects of distance have been and continue to be overcome as a result of the technological and electronic revolutions in transport and communications. Advances in transport have caused the world to 'shrink' geographically in that people and bulk goods can now be speedily conveyed between one part of the globe and another. Advances in communications have shrunk social, economic and political time and distance. When President Lincoln was shot, it took five days for the news to reach London (there was no telegraph cable in 1865). When President Reagan was shot in 1981, a journalist working one block away from the shooting got word of it by telephone from the editor of the *Spectator* in London who happened to see a television re-run of the shooting shortly after it occurred.[6]

Secondly, since about 1500, people have taken advantage of shrinking geographical distance to move around the world in great numbers. The period of exploration and colonisation was marked by the settlement, often permanent, of Europeans in the Americas, Asia, Africa and Australasia; in the post-colonial period, European and North American societies have become more culturally and ethnically mixed as a result of a northwards migration of peoples. The movement and re-settlement of peoples has helped create a complex web of transnational ties, loyalties and sentiments within national communities. It has also been a potent factor in the creation of a shared global culture.

The shrinking of the world and the migration of peoples have both influenced and been influenced by the emergence of an economically-interdependent world. Exploration and colonisation forged the beginnings of a global trading system in which the colonies supplied Europe with food and other resources and, in turn, became consumers of European manufactured goods. Built early into the system of the major colonial powers was a worldwide division of labour so that various zones were 'assigned specific economic roles, developed different class structures, used consequentially different modes of labor control, and profited unequally from the workings of the system.'[7] Not only did the division of labour help integrate the world economically, it also carried the seeds of the unequal distribution of wealth in the contemporary global economy. The demands of industriali-

Multi-ethnic Britain enmeshed in a world trading system

sation in Europe and North America strongly reinforced global economic connections, consolidated the global division of labour and accelerated the widening of the gap between rich and poor lands.[8] Today, we have a world in which the standard of living and lifestyle to which Emily is accustomed is dependent upon legions of people beyond the shores of her own country, many of them poor and disadvantaged and now lending their voices to rising demands for a global redistribution of wealth.

Ecologically, too, there is growing planetary awareness of the effect humankind is having on the global ecosystem and of the fact that the different regions of the world are environmentally interdependent. Acid rain and radiation ignore border posts. The destruction of the tropical rain forest, some scientists predict, may seriously affect oxygen levels across both hemispheres. The spread of deserts, others argue, is in part attributable to a hotting up of the atmosphere caused by carbon dioxide released principally by northern industrial countries.

In the first lesson of our two-year course on world studies, my class of fourth-year students – seated in a circle – were asked to stand on their desks and remove their shoes. 'Examine your shoes and find out where they were made,' I asked. 'If you can't be sure that the raw materials came from Britain and that the shoes were made in Britain, throw them into the centre of the circle.' Most shoes were duly despatched into the circle. Cardigans and pullovers followed, as did ties. The students, new to me, were soon wondering how many more stages I had in mind. The exercise served as a vivid and afterwards well-remembered illustration of our dependency upon places beyond these shores for many of the things we take for granted.

A Leicestershire secondary teacher.

Eco-awareness, itself a response to the damage done to the environment by humankind in the industrial age, is a contributory factor in the transition to globality.

The world, then, is taking on an increasingly systemic quality. To touch any part of the spider's web is to trigger vibrations in many – sometimes all – other parts. A distant political struggle is a luggage search for plane passengers at Manchester airport. An upheaval in Iran is a lowered thermostat in Buenos Aires. An assassination in India sparks off demonstrations in South London. A nuclear power station disaster in the Ukraine is a meat emergency in Cumbria. The uranium requirement of French nuclear power stations is the desecration of sacred homelands in Queensland, a sneeze in Hong Kong becomes an epidemic in the Outer Hebrides. Insights from General Systems Theory help us to comprehend the nature of the emergent global system. According to Systems Theory, nothing can be fully understood in isolation but must be seen as part of a dynamic, multi-layered system; relationship is everything; the activity of the system comprises the simultaneous and interdependent interaction of its many component parts; the nature of the system is always more than the mere sum total of its separate parts.

We speak an Anglo-Saxon form of a Germanic language that contains more original Latin than English words. Our religion is Palestinian, with its specific formulations into denominations made chiefly in Rome, Germany, England, Scotland, and Holland. Our Bible is translated partly from Hebrew, partly from Greek. We drink coffee first grown in Ethiopia and adopted in Arabia, tea discovered in China, beer first brewed in ancient Mesopotamia or Egypt, hard liquor invented in mediaeval Europe. Our bread, beef, and other meats are from plants and animals first domesticated in Asia; our potatoes, corn, tomatoes, and beans were first used by the American Indians; likewise tobacco. We write an Etruscan-Roman variant of a Greek form of an alphabet invented in or near Phoenicia by a Semitic people on the basis of nonalphabetic writing in still more ancient cultures; its first printing took place in Germany, on paper devised in China.

A.L. Kroeber's characterisation of American culture, cited in Lee Anderson, *Schooling and Citizenship in a Global Age*, Social Studies Development Center, Indiana University, 1979.

To see the world as a system is to raise questions about some dearly-held articles of faith and to blur some conventional dichotomies and distinctions. Within an interactive system in which relationship is everything and in which nothing can be understood in isolation, what are we to make of terms such as 'national interest', 'national history', 'national culture' and, indeed, 'nation state'? 'Columbus' voyages,' writes Lee Anderson, 'do not mark the beginning of American history; quite the opposite, they mark the end of an American history as such and the beginning of a world history, part of which transpires in the continents of North and South America.'[9] The still frequently-drawn distinction between 'home', 'domestic' and 'internal' affairs on the one hand, and 'foreign' or 'external' affairs on the other, also fails to mirror today's reality. Seemingly 'domestic' events are often manifestations of global interactions and proceed themselves to impact on the global stage whilst so-called 'foreign' events can have profound domestic repercussions. The conventional dichotomy between 'local' and 'global', so often favoured in the construction of school humanities syllabuses, also begs some important questions. Is the can of Australian peaches Emily finds on a York supermarket shelf a 'local' or 'global' phenomenon? Would a population shift from dormitory villages back to York city centre on account of escalating fuel prices be a 'local' or 'global' trend? Such 'glocal' examples reflect the interactive nature of the contemporary world system; a compartmentalised view of reality is essentially distorting.

There is a tendency, too, to interchange the terms 'global' and 'international' thus disguising the fact that the contemporary world has witnessed a proliferation of *non-state actors* – individuals and organisations – operating across national frontiers. National governments handle and channel a decreasing proportion of all the relations that global interdependence has spawned. There are international and supernational organisations, such as the United Nations and the European Community, which have developed some degree of autonomy from and authority over the nation states of which they are composed. There is also a multitude of non-governmental organisations transcending national boundaries. Emily is a member of one such organisation – the World Association of Girl Guides and Girl Scouts. Others include the International Red Cross, the World Council of Churches, the World Confederation of Labour, transnational terrorist or freedom fighting groups and transnational corporations. The latter are, perhaps, the most influential of all non-state actors. Described by the Brandt Report as 'major actors in the world's political economy', it has been estimated that the major transnationals may control 75% of world trade and employ 20% of the world's pool of labour.[10] Local and regional governments and pressure groups are also beginning to bypass national governments and enter the global arena. The former governor of California, Jerry Brown, negotiated directly with Mexico and Canada for future natural gas supplies.[11] Sheffield has agreed a peace treaty with the Russian city of Donetsk. Representatives of 22 native American tribes travelled to the Middle East to initiate talks with the Organisation of Petroleum Exporting Countries.[12] Then there are the myriad ways in which individuals and groups of individ-

> Today issues are so interconnected that two states may be allies in one issue area and antagonists in another, trading concessions in the latter for continued support in the former. Today situations are so complex that bureaucrats in several countries may form a coalition to oppose convergence among their respective chiefs of state.
>
> James Rosenau, 'Teaching and learning in a transnational world', *Educational Research Quarterly*, Vol. 8, No. 1, 1983, p. 30.

> There is no one single, unambiguous national interest on most issues. In the arena of world politics the interests of organized labor can be quite different and, indeed, conflict with the interests of the managers of multinational firms. The interests of midwest wheat farmers can be very different from the interests of urban consumers. The interests of Idaho potato farmers can be very different from the interests of Connecticut chicken breeders. The interests of California can be different from the interests of North Dakota. In short, in an increasing number of issues of international policy there exists a plurality of conflicting interests in contrast to a single national interest.
>
> Lee Anderson, *Schooling and Citizenship in a Global Age*, Social Studies Development Center, Indiana University, 1979.

uals interact with people in other lands. Correspondence, family visits, holidays abroad, study tours, business trips and school exchanges are but some. A more recent development, to which we will return later in this chapter, has been the growth of loose transnational networks of ecological, feminist, peace and other alternative movements. The trend towards a greater complexity and intensity of contact between peoples globally is unmistakable.

Some educational implications

Emily's present and future are an increasingly global present and future. We are often told that formal schooling aims to help the young make sense of the world in which they live. We are also told that schooling seeks to endow the young with the skills and insights which will enable them to be effective participants in a democratic society. To what extent does Emily's schooling help her to make sense of a world in which the interdependence of lands and peoples is one of its most salient features? In which her life will be buffeted by events often happening on the other side of the globe? To what extent is school equipping Emily with the capacities and skills for effective participation in a fast-changing systemic world? Should Emily, for whatever reason, freely make the extraordinary mental decision to limit her life to the skyline she sees from her front door, she will still not be able to make sense of her narrow world unless she is capable of interpreting what she sees within a global framework. Some suggested activities for setting students on the path towards acquiring that framework are given in the following table. Other techniques can be found in Part Two.

Ideas for teaching/learning about spatial globality/interdependence

Dependency Webs 1

Students, working in small groups, map out on a large sheet of paper some of the ways in which different people in the locality are dependent on each other.

Dependency Webs 2

Students each make a list of the people they have depended upon since waking up that morning, explaining the nature of the dependency in each case. Lists are shared in groups. The students go on to discuss questions such as 'do the people you list in any way depend upon you?', 'who do the people you list themselves depend on?' and 'are there different degrees/kinds of dependency?' Individuals then draw their own dependency webs reflecting points raised in discussion.

Student Survey

Students exchange information about where they were born, where they have lived and where they have travelled (having first had the opportunity to carry out some research at home). On a large world map, each student's route to the locality is marked using coloured pins and wool. Date details can be attached to the wool. Discussion follows as to what the map suggests about the relationship of the locality to the wider world.

Post Survey

Over a two or three-month period, each student keeps a record of all letters, postcards and parcels received and sent from home. Each week time is set aside for students to indicate on a class map what foreign countries, if any, they have received mail from and sent mail to (the countries are linked to the home area by means of pins and wool).

At the end of the survey, the percentage of foreign and domestic post for the class as a whole is calculated and significant features of the map discussed.

World in the Classroom

Students, working in pairs, are given fifteen minutes to write down as many raw materials as possible that they find present in the classroom. The raw materials can be seen, e.g. 'wood in desk tops', or unseen, e.g. 'copper in the electric wires' or 'oil in our nylon shirts'. Then, using reference lists giving details of countries and their principal exports, they make educated guesses as to what countries are actually represented, through their raw materials, in the classroom. Students proceed to draw World in the Classroom maps with arrows going from the exporting country to their own part of the world. Explanations are written along the arrows.

Variations: 1 students can be given a raw materials checklist for the first part of the activity; 2 students can pin or stick notices to things found in the classroom listing the likely raw materials in each and, after research, adding the likely country of origin (total accuracy is neither possible nor essential); 3 each student is given a particular country, researches what it exports and then examines the classroom to determine the degree to which the country might be present on account of its raw materials.

World in the School

A useful continuation of World in the Classroom. Students divide into small groups and each group investigates some aspect of the school's connection with the wider world. One group visits the school's kitchens and dining hall to find out what basic provisions are being used and where they come from. Another group visits the wood and metalwork shops to talk to the teachers about the raw materials they use and their country of origin. Another conducts a simplified *Student Survey* for a whole year group. Another surveys the teaching staff to find out if there are teachers who were born outside Britain and who have studied and worked abroad whilst another interviews the careers teacher about the possibilities for work overseas and about the impact of international events on job prospects. Other groups investigate the extent to which foreign and international books, magazines and works of reference are available in the school library, the language department's links with foreign schools and the head-teacher's perspective on the school's various connections with the wider world.

World in the Pantry

Students make a list of the food items in their home pantry, cupboard or deep freeze and note the place of origin of each item. Back at school they prepare individual or collective World in the Pantry maps with arrows drawn from the exporting country to their own part of the world (name of food along the arrow).

It is likely that students will encounter certain problems in that many food products will have been grown abroad and then processed in the United Kingdom. Such difficulties provide a springboard for introducing the concepts of 'primary', 'secondary' and 'tertiary' industry and for beginning an explanation of 'First World' import controls on finished products and the reasons behind those controls.

Variations: World in the Clothes Cupboard/ World in the Bathroom. Students make a list of clothes in the home and/or items in the bathroom (towels, soaps, toothpastes, cosmetics, etc.) and note the place of origin of as many items as possible.

Supermarket Survey

Students visit a local supermarket and note down products on the shelves and their country of origin. Returning to school, they present their findings in written or illustrative form.

Factory Visits

Groups of students visit local factories to discover the places of origin of the raw materials being used and to determine how dependent the factory is on raw materials from abroad. They also ask for facts and figures concerning the finished products. What proportion are sold to the home market? What proportion are exported? To what countries? By what means and routes are they transported there?

Flower Shop Survey

Students visit a flower shop in mid-winter to find out where the flowers on sale come from and the name of the exporting organisation. Back at school they research into the countries of origin of the flowers.

To what extent are these countries in fact in possession of surplus land for flower production given the needs of their own population? Who benefits from the growing and exporting of flowers?

World in the Garden

Students investigate gardening books and visit a local garden centre to find out about the countries of origin of plants now common features of gardens in the United Kingdom. When were they brought to the country? By whom? They write to environmental and gardening organisations to find out about the current international trade in plants. To what extent are species being endangered in their original habitat by the thirst for ever more beauty and variety in the garden?

Local Newspaper Survey

Students bring to class successive copies of the daily or weekly local newspaper(s). Working in small groups they cut out news items which either directly or indirectly show the connection between the locality and the wider world. As the collection of cuttings grows, students are en-couraged to categorise them under different headings of their own choice (some cuttings will reveal economic and trading links, others cultural links through the migration of peoples, etc.). Group scrapbooks can be built up. Alternatively a World in (name of locality) bulletin board can be regularly refreshed with newly-discovered news items. See p.11.

World in the Furniture Store

Students visit a local furniture store to find out about the types of wood used in the furniture on sale and the countries of origin of different woods. They also enquire about the turnover of the different types of furniture. Back in school, they research into the destruction of the tropical rain forests and discuss the issues raised by the popular demand for mahogany and other tropical woods. Is the destruction of the rain forests a 'local' or 'global' problem?

Foreigners

People from overseas temporarily resident in or visiting the locality are interviewed about the extent to which the United Kingdom is 'visible' in their own country. Are British products on sale? If so, what? Does Britain feature in news and current affairs programmes on radio and television? Are British programmes broadcast? What kind of image of Britain and the British do people have? Are there many British visitors?

Travel Agency

Groups of students visit a travel agency by prior arrangement. They go through the motions of arranging an imagined class trip to a faraway destination they have chosen in advance. Alternative forms of transport, routes and timings for each stage of the journey there and back are negotiated, costs calculated and things to do when they have reached their destination discussed. Practical matters such as passports, visas, foreign languages and necessary injections are also entered into. Back in school, groups prepare to present their journey to the rest of the class using the medium or media of their choice.

A moving reminder of the power of music

District Six; York Arts Centre.

DISTRICT Six played the Arts Centre last night to an enthusiastic audience.

The session opened with a number typical of the South African township jazz style. Jim Dvorak provided some delicate playing on whistles and pipes, followed by a series of expert solos from Mervyn Africa on keyboards, Brian Abrahams, drums, Bill Katz on fretless bass and Harrison Smith on saxes.

The numbers were long but few. All contained a ran... le th...

and technical terms. The sweet rhythmic Soweto sound (South West Township to the uninitiated) moved through some exotic jangled but controlled phrases leading to Blakey-style modern jazz, often returning to finish with the original Soweto melody.

The township themes were beautifully d...

as close to its African roots as we are likely to hear in York.

The expertise of the musicians was unquestionable. Brian Abrahams demonstrated a controlled power of his percussion instruments and a fine sense of timing, Bill Katz opened the last number with a beautiful deep blue solo on bass.

District Six, Capetown, gave a stunning performance in his piano solo in Song For Winnie Mandela. His technique of hitting the keys with the side of his hands, almost chopping out the notes, and at the same time demonstrating incred... ...d and perfect rhythm was ... ...to watch and

Exhibition honours Mandela

AN EXHIBITION on the imprisoned South African leader Nelson Mandela and his wife Winnie is being displayed by York Anti-Apartheid Group at York Central Library.

It includes photographs depicting the life of Mandela and ordinary black people under apartheid.

South African newspapers are seen alongside records, T-shirts and books produced to honour Mandela.

The exhibition was opened by ... Mzamo, a senior member of ... National Congress, ... that

TRYAR TRAVEL LTD.
28/30 CASTLEGATE, MALTON
Telephone: 0653-7638
MINI-CRUISE to DENMARK
Only £18 for 3 Days*
Available: ... 19, 20, 23 &

LEARN KARATE
...e practical self defence
...defending oneself in to-
LEBURY 3rd DAN BLACK
Semi-Contact Champion
... Belts, is starting

Tory vote to keep grain levy shocks MP

MRS ELIZABETH Shields, the MP for Ryedale, is staggered that Conservatives voted to keep a controversial grain-mountain levy.

Britain's farmers are paying £3.37 for every ton of cereal produced, as the Common Market tries to fund its multi-million pound intervention policy.

The National Farmers' Union, the grain merchants and the ma... ...rs were against the ...hields.

...tally, she added, did ...owledge the charge ...posedly made on all ...et farmers to cover ...posing of the grain ...putting millions of ...ore.

...the levy was that ...were growing

Global Town Trails

Teachers devise a town trail leaflet to alert students to the many ways in which the town is linked to the wider world. Students inspect shop windows for goods from overseas, visit local industries to find out about imports and exports, visit local higher education institutions to find out about links with abroad (e.g. foreign students, home students studying abroad, courses with international dimensions), visit local tourist offices to find out about foreign visitors to the area and inspect buildings (pubs, churches, etc.) which have or have had special foreign connections.

The Name Behind the Name

Students watch The Shy Giants, a filmstrip with accompanying cassette produced by the Bedford World Development Action Group (available from the Centre for World Development Education). The filmstrip shows how seemingly local businesses in Bedford are often part of transnational corporations which have outlets in many countries. Students go on to research into shops in the local high street through interviews and visits to the local chamber of commerce and public library. Having identified the corporations behind the high street shops, they write to each corporation for a copy of its annual report *(usually available free of charge). This will give a clear — and usually attractively presented — picture of the corporation's international operation.*

It's a Small World!

The class forms a person to person link with another class in a school in a distant country. Each student writes giving the name and address of the person she knows in the world who lives closest to that school ('closest' may be tens, hundreds or thousands of miles away!). Students in the sister class respond by giving the name and address of the person they know who lives closest to the person their counterpart has named. Each side then writes to the person they have named asking if they know someone who lives even closer to the person the other student has named. The process continues until people

are identified on either side who actually know each other. This experiment, which is done as an occasional project over a period of time, often has startling results in that it usually takes very few steps to make the link.

Some of the above ideas have been developed from suggestions in Taylor, N., and Richardson, R., Change and Choice: Britain in an Interdependent World, Centre for World Development Education, 1980 and Johnson, J., and Benegar, J., Global Issues in the Intermediate Classroom, ERIC/SSEC/GPE, 1981. The World in the Bathroom activity has been used successfully by Sandra Charity of Harehills Middle School, Leeds and The Name Behind the Name is inspired by the work of Paul Weeden of Brislington School, Bristol, on teaching and learning about transnational corporations.

---

2. The temporal dimension

Eastern mystics have long perceived intuitively what twentieth-century physicists have now confirmed – that space and time are inseparably connected. 'We look around,' writes Daisetz Suzuki, 'and perceive that every object is related to every other object not only spatially, but temporally. As a fact of pure experience, there is no space without time, no time without space; they are interpenetrating.'[13] The Eastern sages similarly see past, present and future as in dynamic relationship rather than as a linear succession of two separate blocks of time with a fleeting instant caught between them. This important insight has been taken up by Western futurists. 'What we take to be the present necessarily refers back and forward in time,' writes Richard Slaughter. 'Our reality grows out of past history, but it is powerfully shaped too by what we believe about the future. Similarly, our decisions, the technologies we collectively

deploy, the ideologies and ends we pursue all frame and condition the world of our descendants. In other words, whatever we do *we cannot be uninvolved.* This is immensely important for such a view leads to a deep sense of historical process and connectedness in space and time.'[14] Time is, thus, seamless and interactive. Temporal globality complements and is in symbiotic relationship with spatial globality. Together they provide a framework for making sense of an interdependent world in which the rate of change is constantly quickening.

The pace of change

As with interdependence, it is important to recall that change is not new; what is new is the *degree of change.* Change has in fact changed.[15]

The J curves illustrated below are but a few examples of the geometric or exponential rate of change experienced by most areas of human activity in the recent past. Contemporary global society is beyond the bend of most J curves. Humankind has reached the stage where change occurs so swiftly that it would appear essential that we continuously reassess our values, beliefs and patterns of behaviour. The question is: have we developed the capacities, insights and skills that would enable us to carry out that process of constant re-assessment? Alvin Toffler coined the term 'future shock' in 1970 to describe the 'psychological disease' afflicting the many unable to cope with the velocity and pervasiveness of change.[16]

Alternative futures

The central themes of futurist thinking have been summarised as follows:

- There exist a wide variety of *alternative futures* at all levels.
- These are commonly divided into *possible*, *probable* and *preferable* futures (i.e. futures that *might just* come about, that are *likely* to come about and that we *would like* to come about given our values and priorities).
- They suggest a need for *conscious choice*, *participation* and *purposive action*.
- The future is *not predictable or predetermined*, but may be affected by individuals.

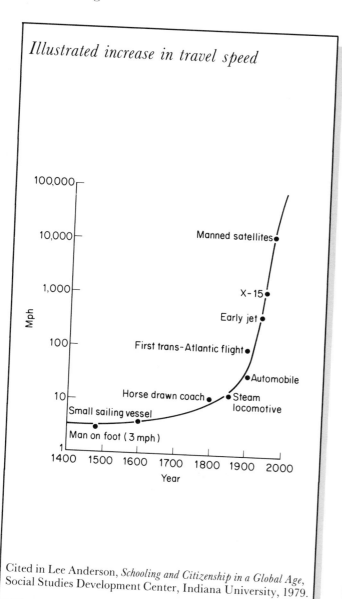

Illustrated increase in travel speed

Cited in Lee Anderson, *Schooling and Citizenship in a Global Age*, Social Studies Development Center, Indiana University, 1979.

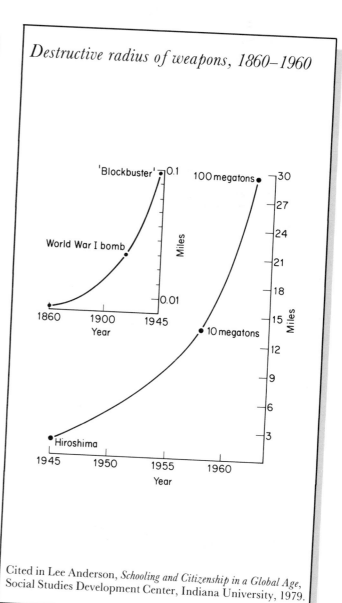

Destructive radius of weapons, 1860–1960

Cited in Lee Anderson, *Schooling and Citizenship in a Global Age*, Social Studies Development Center, Indiana University, 1979.

- Human *actions and decisions* (or their lack) *shape the future*.
- The present period is *unique* and *crucial for all future generations*.
- It is necessary to exert *human control* over *change processes*.
- In so doing, '*preaction*' is preferable to '*crisis learning*'.
- *Holistic, global* and *long range perspectives* are indispensable.
- *Images* of the future guide actions in the present and affect what seems possible in the future.[17]

A major premise underpinning the ten themes is that human beings, individually and collectively, can consciously strive to both anticipate and influence a future that is not predetermined. In so doing, it is implied, they will probably wish to revise their present patterns of behaviour not only in the light of their image of a preferred future but also in the light of a more thorough-going understanding of the present, bred of a profounder appreciation of past trends and developments. A further implication is that humankind should not rely too heavily on experts. 'If we leave the experts to think about the future for us,' says James Robertson, 'we thereby choose a certain kind of future – a future dominated by experts.'[18]

Robertson is but one of a number of contemporary thinkers who have explored possible, probable and preferred futures. In *The Sane Alternative*, he identifies five future scenarios to which people subscribe. His preference is for the fifth but he acknowledges that any one of the five – or, indeed, a blend of two or more – might happen. They are:

- **Business as usual**. The future will not be radically different from the present. Change there will be but the problems we face, the methods by which we handle them and our outlook and attitudes will not fundamentally shift.

- **Disaster**. The future will see an intensification of the crises the world now faces, such as the threat of nuclear war, famine and environmental degradation, leading at some point to global breakdown.

> Time present and time past
> Are both perhaps present in time future,
> And time future contained in time past
>
> T.S. Eliot, *Four Quartets*

> In this spiritual world there are not time divisions such as the past, present and future; for they have contracted themselves into a single moment of the present where life quivers in its true sense... The past and the future are both rolled up in this present moment of illumination, and this present moment is not something standing still with all its contents, for it ceaselessly moves on.
>
> Daisetz Teitaro Suzuki, *On Indian Mahayana Buddhism*, Harper & Row, 1968.

> Imagine a clock face with sixty minutes on it. Let the clock stand for the time men have had access to writing systems. Our clock would thus represent something like three thousand years, and each minute on our clock fifty years. On this scale, there were no significant media changes until about nine minutes ago. At that time, the printing press came into use in Western culture. About three minutes ago, the telegraph, photograph, and locomotive arrived. Two minutes ago: the telephone, rotary press, motion pictures, automobile, aeroplane and radio. One minute ago, the talking picture. Television has appeared in the last ten seconds, the computer in the last five, and communications satellites in the last second. The laser beam – perhaps the most potent medium of communication of all – appeared only a fraction of a second ago. It would be possible to place almost any area of life on our clock face and get roughly the same measurements.
>
> Neil Postman and Charles Weingartner, *Teaching as a Subversive Activity*, Penguin, 1971.

- **Authoritarian Control**. Future disaster will be averted by strong authoritarian government which will conserve and distribute dwindling resources and enforce order.

- **The Hyper-expansionist (HE) Future**. Present problems will be overcome by accelerating the development of, and the more effective use of, science and technology. The acronym

HE, says Robertson, helpfully conveys that a significant number of adherents to this view are male.

- **Sane, Humane, Ecological (SHE) Future**. The future will require a radical change of direction involving decentralisation, ecological concern and supportive human relationships globally. The acronym SHE helpfully conveys that exponents of this view regard current world crises as a crisis of masculine exploitative values.[19]

With due caution, it can be helpful to differentiate two broad modes of thinking amongst futurists. First there are those who envision the future as a fairly strict continuation of the main trends of the past and present. Such *extrapolationists* can either take an optimistic (cornucopian) or a pessimistic stance. Hyper-expansionists usually fall into the former category whilst the exponents of disaster fall into the latter. Ronald Higgins, for instance, in *The Seventh Enemy* identifies seven main threats to human survival: population explosion, food shortage, scarcity of natural resources, pollution and degradation of the environment, nuclear energy, uncontrolled technology and moral blindness coupled with political inertia. His examination of the evidence and his experience of central government leads him to the gloomy conclusion that there can be no better future because, although humankind could hypothetically resolve the first six problems, moral blindness and political inertia are too entrenched for us to act in time.[20]

Whilst extrapolationists project forward from the more prominent trends in contemporary society, *transformationalists* look for, often marginal, shifts in culture, values and patterns of behaviour which might collectively herald a forthcoming leap into new forms of consciousness and social organisation. Willis Harman writes of 'lead indicators of impending social change' that have been visible since the 1960s – such as alienation, purposelessness, lowered sense of community and increased rates of mental illness, violent crime and social disturbance – and which are the early warning signals of a coming transformation to a 'transindustrial society' in which inner growth and quality of life would replace economic growth as the primary concern of society.[21] Marilyn Ferguson detects the stirrings of a 'conspiracy' (literally a 'breathing together') in which, often independent of

---

A transformationalist's view of value shifts in contemporary society

From	To
– considerations of quantity ('more')	– considerations of quality ('better')
– the concept of independence	– the concept of interdependence (of nations, institutions, individuals, all natural species)
– mastery over nature	– living in harmony with nature
– competition	– co-operation
– doing and planning	– being
– the primacy of technical efficiency	– considerations of social justice and equity
– the dictates of organisational convenience	– the aspirations of self-development in an organisation's members
– authoritarianism and dogmatism	– participation
– uniformity and centralisation	– diversity and pluralism
– the concept of work as hard, unavoidable, and a duty	– the concept of work as purpose and self-fulfilment, recognition of leisure as a valid activity in its own right.

Cited in John Haas, *Future Studies in the K–12 Curriculum*, Boulder, Colorado, ERIC Clearinghouse for Social Studies/Social Education, 1980.

each other, people from all walks of life are beginning to challenge assumptions long taken for granted within Western society; assumptions that divorce us from nature, which limit our personal autonomy and which inhibit the development of our human potential. When a critical number conspire together, a transformation in the consciousness of society will occur.[22] Duane Elgin sees the future as one of civilisational decline and breakdown characterised by mounting bureaucratic complexity, an inexorable crumbling of consensus about social, political and economic purpose and a 'lifeboat ethic in global relations'.[23] Either stagnation or revitalisation will follow from civilisational breakdown.

If the former happens, he argues, massive but deadening bureaucracies will attempt to manage virtually every facet of life as all energy is expended on maintaining the status quo. Psychological responses will include denial (i.e. that a crisis exists), indifference, scapegoating, escape or fatalistic resignation. Revitalisation, on the other hand, would demand the release of creativity through conscious acceptance of challenge, a revitalisation of democratic processes through increased participation in decision-making and the transformation of majority behaviour through the acceptance of new ways of living and working now being developed by creative minorities.[24]

Teaching for the future: how we used the bottlebanks but worried about custard...

by **Cathie Holden**, teacher at Bishop Kirk Middle School, Oxford

Stone Age people, the Arabs, Festivals, the Caribbean and the history of Trinidad...all our projects seemed to emanate from the past or feature the past as a prominent component. There was no mention of the future, of how the future might be shaped, or of what part students would take in its creation...the education we were offering pupils looked backwards, not forwards.

And yet these pupils (articulate, many from professional backgrounds with high expectations) would be the decision-makers of the twenty-first century, would be creating the environment in which our grandchildren would live. A decision to teach for and about the future as well as the past, involved two distinct tasks: getting children to focus on the future, and getting them to realise that they could take action to help bring about the type of future they wanted.

The first task was definitely the easier of the two. One of the most fail safe activities is the 'Time Line' (see p. 151). I have used this with many successive classes of nine and ten year olds (and with other teachers) and it always provides a stimulating starting point. If one asks pupils to divide their time lines into preferable and probable futures, the teacher can easily see the concerns which dominate that particular class and channel the discussion along those lines. This year (1986) the children focused on radiation (Chernobyl), a nuclear free world, an end to unemployment, cures for diseases (including AIDS), and commented on their own particular personal hopes (marriage/footballer/computer expert, etc.). Previous years have shown concern with the Falklands war, acid rain and famine in Africa as these events were foremost when the time lines were done.

Another good starting point is 'Ten questions I'd like to ask about the future'; again children are brought to think about the future and how the world may or may not be a desirable place to live in. Children can interview adults following on from this, asking them their answers to the ten questions.

Both these exercises stimulate children to think of the future but they do not in themselves bring about change nor do they help children realise that they themselves have power to effect change. Children generally see themselves as powerless. They regard adults as the holders of power and even then only see *certain* adults (politicians, headteachers) as being in this position. The time when they will be adults seems a long way off, and apart from voting they do not think they will have much power even then.

The best way I've found of encouraging both children and adults to realise that every person *can* work towards a better future is to ask people in small groups to draw up a list of ten things they could give up to help make a better future. With adults the responses range from time (to help a particular organisation), money, and private transport to meat and banking with Barclays. With children I change the title to 'Ten things I could *do*...' as children actually have little to give up. One recent class produced this list:

(see p. 151)

- don't buy smelly rubbers (little children can eat them)
- stop eating meat (it's cruel to animals and the grain can go to poor people)
- don't buy shampoo or make-up that's tested on animals
- tell your parents not to buy apples from South Africa like Beth's mum
- give some of your pocket money to join Greenpeace
- take old bottles to the bottle bank
- save your newspapers and comics for the Oxfam skip for recycling
- eat less sugar because of your teeth
- don't buy food with additives or colouring
- don't eat salt because it's bad for your heart
- eat wholemeal bread because it has 7 times the protein of white bread
- join CND so we don't have nuclear bombs
- make friends with black people and don't be racist

By each group contributing to the class list, children were able to pass on their surprisingly extensive knowledge. One girl thus persuaded quite a few others that Greenpeace was a good organisation to support, another explained why her mother wouldn't buy South African fruit. The children as a class agreed not to buy any more 'smelly rubbers' and one group wrote to Oxfam to ask for details of where their skip would be each Saturday during the following month so that either the children or their parents could take household papers there.

There is a bottle bank which the children pass every week on their way to swimming. A suggestion was made that we collect old bottles and take them down; this then mushroomed into asking the whole school assembly to bring in empty bottles so that all 90 first year children could carry a couple of carrier bags of bottles on their way to swimming. Even if it is true that bottle banks just pay their way, it was a good lesson in caring for natural resources and showing that children can help.

There was a great deal of discussion about what the children ate; they realised that many of the snacks they ate at break time were harmful and one pupil explained about the benefits of wholemeal bread. It was pointed out that one LEA had recently banned all yellow colouring and harmful additives from school meals: the children were fascinated by this – 'But what about the custard, Miss?'

Pupils soon began to see that no action could exist in isolation. One said that if we all stopped buying food with additives, those factories would close down so there'd be more unemployment. Another argued that this would *not* be the case, as people would eat different food that would have to be produced. At this point I introduced them to a futures wheel (see page 154) and this produced the web on page 18.

To an adult there are obvious flaws and the links and statements are rather simplistic, but I think for ten year olds the exercise was valid, showing that all actions have repercussions and encouraging them to think beyond the initial statement.

This particular class had also been working on ways of improving the school in social education lessons, and the two projects linked well. Once the pupils began to realise that they could bring about change they invited a County Councillor in to discuss a better school environment (painted walls, better sports facilities, soft toilet paper) and met with older children to discuss a charter for behaviour in the toilets (see p. 227). But in the end the issues themselves are less important than the realisation that individuals, including children, can do something; that the future does not just come about, it happens as a result of people's decisions and can be worked towards. Teachers can include a future dimension in most topics; pupils can learn to look to the past *and* the future.

The classroom and the future

Emily and other children now in school will live most of their lives in the twenty-first century. We have earlier raised a number of questions about the responsiveness of schools to the interdependent and systemic nature of the contemporary world. But what of the education system's responsiveness to the future? To what extent is Emily being equipped with the 'shock avoidance' skills and capacities she will need to be able to cope with and handle an accelerating rate of social change? Is she being offered the opportunity to study, discuss and reflect upon a range of alternative futures; of possible, probable and preferred futures? Are countervailing visions of the future being offered to balance the 'space ships and battle stars' image of the future projected by the mass media? Is school conveying a 'business as usual' view of the future by default? Is a forward-looking counterpart to history included within the curriculum? It would seem that the school curriculum is heavily past and present orientated even though a major aim of schooling is clearly to prepare young people for the future. 'In contrast with other large scale institutions,' writes Richard Slaughter, 'the education system has made little or no investment in understanding that dimension to which its efforts are ostensibly directed. A careful study of the field suggests that, by and large, we are still attempting to "invent the future backwards". that is to say, in the school curriculum the past has far more weight and reality than the future.'[25] The injection of a future-facing component into the school curriculum would seem to be one important pre-condition if individuals are to shed their sense of powerlessness in the face of rapid change and if they are also to capture more control over the direction change takes. Some suggested first steps towards introducing a futures dimension into the curriculum are given in the following table. Other techniques can be found in Part Two.

In almost any school one cares to visit there is a strange sense of being transported back in time. Part of this sensation is probably a distant echo of childhood. But, on a deeper level, the doors of the school coincide with those of a time capsule drawing us into the world of the past, to our roots, our history. Here, in this often closed, self-referential environment, the rituals and rites of passage of an industrialising society are acted out. Here, the imperatives of an earlier age continue to operate even though the futures they presuppose were dead before the middle of the present century. The blank faces of newly installed VDUs look out on a world that has no future because its future lies in the past.

Richard Slaughter, 'The dinosaur and the dream: re-thinking education for the future', *World Studies Journal*, Vol. 6, No. 1, 1985.

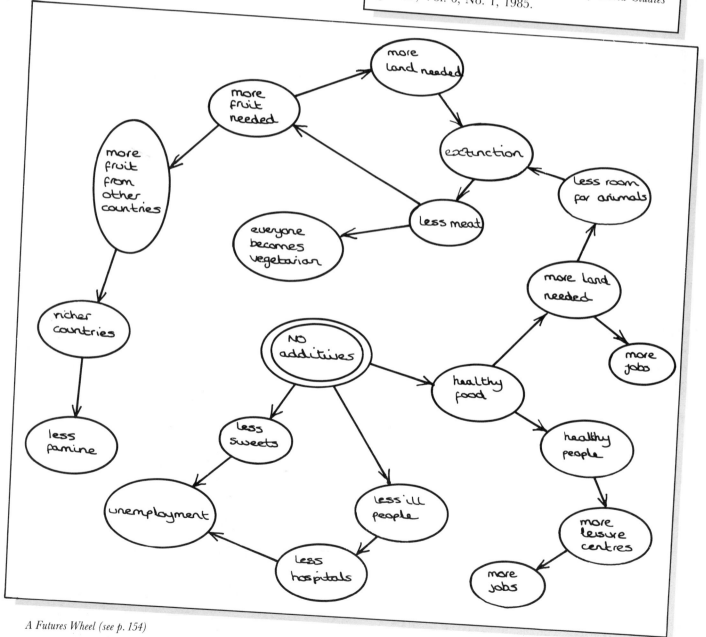

A Futures Wheel (see p. 154)

Futures education?

Ideas for teaching/learning about temporal globality

Time Capsule

Students work in small groups to compile a list of ten items they would like to place in a time capsule in order to provide people of 2050 with an understanding of the best and worst of life today. Each group reports back and the class debates and negotiates a final list of ten items most accurately representing our civilization. The capsule is buried in a corner of the school grounds, to be opened in 2050.

Newspapers Now 1

Students collect newspaper articles with the word 'future' in the title or articles with a strong futures orientation. These are pinned on a 'Futures' noticeboard or categorised in a scrapbook. In introducing the class to articles they bring to school, students can be asked to explain what is being said about the future and how it will affect classmates' lives.

Newspapers Now 2

Students collect articles on world problems which, at first glance, may not seem future-related. In groups, they discuss the contents from a futurist perspective. (This exercise is best done later in a course when students have become more practised and sophisticated in considering the relationship between past, present and future.)

Newspapers in the Future

Groups of students form writing/editorial teams to compile a Future Times (or other title of their choice). They agree on a date ten, twenty or thirty years into the future and cover local, national and global news through reports, editorials and illustrations. Advertisements can also be included! Each newspaper should contain a retrospective 'Life in (present year)' column.

Posters

Students, working individually or in pairs, design posters reflecting their images of the future.

Job Advertisement

Students, working in pairs, are asked to design a job advertisement for the year 2010. The job is to be one that does not yet exist. In deciding upon a job, they are to imagine possible and probable changes in technology, products, services, lifestyles and attitudes. The qualifications for the job are to be stated. Next, they are each to write a letter of application for the position, stating their reasons for applying and their qualifications. The class then shares advertisements and applications. Plenary discussion can focus upon work in the future. What new types of job will be created? What present jobs will become obsolete? Will our understanding of the terms 'employment' and 'unemployment' change? If so, why?

Interviews 1: The Pace of Change

Students interview parents, grandparents and other adults to find out how much life has changed during their lifetimes and whether they feel that the pace of change has quickened. Adult reactions to change and the pace of change are elicited.

Questions about the Future

Students first write their own list of ten questions they would like to ask about the future. Groups of 4–6 are formed and members share their lists. Discussion and negotiation follow with a view to compiling an agreed group list of ten questions. The questions can form the basis of interview and questionnaire work (see Interviews 2 and 3 on page 21).

Visit

Students visit a city planning department or invite a city planner to visit the class to explain how the department sets about planning the local environment of the future.

Model City

Students working in groups are asked to design a self-contained model city of approximately 50,000 people in which all the basic services (education, health care, water, power, waste disposal, recreation, transport, police, etc.) are provided. Groups are given four large sheets of white paper sellotaped together, rough paper and felt pens. They are also given different requirements and constraints under which to work, e.g. the city must be pollution free, it must only have public transport, it must occupy only one square mile of land area. After designing their city, groups present it to the rest of the class and answer questions.

Clock Face

Students, in groups, prepare a sixty-minute clock face on a large sheet of paper. Each minute represents fifty years. Different groups choose different areas of human activity, e.g. farming, transport and communications, medicine, industry. Using encyclopaedias and reference books, they research major inventions and developments in their chosen area and write them in against the appropriate minute of the clock. The results will offer vivid evidence of the quickening pace of change. As a continuation, groups can prepare a second clock face on which one minute equals one year (the clock starts with the present). Keeping to the area of their choice, they discuss and predict likely future developments and when they will occur. These are written onto the clock face. Groups present their work and answer questions.

Interviews 2: Attitudes to the Future

Students interview each other, friends, parents, relatives, teachers, etc., to find out their attitudes to and hopes and fears for the future. Alternatively, students design and use questionnaires.

Interviews 3: Visions of the Future

Students interview prominent local people — councillors, politicians, representatives of local organisations and pressure groups — to ascertain their visions and plans for the future. Attitudes, hopes and fears identified under Interviews 2 can also be put to such people for comment.

Science Fiction

Students are assigned different science fiction short stories and are asked to assess whether the stories have anything significant to say about the future. Conclusions are reported in plenary. Discussion follows.

Desirable Futures

Students, working individually, write a description of the world they would like to live in and of the lifestyle they desire for themselves in thirty years' time. They then form groups of 4—6 and, in turn, read their descriptions and face questions. The role of other members of the group is to play devil's advocate by asking questions concerning the achievability, realism, morality and implications for both the environment and other human beings of the future desired.

Past, Present and Future

The future of the past is in the present
The future of the present is in the past
The future of the future is in the present.
                                    John McHale

Older students can use the above quotation as a basis for speculation upon the relationship between past, present and future.

'The _____ of the ____ is in the ____ '. Using the framework, they insert the words 'past', 'present' and 'future' and discuss the implications of the sentences created for exploring the relationship of the three phases of time.

Brainstorming the Future

Students brainstorm (see p. 133) as many ideas as possible surrounding topics such as the following:

— alternatives to compulsory schooling
— new uses for television
— alternatives to competitive sports
— replacements for the family unit
— means of reducing world inequality
— new uses for rubbish
— new forms of democracy
— ways of reducing people's reliance upon experts and professionals

This lively lateral thinking exercise can be followed by group work aimed at clustering and ranking the ideas put forward.

The above ideas have, in the main, been developed from suggestions put forward in Fitch, R.M. and Svengalis, C.M., Futures Unlimited Washington, DC, NCSS, 1979, pp. 37—44, and Holden, C., 'Teaching about the future with younger children', World Studies Journal, Vol. 6, No. 1, pp. 6–9.

3.   The issues dimension

A global issue we define as a contemporary phenomenon affecting the lives of people and/or the health of the planet in a harmful or potentially harmful way, such as environmental pollution, racism and the threat of nuclear war. To understand any global issue, it has to be viewed within a four-dimensional framework. Two dimensions have so far been suggested; the spatial and the temporal. A global issue by definition, will have an impact across many, if not all, parts of the world. It will have macro and micro implications in that it will affect the lives of large groups of people as well as the inner and outer reality of individuals (for instance, a raw materials shortage can lead to recession and higher national levels of unemployment which will, in turn, seriously harm the material well-being and, hence, self-respect of those cast out of work). Each global issue also has to be seen as a process with a past, present and future; to arrive at possible solutions it has to be set within both a space and time continuum.

The third dimension is that comprising all global issues. Just as interdependence and change have been transformed in the contemporary world, so have issues. Earlier in the transition to globality it was rather more possible to compartmentalise issues and to tackle them in isolation. Today, the problems and crises we face are inextricably interlocked. It is for this reason that Edward Cornish has referred to contemporary times as 'the Era of the Megacrisis',[26] and why John Platt describes humanity's present predicament as a 'crisis of crises'.[27] 'Suddenly – virtually overnight when measured on a historical scale,' write Mihajlo Mesarovic and Eduard Pestel, 'mankind finds itself confronted by a multitude of unprecedented crises: the population crisis, the environmental crisis, the raw material crisis, to name just a few. New crises appear while the old ones linger on with the effects spreading to every corner of the Earth until they appear in point of fact as global, worldwide, crises ... Collectively the whole multitude of crises appears to constitute a single global crisis-syndrome of world development.'[28]

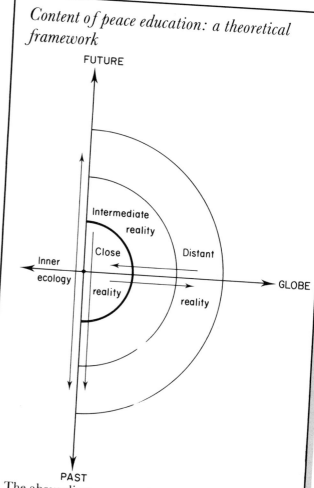

Content of peace education: a theoretical framework

The above diagram was offered by Magnus Haavelsrud, University of Tromso, in a talk on 'Peace Education in the Eighties' in York in October 1984. The diagram offers a useful model for the global educator in that it (a) places issues within interlocking space and time dimensions, (b) suggests a continuous dialectic between near and distant realities, (c) suggests a continuous dialectic between past, present and future. It is a less convincing model in that it (a) seems to compartmentalise spatial levels – the global is often in the local, (b) ignores our inner ecology – the fourth dimension of globality – and, hence, the person/planet relationship (see Section 2).

The systemic nature of global issues carries profound implications for both our perception of the issues themselves and our solution strategies; it also demands a reconceptualisation of the meaning of the term 'solution'. Problems cannot be understood within a simple cause(s) and effect(s) framework. They are locked into a dynamic, interwoven and multi-layered web in which interaction and relationship are the principal features. Hence, a major environmental problem may well impact upon and be impacted upon by, for instance, a raw materials shortage, an energy crisis, rising unemployment, a long-standing issue of wealth maldistribution and a famine crisis, each of which will be simultaneously impacting upon each other at a range of levels, personal to global. It follows that we cannot hope to compartmentalise solution strategies without running the risk of our actions being ultimately counter-productive. As Eugene Schwartz puts it: 'each quasi-solution has a multiplier effect on the residue of problems.'[29] It also follows that solution strategies are not likely to be effective unless they are supported by high levels of transnational assent and co-operation. Within an interactive system of issues we also have to bite our lip when we mention 'solutions'. At best we can talk about provisional solutions because we can never be quite sure in what way an action will reverberate around the system. 'Dealing with a systemic problem is best viewed as an internal adjustment procedure in an ongoing, dynamic process. There is no one-time "solution" to the problem.'[30]

A powerful tide is surging across much of the world today, creating a new, often bizarre, environment in which to work, play, marry, raise children, or retire. In this bewildering context, businessmen swim against highly erratic economic currents; politicians see their ratings bob wildly up and down; universities, hospitals and other institutions battle desperately against inflation. Value systems splinter and crash, while the lifeboats of family, church, and state are hurled madly about.

Looking at these violent changes, we can regard them as isolated evidences of instability, breakdown, and disaster. Yet, if we stand back for a longer view, several things become apparent that otherwise go unnoticed.

To begin with, many of today's changes are not independent of one another. Nor are they random. For example, the crack-up of the nuclear family, the global energy crisis, the spread of cults and cable television, the rise of flexitime and new fringe-benefit packages, the emergence of separatist movements from Quebec to Corsica, may all seem like isolated events. Yet precisely the reverse is true. These and many other seemingly unrelated events or trends are interconnected. They are, in fact, parts of a much larger phenomenon: the death of industrialism and the rise of a new civilization.

So long as we think of them as isolated changes and miss this larger significance, we cannot design a coherent, effective response to them. As individuals, our personal decisions remain aimless or self-cancelling. As governments we stumble from crisis to crash programme, lurching into the future without plan, without hope, without vision.

Lacking a systematic framework for understanding the clash of forces in today's world, we are like a ship's crew, trapped in a storm and trying to navigate between dangerous reefs without compass or chart. In a culture of warring specialisms, drowned in fragmented data and fine-toothed analysis, synthesis is not merely useful – it is crucial.

Alvin Toffler, *The Third Wave*, Pan, 1981, pp.15–16.

Our critical problems... are enormous in size (often involving millions of people), complexity (of bewildering difficulty to comprehend and resolve), and severity (failure to cope with any one of them will ensure much human suffering). Second, we face many different kinds of problems: technical problems (such as energy and resource shortages), normative problems (such as challenges to the appropriateness of the historic social purpose of unending material progress), and process problems (such as trying to cope with overwhelming levels of bureaucratic complexity). Third, these problems are not isolated from one another but comprise a tightly intertwined pattern of problems that reach from local to global scale. As a consequence, they cannot be successfully dealt with through a one-by-one approach; these problems require a pervasive shift in our overall pattern of living. In sum, we confront a fundamental challenge of the workability and meaningfulness of Western industrial civilisation.

Duane Elgin, *Voluntary Simplicity*, New York, William Morrow Co. Inc., 1981.

4. A global cultural crisis

At school, Emily's work books are replete with ticks and crosses. Are such symbols indicative of the school's part in moulding a mental framework which is inappropriate for making sense of the real world? A number of contemporary thinkers have suggested that our several global crises are themselves manifestations of a profounder cultural crisis in which we view reality with distorted and incomplete vision and in which our interpretations of and solutions to crises have the same cultural underpinnings and are, likewise, flawed. Fritjof Capra [31] writes of 'our multifaceted cultural crisis', which is essentially a crisis of perception. Jeremy Rifkin[32] calls for 'a thorough autopsy on the prevailing world view'. Stephen Sterling describes our contemporary ecological crisis as 'at heart a cultural one'.[33] 'Our present problems,' Jean Houston[34] suggests, 'are not primarily political or economic but are rooted in the inadequate use of our humanity or, rather, in our persistence in using those capacities in ourselves that are no longer appropriate to present times.'

The mechanistic paradigm

The cultural worldview to which the above writers refer has its origins in the scientific revolution of the seventeenth and eighteenth centuries. The birth of modern science was accompanied by the emergence of a new paradigm or framework of thought, the principal architect of which was René Descartes. That paradigm eclipsed the worldview of Medieval Christendom. Descartes, a mathematician first and foremost, was fascinated by machines, especially clocks. He translated his knowledge and understanding of machines into a new view of the physical world. Nature itself was a perfect machine 'governed by exact mathematical and mechanical laws. Like a clock or any other machine, it consisted of a multitude of separate parts and could be explained in terms of their arrangement and movement. It was possible, with perfect precision and certainty, to understand phenomena by analysing them and reducing them to their many constituent parts.' De-

scartes' 'reductionist' or 'clockwork universe' philosophy went hand in glove with his separation of mind and matter. His famous dictum was *'Cogito, ergo sum'*. 'I think, therefore I exist.' The only thing that Descartes could not doubt was his existence as a thinker. Mind was more certain than matter. That was what distinguished human beings from nature. Human beings, possessing the ability to reason and analyse, were separate from nature and could investigate the world objectively. There could be complete neutrality between observer and observed. The Cartesian separation of mind and matter also inevitably involved the divorce of the human mind from the human body, itself an animal-machine composed of working parts. The analysis and interaction of facts could be kept in sanitised isolation from (subjective) values.[35]

Cartesian thought provided the conceptual framework for the development of classical science and, in particular, the work of Isaac Newton who postulated small indestructible particles as the basic 'building blocks' of all matter and who added mathematical flesh to Descartes' picture of the universe as a working machine.[36] It has also profoundly influenced the Western worldview up to the present day so that there are few areas of human activity left unaffected by its assumptions and methodologies.

The prevailing mechanistic worldview divorces humanity from nature. It offers a compartmentalised and fragmented 'building blocks' view of reality in which phenomena and events are viewed in isolation. It divides knowledge into subjects or disciplines and into separate modes of perceiving and interpreting reality. Problems are treated in the same way as are clocks in need of repair; all will be well if one can but identify and repair or replace the malfunctioning part(s). A linear problem/solution and cause/effect interpretation of reality prevails. Analysis is preferred to synthesis. Objectivity and neutrality continue to hold sway as perfectly realisable modes of functioning. The Cartesian/Newtonian separation of psychology from physiology has meant that 'most individuals are aware of themselves as isolated egos, existing "inside" their bodies'.[37] The mechanistic worldview also reinforced the long-standing divorce of cerebral thinking from the emotions and the ascendancy of intellectual power over other means of mediating reality. It, likewise, gave new strength to the patriarchal nature of society through the association of 'hard' and preferred qualities (e.g. reason/the domination of nature) with the male, and 'soft' and secondary qualities (e.g. intuition/attunement with nature) with the female.

Critics of the mechanistic paradigm do not suggest that it is wrong; only that it has very limited scope and usefulness and that, taken beyond those limits, it can have adverse, even disastrous, consequences. The orientation of culture towards analysis and reductionism, objectivity and the exploitation of a machine-like physical world has yielded enormous technological advances. It is a good orientation for making cars and putting human beings on the moon. It is a dangerous orientation, however, if applied comprehensively and monopolistically to the sum total of human activity and experience. 'The belief,' writes Fritjof Capra, 'that all these fragments – in ourselves, in our environment and in our society – are really separate can be seen as the essential reason for the present series of social, ecological and cultural crises. It has alienated us from nature and from our fellow human beings. It has brought a grossly unjust distribution of natural resources creating economic and political disorder; an ever-rising wave of violence, both spontaneous and institutionalised, and an ugly, polluted environment in which life has often become physically and mentally unhealthy.'[38] The parallel fragmentation and, hence, disintegration of inner and outer reality is also seized upon by Jean Houston. 'All over the planet,' she writes, 'a Western psychological imperialism has prevailed, one that makes all other imperialisms pale by contrast. The "single vision and Newton's sleep" dominating Western consciousness since the eighteenth century has brought with it the ideal of mind modeled on mechanism, resulting in turn in the materialisation of values, the standardisation of society through industrialisation, and the inability to consider anything other than cause-and-effect relationships as underlying events. In the interests of an extraordinarily narrow notion of "progress", culture is disintegrating, computers are replacing consciousness, and the erosion of human reality is being enacted and mirrored on the stage of nature in the erosion of the planetary ecosystem.'[39]

The mechanistic paradigm has become so embedded, its critics argue, that most of us embrace it unthinkingly and see its various manifestations as rooted in human nature.[40] It equally pervades the goals and workings of capitalist and communist societies.[41] A medical service, for instance, generally regards illness in whatever part of the body as a malfunction of a biological mechanism and attempts to make a person 'well' again by curing that part of the body. The body-mind relationship and the body-mind/personal environment relationship is, all too often, not taken into account. Economists see cost-benefit analysis in strictly financial terms and fail to take on board the environmental, social and psychological costs of economic activity.[42] At Emily's school, the curriculum is fragmented into separate timetable slots and teachers reflect a mechanistic orientation in their emphasis on content and product and their often exclusive interest in intellectual aspects of learning.

The systemic paradigm

Many of the critics of the mechanistic paradigm have detected the recent stirrings of a paradigm shift, a transformational process from one framework of thought and perception to another. The 'systemic' or 'holistic' paradigm has been influenced and invigorated by the findings of modern atomic physics but also draws extensively upon the worldview of Eastern religions and indigenous peoples and upon recent developments in the biological sciences.

Research into the atomic and sub-atomic world has shattered all the principal tenets of the Cartesian/Newtonian mechanistic worldview. First and foremost, research has not revealed a final indissoluble 'building block' of matter but a sub-atomic world made up of particles that can only be understood in terms of their interaction with their surrounding environment. The particles have no meaning save as integrated parts of a dynamic unified whole.[43] 'One is led to a new notion of unbroken wholeness which denies the classical idea of analysability of the world

into separately and independently existing parts,' writes David Bohm.[44] The properties exhibited by a particle depend upon the particular questions asked of it; for instance, the more precise the scientist wishes to be about the momentum of a particle, the less certain she can be about the position within the atom. This *'uncertainty principle'* explodes the notion of the detached objective observer. As Werner Heisenberg, creator of the principle, put it: 'What we observe is not nature itself, but nature exposed to our method of questioning.' What the observer observes also tells us something about the observer herself, her priorities and values. For this reason, John Briggs and David Peat describe reality as a 'looking glass universe'.[45]

Modern atomic physics thus speaks of a universe which is a dynamic, inseparable and systemic whole and which always includes the observer in an essential way. This carries far-reaching implications for other traditional concepts such as cause and effect and local and global. For David Bohm, the 'holomovement' (the flowing, unbroken whole of reality) means that, in the final analysis, everything causes everything else, and what happens anywhere affects what happens everywhere. Although for practical purposes the multitude of causes are negligible and can be set aside, the universe is really 'a moving causal network'. Bohm speaks too, of reality at two levels: the *explicate* and the *implicate*. At the explicate level we can consider objects as (relatively) separate and treat them as such for practical purposes; at the implicate level we need to see the whole as 'enfolded' in every part.[46] Human beings, he suggests, need to be more alive and responsive to the existence of the latter level in their social relationships and in their relationship with the environment. The creation of groups which separate themselves from the rest of the world, for instance, will ultimately break down, because members are really connected to the whole. 'Each member

> . . . 'I'm sure I don't know,' the Lion growled out as he lay down again. 'There was too much dust to see anything. What a time the Monster is cutting up that cake!'
>
> Alice had seated herself on the bank of a little brook, with the great dish on her knees, and was sawing away diligently with the knife. 'It's very provoking!' she said, in reply to the Lion (she was getting quite used to being called 'the Monster'). 'I've cut several slices already, but they always join on again!'
>
> 'You don't know how to manage looking-glass cakes,' the Unicorn remarked. 'Hand it round first, and cut it afterwards.'
>
> This sounded nonsense, but Alice very obediently got up, and carried the dish round, and the cake divided itself into three pieces as she did so. '*Now* cut it up,' said the Lion, as she returned to her place with the empty dish. . . .
>
> Lewis Carroll, *Through the Looking Glass.*

has in fact a somewhat different connection, and sooner or later this shows itself as a difference between him and other members of the group. Wherever men divide themselves from the whole of society and attempt to unite by identification within a group, it is clear that the group must eventually develop internal strife, which leads to a breakdown of its unity... True unity... between man and nature, as well as between man and man, can arise only in a form of action that does not attempt to fragment the whole of reality.'[47]

Bohm and other leading atomic scientists have found some of the most satisfying descriptions of their emergent worldview within Eastern philosophy and religion. They have also drawn inspiration from the holistic worldview of indigenous peoples. To this marriage of traditional culture and contemporary Western physical science we can add a third influence on the emergent systemic paradigm – modern systems biology, a biology that sees organisms as inte-

---

Let's say the council hall in an Indian community needs a new roof... Well everybody knows that. It's been leaking here and there for quite a while and it's getting worse. And people have been talking about it, saying, 'I guess the old hall needs a new roof.' So all of a sudden one morning here's a guy on the roof, tearing off the old shingles, and down on the ground there's several bundles of new, hard-split stakes – probably not enough to do the whole job... Then after a while another guy comes along and sees the first guy on the roof. Pretty soon he's back with a hammer or shingle hatchet and maybe some shingle nails or a couple of rolls of tarpaper. By afternoon there's a whole crew working on that roof... The whole community is involved and there's a lot of fun and laughter... All that because one guy decided to put a new roof on the hall. Now who was that guy? Was he a single isolated individual? Or was he the whole community? How can you tell?

Wilfred Pelletier, *No Foreign Land: the Biography of a North-American Indian*, New York, Pantheon, 1973.

---

grated wholes whose properties cannot be reduced to those of their separate parts and which maximise their survival chances through a dynamic interplay or *complementarity* between their tendency to be self-assertive and their to integrate within a larger e

Writers such as Erich F Roszak, Marilyn Ferguson, James Robertson and Fritjof pointed to the shift in conse taking place as increasing numbers of individuals and groups embrace the systemic paradigm. What is the new worldview now evolving amongst those who hold that the pervasiveness of mechanistic thinking is responsible for a cultural crisis that is both inhibitive of human potential and the critical factor in all the other crises we face globally?

In short, the systemic paradigm views phenomena and events as dynamically interconnected; true understanding lies in accepting that, however much we may have to compartmentalise for practical purposes, everything, in the final analysis, is woven into a multi-layered, multi-dimensional web of interactions. To fragment is dysfunctional upon both people and the environment. The mechanistic divorce of humankind from nature has led to the exploitation of the physical world which is now rebounding upon us in the form of a succession of 'environmental' crises. Humankind, it is argued, should seek 'right' relationships in which a balance between self-assertive and integrative tendencies is struck and in which the 'unit of survival' is not the individual or the part but the system as a whole.[50] This point applies not only to our relationship to the environment but also to global human relationships which currently involve high levels of exploitation and inequity.[51]

If the wider world suffers the effects of mechanistic fragmentation, so, crucially, does the individual. A central tenet of the systemic paradigm is that we can only become 'whole' again if we re-integrate the dualities of the mechanistic worldview. We need to bring 'into interplay the pairs which Descartes divorced (subject/object, value/fact, mind/body, and derivatives such as intuition/reason, spirit/matter, feeling/thought, synthesis/analysis)'.[52] Each pair should be seen not as unconnected opposites but as in constant and dynamic interaction and, thus, complementary. The dominance of the cerebral over other human qualities such as the emotional, the intuitive and the spiritual stunts human potential; it leads to our remaining 'the unfinished animal'. It follows that we cannot hope to achieve personal transformation at a purely intellectual level. If the heart is not engaged and if patterns of behaviour remain unchanged there is no real transformation. It follows, too, that the fuller development of our human potential through the synthesis of our capacities will enable us the better to exercise control over our own lives, thus reducing our present dependency on experts and on the state apparatus and its attendant institutions.

The ancient Chinese belief in the ceaseless interplay of two poles, yin and yang, within all phenomena in accord with nature captures the essence of what those embracing the systemic paradigm seek in both their inner selves and their relationship with the world. The two poles set the limits of a constant oscillation of change. 'The yang having reached its climax retreats in favour of the yin: the yin having reached its climax retreats in favour of the yang.'[53] Yang characteristics are associated with the assertive, the aggressive, the competitive, the rational and the analytic; yin characteristics with the caring, the responsive, the co-operative, the intuitive and the synthesising. Human potential and 'right' relationships with the environment and with other human beings are distorted if one tendency predominates. Yet that is precisely what has happened. The ascendency of yang characteristics, it is held, has created an exploitative relationship with the environment and high levels of inequality globally. It has also stunted the personal growth and fulfilment of millions, not least because, in our patriarchal society, we have become conditioned to seeing 'yin' characteristics as the 'natural' province of women and 'yang' characteristics as the 'natural' domain for men.

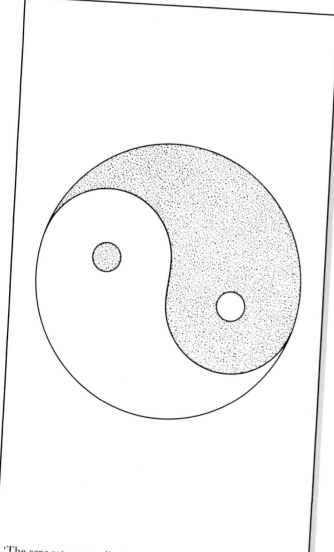

'The *yang* returns cyclically to its beginning, the *yin* attains its maximum and gives place to the yang.' Kuei Ku Tzu, fourth century BC.

Fritjof Capra, *The Tao of Physics*, Flamingo, 1976.

In the heaven of Indra, there is said to be a network of pearls, so arranged that if you look at one you see all the others reflected in it. In the same way each object in the world is not merely itself but involves every other object, and in fact *is* every other object.

The Flower Garland Sutra.

Two Paradigms: Some Principal Features

The Mechanistic Paradigm	The Systemic/Holistic Paradigm
The whole is the sum of its parts.	The system is greater than the sum of its parts. Parts are, in the final analysis, abstractions, the nature and workings of which cannot be understood save in their relationship with the entire system (which is dynamic and multi-layered).
Phenomena and events are viewed in isolation.	Phenomena and events are viewed as dynamically and systemically interconnected in time and space.
The observer is separate from what she observes. Complete objectivity is achievable, especially as the observer can isolate facts from values.	Observer and observed are in reciprocal relationship. What the observer chooses to observe, how she studies and how she interprets what she finds is affected by her priorities, values and framework of thought and perception. Only relative objectivity is achievable.
Rational knowledge and cerebral thinking are separate from and superior to the emotional, the intuitive, the spiritual.	For the full and undistorted realisation of personal potential, the rational and cerebral must be in complementary and synergistic* relationship with the emotional, the intuitive, the spiritual. *Synergy: the combined effect of parts which in their interaction exceeds the sum-total of their individual effects.
A preference for analysis, reduction (understanding phenomena by reducing them to their separate parts) and convergent focus.	A preference for synthesis and divergent overview.
Problems are seen in linear problem/solution and cause/effect terms. A 'technical fix' is possible.	Within the system problems are interlocking aspects of a dynamic, multi-layered causal network; solutions and effects reverberate around the system triggering 'effects' that, given the nature of systems, become 'causes' elsewhere. There is no such thing as a 'technical fix'.
Knowledge is divided into separate subjects/disciplines and into separate modes of experience (economic, environmental, political, social, etc.)	Knowledge is ultimately indivisible into distinct subjects/disciplines and modes of experience.
Humans are distinct from the natural world and natural systems; they can control and dominate both.	Human life is embedded in nature, humans are caught up in natural systems; to act as though this is not the case harms nature and ultimately endangers human survival.
The fragmented nature of reality – and of our own physiology and psychology – occasionally requires the knowledge and skills of experts upon whom we can rely.	An enlarged concept of human potential enables us to gradually acquire the capacity to solve our own problems and to transform our own lives. Our dependence on experts and specialists decreases accordingly.

5. The human potential dimension

Emily has eight thirty-five minute periods each school day. When the school bell sounds, she moves from one classroom to another and from one subject to another. She is then asked to look at the world through the eyes of another subject specialist. Topics are occasionally covered in two or more subjects but little is made of the fact. The fragmented nature of the school experience is but one clear manifestation of the ascendancy of the mechanistic paradigm in education. There are many others. Primacy is given to analytical and memory skills, and to book knowledge; there is all too little opportunity for Emily and her friends to share and explore their inner feelings and personal experiences. Intuition, guesswork and divergent thinking are discouraged. The classroom atmosphere is competitive; the criteria for judging development and performance are in the main confined to what is strictly testable. Emily's teachers (nearly all the senior ones are male) see themselves as 'experts' imparting 'right' information along an often one-way communication channel. Emily is not encouraged to believe that teachers have anything to learn from her. She has come to accept – without every really thinking about it – that the school is a 'building block' divorced, save on rare occasions, from the community.

One question central to this book is: what would a school embracing the systemic paradigm look like? What changes in curriculum, structure and ethos would be needed to create an appropriate context for the education and improvement of the 'whole person'? In what ways would teaching and learning styles need to be transformed? What are the implications for the role of the teacher?

A first step towards schools embracing the new paradigm might be to reconceptualise multicultural education. Multicultural education has been much criticised because its practitioners have tended to treat culture in an exotic and superficial way; the 'Diwali/steel band' approach with an emphasis upon customs, festivals, dress, food, myths and the ritualistic aspects of religion.[54] It has also been roundly condemned for not tackling attitudinal racism head on and for ignoring the economic, political and social effects of racism.[55] If, however, the crisis we face is, at heart, a cultural crisis in which our mechanistic worldview is inadequate for either understanding or dealing with the problems it has created, and of which racism is but one of the ugliest manifestations, then schools could play no more crucial role than that of making succeeding generations aware of alternative paradigms. Bhikhu Parekh describes multicultural education as 'an education in freedom'. 'Monocultural education,' he writes, 'is unlikely to develop the faculty of imagination which represents the ability to conceive alternatives.... Imagination does not develop in a vacuum. It is only with exposure to different societies and cultures that the imagination is stimulated and the consciousness of alternatives becomes an inseparable part of the way of thinking.... Monocultural education stunts the growth of the critical faculty. Children taught to look at the world from the narrow perspective of their own culture and not exposed to any other are bound to reject all that cannot be accommodated within the narrow categories of their own way of looking at the world.'[56] Peter Worsley writes of the 'shocking' and, then, 'liberating' function that the study of anthropology can have in, first, helping us see ourselves more clearly and in, second, helping us to see our way out of a cultural blind alley. 'Despite all these educational virtues, values and strengths,' he adds, 'anthropology is still scandalously absent from the school curriculum.'[57]

We have come to look upon our secondary school experience in terms of subject and not of curriculum. We have fragmented and compartmentalised our school day to the extent that our students have no means of recognising that the parts do add up to an identifiable whole. Indeed, it is doubtful whether in most secondary schools there is even a theory of holism, let alone the practice.

Cyril Poster, 'World studies and the community college', *World Studies Journal*, Vol. 2, No. 1, Autumn 1980.

Multicultural education, so reconceptualised, would not simply be a means of promoting social harmony through understanding and toleration; it would be a central component in education's contribution to a survival strategy for the planet. It would encompass the worldview of indigenous peoples and that of groups and networks operating along what Theodore Roszak has called the 'counter-cultural fringes' of Western society as well as the worldview of major world and ethnic minority cultures. Such a multicultural education programme would carry within it a profoundly radicalising dimension in that it would ask students to confront new perspectives that would powerfully challenge long-held assumptions and that would offer startlingly different conceptions of human potential.

The systemic paradigm, by definition, links our outer world and our inner reality. 'It is essential,' writes Stephen Sterling, 'that we recognise that our "lop-sided" culture generates "lop-sided" individuals and that the realisation of external crises depends on achieving a better internal balance.'[58] Theodore Roszak likewise links the achievement of full and authentic personhood with the well-being of the global environment. 'My argument,' he explains, 'is that *the needs of the planet are the needs of the person.* And, therefore, *the rights of the person are the rights of the planet*...the adventure of self-discovery stands before us as the most practical of pleasures.'[59]

A growing awareness of the spatial, temporal and issues dimensions of globality goes hand in glove with the exploration and exercise of the globality of human potential. As many people who have made voyages of discovery have found, they learn as much about themselves as about the new landscape they enter. *The outward journey is also the inward journey. The two journeys are complementary and mutually illuminating.* Emily brought face to face with new perspectives, new ways of seeing the world, alternative visions of the future, Emily learning that her life is inextricably bound up with the problems and prospects of people thousands of miles away, will inevitably begin to critically examine her own perspectives, attitudes and patterns of behaviour. *The journey outward is the journey inward.* Likewise, carefully and sensitively coaxed, *the journey inwards is the journey outwards.* As Theodore Roszak describes it: 'Suddenly, as we grow more

> The character structure of the average individual and the socioeconomic structure of the society of which he or she is a part are interdependent. The relation between social character and social structure is never static, since both elements in this relationship are never-ending processes. A change in either factor means a change in both. Many political revolutionaries believe that one must first change the political and economic structure radically, and that then, as a second and almost necessary step, the human mind will also change: that the new society, once established, will quasiautomatically produce the new human being. They do not see that the new elite, being motivated by the same character as the old one, will tend to recreate the conditions of the old society in the new sociopolitical institutions the revolution has created; that the victory of the revolution will be its defeat as a revolution – although not as an historical phase that paved the way for the socioeconomic development that was hobbled in its full development. The French and Russian revolutions are textbook examples. On the other side are those who claim that first the nature of human beings must change – their consciousness, their values, their character – and that only then can a truly human society be built. The history of the human race proves them wrong. Purely psychical change has always remained in the private sphere and been restricted to small oases, or has been completely ineffective when the preaching of spiritual values was combined with the practice of the opposite values.
>
> Erich Fromm, *To Have or to Be?*, Abacus, 1979.

introspectively inquisitive about the deep powers of the personality, our ethical concern becomes more universal than ever before; it strives to embrace the natural beauties and all sentient beings, each in her and his and its native peculiarity. Introspection and universality: centre and circumference. Personal awareness burrows deeper into itself; our sense of belonging reaches out further. It all happens at once, the concentration of mind, the expansion of loyalty.'[60]

A 'human potential' paradigm for learning, grounded in the belief that the character and well-being of the individual and the character and well-being of global society are interdependent, will be offered in Section 2. It is also implicit in the classroom activities described in this book. The nature of the person/planet relationship encourages speculation as to how the world system might be transformed should

'The earth is like a tiny oasis in the vastness of space' (James A. Lovell Jr, American astronaut, Apollo VIII, 1968)

enough people awaken to and draw upon the fullness of their potential. The trend towards global interdependence has happened, it needs to be recalled, in the era of 'single vision and Newton's sleep'. To this fact we can trace the inequities and environmental damage that have accompanied the onset of systemness. Virginia Hine and Luther Gerlach have examined contemporary counter-cultural movements, such as the feminist movement and the ecological movement, and have found that, regardless of type or goals, such movements are characterised by similar organisational patterns. Each movement is composed of a whole network of small, relatively autonomous, organisations, voluntarily linked together and sharing some basic assumptions: 'a badly knotted fishnet with a multitude of nodes or cells of varying sizes, each linked to all the others either directly or indirectly.'[61] Virginia Hine describes the advantage of networking as follows:

> ...it encourages full utilisation of individual and small group innovation while minimising the results of failure; it promotes maximum penetration of ideas across socio-economic and cultural barriers while preserving cultural and sub-cultural diversity; it is flexible enough to adapt quickly to changing conditions; and it puts a structural premium on egalitarian, personalistic skills in contrast to the impersonalistic modes of interaction suited to the bureaucratic paradigm.[62]

Such networks, emphasising at one and the same time the integration and differentiation of groups setting great store upon personal transformation and grass-roots participation, provide us with some clue as to what shifts there might be in the nature of the world system were we to break free from the mechanistic paradigm. An all-pervasive human potential paradigm with its emphasis on the empowerment and autonomy of individuals and groups might well give rise to new levels and forms of culture and community within and across the global system and to a corresponding lessening of those features of current interdependencies that are destructive and inequitable.

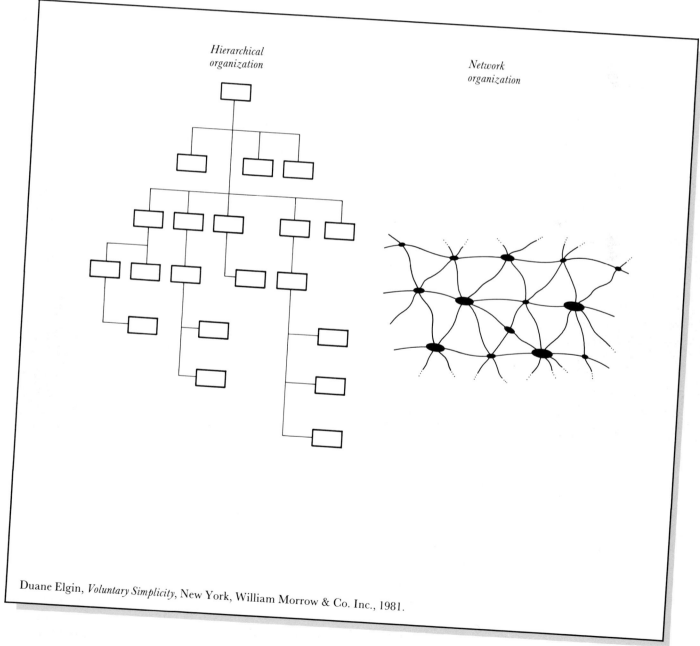

Hierarchical organization

Network organization

Duane Elgin, *Voluntary Simplicity*, New York, William Morrow & Co. Inc., 1981.

6. The aims of global education: a summary

In this chapter we have explored the four interlocking dimensions of globality. We have also raised a number of questions about the implications of the global perspective for schools. What, in summary, are the aims of global education? Below we offer five aims which together constitute the irreducible global perspective. If any of the five are not met, then the school is failing in part to address and prepare students for contemporary reality.[63]

Systems consciousness

Students should:

- **acquire the ability to think in a systems mode.** Simple dualities such as cause/effect, problem/solution, observer/observed, value/fact, reason/emotion, local/global are put aside. In their place, students are encouraged to see phenomena and events as bound up in complex, interactive and multi-layered webs in which relationship is everything. So-called 'effects' loop back and trigger more 'effects' that impact elsewhere in the system. Observers in part determine what is observed. Solutions are, at best, helpful adjustments within the system.
- **acquire an understanding of the systemic nature of the world**. Firstly, in a spatial dimension; on a range of scales intra-personal to global. Secondly, in the temporal dimension, i.e. the interacting nature of past, present and future. Thirdly, in the issues dimension, i.e. the interlocking nature of global issues.
- **acquire an holistic conception of their capacities and potential.** Our true potential can only be realised when the bodily, emotional, intellectual and spiritual dimensions of personhood are seen as equal and complementary dimensions. The character and well-being of person and planet are inescapably locked together. Under this heading, students should be given the scope to exercise and develop their potential and, hence, achieve higher levels of personal autonomy and empowerment.

Perspective consciousness

Students should:

- **recognise that they have a worldview that is not universally shared.** Students are helped to realise that they have their own particular perspective, that they interpret reality from within a particular framework of thought and perception and that there are difficulties and dangers attached to using that framework of reference as a yardstick for interpreting and judging the lifestyles, patterns of behaviour, values and worldview of others. They are also encouraged to see how perspective is shaped by factors such as age, class, creed, culture, ethnicity, gender, geographical context, ideology, language, nationality and race.
- **develop receptivity to other perspectives.** Such receptivity can be profoundly liberating. It can help students challenge previously unexamined assumptions, feed the imagination and promote divergent and lateral thinking; it can lead to a radical reassessment of the nature of both problems and solutions.

Health of planet awareness

Students should:

- **acquire an awareness and understanding of the global condition and of global developments and trends.** Through study and discussion students should learn of global conditions, trends and developments, e.g. wealth distribution, population growth, types of development, the environmental impact of human activity, international tensions, setbacks and success stories in the safeguarding of human rights. They should become equally familiar with the range of, often conflicting, arguments surrounding those conditions, trends and developments.
- **develop an informed understanding of the concepts of justice, human rights and responsibilities and be able to apply that**

understanding to the global condition and to global developments and trends.

- **develop a future orientation in their reflection upon the health of the planet.** Whilst present conditions, developments and trends need to be set within their historical context, it is equally important that students are encouraged to reflect upon the mid and long-term consequences of what is happening in the world today and upon possible, probable and preferred futures.

Involvement consciousness and preparedness

Students should:

- **become aware that the choices they make and the actions they take individually and collectively have repercussions for the global present and the global future.** Choices made and actions taken at any point on the intra-personal to global scale can have contemporaneous impact on all other points on the scale. Likewise, present choices and actions can carry implications for the future well-being of humankind and the environment. Failure to choose and act can have as many repercussions as conscious choice and action.
- **develop the social and political action skills necessary for becoming effective participants in democratic decision-making at a variety of levels, grassroots to global.** Students should explore avenues and techniques for participation in school and society. They should practise participation and, thus, develop discernment and judgement in making choices and in their participation in social and political processes.

Process mindedness

Students should:

- **learn that learning and personal development are continuous journeys with no fixed or final destination.** 'I was partially right before and now I'm a bit more partially right.'[64] Decisions and judgements we reach are, by their nature, impermanent; stills taken from a life-long moving picture. New informa-

tion, new perspectives, new paradigms will help us see things in new ways.

- **learn that new ways of seeing the world are revitalising but risky.** New paradigm vision is double-edged; it enables us to see lots of things in new ways but it may mean that other things are not seen as clearly. The systemic paradigm is not a panacea; it now offers a coherent and challenging framework for present and future thought and action. We need to recognise that it will, in turn, be overtaken.

A parable

Once upon a time there was a class
and the students expressed disapproval of their teacher.
Why should they be concerned with
global interdependency, global problems
and what others of the world were thinking, feeling and doing?
And the teacher said she had a dream in which she
saw one of her students fifty years from today.
The student was angry and said,
'Why did I learn so much detail about the past
and the administration of my country
and so little about the world?'
He was angry because no one told him
that as an adult he would be faced
almost daily with problems of a
global interdependent nature, be they
problems of peace, security, quality
of life, food, inflation, or scarcity
of natural resources.
The angry student found he was the
victim as well as the beneficiary.
'Why was I not warned? Why was
I not better educated? Why
did my teachers not tell me about
the problems and help me understand
I was a member of an interdependent human race?'
With even greater anger the student shouted,
'You helped me extend my hands with incredible machines,
my eyes with telescopes and microscopes,
my ears with telephones, radios, and sonar,
my brain with computers,
but you did not help me extend
my heart, love, concern
to the entire human family.
You, teacher, gave me half a loaf.'

Jon Rye Kinghorn from *A Step-by-Step Guide for Conducting a Consensus and Diversity Workshop in Global Education*, a Program of the Commission of Schools, North Central Association and the Charles F. Kettering Foundation.

References

1 The name Emily was chosen following Roger Scruton's attack on world studies, *World studies: education or indoctrination?*, Institute for European Defence and Strategic Studies, 1985. In his pamphlet, Scruton at one point implies that Emily Brontë achieved a profound human understanding through a life and education in North Yorkshire which was devoid of a global perspective (p. 37). In our reply (*Scrutinizing Scruton*, World studies documentation service, No. 17, Centre for Global Education, 1986), we pointed out that Emily Brontë was actually sent to a finishing school in Brussels to broaden her education. In the light of this interchange, we decided to base much of our book round a modern North Yorkshire Emily.

2 Anderson, L., *Schooling and Citizenship in a Global Age: an exploration of the meaning and significance of global education*, Mid-American Program for Global Perspectives in Education, Social Studies Development Center, Indiana University, 1979, p. 79; Stuart, J. F., *The Unequal Third*, Edward Arnold, 1977, pp. 32–3; File, N. and Power, C., *Black Settlers in Britain 1555–1958*, Heinemann, 1981, p. 1.

3 Anderson, L., op. cit., pp. 80–1.

4 Bailey, S.K., 'International education: an agenda for interdependence', *International Educational and Cultural Exchange*, Vol. XI, 1975, cited in Anderson, L., op. cit., p. 82.

5 Anderson, L. and Becker, J., 'An examination of the structure and objectives of international education', *Social Education*, Vol. 22, November 1968, pp. 639–47.

6 Naisbitt, J., *Megatrends*, Warner, 1984, p. 15.

7 Wallerstein, I., *The Modern World-System*, New York, Academic Press, 1974, p. 162, cited in Anderson, L., op. cit., pp. 135–6.

8 Anderson, L., op. cit., p. 139 *et seq.*

9 Anderson, L., op. cit., p.70.

10 *North-South: a programme for survival*, Pan, 1980, p. 187; Anderson, L., op. cit., pp. 153–4.

11 Naisbitt, J., op. cit., p. 128.

12 Rosenau, J. N., 'Teaching and learning in a transnational world', *Educational Research Quarterly*, Vol. 8, No. 1, 1983, p. 30.

13 Suzuki, D. T., Preface to Suzuki, B. L., *Mahayana Buddhism*, Allen & Unwin, 1959, p. 33, cited in Capra, F., *The Tao of Physics*, Flamingo, 1983, p. 189.

14 Slaughter, R. A., 'The dinosaur and the dream: rethinking education for the future', *World Studies Journal*, Vol. 6, No. 1, 1985, p. 3.

15 Postman, N. and Weingartner, C., *Teaching as a Subversive Activity*, Penguin, 1971, p. 23.

16 Toffler, A., *Future Shock*, Pan, 1971, p. 19.

17 Slaughter, R. A., 'Towards a critical futurism', *World Future Society Bulletin*, July/August 1984, p. 20.

18 Robertson, J., *The Sane Alternative*, James Robertson (Spring Cottage, 9 New Road, Ironbridge, Shropshire) 1983, p. 10.

19 Ibid., pp. 11–13.

20 Higgins, R., *The Seventh Enemy. The Human Factor in the Global Crisis*, Pan, 1980.

21 Harman, W. W., *An Incomplete Guide to the Future*, San Francisco, San Francisco Book Co., 1976, pp. 3–4, 117.

22 Ferguson, M., *The Aquarian Conspiracy. Personal and Social Transformation in the 1980s*, Granada, 1980, pp. 19, 28–9.

23 Elgin, D., *Voluntary Simplicity*, William Morrow, 1981, p. 110.

24 Ibid., pp. 106–13.

25 Slaughter, R. A., 'The dinosaur and the dream: rethinking education for the future', *World Studies Journal*, Vol. 6, No. 1, 1985, p. 2.

26 Cornish, E., *The Study of the Future*, Washington DC, World Future Society, 1977, p. 2.

27 Platt, J., *Perception and Change: projections for survival*, Ann Arbor, University of Michigan Press, 1970, p. 163.

28 Mesarovic, M. and Pestel, E., *Mankind at the Turning Point*, Hutchinson, 1975, cited in Hicks, D. W. and Townley, C., *Teaching World Studies*, Longman, 1982, p. 6.

29 Schwartz, E.S., *Overskill: the decline of technology in modern civilization*, New York, Quadrangle, 1971, p. 72.

30 Schwartz, P., Teige, P.J. and Harman, W. W., 'In search of tomorrow's crises', *The Futurist*, October 1977, Vol. 11, No. 5, pp. 270–2.

31 Capra, F., *The Turning Point*, Flamingo, 1982, p. 7.

32 Rifkin, J., *Entropy. A new world view*, Paladin, 1985, p. 16.

33 Sterling, S. R., 'Culture, ethics, and the environment – towards the new synthesis', *The Environmentalist*, Vol. 5, No. 3, 1985, p. 199.

34 Houston, J., *The Possible Human*, J. P. Tarcher, 1982, p. xv.

35 Capra, F., *The Turning Point*, Flamingo, 1982, pp. 41–8.

36 Ibid., pp. 48–53.

37 Capra, F., *The Tao of Physics*, Flamingo, 1983, p. 28.

38 Ibid.

39 Houston, J., op. cit., p. xiv.

40 Fromm, E., *To Have or to Be?*, Abacus, 1979, pp. 102–3.

41 See, for instance, Fromm, E., op cit., pp. 102–3, 155–6; Toffler, A., *The Third Wave*, Pan, 1980, pp. 59–74.

42 Capra, F., *The Turning Point*, Flamingo, 1982, p. 198.

43 Capra, F., *The Tao of Physics*, Flamingo, 1983, pp. 92, 149–50.

44 Bohm, D. and Hiley, B., 'On the intuitive understanding of nonlocality as implied by quantum

theory', *Foundations of Physics*, Vol. 5, 1975, cited in Capra, F., *The Tao of Physics*, op. cit., pp. 149–50.

45 Briggs, J. P. and Peat, F. D., *Looking Glass Universe. The emerging science of wholeness*, Fontana, 1984, p. 33.

46 Ibid., pp. 126–7, 154–5.

47 Bohm, D., *Wholeness and the Implicate Order*, Routledge & Kegan Paul, 1980, cited in Briggs, J. P. and Peat, F. D., op cit., p. 111.

48 Sterling, S., op. cit., p. 200; see also, Lovelock, J. E., *Gaia. A new look at life on earth*, OUP, 1982.

49 Fromm, E., op. cit., pp. 170–97; Roszak, T., *Unfinished Animal*, Faber & Faber, 1976, pp. 19–43; Ferguson, M., op. cit., pp. 23–45; Houston, J., op. cit., pp. xii–xxi; Robertson, J., op. cit., pp. 87–105; Capra, F., *The Turning Point*, Flamingo, 1982, pp. 1–34.

50 Sterling, S., op. cit., p. 201.

51 Ibid., pp. 200–2.

52 Ibid., p. 200.

53 Capra, F., *The Turning Point*, Flamingo, 1982, pp. 17–18.

54 See, for instance, Clarke, H., 'Multi-cultural education – a whole school approach', *Cambridge Journal of Education*, Vol. 12, No. 2, 1982, pp. 82–6.

55 See, for instance, Richardson, R., 'Some polemical notes for the conference', *World Studies Journal*, Vol. 4, No. 1, pp. 5–6.

56 Parekh, B., 'The gifts of diversity', *Times Educational Supplement*, 29.3.1985, pp. 22–3.

57 Worsley, P., 'Making anthropology popular' in Corlett, J., and Parry, G. (eds), *Anthropology and the Teacher*, Association for the Teaching of the Social Sciences, 1985, pp. 8–10.

58 Sterling, S., op. cit., p. 202.

59 Roszak, T., *Person/Planet*, Granada, 1978, pp. 4, 26.

60 Roszak, T., *Unfinished Animal*, Faber & Faber, 1976.

61 Hine, V., 'The basic paradigm of a future socio-cultural system', *World Issues*, April/May 1977, p. 19, cited in Elgin, D., op. cit., p. 292.

62 Hine, V., op. cit., p. 20, cited in Elgin, D., op. cit., p. 293.

63 The idea of five dimensions constituting a global perspective is derived from Hanvey, R. G., *An Attainable Global Perspective*, Global Perspectives in Education, 1982. Hanvey's work is seminal but, in our view, insufficiently forceful in its promotion of the need for a global perspective. Our global perspective we call *irreducible* rather than *attainable*. It is irreducible in two senses. First, each of the five dimensions must be present in a school that lays claim to offering a global perspective. Secondly, if the school is not offering the five dimensions then it is not preparing its students adequately for participation in an interdependent and fast-changing world system.

64 Ferguson, M., op. cit., p. 76.

2 Journey outwards, journey inwards

The human potential dustbin

In nearly nine years of schooling, Emily has learnt the survival code well. She has learnt that conformity to rules is easier than fighting against them, even though some of the 'Regulations' printed in the school handbook seem, to her way of thinking, nonsensical. Why, for example, is she allowed to wear certain items of jewellery, but not others? Who has made this decision, and in whose interests? But such thoughts are merely fleeting moments of adolescent rebellion; there's no point, after all, in trying to change the system. Some of her friends *have* tried, only to discover the system's many means of control, from punishment to humiliation, isolation and boredom. Emily prefers to direct her energies towards more creative pastimes outside school. She thrives in the positions of responsibility she has earned in the Girl Guides; she experiences a wondrous sense of freedom and unity with the natural world on her walks into the heart of the Moors; and she blossoms into full personhood on the dance floor, a self-assured teenager expressing her personality to the rhythm of her favourite music.

Emily has learnt, too, the priorities of school life: obedience and demureness (a particular virtue in girls), memorisation of factual information for the purpose of regurgitation in tests, suppression of intuitive thoughts and actions which are not considered right or proper for school life. She notices some inconsistency, however; in Drama lessons, and sometimes in English, the tap of creativity is required to be turned on full; occasionally in Humanities her opinion is sought, and given with some trepidation; and in her favourite lesson, Biology, Emily is invited, from time to time, to consider issues which do

seem to have direct relevance to her life outside and beyond school. On her way to meet the school bus every morning she passes the village primary school and often reminisces about her experiences there. She can remember, with remarkable clarity, the anxieties of the first day at school, but then the wide-eyed excitement as a whole new vista of learning experiences opened up before her: a multi-sensory feast of bright colours, harmonious sounds, tactile substances and the warmth of human contact and companionship. She can recall, too, the bitter taste of failure over many years as she struggled to interpret the black lines which seemed to bear little significance to the picture on the opposite page. She was either 'not trying', or 'not concen-

trating', or she was 'lazy'; whatever the accusation – or the incentive that was sometimes proffered – her 'reading problem' remained with her until she was ten years old. And what misery it had brought her! She can sense, even now in the pit of her stomach, that sickening feeling which accompanied the certain knowledge that she would be asked to read aloud to the rest of the class, the certain knowledge that she would mumble and stumble over words which she had read clearly to herself many times over. Yet again she was a failure, not only to herself but also in the eyes of her friends. Although the skills of reading no longer present any difficulty, the numbing fear of failure still haunts Emily from time to time in the secondary school, particularly during class tests when the sense of personal competition is greatest. The prospect of GCSE examinations in a little over two years' time is one she contemplates with dread.

> How can the bird that is born for joy
> Sit in a cage and sing?
>
> William Blake, *The School Boy.*

There is plenty of evidence to suggest that Emily's school experiences are common: the rampant curiosity and enthusiasm for learning of the five year old is slowly but surely subdued during a rigid process designed to convert unruly raw material into neat and tidy finished products.[1] Such a process represents an enormous, and damaging, waste of human potential; as Carl Rogers points out, 'we are working hard to release the incredible energy in the atom and the nucleus of the atom. If we do not devote equal energy - yes, and equal money – to the release of the potential of the individual person then the enormous discrepancy between our level of physical energy resources and human energy resources will doom us to a deserved and universal destruction.'[2] This gloomy outlook is echoed by Theodore Roszak, arising from his own frustrating experience of trying to find an appropriate education for his daughter who, from the age of three, was determined to become a ballerina. Kathryn had an obvious talent and determination to succeed in her chosen vocation, but, as Roszak points out: 'We are all born as mavericks gifted with strange vocations... This is what all of us bring into life and to school: a wholly unexplored, radically unpredictable identity. To educate is to unfold that identity – to unfold it with the utmost delicacy, recognising that it is the most precious resource of our species, the true wealth of the human nation.'[3]

> *About school*
>
> He always wanted to say things. But no one understood.
> He always wanted to explain things. But no one cared.
> So he drew.
>
> Sometimes he would just draw and it wasn't anything. He wanted to carve it in stone or write it in the sky.
> He would lie out on the grass and look up in the sky and it would be only him and the sky and the things inside that needed saying.
>
> And it was after that, that he drew the picture. It was a beautiful picture. He kept it under the pillow and would let no one see it.
> And he would look at it every night and think about it. And when it was dark, and his eyes were closed, he could still see it.
> And it was all of him. And he loved it.
>
> When he started school he brought it with him. Not to show anyone, but just to have it with him like a friend.
>
> It was funny about school.
> He sat in a square, brown desk like all the other square, brown desks and he thought it should be red.
> And his room was a square, brown room. Like all the other rooms.
> And it was tight and close. And stiff.
>
> He hated to hold the pencil and the chalk, with his arm stiff and his feet flat on the floor, with the teacher watching and watching.
> And then he had to write numbers. And they weren't anything.
> They were worse than the letters that could be something if you put them together.
> And the numbers were tight and square and he hated the whole thing.
>
> The teacher came and spoke to him. She told him to wear a tie like all the other boys. He said he didn't like them and she said it didn't matter.

After that they drew. And he drew all yellow and it was the way he felt about morning. And it was beautiful.

The teacher came and smiled at him 'What's this?' she said. 'Why don't you draw something like Ken's drawing? Isn't that beautiful?'
It was all questions.

After that his mother bought him a tie and he always drew airplanes and rocket ships like everyone else.
And he threw the old picture away.
And when he lay out alone looking at the sky, it was big and blue and all of everything, but he wasn't anymore.

He was square inside and brown, and his hands were stiff, and he was like anyone else. And the thing inside him that needed saying didn't need saying anymore.

It had stopped pushing. It was crushed. Stiff. Like everything else.

R. Nukerji in Striker, S., *The Third Anti-colouring Book*, Scholastic Publications, 1981.

Perhaps Emily, likewise, could best reveal her true identity through the medium of dance, or poetry, or wood-carving – or any of the myriad ways that humankind has devised to express its essential creativity. She will have precious few opportunities to find out at school, perhaps a timetabled thirty-five minutes here and there before being submerged again in the knowledge-oriented, right-answer-dominated process of learning which characterises so much of schooling. Emily's school, like so many others, is an overflowing dustbin of human potential.

'Alone among all the creatures we can fail to become what we were born to become.' We are 'the unfinished animal.'[4] The capacity to express ourselves creatively – one of the characteristics of humankind which sets us apart from the rest of the animal world – has been stifled in all but a few individuals whose exceptional talent has enabled them to break free from the oppressive influence of what Jean Houston calls the 'extremely limited consciousness' of our time. She reminds us of the dangers inherent in such a myopic condition:

> We find ourselves in a time in which extremely limited consciousness has the powers once accorded to the gods. Extremely limited consciousness can launch a nuclear holocaust with the single push of a button. Extremely limited consciousness can and does intervene directly in the genetic code, interferes with the complex patterns of life in the sea, and pours its wastes into the protective ozone layers that encircle the earth. Extremely limited consciousness is about to create a whole new energy base linking together computers, electronics, new materials from outer space, biofacture, and genetic engineering, which in turn will release a flood of innovation and external power unlike anything seen before in human history. In short, extremely limited consciousness is accruing to itself the powers of Second Genesis. And this with an ethic that is more Faustian than godlike.[5]

What are the symptoms of this disturbing condition that currently afflicts humankind? Jean Houston's diagnosis includes:

the divorce of mind from body The human body is a complex, but flexible organism which can withstand many of the physical and mental abuses of twentieth-century industrial life such as lack of exercise, addiction to noxious substances, poor posture and stress. But the tendency, in the Western world at least, to view the body as separate from the mind – as can be seen, for example, in Western medical practice – has seriously limited the potential of the body-mind system, by becoming 'centred': 'to feel centered is to experience one's psychological centre of gravity – a solid integration of mind and body'.[6] The divorce of mind from body, or lack of 'centering', it is claimed, leads to a progressive deterioration of human capacities such as perception, conceptualisation and creativity – in short, our ability to learn and to understand our environment. 'Quite simply,' writes Jean Houston, 'the holocaust of body-mind has led to the ecological holocaust and to the awful inadequacy of present political and economic solutions.'[7]

How do you feel?

The British Museum's Human Touch exhibition is designed with the visually and physically handicapped in mind, but you can have a great time even if you're sighted and able-bodied. I strongly urge you not to go and see it. Go by all means, but don't look at the sculptures – not, at least, until you have felt them.

Handling sculpture tells you things you would never learn simply by looking. The sense of touch tells you not only about the proportions, and three-dimensional form, the difference in texture between such materials as granite, jade and wood, but also unexpected things such as the temperature. Intellectually you may know and expect that basalt or marble will be colder than wood, but just how much colder? Your eyes won't give you the answer, but your hands do. The student of human behaviour can have a field day as well as a feeled day. While I was there everyone was in fact sighted. After watching a while I saw a consistent pattern emerge. They come in and look at the first sculpture from a respectful distance.

Around the third or fourth sculpture they overcome a lifetime's Do Not Touch inhibition and put out a tentative finger-tip. Finding that they have not received an electric shock and that bells haven't started ringing, they become bolder. They smile. They progress from using the finger-tips to the whole hand. Some people end up actually hugging the sculptures. It's wonderful.

Richard Boston in *The Guardian*, 18 February 1986.

---

the blunting of the senses Technological sophistication has, in diverse ways, distanced us from being able to adequately interpret reality through the senses. Through the television screen we receive distorted and disjointed images of the world, employing only the senses of sight and hearing; in the supermarket, the pervasive odour of refrigeration plant, cardboard packaging and chemical cleaning agents robs our senses of the pleasures attaining in fresh, unprocessed food; in the modern office block, factory or school, artificial light and heat, and the persistent buzzing of machinery, block out the ever-changing natural world outside. And yet we can also employ this technology to transport us, complete with our limited sensory awareness, to distant lands where our senses are indulged in unfamiliar sights, sounds and tastes. Is it any wonder that we fail to understand, in a profound way, the beliefs and practices of people who are foreign to us? As Jean Houston maintains, 'the capacity for awareness of sensory experiences is critical to the development of meaning... Meaning derives from a profoundly held relation to the revelatory power of the symbol. Yet the symbol becomes an objectified "other" if it is not grounded in the senses.'[8]

outmoded physiological responses Scientists working in the fields of ethnology and brain evolution have shown that the parts of the brain which control our physiological responses to hostile or threatening situations were developed at a time in our evolution when the threat demanded displays of overt aggression. The brain mechanisms, they argue, have changed very little, though the environment in which we live has. The result is a residue of inappropriate and ritualistic behaviour, as witnessed daily in the newspaper reports of violence and destruction, or even in our own lives as instances of over-reaction to provocation. Recognising that, in a world of sophisticated nuclear armaments, an extreme case of over-reaction could precipitate our own destruction, it is time to develop a more appropriate response pattern, one that, in Arthur Koestler's words, 'rings the bell of man's departure from the rail of instinct... signals his rebellion against the single-mindedness of his biological urges, his refusal to remain a creature of habit governed by a single set of "rules of the game".[9]

the failure to empower each other In a world increasingly dominated by 'things', material and abstract, the power of the person tends to be relegated in importance. 'The greatest of human potentials,' writes Jean Houston, 'is the potential of each one of us to empower and acknowledge the other.'[10] That acknowledgment is crucial in times of stress, despair or uncertainty; it can also enhance the quality of everyday experience when offered as encouragement, support and love. It is a characteristic of the contemporary world that we meet very many people, yet acknowledge – in a meaningful way – very few. Offices, schools, shops, buses, housing estates are full of people busily avoiding each other, failing to help realise each other's potential. Through this process of neglect we not only miss the opportunity for empowerment of ourselves, but also fail to recognise and value the richness, and diversity of experience in others. Possessing no evidence to the contrary, we all too readily judge other peoples and cultures from our own limited perspective, thereby nurturing our own assumptions and prejudices.

> In contrast to insects, as someone said, human beings start out as butterflies and end up in cocoons.
>
> Marilyn Ferguson, *The Aquarian Conspiracy.*

The condition of extremely limited consciousness is endemic in schools. It profoundly affects the curriculum, teaching and learning methods, the classroom and school environment, and the role of the school in the wider community. During her school career, Emily is likely to experience most, if not all, of its manifestations:

- compartmentalisation of mental and physical activity, with a higher value placed on the development of the mind;
- failure to help students become 'centred', resulting in learning difficulties, anxiety and neurosis;
- an emphasis on learning through abstract concepts, rather than through actual experience;

- little contact with the community, thereby underlining the isolated, unreal nature of schooling;
- little value given or time allocated to the development of sensory awareness, except in the first few years of primary school;
- a pervading atmosphere of individualistic competition, thereby fostering selfishness, self-importance and aggression;
- little attention paid to an exploration of personal attitudes and values, and the development of positive feelings towards others;
- failure to recognise and nurture the richness and diversity of each individual's talent.

> For school in my day, that day, Crabby's day, seemed to be designed simply to keep us out of the air and from following the normal pursuits of the fields. Crabby's science of dates and sums and writing seemed a typical invention of her own, a sour form of fiddling or prison labour like picking oakum or sewing sacks.
>
> So while the bright times passed, we sat locked in our stocks, our bent backs turned on the valley. The June air infected us with primitive hungers, grass-seed and thistle-down idled through the windows, we smelt the fields and were tormented by cuckoos, while every out-of-door sound that came drifting in was a sharp nudge in the solar plexus. The creaking of wagons going past the school, harness-jingle, and the cries of the carters, the calling of cows from the 17-Acre, Fletcher's chattering mower, gunshot from the warrens – all tugged and pulled at our active wishes till we could have done Miss B a murder.
>
> Laurie Lee, *Cider with Rosie.*

> There are just two things you can do in my lessons without permission. The first is to work hard, the second is to breathe. The latter is less important.
>
> *Teacher in North Yorkshire, 1984, on meeting her 11 year old students for the first time.*

If a fundamental aim of education is to 'unfold the identity' of every child then we need to develop a much broader consciousness within schools. This demands a re-appraisal of the quality of inter-personal relationships amongst teachers and students, a commitment to creative, open and co-operative approaches to teaching and learning, an examination of the implicit messages of the 'hidden curriculum', and the development of productive school-community links. It demands, too, urgent action for the development of the person and the development of the planet are inextricably related:

> Never before has the responsibility of the human being for the planetary process been greater. Never before have we gained power of such magnitude over the primordial issues of life and death. The density and intimacy of the global village, along with the staggering consequences of our new knowledge and technologies, make us directors of a world that, up to now, has mostly directed us. This is a responsibility for which we have been ill-prepared and for which the usual formulas and stop-gap solutions will not work.[11]

Person-centred, planet-conscious learning

In Section 1 we suggested that the exploration of the globality of human potential exists in dynamic interrelationship with a growing awareness of the spatial, temporal and issues dimensions of globality. The outward journey is also the inward journey; similarly, the journey inwards is the journey outwards. For the majority of people in the contemporary world, the two journeys are not only interrelated, but also *interdependent*. An understanding of global problems is likely to be enhanced through a deeper awareness of self: racism, for example, is made more comprehensible through an exploration of the assumptions, perspectives and prejudices which make up the worldview of each and every one of us. Likewise, the development of human potential, in a constructive and planet-conscious way, can be heightened through a concomitant growing awareness of wider global issues and perspectives.

Global learning

What, then, are the essential characteristics of learning which can facilitate both journey outwards and journey inwards, the development of the planet and the fulfilment of the person? A number of central features readily come to mind from an analysis of the educational implications of the four dimensions of globality. Person-centred, planet-conscious learning is:

affirmative of self and others There has been much research undertaken, and many claims made, concerning the relationship of self-concept (or self-esteem, self-image) and learning capacity. Michele and Craig Borba cite research which shows that self-concept is a better predictor than intelligence test scores of a child's future academic success;[12] Stephanie Judson claims that positive self-concept is a requisite for the desire to reach out into new areas of learning.[13] In a similar vein, Jack Canfield and Harold Wells have developed the 'poker chip theory of learning' to explain the 'extensive and overwhelming evidence' that cognitive learning increases when self-concept increases: learning is a risk-taking business, the more poker chips (the higher the self-concept) a student has, the more prepared she is to take chances, to risk failure.[14] Priscilla Prutzman *et al.* argue that 'poor self-image is at the root of many conflicts that exist in school today', on the grounds that it is difficult to feel positive about others if we don't feel positive about ourselves;[15] Edward Cell postulates that 'perhaps the dominant factor in sapping our courage to stand against injustice is the erosion of our sense of worth.'[16] Many writers, in Britain and the United States, have pointed to the contribution of low self-concept to the underachievement of ethnic minority children, though the Swann Report concludes that the 'issues involved are complex' and the 'research evidence is conflicting and confusing.'[17] There can be little doubt, however, about the overall significance of self-concept levels in school and classroom; if the aims of global education are to be met, an affirmative environment is required – one in which students' self-concept, and their appreciation of each other, can be enhanced.

Full Charge

Each participant has a sheet containing a line picture of a car battery. Students sit in a circle and write their names on the battery. They pass their sheet to the person to their left who writes something positive about the strengths of the person whose sheet it is. The papers continue around the circle until everyone has written something about everybody else. When the papers have gone full circle, they are returned to their owners who receive a 'full charge' from reading good things about themselves.

Students form into groups of 5–6 and share with the group the strengths that have been recorded and discuss their feelings about each strength. As each student talks, the rest of the class ask 'encourager' questions to promote further self-reflection.

Primary/Secondary, 30 minutes.

▼ Source

Jon Kinghorn and William Shaw, *Handbook for Global Education,* Charles F. Kettering Foundation, 1977.

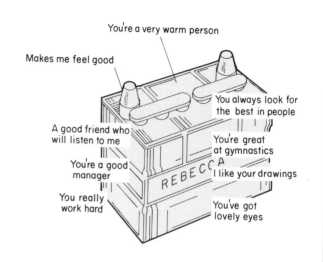

This can be encouraged through the use of affirmative exercises such as 'Full Charge' (see above; for others see Section 6).

participatory A feature of Carl Rogers' person-centred mode of learning is that responsibility for the learning process is shared among teachers, students and, possibly, parents and community members.[18] Participatory learning means more than simply receiving information; it requires student involvement in the initiation, direction and evaluation of what is learnt. It is also a way of processing information; as Erich Fromm points out, students can either memorise information for the purpose of passing examinations but 'remain strangers' to it (the 'having mode' of learning), or they can use the information received to stimulate their own thinking processes, thereby engendering new ideas and perspectives (the 'being mode' of learning).[19]

co-operative David and Roger Johnson identify three types of goal structures (ways in which students relate to each other and the teacher in working towards a goal):[20]

- **individualistic** when a student's achievement of the goal is unrelated to the achievement of the goal by other students;

- **competitive** when a student perceives that she can obtain her goal if, and only if, all other students with whom she is linked fail to obtain theirs;

- **co-operative** when students perceive that they can achieve their goal if, and only if, all other students with whom they are linked achieve theirs.

Participatory learning stimulates thinking processes and engenders new ideas

'Four Hands on Clay' in action (see p. 46)

Based on extensive research evidence,[21] the Johnson brothers conclude that co-operative goal structures:

- encourage positive interpersonal relationships;
- decrease levels of students' anxiety;
- encourage open, effective and accurate communication;
- decrease student apathy and disruption;
- encourage peer learning;
- facilitate conceptual learning;
- promote divergent thinking.

Why is co-operation (even called 'cheating') so frowned upon in education when work is always organised around co-operating, sharing groups? Do schools falsely encourage an individualist approach to work because that suits their examination system?

Charles Handy, *The Future of Work*, Basil Blackwell, 1984.

Contrary to the evidence of most classrooms, co-operation (not competition) is an instinctive form of human behaviour: the vast majority of all human interaction is co-operative. Co-operation is a non-conscious goal of interaction.[22] The term *interactive learning* is sometimes used to denote this feature.

experiential 'Experiential learning occurs,' writes Edward Cell, 'when direct interaction with our world or ourselves results in a change in behaviour, interpretation, autonomy or creativity.'[23] The two key elements are the direct involvement of the learner, who is not controlled or guided by an external agent; and the change that takes place in terms of the learner's awareness and understanding of self. Experiential learning essentially involves an exploration of personal feelings, attitudes and values through which the development of cognitive skills can take place, either during the experience, or on reflection thereafter. It often involves one of the primary senses of touch (as in the example on p. 46, **Four Hands on Clay**), taste or smell, or a significant level of emotion. It is, in short, how children learn *before* they go to school.

Four Hands on Clay

▼ Resources

A c.20cm × 20cm × 20cm block of clay for each two participants. The clay should be soft enough for moulding but not too wet. A table and two chairs for each two participants arranged so that participants face each other across the table; the tables so arranged that individuals can be led, eyes shut, between them. Blindfolds (optional). Soothing or relaxing music (optional).

▼ Procedure

Students stand around the walls of the room. It is explained that the activity involves working in pairs and modelling something out of clay; also, that it can be a very profound experience for those who keep to two basic rules, i.e. eyes should be kept shut throughout and no one should reveal their identity by laughing or talking.

It is particularly important with this activity to indicate that participation is optional; students opting not to model can play a most useful part as observers and rapporteurs. Those intending to take part should be advised to remove watches, bracelets and rings and to roll up their sleeves.

With eyes shut and avoiding talk and laughter, participants are led carefully and protectively to chairs. Once in place, they are asked to fold their arms and wait silently until everybody is seated. During this period — and throughout the activity — soothing music can be played. The facilitator may wish to bear a variety of factors in mind in creating pairings. The problem of uneven numbers can be handled by putting three students together in one group.

With everyone in position, the facilitator goes to each pair in turn, brings their hands together on the clay and says: 'With your four hands working together on the clay, make one model.' The pairs will usually be finished in 15–20 minutes at which point they can be asked to open their eyes. An excited and spontaneous sharing of experiences and feelings normally follows. Allow 5 or so minutes for this before attempting plenary discussion.

▼ Potential

Students are also usually keen to share their experiences and feelings with the class as a whole. How did they feel being led with eyes shut? Did they trust the facilitator? What feelings did they have during the decision period about what to model, during the modelling and when things seemed to be going well or badly? What pleasures or frustrations did they encounter in reaction to their unknown partner, from not talking or seeing, from the music that was being played?

Out of this sharing, a number of key areas for further discussion will probably emerge:

- **Non-verbal communication**—did pairs communicate in deciding what model to make, if so, how; later on, were feelings about what was happening communicated; if so, how; were communications clearly understood by the other partner, etc?
- **Decision making**—how was the decision reached as to what to make; was it a joint decision; did one partner in some way take the initiative; which kinds of initiative-taking proved acceptable, which did not; how did participants react to what they felt was a dominating partner, etc?
- **Gender issues**—were many guessing who their partner was; why; was it important to know whether the partner was a boy or girl; did participants in fact decide whether they were working with a boy or girl; on what evidence did they make the decision; was that evidence, on reflection, reasonable evidence; etc?
- **Touch**—were participants comfortable touching another person's hands; did it become more or less comfortable or uncomfortable once they had decided in their minds whether a partner was female or male; etc? (This area can usefully lead into consideration of tactile and non-tactile cultures.)

This is an excellent unit for filming with a video camera but only if the group is highly affirmed. The playback can be a powerful emotional experience and sections can be replayed to facilitate deeper exploration of the issues raised above.

Primary/Secondary, 30 minutes.

creative The aims of global education, if they are to be met, demand the development of 'higher order' cognitive skills such as divergent and creative thinking, problem-solving and perspective-taking. They demand that students transgress the bounds of normal consciousness in order to seek radical alternatives and grasp new perspectives. As Jean Houston puts it: 'We must think in multimodal ways – kinesthetically, in words and in images, and above all we must have sensuous bouts with ideas. For the more complex and interactive a creative nonequilibrium you have, the more "hooks and eyes" you develop to catch and bring back the forms of possibility.'[24] Jean Houston's research indicates that creative work and expression need not be the preserve of the artist or scientist, but that they are the natural activities of the human being who is able, at least temporarily, to break through the inhibitions of culture, habit and time – to become 'the possible human'.[25]

> Time past and time future
> Allow but a little consciousness.
> To be conscious is not to be in time
> But only in time can the moment in the rose-garden,
> The moment in the arbour where the rain beat,
> The moment in the draughty church at smokefall
> Be remembered; involved with past and future.
> Only through time time is conquered.
>
> T.S. Eliot, *Four Quartets*.

These characteristics of person-centred, planet-conscious learning (affirmative, participatory, co-operative or interactive, experiential and creative) are sometimes referred to as *types* of learning. Such a classification, however, is not always helpful as there is obviously a considerable degree of overlap between them (experiential learning, for example, is clearly participatory and may well be co-operative, affirmative and creative). We prefer to regard them as essential features of a learning process directed towards the development of the planet and the fulfilment of the person. That process we shall call *global learning*.

Global learning: a rationale

Let us summarise what has been discussed so far. We have argued that schools are human potential dustbins: the prevailing condition of extremely limited consciousness is manifestly dominant in the way in which the learning process is organised and structured in schools. An interdependent relationship was then suggested between an awakening of human potential and a deeper understanding of the world: the journey inwards and the journey outwards are mutually illuminating. That led on to an exploration of the essential characteristics of a learning process, called global learning, which can best facilitate the two complementary journeys. What now follows is a rationale for global learning as a *necessary* approach for global education.

An exploration of the four dimensions of globality, we would submit, demands a recon-

sideration of commonly practised, or 'traditional', approaches to learning and a careful scrutiny of the pervading climate of the school – the quality of interpersonal relationships and the implications, or hidden messages, of the school's structure and management style. In offering this rationale, we are not aiming to sell global learning as a complete learning package, a do-it-yourself global education kit; nor are we suggesting that other learning styles – those which are not intrinsically affirmative, participatory, co-operative, experiential or creative – have no place in global education. Section 4 will explore the place of global learning within the overall life and rhythm of a course, whilst Part Four will discuss in more detail the implications of global learning for the personal and professional development of the teacher. There is the implicit assertion, however, that the prevailing teaching and learning styles in many British schools, primary and secondary, are not in themselves conducive to meeting the aims of global education. A rather different pedagogical philosophy is required; the following rationale attempts to explain why.

1 The medium is the message

On Emily's timetable there is a range of subjects such as Maths, French, Music, Biology, Physical Education, and so on. Emily can differentiate between these subjects because of their distinctive content, each requiring certain skills: Maths is to do with numbers and computation skills, French is to do with the French language and communication (mostly writing) skills, Music is to do with musical appreciation, involving listening to, and sometimes making music. The message of each subject – arising out of its content – is, it seems, quite clear. But Emily is receiving other, subliminal messages, too:

- Significant knowledge is that which comes from the mouths of teachers or the pages of books or worksheets.
- The most important skill is memory recall.
- One's own opinion is not valuable, being under-informed and poorly expressed.
- Feelings are irrelevant and should be controlled.
- The basic aim of education is to do things better or faster than anyone else.
- Knowledge comes in separate packages.
- Success is rewarded, failure is punished.
- One's programme of learning must be regulated by someone in authority.

Such messages have little to do with the subject content but are received intuitively from the medium in which they are conveyed: the character and structure of the learning environment and the teaching methods employed.

To be a pupil in a large school is a strange experience. How many of us, if asked to organize an office, would so arrange things that people worked for eight or nine bosses in a week, in perhaps five different work groups, in seven different rooms, without any desk or chair to call their own or put their belongings and discouraged, if not prohibited, from talking to anyone while working? Furthermore, which of us would then interrupt them thirty minutes into each task and move them on to the next? Only slightly caricatured, that is the experience of a pupil in a large secondary school.

Charles Handy, *The Future of Work*, Basil Blackwell, 1984.

In global education the medium is of crucial importance because it is directly related to the message; indeed, it *is* the message. Let us consider, in brief, some objectives – the 'messages' – of global education (to be explored fully in Section 3):

- to understand the process of global interdependence;
- to develop a sense of one's own worth and encourage respect for others;

- to develop the skill of critical thinking;
- to understand the concept of peace – at all levels, personal to international – and to develop conflict avoidance and conflict resolution skills;
- to understand the concept of human rights and to encourage rights' respectfulness;
- to understand the nature of prejudice and to develop means of combating it.

If Emily's school were to adopt such objectives without changing teaching methods or the school environment, a critical disharmony between medium and intended message would soon become evident. Two different and conflicting messages, one overt, the other covert, would be received by students; the overt, intended message could well be undermined by contradictory signals emanating from the climate of the classroom.

The global learning approach aims to preclude such conflict. A good example of medium and message harmony in global education can be found in a field experiment in the United States by Steve Jongewaard, in which he taught about the concept of interdependence to sixth grade social studies classes. In addition to providing a sequence of learning materials for all students, Jongewaard organised them into two groups, each following different learning approaches. In one group students worked according to an individualistic model, with each student working towards the goal independently of others; the other group adopted a co-operative approach, in which students could only achieve the goal if others in the group were also to achieve it. Thus, a condition of interdependence existed in the classroom. Jongewaard concluded that the co-operative approach, which was activity-oriented, was not only an effective teaching strategy in global education, but also enhanced student understanding of the concept itself.[26] If the medium is constructed so as to synthesise the overt (intentional) and covert (hidden) message, the resultant learning is likely to be all the more meaningful.

2 Learning *about*, learning *for*, learning *in* (or *through*)

In Emily's school, learning *about* is the predominant mode. It is primarily a knowledge-oriented process concerned with the assimilation and interpretation of facts, concepts, data and evidence. In some classes, Emily experiences the learning *for* approach: the acquisition or development of skills (for example, research and communication skills) which will enable her to apply the knowledge she has gained. Rarely has she experienced learning *in*, or *through*, whereby the actual process of learning is also a significant part of the intended substance of learning. Let us turn to global education for clarification of these three modes, and consider a series of lessons on human rights. A student will learn *about* the key international documents on human rights (such as the UN Declaration of 1948 and the European Convention of 1950), the principal concepts (civil and political rights, social and economic rights, fair treatment, due process, etc.) and will, perhaps, explore the violation of human rights through individual case studies (Mahatma Gandhi, Martin Luther King, Andrei Sakharov, for example). Learning *for* human rights will require not only the acquisition of relevant knowledge, but also the development and practice of the skills necessary for the defence and promotion of human rights. These would undoubtedly include effective communication skills, skills of co-operation, negotiation and decision-making and, probably, non-violent action and campaigning skills. Learning *in* or

> Teaching to groups of children rather than to the class or individual is currently prescribed by HMI (1980). This report reiterated the suggestions made in the Plowden Report (1967) concerning the utilisation of groups since it was recognised that teachers could not be expected to individualise instruction in large classes of children. Unfortunately the use of classroom groups in practice has emerged as no more than a convenient seating arrangement rather than as a specific site for teaching...The assumption appears to be that simply sitting children together will further intellectual and social development. Research on groups does not support this assumption and neither do the findings reported in this study, where it has been shown that interaction is usually of dubious quality.
>
> Neville Bennett, *et al.*, *The Quality of Pupil Learning Experiences*, Lawrence Erlbaum Associates, 1984.

through human rights goes one stage further. The knowledge and skills elements remain, but in addition learning is reinforced through the very nature of the classroom environment: the quality of interpersonal relationships and the methods of teaching and learning exhibit an intrinsic respect for the rights (whilst, of course, reaffirming the duties) of students and of the teacher.

In the global classroom, where medium and message harmonise, learning *in* or *through* is the prevailing mode; as Ian Lister puts it, learning will be that much more efficacious in 'classrooms of affirmation' than in 'classrooms of negation'.[27] Research supports this assertion: the Johnson brothers and Douglas Anderson have found that an affirmative classroom climate is positively related to frequent student participation in co-operative learning experiences.[28] The findings of the monumental research project directed by David Aspy and Flora Roebuck, involving more than two thousand teachers and twenty thousand students in eight countries over seventeen years, are summarised in one statement: 'Students learn more and behave better when they receive high levels of understanding, caring and genuineness, than when they are given low levels of them.'[29] The findings of this important research will be explored fully later in this Section; for now we need only reaffirm the message of this summary – that the quality of the learning environment has a direct bearing on the quality of learning.

3   Learning for the global mind

The process of learning at school is, for Emily, essentially rational, logical and sequential. What she should learn is decided for her and neatly parcelled into student-size chunks. How to learn, too, is a preordained pathway, consisting mainly of recording and organising information into categories and compartments so that it can be reproduced at will, in as near-perfect a form as possible, whenever required for the purpose of 'assessment'. She does not see, nor is she expected to see, any relationship between the chunks of knowledge (the cry of 'We've done that, Miss, in Geography!' indicates the extent of student conditioning); nor is she often given questions or problems to which there is more than one answer.

Recent medical research into the workings of the brain, an organ so complex that we are only just beginning to understand it, has given birth to the suggestion that the stifling of human potential in schools may be due, in no small part, to a process of learning which engages one

> English is not history and history is not science and science is not art and art is not music, and art and music are minor subjects and English, history and science major subjects, and a subject is something you 'take' and, when you have taken it, you have 'had' it, and if you have 'had' it, you are immune and need not take it again. (The Vaccination Theory of education?)
>
> Neil Postman and Charles Weingartner, *Teaching as a Subversive Activity*, Penguin, 1971.

part of the mind much more than another. The research, involving cutting the *corpus callosum* (the bundle of fibres connecting the two hemispheres of the brain) in severely epileptic patients, indicates that the two hemispheres of the brain process information in different and yet complementary ways. The left hemisphere tends to break up pieces of information into component parts;[30] to analyse these parts, to label, categorise and compartmentalise them, and to control verbal and auditory processes. The right hemisphere synthesises information, sees wholes rather than parts, detects meaning from patterns and tends to control visual and spatial processes. The left hemisphere tends to deal with the abstract and the rational, the right with the emotional and the intuitive (see diagram opposite).

The educational hypothesis which has evolved from this medical research is that most learning in schools is, as in Emily's experience, heavily left-brain oriented, thereby disadvantaging those children who learn, more naturally, through right-brain processing. A word of caution is necessary before examining this hypothesis. Many books have been written[31] on the educational implications of split-brain theory, and many claims made for hemispheric specialisation as providing answers to all learning difficulties, from dyslexia to inability to tell the time. There has clearly, and ironically, been much left-brain thinking – seizing on a particular part of a scientific theory and not seeing the of functions normally attributed to the other. Thirdly, however, learning will be at a profounder, more significant level if it takes place through a fusion of diverse styles and complementary dimensions: abstract and experiential, verbal and visual, analytical and holistic, rational and intuitive. Fourthly, each child has an optimum, or preferred learning style; in any one classroom, students are likely to have a wide range of optimum learning styles on a continuum from left-brain dominance to right-brain dominance. The educational implications of this will be considered in Section 4. Fifthly, irrespective of the preferred style, it seems probable that the full development of human potential in any individual is dependent upon a unique synthesis of a variety of learning approaches. As Barbara Meister Vitale puts it: 'this potential is achieved when both hemispheres are working to their capacity and the information from both is integrated into a whole. This integration creates an intelligence far greater than the sum of its parts. It is an intelligence that exists beyond specializtion and beyond the individual modes of processing present in each hemisphere. It is this intelligence that is the unknown.'[34]

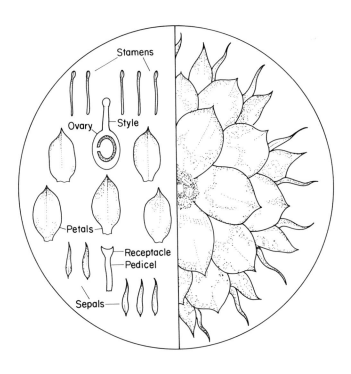

Left and right hemisphere processing (from Linda Verlee Williams, Teaching for the Two-sided Mind, *Simon & Schuster, 1983)*

Your reason and your passion are the rudder and the sails of your seafaring soul.
If either your sails or your rudder be broken, you can but toss and drift, or else be held at a standstill in mid-seas.
For reason, ruling alone, is a force confining; and passion, unattended, is a flame that burns to its own destruction.

Kahlil Gibran, *The Prophet.*

whole. As Theodore Roszak, an ardent critic of 'the split-brain follies' points out, 'to play any role in life – whether that of logician or poet, operations analyst or saint – requires the use of a whole, functioning brain'.[32] 'The brain is a hologram,' writes Marilyn Ferguson, 'interpreting a holographic universe';[33] a significant feature of a hologram is that the code of the whole is resident in each of its parts.

So what are the relevant implications for learning, and for schools, that can be reasonably deduced from split-brain theory, in conjunction with other theories of learning? First, learning is a whole-brain process; it is too simplistic to say that intuitive learning, for example, is a function solely of the right hemisphere. Secondly, the brain is infinitely adaptable. Learning will take place through whatever information it is fed, and however it is received; it has been known, for example, for one hemisphere to take over control

In the context of the rationale for global learning, the primary significance of the hemispheric specialisation theory lies in its support for the notion that the global mind thrives on a global approach to learning, an approach which values imagination, fantasy and intuition as highly as, and complementary to, analysis and logicality. Linda Verlee Williams suggests a variety of learning approaches to counteract the left-brain orientation of most classroom activity; these include the use of metaphor, visual thinking and fantasy, multisensory learning and learning through direct experience.[35] Jean Houston cites the power of a programme of imagistic thinking, a natural capacity of the human being which is inhibited by an emphasis on verbal processes in school and elsewhere, to reactivate creative and problem-solving processes.[36] Such processes are critical, not only to the awakening of human potential, but also in the search for solutions to the problems of the planet.

4 Learning for global perception

It was suggested in Section 1 that our mechanistic worldview is inadequate for either understanding or tackling the problems of its own creation. A central feature of this inadequacy is our propensity to perceive, and henceforth make judgements upon, our world from within a fixed framework of subconscious assumptions and perspectives. Fritjof Capra cites the power of patriachy, which 'has influenced our most basic ideas about human nature and our relation to the universe ... It is the one system which, until recently, had never in recorded history been openly challenged, and whose doctrines were so universally accepted that they seemed to be laws of nature; indeed they were usually presented as such.'[37] The resilient influence of patriarchal assumptions is clearly evident when attempting to find a solution to the **My Son, My Son** exercise.

In all groups, female, male and mixed, with whom we have worked, the majority of participants have failed to arrive at the simplest explanation; the idea that a woman can be a surgeon is not part of our subconscious worldview. It is, of course, inevitable that our perception of the world is limited in focus. Perception is a process of understanding reality by filtering whatever is 'out there' through the mechanism of the brain; as such, it is influenced by both our past experiences and our present needs.[38] A shower of rain is perceived very differently by cricket spectators in Jamaica from villagers in a drought-stricken area of Sudan. The crucial point is that a narrow worldview no longer provides an adequate framework in which to interpret, in a meaningful and creative sense, a world which is characterised by increasing interdependence and rapid change. It is time to challenge existing assumptions and broaden

My Son, My Son

▼ Resources

A six-sentence story for every pair of students, each sentence appearing on a separate slip of paper:

> There is a road accident.
> A lorry ran over a man and his son.
> The father was killed outright.
> The boy was taken to hospital.
> The surgeon at the hospital recognised him.
> 'My son,' cried the surgeon, horrified, 'that's my son.'

▼ Procedure

Students working in pairs receive six slips of paper, not in the above order, which they have to arrange in a sequence which makes sense. Those pairs who finish quickly should not divulge their solution to the problem. After a few minutes those who are struggling could be asked to express their difficulties.

▼ Potential

A simple, but very effective means of stimulating discussion about sex roles and stereotyping, and of illustrating the idea that we tend to view the world on the basis of a fixed set of assumptions. Some pairs will probably work out the 'answer' (that the surgeon is the boy's mother), but there will usually be a number who fail to solve the problem, or who offer a tortuous alternative solution, and who will be startled when they are told. Therein lies the power of this exercise: the sudden self-discovery of one's own assumptions and limited perspective. Because of the 'trick' element of this exercise, it may need to be handled with some sensitivity, particularly for those who did not get the 'right answer'.

Primary/Secondary, 10 minutes.

▼ Source

Doing Things Pack (Maidenhead Teachers Centre, 1983).

The maligned wolf

by **Leif Fearn**, San Diego, California

The forest was my home. I lived there and I cared about it. I tried to keep it neat and clean.

Then one sunny day, while I was cleaning up some garbage a camper had left behind, I heard footsteps. I leaped behind a tree and saw a rather plain little girl coming down the trail carrying a basket. I was suspicious of this little girl right away because she was dressed funny – all in red, and her head covered up so it seemed like she didn't want people to know who she was. Naturally, I stopped to check her out. I asked who she was, where she was going, where she had come from, and all that. She gave me a song and dance about going to her grandmother's house with a basket of lunch. She appeared to be a basically honest person, but she was in my forest and she certainly looked suspicious with that strange getup of hers. So I decided to teach her just how serious it is to prance through the forest unannounced and dressed funny.

I let her go on her way, but I ran ahead to her grandmother's house. When I saw that nice old woman, I explained my problem, and she agreed that her granddaughter needed to learn a lesson, all right. The old woman agreed to stay out of sight until I called her. Actually, she hid under the bed.

When the girl arrived, I invited her into the bedroom where I was in the bed, dressed like the grandmother. The girl came in all rosy-cheeked and said something nasty about my big ears. I've been insulted before so I made the best of it by suggesting that my big ears would help me to hear better. Now, what I meant was that I liked her and wanted to pay close attention to what she was saying. But she makes another insulting crack about my bulging eyes. Now you can see how I was beginning to feel about this girl who put on such a nice front, but was apparently a very nasty person. Still, I've made it a policy to turn the other cheek, so I told her that my big eyes helped me to see her better.

Her next insult really got to me. I've got this problem with having big teeth. And that little girl made an insulting crack about them. I know that I should have had better control, but I leaped up from that bed and growled that my teeth would help me to eat her better.

Now, let's face it – no wolf would ever eat a little girl – everyone knows that – but that crazy girl started running around the house screaming – me chasing her to calm her down. I'd taken off the grandmother clothes, but that only seemed to make it worse. And all of a sudden the door came crashing open and a big lumberjack is standing there with his axe. I looked at him and it became clear that I was in trouble. There was an open window behind me and out I went.

I'd like to say that was the end of it. But that grandmother character never did tell my side of the story. Before long the word got around that I was a mean, nasty guy. Everybody started avoiding me. I don't know about that little girl with the funny red outfit, but I didn't live happily ever after.

parochial perspectives. This might be achieved, it was argued in Section 1, through a study of anthropology; Neil Postman and Charles Weingartner concur, arguing that schools should be 'cultivating in the young that most "subversive" intellectual instrument – the anthropological perspective. This perspective allows one to be part of his own culture and, at the same time, to be out of it. One views the activities of his own group as would an anthropologist, observing its tribal rituals, its fears, its conceits, its ethnocentrism. In this way one is able to recognise when reality begins to drift too far away from the grasp of the tribe.'[39]

'Perspective consciousness', one of the five aims comprising the irreducible global perspective, requires the student to take an imaginative leap outside her own cultural framework, to assume, in her mind, a 'fly on the wall' position. Attaining that position demands more than cognitive reasoning, which itself helps to construct the limited framework; it requires a constant interplay between cognitive and affective learning. That emotional 'slap on the face' which so often accompanies the sudden self-awareness of one's limited worldview is a powerful tool for learning, a deep-felt dawning which can stimulate the intellect into accommodating the new horizons glimpsed. But established worldviews are profoundly constructed and persistent in their influence: imagination and creativity are needed if they are to be consistently challenged and adapted. Learning for global perception is whole brain learning.

5 Valuing diversity, promoting equality

A narrow worldview is not only limiting of one's personal development, it is also potentially inhibiting of the life-fulfilment of others. A failure or unwillingness to question personal assumptions and be open to new perspectives is likely to result in prejudiced views towards people and experiences that do not conform to one's established worldview. As Michael Banton explains, 'one of the major characteristics of prejudice is this mental rigidity which the prejudiced individual maintains by twisting new information to accord with his stereotyped preconceptions.'[40]

Schools have a vital role to play in developing positive attitudes towards other peoples and cultures; research indicates that there is probably a significant period between the ages of seven and twelve when children are most open to and accepting of differences.[41] Subsequent to that period, when intolerance tends to increase, students' prejudices can be combated, but as educators at all levels of schooling have testified, the character of the classroom environment and the type of learning process is crucial. Nancy Schniedewind and Ellen Davidson suggest that an 'egalitarian classroom' is necessary, an atmosphere that promotes personal growth, self-worth, concern for others and equity in education; a powerful reinforcer of inequality, they claim, is the emphasis in schools on 'competitive individualism', the notion that a student's success or failure depends *solely* on her efforts and merits, and based on the false premise that each student has an equal chance to compete and succeed.[42] David and Roger Johnson have found that co-operative learning experiences, compared with competitive and individualistic learning situations, promote more positive relationships between ethnic majority and minority students: the interdependence of group participants working towards a common goal tends to result in interpersonal attraction which, in turn, enhances the self-esteem of all participants.[43] The Johnson brothers also claim that differences of all kinds, whether to do with ethnicity, gender, class or handicap, are positively respected and valued in co-operative group structures if they are perceived as resources which can help the group accomplish a variety of goals.[44] Similarly, Alfred Davey's research with primary school children in diverse areas of England indicates that ethnicity will significantly drop in importance as a factor in friendship choice if the children are consistently placed in 'contexts of neutral and mutual dependency', i.e. in group situations where co-operation is needed to achieve a particular goal.[45] From their two-year study in four classrooms employing collaborative learning approaches in two inner city comprehensive schools, Phillida Salmon and Hilary Claire conclude that despite strong evidence of racial barriers and tensions amongst student groups studied, instances of interracial hostility were markedly absent in all four classrooms.[46]

On the basis of the evidence concerning co-operative behaviour and attitudes towards ethnicity, we would postulate that similar results might obtain with regard to gender difference and the promotion of sex equality in schools. The cry from some educators for a return to single-sex schooling as the way to provide genuine equality of opportunity for girls is understandable in the light of evidence to indicate that co-education benefits boys more than girls.[47] An alternative approach, and one which would incorporate the necessary education of boys about sexism and its pervasive effects, might be to change significantly the classroom environment and the quality of interpersonal relationships. As Schniedewind and Davidson point out, a competitive climate is, in the long-term, disadvantageous for both sexes: 'girls often develop the low self-concepts and dependency traits which are disadvantages in personal, and later career, development. The early pressure for boys to compete, to be rational, and achieve at all costs produce behavior patterns that lead to stress-related diseases in adult men and premature death.'[48] The research study by Salmon and Claire cited above found that gender, as well as racial, hostility gradually lessened: 'collaborative learning in mixed classrooms may carry a positive spin-off for gender relations'.[49] From their review of American research into the relevance of classroom organisation and climate to gender inequalities, Marlaine Lockheed and Susan Klein recommend the restructuring of classrooms to utilise co-operative, cross-sex learning and discussion groups and the assigning of specific task-oriented roles to group members. They also point to the need for teachers to monitor their own behaviour towards, and expectations of, both sexes.[50]

But simply improving interpersonal relations and enhancing self-esteem may fail to tackle the critical issues of prejudice and discrimination, which are nurtured by social structures and processes and sustained through deep-seated attitudes. A broad understanding of the processes and effects of discrimination and oppression is required, together with a realisation of the limitations of individual perspective. It is through this interplay between cognitive and affective learning, the analytical and the experiential, learning through reasoned argument and emotional insight, that diversity can be valued yet equality promoted.

6 Realising cognitive and affective goals

We have suggested that learning needs to take place in both affective and cognitive domains if the aims of global education are to be met. But how does the global learning approach contribute to the realisation of specific cognitive and affective goals? What about 'attainment' (to borrow a term revered in Emily's school), in its intellectual, emotional, social and cultural dimensions? How can global learning help a student pass examinations, secure a job, assume responsibility for herself and others, become an effective participant in a democratic society? The most extensive and detailed research undertaken in attempting to answer such questions is that carried out by David Aspy and Flora Roebuck, whose summary conclusion we quoted earlier in this Section. It is important to note, before looking at the findings in detail, that this American research was replicated over a decade in West Germany by Reinhard and Anne-Marie Tausch: their findings, in all essential respects, corroborated those of Aspy and Roebuck.[51]

Through a variety of approaches, involving both quantitative research and illuminative evaluation, at all levels of schooling, Aspy and Roebuck set out to discover relationships between Carl Rogers' 'facilitative conditions' and factors such as attitudes (towards self, school, others), discipline problems, physical health, IQ changes and cognitive growth. The 'facilitative conditions' can be summarised as:

1 realness or genuineness on the part of the facilitator (teacher);

2 prizing of the learner, involving acceptance of her feelings and her trustworthiness;

3 empathetic understanding of the learner.[52]

With regard to affective goals, the research found that students in classrooms characterised by facilitative conditions:

- had higher levels of self-concept;

- had more positive attitudes towards school (less absenteeism, fewer disciplinary problems, fewer acts of vandalism to school property);

- were more involved in learning (more student talk and problem-solving, more asking of questions and eye-contact with the teacher);
- were more spontaneous and creative.

The findings with respect to cognitive goals were equally encouraging. Students learning under facilitative conditions:

- made greater gains on academic achievement measures, including both maths and reading scores;
- increased their scores on IQ tests (kindergarten to fifth grade);
- used higher levels of cognition, including problem-solving and decision-making.

Similar results were recorded, in both cognitive and affective domains, for students regarded as having significant learning difficulties. The control groups, classes in which there were low measures of facilitative conditions, also provided some significant data: in one study, the control students had suffered a decrease in self-concept scores during the research, whilst in another it was discovered that typically both students and teachers employed the lowest order of cognitive behaviour (memory) almost exclusively.[53]

Rogers' 'facilitative conditions' lie at the heart of a global learning approach, though they do not necessarily incorporate all the principal features. David and Roger Johnson's research has found that co-operative, as compared with competitive, learning creates more positive attitudes towards the task and the subject area, and may be crucial to understanding other perspectives and the development of empathy. Whereas a competitive structure is superior in the achievement of a simple task, or task requiring little help, co-operative learning promotes divergent thinking and problem-solving, necessary features for the attainment of more complex goals. Interestingly, co-operation has also been found to be more efficient for individual memory recall.[54] Overall, the Johnson brothers conclude that, though co-operative procedures may be used successfully with any type of academic task, the *greater the conceptual learning required, the greater will tend to be the efficacy of co-operation*; additionally, higher cognitive learning will result from co-operative situations in which the task undertaken generates controversy or conflict of ideas,

opinions and theories (as compared with individualistic study of controversy, or a group task based on a non-controversial issue).[55] Such conclusions would seem to carry great significance for global education in which, typically, relevant concepts are complex (e.g. interdependence, prejudice, justice) and the issues tackled controversial.

7   Learning in a rapidly changing world

The rationale we have offered so far for global learning as a necessary approach to global education has related principally to three dimensions of globality, namely the spatial dimension, the issues dimension and the globality of human potential. The rationale can also be extended to the temporal dimension.

In Section 1 we posed a number of questions about Emily's preparation for life in the twenty-first century. Is she being encouraged to develop 'shock avoidance skills', to cope with an accelerating rate of social change? Does she have the opportunity to creatively explore her 'possible' and 'preferred' futures, or is the 'probable' future implicitly accepted as an inevitability? Does the curriculum acknowledge the fact that a major aim of schooling must be to educate children for the future? For Emily, and many like her, an emphasis in school on knowledge acquisition and the development of lower order cognitive skills, such as memory, inevitably limits her education to considerations of past and present. Robert Hilliard has attempted to quantify the rapid acceleration of growth in new knowledge: 'At the rate at which knowledge is growing, by the time the child born today graduates from college, the amount of knowledge in the world will be four times as great. By the time that same child is fifty years old, it will be thirty-two times as great, and 97 per cent of everything known in the world will have been learned since the time he was born.'[56] Such statistics are obviously speculative, though the general thrust of the argument deserves our attention. Who can predict whether the 'facts' which children are required to internalise at school will be those of greatest value to them in later life? How can students be best equipped to acquire, beyond schooling, the new knowledge necessary for survival? And in what way can students adequately be prepared for the inevitable realisation that 'fact' may be just opinion or perspective, or the current transient position in the continuous process of trying to make sense of the world?

> Our village school was poor and crowded, but in the end I relished it. We learnt nothing abstract or tenuous here – just simple patterns of facts and letters, portable tricks of calculation, no more than was needed to measure a shed, write out a bill, read a swine-disease warning. Through the dead hours of the morning, through the long afternoons, we chanted away at our tables. Passers-by would hear our rising voices in our bottled-up room on the bank; 'Twelve-inches-one-foot. Three-feet-make-a-yard. Fourteen-pounds-make-a-stone. Eight-stone-a-hundred weight.' We absorbed these figures as primal truths declared by some ultimate power. Unhearing, unquestioning, we rocked to our chanting, hammering the gold nails home. 'Twice-two-are-four. One-God-is-Love. One-Lord-is-King. One-King-is-George. One-George-is-Fifth ...' So it was always, had been, would be for ever; we asked no questions; we didn't hear what we said; yet neither did we ever forget it.
>
> Laurie Lee, *Cider With Rosie.*

> Our sociological theories, our political philosophy, our practical maxims of business, our political economy, and our doctrines of education are derived from an unbroken tradition of great thinkers and of practical examples from the age of Plato ... to the end of the last century. The whole of this tradition is warped by the vicious assumption that each generation will substantially live amid the conditions governing the lives of its fathers and will transmit those conditions to mould with equal force the lives of 'its children'. We are living in the first period of human history for which this assumption is false.
>
> Alfred North Whitehead, *The Adventure of Ideas.*

The acquisition of knowledge is but one component of global education; it needs to be accompanied by, and integrated with the development and refinement of skills and an exploration of personal attitudes and values. A range of knowledge, skills and attitudinal objectives relevant to global education will be considered fully in Section 3. In the context of learning for a rapidly changing and unpredictable world we will just outline a few significant areas:

- an understanding of relevant trends and developments from which *informed* decisions can be made in personal and professional life;
- an understanding of change and a preparedness to participate in personal and planetary growth;
- the skills through which new information can be procured and applied;
- 'shock avoidance skills', through which unexpected, challenging or disturbing experiences can be constructively managed;
- a willingness to explore new perspectives and paradigms;
- a capacity for problem-solving, creativity, envisioning and realising alternatives.

The achievement of such objectives, we submit, can be met most efficaciously through global learning. Learning for the twenty-first century must recognise and reflect the systemic and holistic qualities of the world which that century will witness, rather than upholding the mechanistic traditions of nineteenth-century schooling.

Some implications of global learning

Learning does not take place in a vacuum. As suggested in the above rationale, the quality and character of learning is in interdependent relationship with the type of environment in which it takes place: global learning has profound implications for the teacher and the school. We end this Section with a brief consideration of the role of the teacher and the structure of the school in the light of the learning approach we have advocated.

For the teacher

'Teaching,' says Carl Rogers, 'is a vastly over-rated function.' In a time of undoubted and increasing pressure on teachers, that may appear a heartless remark; however, he goes on to argue that teaching as the imparting of knowledge makes sense only in an unchanging world: 'We are, in my view, faced with an entirely new situation in education where the goal of education, if we are to survive, is *the facilitation of change and learning.*'[57] For similar reasons, Postman and Weingartner suggest there is a need for a new term to describe the adult who arranges the school learning environment; the notion that 'teaching' may be unrelated to 'learning', as in the commonly held view that something can be 'taught' by a teacher but not 'learnt' by her students, is on the same level, they argue, as a salesman remarking: 'I sold it to him, but he didn't buy it.'[58] Although, for reasons of clarity we have retained the term

> No man can reveal to you aught but that which already lies half asleep in the dawning of your knowledge.
>
> The teacher who walks in the shadow of the temple, among his followers, gives not of his wisdom but rather of his faith and his lovingness.
>
> If he is indeed wise he does not bid you enter the house of his wisdom, but rather leads you to the threshold of your own mind.
>
> Kahlil Gibran, *The Prophet.*

'teacher' throughout most of this book, we would strongly contend that global teaching is essentially the *facilitation of a learning process* (global learning); consequently *facilitator* would be a more suitable term. Socrates speaks of himself as 'midwife' to his students, bringing forth what is already there waiting to be born; putting aside its sexist implications, this is a powerful image.[59]

But we are not simply proposing semantic variations. At the heart of the distinction between 'teacher' and 'facilitator' lies the issue of power in the classroom. Edward Cell identifies three forms of power, each susceptible to destructive as well as creative uses.[60]

- **personal power** is essentially private, rooted in our self-awareness; from this power is derived our sense of worth, our creativity and fulfilment.

- **interpersonal power** involves others directly in face-to-face relationships; sometimes when power meets power, each is increased (as in a creative dialogue), at other times each is threatened or diminished (as in an unresolved conflict).

- **impersonal power** involves others through the structure of an institution; it involves the use of personal and interpersonal power but, as in the case of a dictator, it may be vastly disproportional to them.

Both the 'teacher' and the 'facilitator' use impersonal power, the difference being in the way in which they engage the powers of their students. For the 'teacher', impersonal power is a weapon for manipulation, for overriding the autonomy of her students, for limiting their personal power; the 'facilitator', however, encourages the creative use of personal and interpersonal power in her classroom. In other words, she distributes the power she has among her students, so as to engender more power; it is a system of creative devolution, of *empowerment*.

We are arguing for a shift in the locus of power and decision-making in the classroom, a change in what Neville Bennett *et al.* have called 'the ecological balance of the classroom'.[61] The argument is based on the belief that empowerment, of self and others, is the most productive use of human energy. It is also pertinent, as Theodore Roszak reminds us, to a consideration of the rights and interests of children: 'What could be more self-evident than that our desire to have hard-working, superbly trained *successful* children – the sort of children who are produced by good schools – is all for the children's own good? What could be more in *their* interest than an education that will gain them jobs, status, rich rewards? Meaning an education that affirms *our* world.'[62] Furthermore, such a shift is fundamental to eroding the restrictive differentiation between 'teacher' and 'learner'. If, in the global classroom, a student is encouraged to contribute her own opinions and perspectives then she must, at times, be the 'teacher'; conversely, if that contribution is to be valued and cherished the 'teacher' must assume the role of 'learner'. Students participating in co-operative group tasks are both teaching and learning. The ceaseless interplay between teaching and learning is one of the salient features of the global classroom; it can only come about through a continuous channelling of power. In this respect the global classroom can be likened to a complex electrical circuit: the power (current) flows through all students (points), empowering each of them but not being monopolised by any one.

The Geranium on the Window Sill Just Died, but Teacher You Went Right On.

Book title.

The channelling of power serves another important function. All education, even of the most formal, 'traditional' kind, is concerned with values, attitudes and beliefs; so-called 'value-free' or 'neutral' teaching is an impossibility. The 'traditional' curriculum necessitates selectivity in what should be taught and choice in how it should be transmitted: such choices involve judgements based on values and perspectives. Global education is certainly no different, save that it openly accepts that values are involved and acknowledges the responsibility of the teacher to safeguard against indoctrination or manipulation of credulous minds. Indoctrination – the instruction of a doctrine – is feasible whenever the available power is located solely within the hands of the instructor; it becomes much less of a possibility if that power is shared amongst all those involved in learning. As Salmon and Claire observe:

> Collaborative learning modes rest on the assumption that people essentially construct their own knowledge, and cast what they learn into what makes sense within their own experience ... In so far as they give children autonomy and responsibility in their own learning efforts, they [collaborative modes] remove the curriculum from its sole possession by the teacher. By inviting pupils to negotiate with each other, they offer the possibility of grounding learners' understanding within their shared everyday world. From our study, it is clear that this did indeed often happen ...[63]

One must, however, acknowledge the persuasive power of the group to stifle or subvert the nonconformist individual opinion; the role of the global teacher is to ensure that such opinion is listened to and considered.

For the school

Charles Handy, in *The Future of Work*, argues that 'the secondary school is not organised around the pupil as *worker* but around the pupil as *product*. Raw material is passed from work station to work station, there to be stamped or worked on by a different specialist, graded at the end and sorted into appropriate categories for distribution... The secondary school is the definitive sorting mechanism and it leaves an indelible impression. That so many come through it, smiling, grateful and grown up, is a tribute to the dedication of many teachers who impose their humanity and personality on those huge processing plants. But many do not come through as well. They leave alienated by an institution that seems to them oppressive, irrelevant and dismissive of their possible contribution to the world. Truly, for them, it is a disabling system.'[64] For global learning to flourish, the secondary school (and the primary school, too – though less fundamental change is required) must become an empowering system, not a disabling one.

In the global school, as in the global classroom, the medium is the message. The development of co-operative, affirmative attitudes among students is largely dependent upon teachers displaying those same attitudes, in the staffroom as well as the classroom. A respect for the intrinsic worth and rights of other people must be enshrined in school regulations, disciplinary and complaints procedures. The encouragement of students to actively participate in their own learning and development needs to be supported through opportunities to share responsibility for the management and direction of the school. A belief in open communication is effectively supported through meaningful dialogue between parents and teachers. A commitment to experiential learning can be positively expressed through sending students out into the local community, to learn from its expertise and to contribute to its growth. In short, the empowering school is an embodiment of the ideals and aspirations it has for its students.

References

1   See, for example, Shostack, J., 'The black side of school', *Times Educational Supplement*, 25 June 1982. In a series of interviews with students John Shostack found that over fifty per cent of fifth year secondary students were highly critical of their school experiences with twenty per cent expressing hatred or intense dislike. Only five per cent expressed unreserved enthusiasm for their school. (Cited in Whitaker, P., *Education as if people really mattered*, Centre for Peace Studies, Occasional Paper No. 3, 1983, pp. 9–10.)

2   Rogers, C., *Freedom to Learn for the 80s*, Charles E. Merrill, 1983, p. 132.

3   Roszak, T., *Person/Planet*, Granada, 1981, p. 196.

4   Roszak, T., *Unfinished Animal*, Faber & Faber, 1976, pp. 84–5.

5   Houston, J., *The Possible Human*, J.P. Tarcher, 1982, p. 213.

6   Hendricks, G. and Wills, R., *The Centering Book*, Prentice-Hall, 1975, p. xi.

7   Houston, J., op. cit., p. xix.

8   Ibid, p. 35.

9   Koestler, A., *The Act of Creation*, Macmillan, 1964, cited in Houston, J., op. cit., p. 98.

10 Houston, J., op. cit., p. 123.

11 Ibid, p. 213

12 Borba, M. and Borba, C., *Self-esteem: a Classroom Affair*, Winston Press, Minneapolis, 1978, p. 2.

13 Judson, S. et al., *A Manual on Non-Violence and Children*, New Society, Philadelphia, 1984, p. 4.

14 Canfield, J. and Wells, H.C., *100 Ways to Enhance Self-Concept in the Classroom*, Prentice-Hall, 1976, p. 7.

15 Prutzman, P. et al., *The Friendly Classroom for a Small Planet*, Avery, 1978, p. 35.

16 Cell, E., *Learning to Learn from Experience*, State University of New York, Albany, 1984, p. 24.

17 Department of Education and Science, *Education for All* (the Swann Report), HMSO, 1985, p. 78, para. 4.26.

18 Rogers, C., op. cit., p. 188.

19 Fromm, E., *To Have or to Be?*, Abacus, 1979, pp. 37–8.

20 Johnson, D.W. and Johnson, R.T., *Learning Together and Alone: Cooperation, Competition and Individualization*, Prentice-Hall, 1975, p. 7.

21 See Johnson, D.W. and Johnson, R.T., op. cit., pp. 185–99, for a review of research.

22 Johnson, D.W. and Johnson, R.T., op. cit., p. 14.

23 Cell, E., op. cit., p. 60.

24 Houston, J., op. cit., p. 197.

25 Ibid, p. 163.

26 Jongewaard, S.M., 'Learning the concept of interdependence using selected curricular materials and/or co-operative goal structures', unpublished doctoral dissertation, University of Minnesota, 1981, cited in Kobus, D.K. (ed.), 'The developing field of global education: a review of the literature', *Educational Research Quarterly*, Vol. 8, No. 1, 1983, p. 25.

27 Lister, I., *Teaching and Learning about Human Rights*, School Education Division, Council of Europe, Strasbourg, 1984, p. 27.

28 Johnson, D.W., Johnson, R. and Anderson, D., 'Social interdependence and classroom climate', *The Journal of Psychology*, 1983, No. 114, p. 135.

29 For a summary of the research, see Rogers, C., op. cit., pp. 199–217.

30 Statements about left and right hemisphere specialisation are thought to be accurate for right-hand dominant people and for some left-hand dominant people. For many left-handers, however, the functions are reversed or are represented in both hemispheres. For a fuller explanation of right and left hemisphere processing and relevance to education see: McCarthy, B., *The 4 Mat system: teaching to learning styles with right/left mode techniques*, Excel, Illinois, 1980, pp. 67–80, and Williams, L.V., *Teaching for the two-sided mind*, Prentice-Hall, 1983, pp. 13–38.

31 A useful annotated bibliography can be found in Williams, L.V., op. cit., pp. 197–207.

32 Roszak, T., 1976, op. cit., p. 56.

33 Ferguson, M., *The Aquarian Conspiracy: Personal and Social Transformation in the 1980s*, Granada, 1980, p. 198.

34 Vitale, B.M., *Unicorns are real: a right-brained approach to learning*, Jalmar Press, California, 1982, p. 107.

35 Williams, L.V., op. cit., pp. 54–179.

36 Houston, J., op. cit., pp. 134–5.

37 Capra, F., *The Turning Point: Science, Society and the Rising Culture*, Flamingo, 1983, p. 11.

38 Postman, N. and Weingartner, C., *Teaching as a Subversive Activity*, Penguin, 1971, pp. 92–4.

39 Ibid., p. 17.

40 Cited in *Education for All* (the Swann Report), op. cit., p. 13, note 2.

41 Torney-Purta, J., 'Research and evaluation in global education: the state of the art and priorities for the future', cited in Kobus, D.K. (ed.), op. cit., p. 24.

42 Schniedewind, N. and Davidson, E., *Open Minds to Equality: a Sourcebook of Learning Activities to Promote Race, Sex, Class and Age Equity*, Prentice-Hall, 1983, pp. 6–15.

43 See Johnson, D.W., Johnson, R. and Maruyama, G., 'Interdependence and interpersonal attraction among heterogeneous and homogeneous individuals', *Review of Educational Research*, 52, 1983, pp. 5–54.

44 Johnson, D.W. and Johnson, R.T., op. cit., pp. 195–6.

45 Davey, A., *Learning to be Prejudiced. Growing up in multi-ethnic Britain*, Edward Arnold, 1983.

46 Salmon, P. and Claire, H., *Classroom collaboration*, Routledge & Kegan Paul, 1984, p. 233.

47 See for example, Dale Spender's analysis of R.R. Dale's research on the benefits of co-education in Spender, D., *Invisible Women: the schooling scandal*, Writers and Readers, 1982, pp. 119–20.

48 Schniedewind, N. and Davidson, E., op. cit., p. 9.

49 Salmon, P. and Claire, H., op. cit., p. 235.

50 Lockheed, M.E. and Klein, S.S., 'Sex equity in classroom organisation and climate', in Klein, S.S. (ed.), *Handbook for Achieving Sex Equity through Education*, Johns Hopkins University Press, 1985, p. 212.

51 See Rogers, C., op. cit., pp. 217–9, for an outline description of this research.

52 Rogers, C., op. cit., pp. 121–6.

53 See Rogers, C., op. cit., pp. 199–224 for a summary of Aspy and Roebuck's research. See, also, Brandes, D. and Ginnis, P., *A Guide to Student-centred Learning*, Basil Blackwell, 1986, for a detailed account of innovative teaching in a Birmingham TVEI project, based on Carl Rogers' assumptions.

54 Johnson, D.W. and Johnson, R.T., op. cit., pp. 191–9.

55 Johnson, D.W. and Johnson, R.T., 'The socialisation and achievement crisis: are cooperative learning experiences the solution?', in Bickman, L. (ed.), *Applied Social Psychology Annual 4*, Sage Publications, 1983, pp. 145–7.

56 Hilliard, R. cited in Toffler, A., *Future Shock*, Pan, 1971, p. 149.

57 Rogers, C., op. cit., pp. 119–20.

58 Postman, N. and Weingartner, C., op. cit., p. 46.

59 Cited in Roszak, T., 1981, op. cit., p. 201.

60 Cell, E., op. cit., pp. 5–6.

61 Bennett, N. *et al.*, *The Quality of Pupil Learning Experiences*, Lawrence Erlbaum Associates, 1984, p. 212.

62 Roszak, T., 1981, op. cit., p. 202.

63 Salmon, P. and Claire, H., op. cit., p.238.

64 Handy, C., *The Future of Work. A Guide to a Changing Society*, Basil Blackwell, 1984, pp. 135–7.

3 Learning for the twenty-first century

In Sections 1 and 2 we have argued for fundamental and far-sighted changes in educational practice so as to better equip children with the necessary tools for meeting the challenges of an increasingly interdependent and unpredictable world. Others within and outside education have also responded to the problems and pressures of the contemporary world by demanding a restoration of traditional values and processes in schools. In Emily's school a sizeable body of parents has made frequent and vociferous calls for more time to be spent on the teaching of basic numeracy and literacy. Another group is pressing for more courses to develop computer skills, whilst yet more parents argue that in a society increasingly dominated by technology the curriculum should reflect this trend with an emphasis on teaching the skills and knowledge of applied science. The various demands, though differing in substance, emerge from a similar concern: that education should develop in children the basic skills for life. But are we so sure, asks Theodore Roszak, that we know what the basic skills for life are?

> Bad enough that Johnny can't read or write. But why do we stop worrying there? Why are we not every bit as concerned that Johnny is such a stranger to his organism and emotions that he will (like most of the rest of us) spend the rest of his life struggling under the burden of his ignorance? Why do we not worry that Johnny's body is gripped by thwarted anger and desire, that his metabolism is tormented by a diet of junk foods and nervous tension, that his dream life is barren, his imagination moribund, his social conscience darkened by competitive egotism? Why not worry that Johnny can't dance, can't breathe, can't meditate, can't relax, can't cope with anxiety, aggression, envy, can't express trust and tenderness? Why do we not spare some concern that Johnny does not know who he is, or even that he has a self to find? If the basic skills have nothing to do with all this, then let us admit that they have nothing to do with Johnny's health, happiness, sanity or survival but only with his employability. Whose interest, then, is Johnny's education serving?[1]

For Emily, literacy and numeracy are vital skills but not sufficient on their own to give her the confidence and capacity to cope constructively with life in the twenty-first century. Computer literacy and technological competence will give her, perhaps, a better chance in the search for meaningful employment. But such skills are only some of the necessary life skills. They will enable Emily to receive, process and express informa-

REPORT Emily
Student:
Visualisation: Emily has ... to adapt her own ... and, is making effort ...
Creative Thinking: Emily shows a ... ideas and organ ... friendly. She tea ...
Forecasting: Emily understa ... elements of thi ... and understan ...
Problem Solving: Emily has learne ... identify the proble ... development of id ...
Decision Making: Emily works in ... situation. She ... hesitates in ...
Empathy: Emily underst ... reasons. She is ...
Conflict Management: Emily keen to ...

tion, but will they help her to understand, interpret and manage the diverse emotions, perspectives and values which information so often conveys or conceals? They will help her to satisfactorily complete the tasks she is set at her place of work, but will they give her the sensitivity and awareness necessary for forming meaningful personal relationships with her colleagues? Will they enable her to cope with the stresses of intimate friendships, of marriage, divorce and bereavement, of unemployment and change of occupation, of economic and emotional insecurity, of challenges to her life-style, belief system and worldview? Will such skills endow her, furthermore, with a firm belief in her potential to turn every experience, no matter how distressing, into a creative force for life? Emily's education, certainly, serves only a part of her interest.

Learning for the twenty-first century demands the acquisition of a range of skills and a broad area of knowledge and the development of a set of attitudes which together constitute a far more fundamental critique of current educational practice than that promulgated by the 'back to basics' movement or those advocating a technocratic education. What, then, are the knowledge, skills and attitudinal objectives of global education which, if met, will satisfy the five broad aims outlined in Section 1? The following list of objectives is by no means comprehensive but it attempts to illustrate the breadth of learning required for life in the next century. For convenience and ease of reference, the objectives are categorised under generic sub-headings and listed in sequential form. It should of course be recognised that, in keeping with the holistic and systemic approach of global education, the categories should not be regarded as definitive or exclusive and the capacity for interrelatedness and interdependence within and between them is limitless.

Global Education Objectives

KNOWLEDGE OBJECTIVES[2]

---

1 PERSONAL

(a) *Self-awareness:* students should acquire an understanding of their own physical, intellectual, emotional and spiritual capacities and potential, their strengths, weaknesses and principal areas for development.

(b) *Own perspective:* students should understand that their own perspective is not universally shared and become aware of how their perspective is shaped.

(c) *How others see us:* students should learn about their own culture, lifestyles and identities through studying how other peoples view them.

---

2 SYSTEMS

(a) *Systems theory:* students should develop an understanding of the nature of systems and how they operate, evolve and change.

(b) *World systems:* students should know about the workings of some principal world systems, eg. trading systems, ecological systems, political systems.

(c) *Interdependence:* students should understand the concept of interdependence and how people, places, events and issues are linked through interdependent relationships.

(d) *Commonality:* students should become aware of the commonality of needs, behaviour, talents and aspirations shared by humankind.

3 DEVELOPMENT

(a) *Forms of development:* students should understand the concept of development and some principal forms of development (including capitalist, socialist and alternative) in operation in their own and other societies.

(b) *Trading relationships:* students should know about the principal commodities traded between countries, the places and processes of growing/extraction, manufacturing and retailing of those commodities, and the relative positions of power and wealth between countries, regions and companies in a trading relationship.

(c) *Aid:* students should understand the historical background to development aid, its forms and processes, and the principal political, economic, social and cultural arguments surrounding its use.

(d) *Colonialism:* students should understand the concepts and processes of colonialism, neo-colonialism and imperialism, and their historical and contemporary influences in the world.

(e) *Role of women:* students should know about the role of women and their contribution to the development process in a range of societies.

(f) *Population:* students should know about the current demographic trends and developments in the world and the principal arguments surrounding population issues.

(g) *Health and nutrition:* students should know about the causes and effects of major diseases in the world and understand the importance of a balanced diet and safe water supplies to health. They should also know about developments in primary health care.

(h) *Education and literacy:* students should know about current educational trends and developments in a range of societies and understand the significance of literacy to development.

4 ENVIRONMENT

(a) *Destruction of ecosystems:* students should know about the causes and effects of the destruction of, or threat to, principal local and global ecosystems and a range of alternative solutions put forward for their protection.

(b) *Natural resources:* students should know about the location, extraction processes and usage of the world's natural resources and understand the causes and effects of the depletion of non-renewable resources.

(c) *Conservation:* students should understand the principles of conservation and know about conservation projects from local to global levels.

(d) *Pollution:* students should understand the causes and effects of pollution – of ground, sea and air – locally and globally and know about the principal measures which are or could be taken to combat it.

(e) *Land use and reform:* students should know about the current usage of available land and the principal developments and arguments concerning land use reform and land reclamation.

(f) *Built environments:* students should understand the environmental problems within, and resulting from, major urban centres and know about a range of alternative solutions proposed.

5 PEACE AND CONFLICT

(a) *Negative and positive peace:* students should understand the concepts of negative peace and positive peace and should be conversant with examples of each condition at a range of levels, local to global.

(b) *Interpersonal peace:* students should understand some of the major causes of conflict at an interpersonal level, at school, home or in the community, and know a range of appropriate conflict management techniques.

(c) *Inter-group peace:* students should understand some of the major causes of conflict between different groups in society and know about the strategies in operation to restore peace or avoid conflict.

(d) *International peace:* students should understand some of the major causes of conflict between nations and know about historical and current attempts to establish peace.

(e) *Armaments:* students should know about the major suppliers and purchasers of armaments (conventional and nuclear) and the economic, political and social ramifications of the arms race. They should also know about past and present movements towards disarmament and understand the principal arguments in the debate concerning nuclear disarmament.

(f) *Terrorism/freedom fighting:* students should understand the reasons for and implications of terrorist or freedom fighting activities and know about the historical development and aims of some of the major active movements.

(g) *Non-violent protest:* students should know about the aims and influences of historical and contemporary non-violent protest movements and their leaders, in their own and other societies. Students should also know what opportunities for non-violent protest are open to them.

---

6 RIGHTS AND RESPONSIBILITIES

(a) *Human rights and responsibilities:* students should know about the Universal Declaration of Human Rights, its strengths and weaknesses, and understand the implications of this document for themselves and for humankind in general.

(b) *Moral and legal rights and responsibilities:* students should understand the concepts of moral rights and legal rights, and their relation to human rights, and be aware of their own moral and legal rights and responsibilities.

(c) *Liberty-oriented and security-oriented rights:* students should understand the distinction between liberty-oriented rights (concerned with individual liberties) and security-oriented rights (concerned with material and physical well-being), and that the prioritisation of these rights varies according to ideology and perspective.

(d) *Freedom from, freedom to:* students should understand the concepts of 'freedom from' and 'freedom to' and know about some of the major incidents in the world in which personal freedoms are violated.

(e) *Prejudice and discrimination:* students should understand the nature and workings of prejudice, in themselves and others, and how such prejudices can lead to personal and social discrimination by means of age, class, creed, ethnicity, gender, ideology, language, nationality or race. They should also know about measures to combat discrimination at personal, societal and global levels.

(f) *Oppression:* students should know about the oppression of groups, in their own and other societies, for reasons of their age, class, creed, ethnicity, gender, ideology, language, nationality or race. They should have an understanding of the personal attitudes and social structures which nurture oppression, the part they as individuals play in this process and the contribution each can make towards its diminution.

(g) *Self-determination:* students should have an understanding of the right to self-determination for individuals and social groups, and should know about cases in which this right is violated.

(h) *Animal rights:* students should understand the various arguments concerning the rights of animals and should know about cases in which animals are subjected to cruelty or mistreatment.

7 ALTERNATIVE VISIONS

(a) *Futures:* students should be aware that there are a range of alternative futures open to humankind and they should know what contribution they can make to the realisation of their personally preferred futures.

(b) *Sustainable life-styles:* students should know about the arguments and practices concerning the limiting of economic growth and how their own life-styles can contribute to or negate a process of sustainable development for the planet.

(c) *Human and planetary health:* students should understand the holistic concept of health as being the fusion of the bodily, emotional, intellectual and spiritual dimensions of a person living in harmonious relationship with the planet. They should also know about personal, social and global action to restore and maintain human and planetary health.

SKILLS OBJECTIVES[3]

1 INFORMATION MANAGEMENT

(a) *Receiving and expressing information:* students should have competence in receiving and expressing information through observing, reading, writing, listening, talking, questioning, graphical and other non-verbal communication processes.

(b) *Organising and processing information:* students should have competence in classifying, defining, analysing, synthesising and sequencing information, relating and contrasting one idea or experience to another and deductive and inductive reasoning.

(c) *Evaluating information:* students should have competence in determining the quality, appropriateness or priority of information, in distinguishing between evidence and opinion, and in recognising bias and perspective.

(d) *Storing and retrieving information:* students should have competence in memorising information, including facts, concepts, physical movements and processes, in recalling and utilising stored information, and in storing and retrieving information from manual or computerised information systems.

(e) *Systems analysis:* students should be able to use systems analysis techniques so as to perceive the interrelationships and interdependencies within and between systems.

2 PERSONAL GROWTH

(a) *Centering:* students should be able to utilise a range of skills, such as relaxation, correct breathing and imagery, so as to integrate mind and body, i.e. to become centred.

(b) *Physical well-being:* students should be able to maintain their physical well-being by means of a balanced diet, sufficient exercise and an appropriate life-style.

(c) *Manual:* students should have competence in a wide range of manual skills, including domestic, horticultural and technical skills, so as to facilitate personal and planetary development.

(d) *Creative potential:* students should be able to identify and develop their own areas of potential and have competence in expressing themselves creatively.

(e) *Values, beliefs and perspectives:* students should be able to identify and clarify their own values and belief systems, and be able to modify personal values and beliefs to accommodate appropriate new perspectives and ideas.

(f) *Shock avoidance:* students should be able to cope with stress and be prepared to manage and gain from major shocks, setbacks and transitions in personal and professional life.

(g) *Time management:* students should be able to manage their time effectively through planning, prioritisation and time-saving techniques.

3 INTERPERSONAL

(a) *Assertiveness:* students should be able to clearly state desires, feelings and preferences without infringing the rights of others.

(b) *Empowerment:* students should be able to express feelings about themselves and others constructively and be able to both give and receive help, encouragement and feedback.

(c) *Trust building:* students should be able to build and maintain trust through openness and sharing in their personal relationships, whether at home, school or in the community.

(d) *Co-operation:* students should be able to work and play co-operatively, ensuring the effective participation of all members of a group in the achievement of a common goal.

(e) *Negotiation:* students should be able to make contracts, compromise and reach mutually satisfactory agreements or conclusions.

(f) *Conflict management:* students should be able to handle controversy and resolve conflict in such a way as to maximise the creative force of conflict. They should also be competent in using conflict avoidance techniques where appropriate.

4 DISCERNMENT

(a) *Decision-making:* students should be able to make informed decisions in all spheres of their lives on the basis of sound information gathering, organising and evaluating, and intuition.

(b) *Ethical judgement:* students should be able to select and use criteria to determine the moral rightness or wrongness of an idea or a course of action.

(c) *Aesthetic appreciation:* students should be able to judge, appreciate and express qualities of beauty in the creative arts and in natural or built environments.

5 IMAGING

(a) *Creative thinking:* students should be able to make lateral moves outside their established frameworks of thought so as to generate fresh insights and perspectives.

(b) *Problem-solving:* students should be able to solve problems in all spheres of their lives through a combination of effective information management, creative thinking and intuition.

(c) *Perception of relationships:* students should be able to perceive and identify patterns, commonalities and relationships between phenomena.

(d) *Holistic perception:* students should be able to transcend their own personal and cultural experience so as to see a particular situation, idea or event as a part of a whole.

(e) *Empathy:* students should be able to use their own experience and imagination so as to understand the attitudes, feelings and actions of others.

(f) *Visualisation:* students should be able to reawaken and develop their powers of imaging and visualisation so as to help realise their full creative potential.

(g) *Forecasting:* students should be able to make realistic predictions about personal and global futures and the consequences of proposed actions, based on a reasoned analysis of past and present trends.

ATTITUDES OBJECTIVES[4]

1 POSITIVE SELF-IMAGE

(a) *Belief in own potential:* students should have a sense of their own worth and a belief in their own physical, intellectual, emotional and spiritual potential.

(b) *Genuineness:* students should have the capacity to identify, own and transmit their thoughts, feelings and emotions.

(c) *Curiosity:* students should want to find out more about themselves and their interdependent relationship with other people and the planet.

2 APPRECIATION OF OTHERS

(a) *Diversity:* students should be willing to find the beliefs and practices of other cultural and social groups of value and interest, and be prepared to learn from them.

(b) *Commonality:* students should appreciate the essential worth of others and the commonality of needs, rights, aspirations, behaviour and talents which binds humankind.

(c) *New perspectives:* students should have a receptivity to perspectives different from their own and be prepared to modify their own ideas and beliefs where appropriate.

3 RESPECT FOR JUSTICE AND RIGHTS

(a) *Defence of rights:* students should have a commitment to defending their own rights and the rights of others and a correlative commitment to carrying out responsibilities.

(b) *Concern for justice:* students should be prepared to show solidarity with victims of injustice in their own and other societies.

(c) *Commitment to equality:* students should have a commitment to principles of equality as the basis on which relationships between individuals, groups and societies should be organised.

4 TOLERANCE OF UNCERTAINTY

(a) *Ambiguity:* students should be prepared to tolerate ambiguity in their lives, be willing to explore alternative paths before reaching decisions or conclusions and be prepared to struggle with problems for which there are no single, simple, specific or final solutions.

(b) *Insecurity:* students should be prepared to accommodate moments of self-doubt and temporary feelings of insecurity in their personal relationships and in their lives.

(c) *Conflict and change:* students should perceive conflict and change as inevitable and natural and be prepared to respond through appropriate modifications of their values, beliefs and life-styles.

5 CAPACITY FOR CREATIVITY

(a) *Risk-taking:* students should be willing to explore new patterns of interaction and to take calculated risks in all spheres of life.

(b) *Paradigm shift:* students should be prepared to take the creative mental leaps necessary to perceive alternative visions and versions of reality.

(c) *Imagery and intuition:* students should be prepared to utilise and value their natural capacities for intuition and imagistic thinking.

6 WORLD-MINDEDNESS

(a) *Respect for life:* students should have a respect for all living things and their place and function in the overall planetary ecosystem.

(b) *Altruism:* students should appreciate that in an interdependent world system, consideration of the overall good of humankind and the planet should influence their decisions and actions.

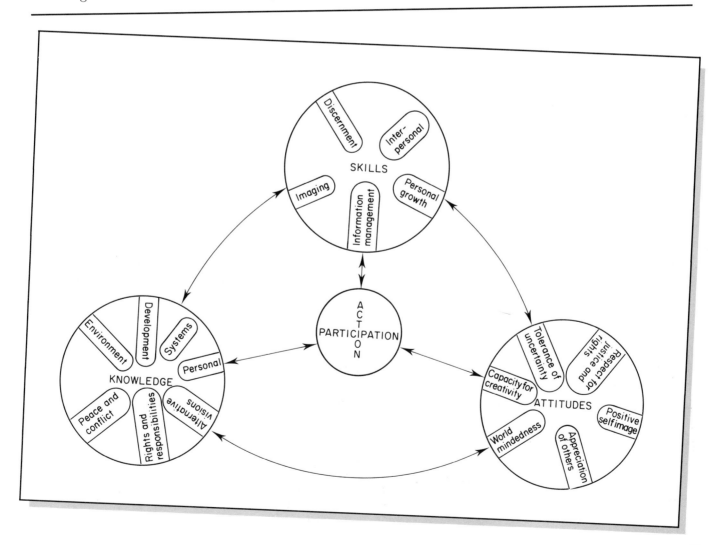

The diagram on page 69 illustrates the inter-relatedness of knowledge, skills and attitudes objectives, and their relationship to participation and action. Non-participation and inaction in the global system is not possible: even a position of apathetic non-involvement requires a combination of knowledge, skills and attitudes which themselves influence and are influenced by other parts of the system. Positive and constructive participation and action likewise depend upon a balance of appropriate knowledge, skills and attitudes, each of which informs, facilitates and nurtures the others. An inadequacy in one area is likely to lead to imbalanced learning and, consequently, less effective or constructive participation and action.

For Emily, life in the twenty-first century is an unknown, exciting and intimidating prospect. To forecast from present trends and developments in a fast-changing world is inevitably speculative. However, it seems likely that her information management skills will be severely put to the test in her personal and professional life and will probably, at times, result in 'information overload'. The resulting stress, ambiguity and uncertainty will have to be effectively managed. We can postulate, too, with some degree of certainty, that Emily will have to make a range of critical choices at stages throughout her life. What career? What personal relationships? What kind of economic and material security? What kind of life-style? Which values and beliefs? Which freedoms, rights, challenges and risks? Her decision-making skills will become highly tuned and sophisticated with experience, but even so she will have to be prepared and able to allow her imagination and intuition to take her places where reason and intellect cannot go. She will need to be able to cope with the consequences of those choices, all of which will have implications for the lives of people with whom she is linked. Conflict in the home, at work and in the community will be unavoidable; she will need to be an accomplished negotiator, assertive in expressing her own demands and feelings, yet empathetic in her understanding of others' perspectives.

And what of knowledge? It is a reasoned assumption that much knowledge vital to Emily's participation in twenty-first century life does not in fact exist today in any accessible form. If she is proficient in information management skills, the acquistion and processing of new information will present no problem. But we can reasonably forecast that, save for a major global environmental or human catastrophe, the present trend towards increasing interdependence of lands and peoples will continue. Ever more sophisticated communication and transportation systems will provide Emily with first or second-hand experiences of war, environmental disaster, rights denials, interpersonal and group violence, famine, poverty and oppression; they will also, hopefully assuage this depressing image of the planet by allowing her to experience the rich delights and insights of diverse cultural practices, perspectives and beliefs, success stories of human achievement, the remarkable creativity of humankind in aesthetic expression and the beauty, symmetry and regenerative capacity of the natural world. Emily will not be able to make sense of many of these experiences without an understanding of the contributory factors and perspectives; she will not be able to take full control of her own life and destiny without understanding her unique yet interconnected position in the global system; she will not be able to contribute to the constructive development of her local and global societies without having a firm grasp of their complex interdependent relationship; and if her contribution to humankind's development is to be significant, she will need vision and imagination and the skills with which to translate her preferred future into reality.

As we suggested in Section 1, the outward journey is also the inward journey. Emily's part in the planet's growth is finally dependent upon her realisation of her own personhood and potential. For that she will need a stalwart belief

'I took my first degree in chemistry at Oxford in 1931.' Looking at the questions asked in chemistry exams at Oxford today, he continues, 'I realise that not only can I not do them, but that I never could have done them, since at least two-thirds of the questions involve knowledge that simply did not exist when I graduated.'

Lord James, former Vice-Chancellor of the University of York, cited in Alvin Toffler, *Future Shock*, Pan, 1971.

in her own worth, an intimate knowledge of her strengths, weaknesses, values and perspectives and the skills to enable her to cope with problems, crises and transitions and with which to restore her mental, physical and spiritual equilibrium.

Global education is lifelong education. Schools cannot expect, nor should they hope, that students will be fully prepared for all the demands of life by the time they finish their formal education. The objectives outlined above are lifelong objectives. Our argument, however, is that schools have a unique opportunity and a responsibility to set and guide students on the paths towards the achievement of those objectives. There are obviously degrees of knowledge and insight, scales of commitment, tolerance and respect, levels of competence and ability; but if students are not given the opportunity and encouragement to achieve *to some degree* the

objectives of global education and, moreover, to acquire the skills of self-education, then life for them in the twenty-first century will be the more mystifying and uncontrollable. It is no longer acceptable in our fast-changing, technologically sophisticated age to argue, for example, that some knowledge of complex global issues, concern for justice and human rights are not appropriate or attainable components of the school curriculum. Apart from ignoring the concurrent learning forces outside the school – such as the home, peer groups and the media – education based on that argument would turn out globally semi-literate young people into a world which demands that they quickly make critical choices for themselves and the planet. Ignorance, tunnel vision and naïvety have never been very useful tools for purposeful decision-making.

Linking pictures

▼ Resources

A set of pictures such as those shown overleaf for each group of eight to ten students. Each set should be cut up into separate pieces and placed in an envelope.

▼ Procedure

The groups form circles. Each group member is given one and, in some cases, two pictures. They are given two minutes to look at their pictures permitting nobody else to see them and avoiding talking. At the end of the two minutes they hide their pictures away and, going around the circle, describe their pictures to each other (it is best to go around the circle twice so that those with two pictures do not describe both pictures at once). Then, still avoiding looking at the pictures, they discuss and negotiate the sequence or arrangement in which they think the pictures should be placed. As they move closer to agreement, they can be asked to actually place the pictures face downwards on the floor/table. When this has been accomplished to the group's satisfaction, the group can turn the pictures over, reflect upon what they have done and then re-negotiate the sequence or arrangement, if necessary.

▼ Potential

An excellent activity for developing/reinforcing a range of important skills such as memory, observation, oral description, discussion, negotiation, lateral

thinking, consensus-seeking, decision-making and reflection. The choice of topics/themes for pictures is virtually limitless.

▼ Follow-up

Two additional stages can be added to the activity as described above. In the first, groups are given three blank sheets of paper. They discuss what they think is likely to happen next in the sequence/arrangement before drawing three pictures illustrating their thinking. In the second, groups receive a further three sheets of paper. This time they discuss what they would like to happen next before drawing three pictures illustrating their hopes and aspirations. Both stages involve the further practice of many of the skills listed above. In addition, the first stage involves students in forecasting and prediction whilst the second stage introduces an important element of values clarification work.

▼ Variation

The activity has been carried out with very good results using pictures randomly chosen from colour supplements and magazines.

Primary/Secondary, 20 minutes.

▼ Source

Developed from an idea in Fisher, S., and Hicks, D.W., World Studies 8–13. A Teacher's Handbook, Oliver & Boyd, 1985, pp. 142–5. Variation suggested by Richard Hedge, Southway School, Plymouth.

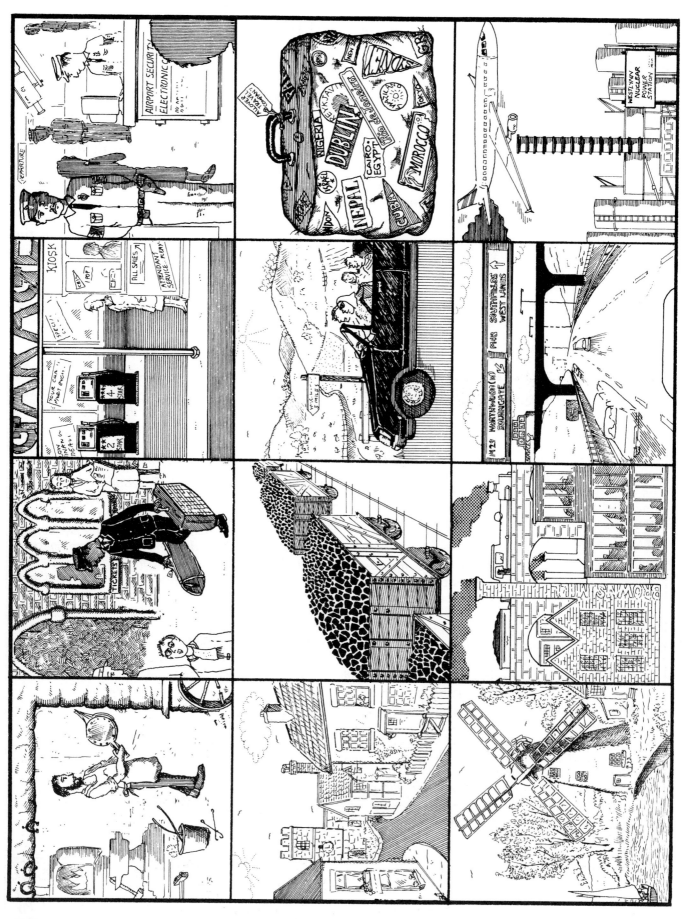

The question remains, however, as to how schools can realistically achieve these objectives, even to a degree, given the limited time and resources at their disposal. We would suggest that the knowledge objectives can be best attained through providing a global perspective right across the primary and secondary curriculum; some examples of this approach can be found in Part Three. As far as the development of skills and exploration of attitudes is concerned, the style of teaching and learning and the quality of the school environment would seem to be of crucial importance. As Edward Cassidy and Dana Kurfman observe, 'a classroom atmosphere which encourages expression of diverse viewpoints is essential for decision making. Decisions are never right or wrong; they are more or less appropriate in terms of a particular situation and an individual decision

maker's values... Moreover, an open atmosphere is necessary for fostering such related affective objectives as self-confidence, tolerance for ambiguity, and a willingness to accept the consequences of one's actions.'[5]

Let us consider one particular activity, **Linking Pictures**, which is extensively used in primary and secondary school world studies lessons. The range of skills being utilised and developed during the various stages of this one activity is vast. During stage one, observation, interpretation and information storing skills are employed, stage two demands information recall, verbal expression, listening skills and visualisation; in stages three and four participants are encouraged to analyse, synthesise and sequence the information and to perceive patterns and relationships through processes of cooperation, negotiation and decision-making;

An appropriate preparation for life in the twenty-first century?

during the final stage any further negotiation results from co-operative evaluation and reflection on the arrangement or sequence of pictures so far created. In order to achieve the goal set – a negotiated and agreed arrangement or sequence of pictures – participants will probably have to be willing and able to manage ambiguity in the information, to explore alternative ideas and perspectives and to adopt the self- and group-affirmative attitudes necessary for effective group co-operation. In the discussion following the activity, verbal communication skills are further utilised, along with analytical, reflective and conceptual thinking. The themes and content of the pictures might prove to be a stimulus for research or study. The extensions to the activity suggested can lead to some very interesting work on probable and preferred futures incorporating forecasting and problem-solving skills. Other activities described in this book promote a similarly wide range of skills development, whilst some provide an emotional or sensory experience which develops understanding of concepts, attitudes and perspectives. We are not suggesting for one moment that the objectives of global education can be met entirely through the use of such activities; a suggested rhythm of courses is discussed in Part Two. We would submit, however, that the use of these and other activities incorporated into a global learning approach will considerably facilitate attainment of the objectives.

Assessment

For Emily, success at school will be measured in terms of grades obtained in GCSE and, if she takes them, A level examinations. Such indicators of her abilities and character will probably be used as principal selection criteria for her entry into a career or further education, but they will not give evidence of her full personhood or potential. Examinations, particularly those undertaken through a process of individual writing against the clock, can only assess a narrow range of skills, of which memory recall and speedwriting are crucial; futhermore, they tend to favour those who work best under pressure in a competitive atmosphere. The achievements of those who succeed in this process should not be belittled, but they are not necessarily sufficiently equipped for life in the

twenty-first century. The tragedy of the traditional examination system is that those who fail may be no less equipped but are deemed to be so by most employers, educators, parents and themselves.

The ultimate paradox is that the public examination system is set up to be an objective measure of learning achievement, an evaluation of an individual student's career in school; in actuality, the system dictates what should be learnt and how it should be learnt. The assessment procedure determines the relative value of a student's abilities, rather like judgement in a beauty contest dictates ideas about beauty. As the orientation of learning in global education is student-centred, rather than examiner-centred, there is a powerful argument for doing away with traditional assessment procedures al-

Robin Richardson, *Fighting for Freedom*, World Studies Series, Nelson, 1978. Copyright World Council of Churches.

together. How can empathy, or concern for injustice, or imagistic thinking be objectively assessed? They cannot, and should not be, at least in a formal sense by an outside agency. Personal assessment is a different matter and should be an ongoing process.

Yet, despite the case against formal assessment, many teachers have argued persistently for a world studies examination at 16+.[6] Mode III CSE and O level syllabuses were operating in many schools prior to the introduction of the GCSE system;[7] a World Studies GCSE syllabus is now offered by the Southern Examining Group.[8] These syllabuses have attempted to mitigate the contradiction between the overall philosophy of world studies and the practices of formal assessment through the development of processes such as oral assessment, assessment of an individual's contribution to groupwork and student profiling. In so doing they are contributing in small but significant ways to a much needed reform of school assessment procedures, a move towards an holistic evaluation of a student's capacities and potential.

It should be recognised that the argument for a world studies examination is based largely on political rather than educational motives. 'Because of the crowded nature of the curriculum for 14–16 year olds,' writes John Turner, 'and the importance of examinations, it is hard to see how World Studies will find a secure place on the curriculum unless it is offered as an exam subject.'[9] The pressure exerted by employers and parents, too, for paper qualifications in every subject studied provides yet more justification for the legitimisation of world studies through public examination. The argument, of course, presupposes that world studies is a subject in its own right, rather than a global perspective in other subjects or right across the curriculum; the relative merits of these approaches will be discussed in Part Three. But so long as secondary schooling remains examination oriented, even the 'global perspective' approach would attract some kind of formal assessment, as everything in the Biology, or RE or Geography syllabus is considered fair game by the examiners.

If, as we have intimated, global education is likely for the foreseeable future to be subject to the public examination system in secondary schools, serious consideration should be given to the formal assessment of the objectives outlined in this section. It would seem logical and feasible to categorise the objectives into those which are *assessable* and those which are *non-assessable*. This would not be inconsistent with present practice in secondary schools, where objectives such as respect for others, time-management and co-operation are considered significant elements in the educational process but not subject to assessment. The difference occurs in the perception of global education as an holistic learning experience rather than just a knowledge- and skills-oriented subject, like History or Chemistry. One problem with this approach is the almost inevitable emphasis that would be given in the final years of secondary schooling on the easily testable objectives, principally those concerned with knowledge and information management skills, thereby distorting the holistic learning process. Consistent pressure for further reforms in assessment procedures is required to convince examiners and others that some of the more problematic objectives, in testing terms, can at least be adequately assessed through a variety and combination of procedures. This may not be 'testing' in the so-called objective sense, but as Pat Burdett points out, even in science subjects traditional assessment is often ethnocentric and disadvantages those who do not share the values, perspectives and the mother tongue of the examiners.[10] A move towards the assessment of the student as a whole person, rather than simply of her knowledge and information management skills, may go some way towards eliminating the discriminatory effect of the present examination system.

Aims and objectives

In Section 1 we identified five aims of global education which together constitute the irreducible global perspective. The following chart explores the relationship between those aims and the objectives of global education, suggesting which objectives are the most important to the satisfaction of each aim. The limitations of a two-dimensional matrix to express an holistic learning programme should again be borne in mind!

GLOBAL EDUCATION: A MATRIX OF AIMS AND OBJECTIVES

KNOWLEDGE OBJECTIVES	AIMS	SYSTEMS CONSCIOUSNESS	PERSPECTIVE CONSCIOUSNESS	HEALTH OF PLANET AWARENESS	INVOLVEMENT CONSCIOUSNESS AND PREPAREDNESS	PROCESS MINDEDNESS
1 PERSONAL						
(a) Self-awareness		*			*	*
(b) Own perspective			*			*
(c) How others see us			*			*
2 SYSTEMS						
(a) Systems theory		*				*
(b) World systems		*		*		
(c) Interdependence		*			*	
(d) Commonality		*				
3 DEVELOPMENT						
(a) Forms of development			*			
(b) Trading relationships		*		*		
(c) Aid		*		*		
(d) Colonialism		*		*		
(e) Role of women		*		*		
(f) Population		*		*		
(g) Health & nutrition		*		*		
(h) Education & literacy		*		*		
4 ENVIRONMENT						
(a) Destruction of ecosystems		*		*		
(b) Natural resources		*		*		
(c) Conservation		*		*		
(d) Pollution		*		*		
(e) Land use & reform		*		*		
(f) Built environments		*		*		
5 PEACE AND CONFLICT						
(a) Negative & positive peace			*	*		
(b) Interpersonal peace		*		*		
(c) Inter-group peace		*		*		

KNOWLEDGE OBJECTIVES

	C1	C2	C3	C4	C5
(d) International peace	*		*		
(e) Armaments	*		*		
(f) Terrorism/freedom fighting	*		*		
(g) Non-violent protest	*		*		
6 RIGHTS AND RESPONSIBILITIES					
(a) Human rights & responsibilities			*	*	
(b) Moral & legal rights & responsibilities		*			
(c) Liberty oriented & security oriented rights		*	*		
(d) Freedom from, freedom to	*		*		
(e) Prejudice & discrimination	*	*	*		
(f) Oppression	*	*	*		
(g) Self-determination	*		*		
(h) Animal rights	*		*		
7 ALTERNATIVE VISIONS					
(a) Futures	*	*	*	*	
(b) Sustainable life-styles	*		*	*	
(c) Human & planetary health	*		*		*

SKILLS OBJECTIVES

	C1	C2	C3	C4	C5
1 INFORMATION MANAGEMENT					
(a) Receiving & expressing information			*	*	
(b) Organising & processing information	*		*	*	
(c) Evaluating information		*	*	*	*
(d) Storing & retrieving information			*	*	
(e) Systems analysis	*				*
2 PERSONAL GROWTH					
(a) Centring	*			*	*
(b) Physical well-being	*		*		
(c) Manual	*			*	
(d) Creative potential	*			*	
(e) Values, beliefs and perspectives		*	*		*
(f) Shock avoidance				*	*
(g) Time management			*	*	
3 INTERPERSONAL					
(a) Assertiveness		*		*	
(b) Empowerment		*		*	
(c) Trust building		*		*	
(d) Co-operation			*	*	
(e) Negotiation			*	*	

SKILLS OBJECTIVES

(f) Conflict management			*	*	
4 DISCERNMENT					
(a) Decision-making	*	*		*	*
(b) Ethical judgement	*	*	*	*	
(c) Aesthetic appreciation	*	*			
5 IMAGING					
(a) Creative thinking	*	*	*	*	*
(b) Problem solving	*	*		*	
(c) Perception of relationships	*			*	*
(d) Holistic perception	*	*	*	*	*
(e) Empathy		*	*		
(f) Visualisation	*	*			
(g) Forecasting	*		*	*	*

ATTITUDES OBJECTIVES

1 POSITIVE SELF-IMAGE					
(a) Belief in own potential	*			*	
(b) Genuineness	*			*	
(c) Curiosity	*	*	*		*
2 APPRECIATION OF OTHERS					
(a) Diversity		*			*
(b) Commonality		*			*
(c) New perspectives		*			*
3 RESPECT FOR JUSTICE & RIGHTS					
(a) Defence of rights			*	*	
(b) Concern for justice			*	*	
(c) Commitment to equality			*	*	
4 TOLERANCE OF UNCERTAINTY					
(a) Ambiguity			*	*	*
(b) Insecurity				*	*
(c) Conflict and change			*	*	*
5 CAPACITY FOR CREATIVITY			*		
(a) Risk-taking	*	*		*	*
(b) Paradigm shift	*	*	*	*	*
(c) Imagery and intuition	*	*	*		
6 WORLD-MINDEDNESS					
(a) Respect for life	*		*		
(b) Altruism	*		*	*	

World studies and assessment

by **Richard Hedge**, Southway School, Plymouth

1 Is World Studies assessable?

It was tempting to pose this question as 'Can we nail jelly to the ceiling?' A glance at the Aims section of the Southern Examining Group's World Studies syllabus (see Appendix) reminds us what we are trying to achieve: individuals with a real under-standing of the world in which they live and an ability and willingness to make it better. Clearly these are far longer-term aspirations than could be evaluated by any on-the-spot assessment procedure and in this sense any attempt to make a summative statement about an individual's 'success' at world studies is an educational equivalent of chasing after rainbows.

All we can hope to do, therefore, is make an interim judgement about the potential of sixteen year-olds to develop into globally-oriented citizens. At this stage, however, we must beware lest our search for the assessable means we limit ourselves to the unimportant. There is a tension between what we want to measure and what we can measure. A set of appropriate world studies assessment objectives is most likely to be achieved if we start from the former and make concessions to the latter as carefully and reluctantly as possible.

It was in this spirit and amidst considerable agonising that the assessment objectives of the GCSE course were formulated. The division of the objectives into three groups relating to understand-ing, ability and capacity recognises the need for a combination of cognitive and affective qualities described above. As teachers we are usually con-fident of our ability to assess students in the realms of knowledge and skills (although there are some new departures in these areas) but the 'capacity' section is unfamiliar to most and has already proved a cause of concern in our own department. In the light of the argument above, however, it will be seen that the need is not to change these objectives but to establish a national network of people thinking creatively about practical procedures for assessing them. I will return to this theme when considering guidelines for an overall assessment programme, but first there is another question to be considered.

2 Who needs assessment anyway?

It may be this should have been our first question. There is a general sense in which all assessment is anti-educational. More particularly, because any assessment will lay stress on individual achievement and, implicitly, competition between students, there is an obvious danger that assessment processes will actually work against the aims of a World Studies course. Even if procedures can be devised to minim-ise the danger, why not remove the risk altogether by devoting all our efforts to producing stimulating and enriching courses rather than obstructing students with a series of hurdles?

Sadly, the answers to this question are largely pragmatic. At Southway we soon discovered that if the course was to be accepted as credible by students, parents and staff it needed the 'seal of approval' of external validation at CSE and O level. This was especially significant in the context of a core curriculum in which the course had to be seen to earn its place alongside the more traditional subject areas of English, Maths, Science and French. In a sense the radical nature of the course content and methodology made this formal recognition more important. Bernard Shaw observed that in England one should not try to combine unconventional views with unconventional dress and it may be that the suspicion with which global education is viewed in some quarters means that we need to take extra steps to reassure people in other ways.

If, in the light of these considerations, we decide that some form of assessment is necessary, it is important to beware of the danger of too readily limiting the course and restricting the students by subjecting them to a series of written assignments which continually disrupt the flow of activities and, for some, repeatedly reinforce a sense of inadequacy and alienation. Several members of our World Studies team feel, in retrospect, that we did our students and our course a mis-service by 'selling out' too early and too easily to the requirements of exam boards – in our case the South Western Board Examinations Board Mode III World Studies and the Joint Matriculation Board Integrated Humani-ties. The tail will always tend to wag the course unless the assessment procedure is actively regarded as secondary to the provision of worthwhile learning experiences and unless it is designed with the aims of the course clearly in mind.

3 What are we looking for?

It seems to me that there are, perhaps, five criteria by which we will want to evaluate any assessment programme. It may well be that this list is not exhaustive; these guidelines simply represent the most memorable lessons learned over four years of not entirely happy experiences working with the assessment schemes previously available at O level and CSE.

(a) We should be assessing important qualities. I vividly remember a student handing back to me an assessment exercise testing ability to 'locate and select information' for the JMB Integrated Humanities. 'It was just like an English com-prehension really' was the verdict. Indeed as humanities courses generally have moved away (quite rightly!) from knowledge testing as the focus for their assessment, they have tended more and more to parallel and even duplicate English in its testing of comprehension and communication skills.

While these skills have a part to play in equipping students for responsible global citizenship, they fall well short of any remotely satisfying measure of the aims of our courses. It was for this reason that the GCSE assessment package broke new ground by seeking to evaluate students in the distinctively 'World Studies' areas of perspectives, futures, interrelationships, co-operative skills and individual action. A practical benefit of this will be that assessment activities play a positive part in furthering the aims of the course rather than being at best a pause and at worst a backward step.

(b) The assessment procedure should be under school control. Perhaps the greatest problem we have experienced with the assessment of World Studies has been the extent to which we have had to accommodate our courses to the inflexible requirements of exam boards. We have had, for example, to assess a course which naturally has four broad dimensions under five topic headings. Almost 50% of our assessment has had to be knowledge testing. The majority of our students have had to be prepared for a final exam. The constraints thus imposed have been considerable and almost always they have detracted from the quality of the learning experience we would like to provide.

Clearly, there is always likely to be some tension between the needs of schools seeking to provide the best possible courses and those of exam boards primarily concerned with ensuring comparable schemes of assessment and grades which can be externally scrutinised. It would be foolish to suppose that any exam scheme could totally resolve this and it is certainly likely to remain in some areas of the World Studies GCSE. The scheme does, however, make some important steps in the right direction. It was, for example, written in part by World Studies teachers with the needs of schools clearly in mind. Secondly, every component of the assessment package is devised and administered by teachers in the schools. Thirdly, the appointment by the exam group of locally-based Adviser-Moderators institutionalises a process of negotiation and co-operation between teachers and examiners which has been lacking in most earlier schemes.

(c) The assessment should be as streamlined as possible. One of the most common pitfalls of coursework-based assessment packages as they have developed over recent years has been the tendency to over-assess students. We have been in the position of setting twenty pieces of work to

assess four assessment objectives five times each. The arrival of GCSE and coursework across the curriculum makes the need to reduce the pressure that this imposes on students' time and nervous energy even more urgent.

The World Studies GCSE takes two significant steps towards achieving this aim. First, the balance is shifted from highly intensive assessment units to more genuine continuous assessment in the form of the profile. Second, and obviously related to this, there are only three occasions in the course where students are involved in formal assessment exercises. It may be that, as confidence in the profiling component increases, there is pressure from teachers to reduce this number still further.

(d) A large proportion of the assessment should be oral. Most students are far more confident – and therefore perform to higher levels – when exploring ideas orally. In terms of life skills it is also true that almost all involvement of the student in global issues after school will be achieved through oral discussion. Our experience of a terminal oral exam for 200+ candidates a year at CSE gives us great confidence in this mode of assessment. We have found that it allows us a powerful insight into the strengths and weaknesses of candidates as well as being almost infinitely flexible and thus enabling us to create situations where almost all candidates can experience some level of positive achievement.

For these reasons, the inclusion of a terminal oral in the GCSE scheme, and its allocation of 25% of the total mark will be welcomed by many teachers. The syllabus provides guidelines for the conduct and moderation of these examinations which should enable worries about standardisations to be at the very least suspended pending experience of the course.

(e) Assessment should be based in part on a process of negotiation between teacher and student. One of the greatest concerns about assessment in general and school-based assessment in particular is that it tends to cast the relationship between teacher and student into a hierarchical framework which undermines the co-operative spirit which the rest of the course seeks to promote.

Clearly the negotiated profiling component of the assessment package is its most innovatory element. There will doubtless be teething problems in many schools and it will be important for teachers to share and jointly evaluate possible strategies. We shall certainly be looking to focus each of the four statements on a particular assessment objective and to arrange that, in addition to the activities prescribed in the syllabus, students experience in the appropriate terms other situations where they can reflect on the objective concerned. There is almost bound to be an element of trial and error in this at first but the experience is one which we welcome for both teachers and students. If the profiling approach is to work, however, it is essential that it is genuinely incorporated into the students' overall experience of the course. This issue is so fundamental it must now be explored in more detail.

4 Bolting on or building in?

If, for all the reasons discussed above, profiling is regarded as a highly significant part of the assessment package then it is important that the principles which underlie the process become truly integrated into the whole of the students' experience. The distinctive features of profiling are, it seems to me, those of reflection, self-assessment and negotiation and it is these which need to be experienced by students over a long period if the profile is to succeed. It is clearly unrealistic to expect students to exercise these skills successfully if they are only called for on four occasions in their school career. World Studies teachers need not only to build these approaches into their courses but also to press for their adoption on a school-wide scale.

Taking the three features in turn. As our course has included more and more participatory activities in recent years, we have become increasingly aware of the need to provide opportunities and structures for students to reflect on what they have learnt. There is a danger that our courses become so action-packed that students hurtle from one activity to the other so quickly that the learning is almost diluted out of the process. We have been particularly concerned to involve students in consideration of group activities – discussing the prerequisites of a successful group and evaluating the extent to which their group has shown these qualities. It is also interesting to note that students are familiar with many of these ideas through their social education programme.

Also on a school-wide scale, for the past four years students have been involved in compiling Personal Records. These records build up through a school career into a file of reflections on activities in and out of school with an emphasis on the personal qualities that are involved. It would be true to say that the success of this process has been somewhat patchy but there is no doubt that most students have gained some level of confidence in self-reflection as a result.

Self-assessment is an area which many students need practice to develop. Some years ago we developed a simple self-assessment form which we now use with third-year students and which will, we hope, enable them to enter the GCSE profiling process with confidence. The form has three sections. The first allows students to respond to each activity as it is completed. These activities may involve part of a lesson's work or may stretch over a week or more and it is likely that students will often complete the forms at different times. The second section identifies a set of skills which are judged as applying across all course units. In the light of the comments made above, it may well be that this list should be reassessed with a view to incorporating more which relate more directly to World Studies. Finally, for each course unit, a set of key ideas is identified which students consider at the end of the topic. The use of four point scales in every case is quite deliberate as it puts students in the position of having to come 'off the fence' and express a more definite view.

Across the school, students are also involved once or twice a term in a self-monitoring procedure. Approximately every six weeks staff assess students on three point scales relating to effort and attainment and this is paralleled by students assessing their own identical form.

Negotiation is not a process which we have yet made as explicit a part of our course as it should be. We have not, for example, arrived at the point where, like some schools, the subject matter of the course is, to some extent, determined each year in conjunction with students. There is, however a sense in which strong emphasis on the processive classroom recasts the relationship between student and teacher in such a way as inevitably to create an environment in which negotiation can more naturally take place. Certainly it has been our experience that as the nature of our learning activities has changed so the quality of discussions between teachers and students has increased considerably.

In addition our school is also a pilot school for a South Western Records of Achievement scheme. The aim of this scheme is for each student to leave school with a positive description of personal qualities as well as activities undertaken in and out of school. This statement is produced in two stages with an interim third-year version preceding the production of the final document in the fifth year. On each occasion both tutor and student draft a statement and then collaborate to produce a final version by negotiation. Characteristically this takes place in a fifteen minute discussion which has been found intrinsically very useful for both parties as well as laying an excellent foundation for World Studies profiling.

Other ideas for student self-evaluation are given in Section 12.

Each one of us possesses gifts and abilities and it is up to all of us to develop and use them as well as we can.

How well do you think you are doing?

Use the table below to comment on your course and performance.

Use the following shorthand:

1 : EXCELLENT   3 : FAIR
2 : GOOD   4 : POOR

DATE	TITLE	INTEREST	ENJOYMENT	UNDERSTANDING	CONTRIBUTION	COMMENT
	ACTIVITY 1					
	ACTIVITY 2					
	ACTIVITY 3					
	ACTIVITY 4					
	ACTIVITY 5					
	ACTIVITY 6					
	ACTIVITY 7					
	ACTIVITY 8					
	ACTIVITY 9					
	ACTIVITY 10					
	ACTIVITY 11					
	ACTIVITY 12					

Use this section to comment on your work. You will probably be invited to do this every three or four weeks during the topic.

Use this shorthand when answering the question:

1 : VERY WELL   3 : WITH DIFFICULTY
2 : QUITE WELL 4 : HARDLY AT ALL
                X : DOES NOT APPLY

HOW WELL DO YOU THINK YOU HAVE BEEN ABLE TO ... ?	DATE		
organise yourself and your work			
cooperate with others in a group			
express your ideas clearly when speaking			
express your ideas clearly in writing			
listen carefully to the ideas of others			
read and understand passages of writing			
take in information from films / videos			
weigh up differing points of view			
put yourself in the position of others			

Complete this section at the end of the topic.

During the study of this topic we have tried to help you to improve your appreciation of the ideas listed below.

Use this shorthand to comment on any change in appreciation that has happened:

1 : I understand this much more clearly.

2 : I have a slightly better understanding.

3 : There has been no real change in my understanding.

4 : I am now more confused than I was to begin with.

People need to be seen both as special individuals and members of groups
People are special : we are different from animals.
People are special because we make decisions and communicate
Decision making and communication are both skills we can develop by practise

If you have any comments on your work and/or the topic, write them in this space.

World Studies Pupil Profile: Southway School

References

1 Roszak, T., *Person/Planet*, Granada, 1981, p. 210.
2 Sources used for ideas on knowledge objectives: Fisher, S. and Hicks, D. W, *World Studies 8–13. A teacher's handbook*, Oliver & Boyd, 1985, p. 25; Fisher, S., Magee, F. and Wetz, J., *Ideas into action: curriculum for a changing world*, World Studies Project, 1980, p. 52; Richardson, R., Flood, M. & Fisher, S., *Debate and decision: schools in a world of change*, World Studies Project, 1980, 29; Southern Examining Group, *World Studies: a GCSE group mode III scheme for first examination in 1988*, p. 9 (see Appendix).
3 Sources used for ideas on skills objectives: Carpenter, S., *A Repertoire of Peacemaking Skills*, Consortium on Peace Research, Education and Development, 1977, pp. 24–34; Cassidy, E.W. and Kurfman, D. G., 'Decision making as purpose and process' in Kurfman, D. G. (ed.), *Developing Decision-making Skills*, National Council for the Social Studies, 47th Yearbook, Virginia, 1977, pp. 17–24; Cell, E., *Learning to Learn From Experience*, State University of New York, Albany, 1984, pp. 194–207; Fisher, S. and Hicks, D. W., op. cit., p. 25; Fisher, S., Magee, F. and Wetz, J., op. cit., p. 52; Haas, J. D., *Future Studies in the K-12 Curriculum*, ERIC Clearing House for Counselling and Personnel Services, University of Michigan, Ann Arbor, 1980, pp. 55–60; Hendricks, G. and Wills, R., *The Centering Book*, Prentice-Hall, 1975, p. 5 *et seq*; Hopson, B. and Scally, M., *Lifeskills Teaching*, McGraw-Hill, 1981, pp. 63–73; Houston, J., *The Possible Human*, J. P. Tarcher, 1982, pp. 134–64; Johnson, D. W. and Johnson, R. T., *Learning Together and Alone: Co-operation, Competition and Individualization*, Prentice-Hall, 1975, pp. 95–113; Johnson, D. W., Johnson, R. T., Holubec, E. J. and Roy, P., *Circles of Learning: Co-operation in the Classroom*, Association for Supervision and Curriculum Development, Virginia, 1984, pp. 43–53; Richardson, R., Flood, M. and Fisher, S., op. cit., p. 29; Southern Examining Group, op. cit., pp. 2–4; Toffler, A., *Future Shock*, Pan, 1971, pp. 374–8.
4 Sources used for ideas on attitudes objectives: Anderson, C. C. and Winston, B. J., 'Acquiring information by asking questions, using maps and graphs, and making direct observations' in Kurfman, D. G. (ed.), op. cit., pp. 75–7; Carpenter, S., op. cit., pp. 24–34; Fisher, S. and Hicks, D. W., op. cit., p. 25; Fisher, S., Magee, F. and Wetz, J. op. cit., p. 52; Haas, J. D., op. cit., pp. 55–60; Houston, J., op. cit., pp. 134–64; Richardson, R., Flood, M. and Fisher, S., op. cit., p. 29; Southern Examining Group, op. cit., pp. 2–4.
5 Cassidy, E. W. and Kurfman, D. G., op.cit., in Kurfman, D. G. (ed.), op. cit., p. 22.
6 See, for example, Turner, J., 'Examining world studies – problems and possibilities', *World Studies Journal*, Vol. 3, No. 4, Summer 1982, pp. 38–44.
7 Some examples of syllabuses can be found in the Global Education Documentation Service of the Centre for Global Education, University of York: Document No. 1, World Studies syllabus, Groby Community College; Document No. 3, World Studies syllabus, City of Ely College; Document No. 12, World Studies mode III syllabus, Central Foundation Girls School, London; Document No. 15, South West mode III CSE World Studies syllabus.
8 See Appendix.
9 Turner, J., op. cit., p. 40.
10 Burdett, P., 'What have science, education in a multicultural society and all-white schools to do with each other?', *World Studies Journal*, Vol. 5, No. 4, 1985, p. 55.

Part Two
THE GLOBAL CLASSROOM

4 The style and rhythm of courses

Learning styles

Reformers in British education, argues Ian Lister, have tended to concern themselves with reform of *access* (so as to open educational institutions at various levels to majorities) or reform of *content* (so as to make the curriculum more relevant to perceived needs). The 'main riddle of reform' – the reform of *process* (i.e. teaching and learning styles, classroom relationships and the hidden curriculum of schooling) – has generally been overlooked especially 'in those schools adjacent to the labour market'. 'Alternative forms of teaching and learning,' he adds, 'are hard to find as teachers are trained with manuals which view the child as the enemy, in which they are recommended to act like Clausewitz in the classroom (with the observed response of some pupils that they follow the maxims of guerilla warfare).'[1] Interestingly, the debate in Britain in the 1980s about 'balance' in education has concentrated almost exclusively on achieving what is seen as a fair representation of opinions and perspectives in the classroom. There has been little debate about the marked imbalance in teaching and learning styles as experienced by the majority of students and little recognition of the political implications of that imbalance. It is to US educational reformers that we principally need to turn for insights into the place that learning styles should have in educational planning at both school and classroom level. One such reformer is Anthony Gregorc.

According to Gregorc learning style is the outward expression of the human mind's *mediation abilities* (i.e. the means and capacities we employ to receive and express information). Two principal factors in determining learning style, he maintains, are the ways in which we perceive and order the information we encounter. *Perceptual abilities* are the means whereby we grasp information; our perception may be *abstract* (through reason, emotion or intuition) or *concrete* (through the physical senses of hearing, sight, smell, taste and touch). *Ordering abilities* are the ways in which we arrange, systematise and dispose of information; our ordering may be *sequential* (linear, step-by-step and methodical) or *random* (non-linear, leaping and multifarious with 'multiplex patterns of data' being processed 'simultaneously and holistically').[2]

The coupling of the qualities of abstract and concrete perception and sequential and random ordering, says Gregorc, creates four distinct learning styles: Concrete Sequential (CS), Abstract Sequential (AS), Abstract Random (AR) and Concrete Random (CR). 'Each of these combinations reveals a particular qualitative orientation to life. Although each and every one of us is equipped, so to speak, with all four qualities, most individuals are predisposed strongly towards one, two, or even three channels. Few individuals are equally strong in all four channels. Given the holistic nature of human personality no one is a "pure" type working exclusively within one style.'[3] What, in brief, are the four learning styles Gregorc has identified?

Concrete Sequential (CS) The dominant Concrete Sequential, Gregorc explains, derives information primarily through direct sensory experience. The 'real' world is the concrete world of the senses. Her thinking is methodical and deliberate – a 'train of thought'. With finely-tuned physical senses, she registers objects in the concrete world extraordinarily well. This same outward orientation can lead her to attribute the cause of intuitive experiences and feelings to something within her environment. Task-oriented and consistently striving for perfection, the dominant Concrete Sequential is at ease with detail, categorises and organises, lacks interest in abstract theories and tends to interpret everything literally. *Learning activities to suit the dominant Concrete Sequential include keeping records of experi-*

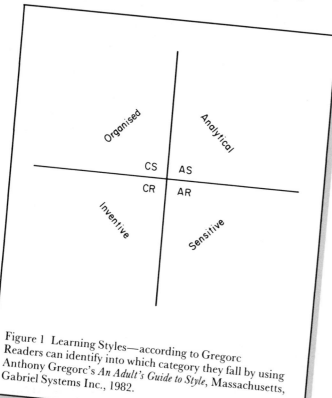

Figure 1 Learning Styles—according to Gregorc
Readers can identify into which category they fall by using Anthony Gregorc's *An Adult's Guide to Style*, Massachusetts, Gabriel Systems Inc., 1982.

ences and experiments, conducting surveys, writing computer programmes, observing and classifying phenomena, undertaking practical work and preparing displays.[4]

Abstract Sequential (AS) The dominant Abstract Sequential lives mostly in the abstract, non-physical world of thoughts, theories and mental constructions. Reality consists of words and concepts, such as justice and peace, which generalise beyond concrete examples and form the scaffolding for a worldview. Her thinking is logical, analytical and evaluative and her ability to outline, correlate, compare and categorise is unsurpassed. She is a first-rate eclectic and synthesiser of information and ideas. She is also an articulate communicator. *Learning activities to suit the dominant Abstract Sequential include listening to lectures, comparing and contrasting different accounts and interpretations of events, project research and the synthesising of ideas and information in essay or project form, library study and group or plenary discussion.*[5]

Abstract Random (AR) The 'real world' of the dominant Abstract Random is the non-physical world of feelings, emotions and imagination. Possessing uncanny intuition and antennae which sense nuances of atmosphere and mood, her thinking processes are anchored in feelings surrounding experiences. Gregorc calls the dominant Abstract Random's mind a 'psychic "sponge" that can absorb ideas, information, vibrations, and impressions' as they flow around and through her. She easily establishes rapport with others, feeling both empathy and sympathy, and cares more about the quality and refinement of experiences than their quantity. She prefers to communicate through personal experiences, story, metaphor, symbol, poetry and music and does not care much for humdrum routine tasks and tightly-structured assignments. *Learning activities to suit the dominant Abstract Random include group discussion work, interpersonal work in small groups, role plays, guided fantasy and imagery, imaginative writing and the preparation and production of multi-media presentations.*[6]

Concrete Random (CR) For the dominant Concrete Random, the concrete physical world is the starting point. Her instinct and intuition are keys for unlocking the meaning to be found in everything experienced. Her thinking processes are impulsive and can make intuitive leaps towards identifying underlying and unifying principles behind what she experiences. Equally, she operates on insight in jumping from fact to theory. An experimenter, risk-taker and divergent thinker, she will often arrive at unconventional and unusual solutions and a range of surprising opinions and perspectives. She rarely accepts anything on outside authority and resents restrictive and over-obtrusive authority figures. Validation of ideas comes through probing, practical demonstration and personal proof. *Learning activities to suit the dominant Concrete Random include experiential units, simulation games, role plays, problem-solving exercises, independent study, practical experiments and exercises which challenge the student to find alternative paths to a particular goal.*[7]

Gregorc is at pains to point out that style applies to all persons irrespective of age, creed, gender or race. He also emphasises that there is no right or wrong style and that there is no connection between style and intelligence. Although we may

be one-style dominant, no person operates totally in that style. Some people are 'squares' in that their learning style profile indicates almost equal comfortability and strength in all four quadrants.[8] Others can be encouraged to operate through styles in which they initially feel neither comfortable nor strong.[9]

Another US educator who has addressed learning style is Bernice McCarthy whose *4 MAT System* draws together the insights of a broad spectrum of learning style researchers but especially David Kolb and ongoing split-brain reasearch. Kolb developed a four-quadrant model for mapping the ways in which people perceive and process information (see Figure 2). Having placed the two dimensions of sensing/feeling and thinking along one axis of the model and the two dimensions of acting and watching along the second axis, Kolb found that people fall into one of the four quadrants thus created.

Organised (CS) quadrant

Analytical (AS) quadrant

Inventive (CR) quadrant

Sensitive (AR) quadrant

Some experience and take in information *concretely* and process it *reflectively*, i.e. they start with what they see and then generalise (the top right-hand quadrant); others take in experience *abstractly* and process it *reflectively*, i.e. they start with an idea and 'play' with it (the lower right-hand quadrant; others take in experience *abstractly* and process it *actively*, i.e. they start with an idea and test if it works (the lower left-hand quadrant); others take in experience *concretely* and process it *actively*, i.e. they start with what they sense and feel and plunge into action (the top left-hand quadrant).[10]

Using Kolb's model and his subsequent analysis of different types of learner and also drawing upon the findings of other learning style researchers, McCarthy developed the four learning style modes that comprise her *4 MAT System* (see Figure 3); to her model, she added insights from research findings on the respective functions of left and right brain hemispheres. Split-brain research, it will be recalled from Section 2, has discovered that the left hemisphere performs a linear/sequential type of processing whereas the right hemisphere uses holistic/synthesising forms of processing. A left-brain dominant person is analytical; prefers verbalising; likes sequence and structure and approaches problems by breaking them down into separate parts and treating them logically. A right-brain dominant person is intuitive and synthesising; likes random patterns, fluidity and spontaneity and solves problems by looking at the whole and by relying upon hunch, intuition and pattern. Each of the four learning modes, says McCarthy, needs to be approached giving due consideration to both left and right brain processing techniques (see Figure 4).[11]

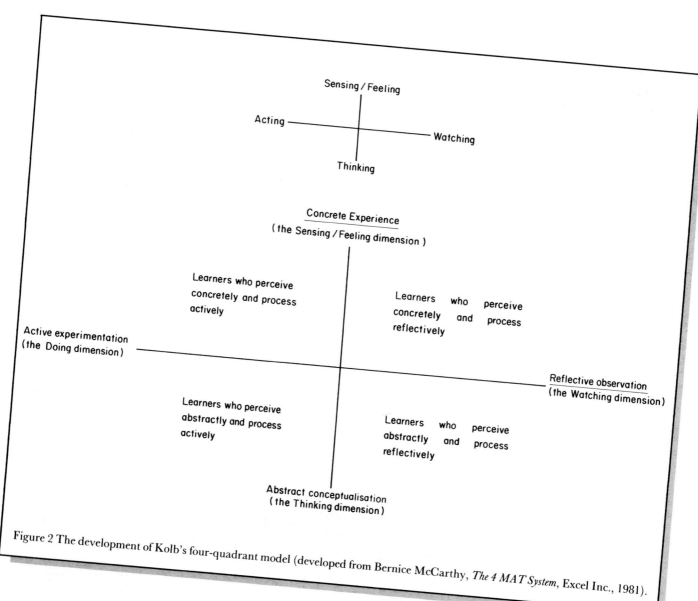

Figure 2 The development of Kolb's four-quadrant model (developed from Bernice McCarthy, *The 4 MAT System*, Excel Inc., 1981).

SENSING/FEELING

STYLE FOUR – 'THE DYNAMIC LEARNER'

- integrates experience and application
- seeks hidden possibilities and excitement
- needs to know what can be done with things
- learns by trial and error
- perceives information concretely and processes it actively
- adaptable to and relishes change
- excels in situations calling for flexibility
- tends to take risks
- often reaches accurate conclusions in the absence of logical evidence
- functions by acting and testing experience
- *Strengths*: action and carrying out plans
- *Goals*: making things happen, bringing action to concepts
- *Favourite Questions*: If? What can this become?

STYLE ONE – 'THE INNOVATIVE LEARNER'

- integrates experience with 'self'
- seeks meaning, clarity and integrity
- needs to be personally involved
- absorbs reality
- perceives information concretely and processes it reflectively
- interested in people and culture
- divergent thinkers who believe in their own experience and excel in viewing concrete situations from many perspectives
- model themselves on those they respect
- learn by listening and sharing ideas
- function through social interaction
- *Strengths*: innovation and imagination (ideas people)
- *Goals*: self-involvement in important issues, bringing unity to diversity
- *Favourite Questions*: Why? Why Not?

DOING

WATCHING

STYLE THREE – 'THE COMMON SENSE LEARNER'

- seeks usability, utility, results
- needs to know how things work
- learns by testing theories that seem sensible
- skill-oriented
- perceives information abstractly and processes it actively
- needs hands-on experiences
- enjoys problem solving
- restricts judgement to concrete things
- resents being given answers and limited tolerance of 'fuzzy' ideas
- needs to know how things she is asked to do will help in real life
- functions through inferences drawn from sensory experience
- *Strengths*: practical application of ideas
- *Goal:* bringing their view of the present into line with future security
- *Favourite Question*: How does it work?

STYLE TWO – 'THE ANALYTIC LEARNER'

- seeks facts
- needs to know what the experts think
- learns by thinking through ideas
- values sequential thinking, needs details
- perceives information abstractly and processes it reflectively
- less interested in people than ideas
- critiques information and collects data
- thorough and industrious, re-examining facts if situations are perplexing
- enjoys traditional classrooms
- functions by thinking things through and adapting to experts
- *Strengths*: creating concepts and models
- *Goals*: self-satisfaction, intellectual recognition
- *Favourite Question*: What?

THINKING

Figure 3 Bernice McCarthy's four learning style quadrants (extracted from *The 4 MAT System*, Excel Inc., 1981, pp. 37–43 and workshop handouts). Tests for identifying preferred learning style are available from the publisher of *The 4 MAT System* (see Select Bibliography).

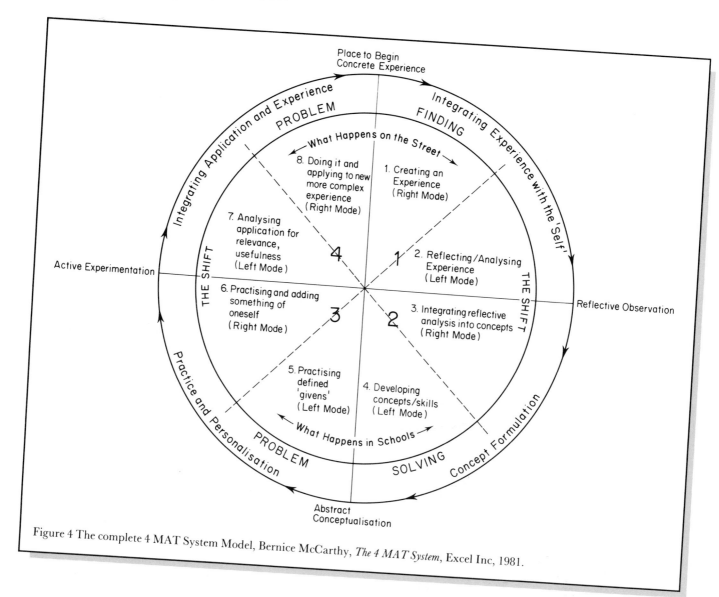

Figure 4 The complete 4 MAT System Model, Bernice McCarthy, *The 4 MAT System*, Excel Inc, 1981.

Whilst both Gregorc and McCarthy would be amongst the first to concede that much remains to be done to refine our understanding of learning styles, it is clear that their work, however qualified our acceptance of its every detail, carries profound implications for the classroom.

First and foremost, there is the question of equality of educational opportunity. If we accept that most of us have a preference for one of four broadly defined learning styles, each of which is likely to be well represented in any class of thirty students, than we have to ask ourselves as teachers whether we are equally catering for each style so that each student has an equal opportunity to learn and succeed. As Gregorc puts it: 'equal educational opportunities for children requires equal access to those opportunities for different types of thinker'.[12] McCar-

thy pulls no punches in making her assessment that schools, in their emphasis upon frontal teaching, facts and analysis, considerably favour Style Two Analytic Learners (Gregorc's dominant Abstract Sequentials). Her own research with 17–18 year olds in two suburban Chicago High Schools revealed that approximately equal percentages of male and female students fell into each of the four learning style quadrants, that 60% of the sample still favoured the Concrete Experience dimension (i.e. although towards the end of compulsory schooling, most were still not comfortable with abstract learning) and that more students (46%) were right-brain dominant as against left-brain dominant (28%) and integrated–dominant (25%). Only the Analytic Learners contained a higher percentage of left-brain dominant students. These findings, she concluded, were particularly striking given that schools are 'designed to instruct primarily in the left mode' and are 'structured for Analytic Learners'.[13] Considerations of equality of opportunity and the need to build positive self-image in each and every student demanded that 'all students get the chance to shine 25% of the time' by learning within their favoured quadrant.[14]

What are the implications of the work of Gregorc and McCarthy for the planning and conduct of courses and topics? Both are at one in recommending that students should learn 'style flexibility', i.e. that they acquire comfortability and strengths in other styles as well as being given the opportunity to operate for a fair share of the time in their preferred style. The means whereby 'flexability' can be achieved are, of course, various. A particular topic, for instance, can be given over *in toto* to one stylistic approach thereby allowing some students to learn through their preferred style whilst stretching the style of all the other sudents. The danger of this single-style approach is that it can engender loss of self-esteem, underachievement, a sense of failure, stress and alienation in some, if not the majority. Another approach is to offer different tracks through a topic, each suitable to different learning styles. The teacher negotiates with the student as to whether she will work in her own style or 'stretch' to another style. A third approach – the multiple approach – is to design a topic to offer a smörgåsbord of the quadrants so that all styles are met on a rotating basis.

The multiple approach is the basis of McCarthy's *4 MAT System*. 'If we consider the circle as a clock,' she writes, 'and begin at 12 o'clock with Concrete Experience, then by moving clockwise around the circle we next develop the skills of Reflective Observation. From that point we move the students to Abstract Conceptualization and finally to Active Experimentation. Then the cycle begins again, with new, richer experiences in ever-widening spirals.'[15] McCarthy and teaching colleagues have developed and tested exemplars of how *4 MAT* can operate in various school subjects.[16] Let us take Marlene Wieczorek Bowen's middle-school science unit on energy as an example (see Figure 5). The topic begins in the right mode of quadrant one (the Innovative Learner's most comfortable place) with students using checklists at home to raise their curiosity and obtain information about family energy usage and energy consciousness.

It continues in the left mode of quadrant one with students working in small groups to combine, examine and plot graphs about their gathered data. In the right mode of quadrant two (the Analytical Learner), students examine examples of energy loss before drawing their image of a world without energy; in the left mode, the teacher develops theories and concepts through a lecture on themes such as energy in appliances, home insulation, calculating energy usage and energy-intensive lifestyles. The concepts are reinforced through worksheets and workbooks in the left mode of quadrant three (the Common Sense Learner). In the right mode ('adding something of oneself'), students draw up their own plans to increase energy efficiency in their homes – which their parents must sign and approve. In the left mode of quadrant four (the Dynamic Learner), students discuss and then write essays on difficulties encountered in attempting to improve energy efficiency in their homes. In the right mode, students carry out their plans later returning to their small groups to report on their degree of success.

The work of Gregorc and McCarthy also has important implications for the teacher. Teachers feel most at ease, confident and creative in employing learning styles to which they themselves are predisposed. Some, it seems, can readily adjust to take on board other styles (Gregorc calls this 'flexing'), some have difficulty adjusting, some will not adjust their style whilst some cannot adjust their style.[18] Clearly, in-service training and the regular use of checklists reflecting activities favoured by those in each learning quadrant can be most helpful to teachers falling into the first two categories. In the case of teachers in the latter two categories, possibilities include team teaching and course/ class sharing.

Should students be made familiar with learning style theory and made aware of their own learning style predispositions? There seem to be very sound reasons why they should and very little to be gained from avoiding open consideration and discussion of style. A student's identification of her personal learning predisposition – and equally of styles with which she is uncomfortable – is clearly a crucial factor in the learning process. Familiarity with style is also an important aspect of self-awareness and crucial for developing and maintaining positive self-

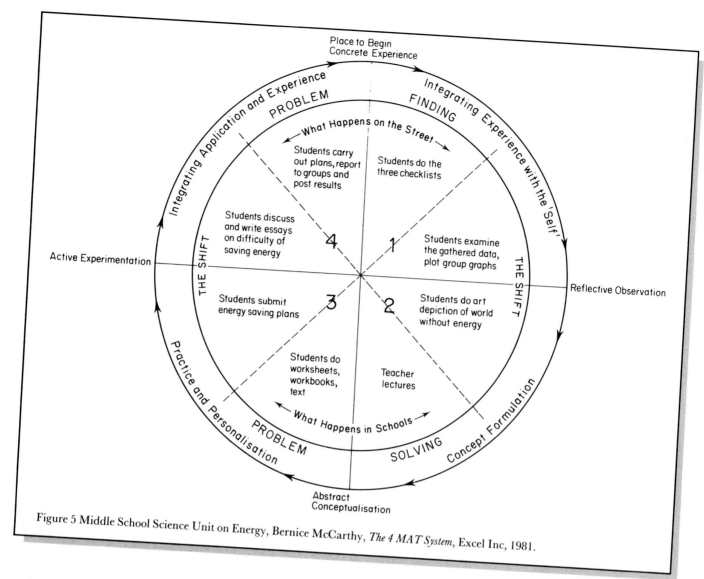

Figure 5 Middle School Science Unit on Energy, Bernice McCarthy, *The 4 MAT System*, Excel Inc, 1981.

image. Students will be better able to understand why certain parts of a course leave them feeling inadequate and uneasy. They will be helped by realising that others, too, go through uncomfortable patches because of their own learning predispositions and that such patches are no reflection on individual worth. Regular counselling with the teacher can take place so that most advantage is taken from learning opportunities requiring different learning styles. Awareness of style may also lead to a more judicious choice of options ('am I opting for Geography as Geography or because the balance of learning styles has suited me and will the balance be similar with the teacher next year?'). An understanding of learning style theory can also play an important part in building intragroup respect. The knowledge that we all have strengths and predispositions and that each of us is trying to capitalise upon and stretch those

strengths and predispositions can, as Bernice McCarthy puts it, help to 'develop a healthy respect for the uniqueness of others'.[19]

In the democratic/humane classroom, with its emphasis upon equal opportunity, interaction, participation and respect, students have both a right and a need to know about learning styles. The teacher needs to encourage and allow opportunities for peer teaching and co-operative learning in which class members dominant in one mode demonstrate that mode to the others and lead them in the learning task. There needs to be opportunities for regular group co-counselling about style. Equally, teachers and students can work together to negotiate a sequence of activities to suit their various style predispositions. Finally, procedures need to be established so that students can seek redress if an insufficiently facilitative teacher continually fails to heed their learning style needs.

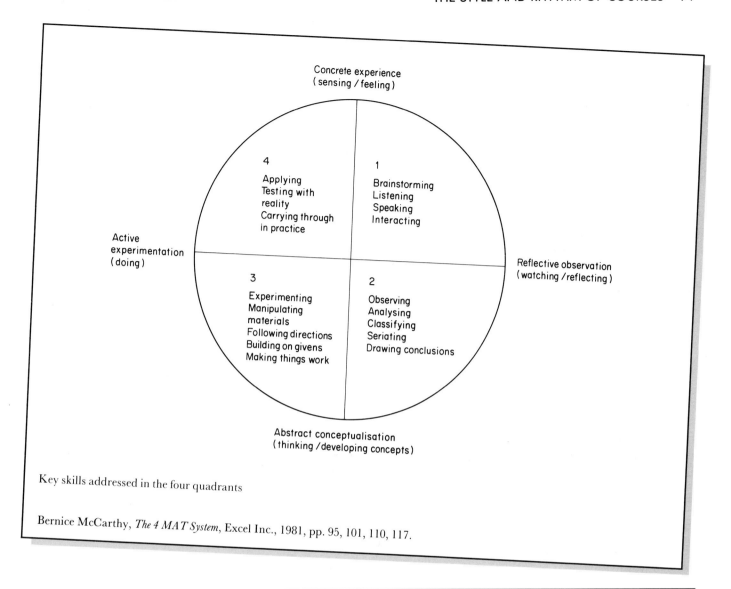

Key skills addressed in the four quadrants

Bernice McCarthy, *The 4 MAT System*, Excel Inc., 1981, pp. 95, 101, 110, 117.

The rhythm of courses

If teachers need to address questions of learning style in topic design, it is also important that they give careful thought to the overall climate and rhythm of courses. Robin Richardson has put forward the following simple four-phase model as appropriate for the treatment of global issues within a humane, person-centred and rights' respectful classroom (as below).[20]

This section in general follows Richardson's model, elaborating and extending it and revising and re-ordering its detail where deemed necessary.

The overall task of building and maintaining an appropriate *climate* (phase one), Richardson maintains, can be broken down into eight smaller tasks. The first four of these relate principally

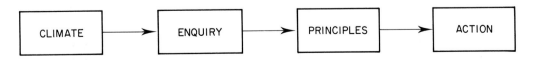

to the *establishment of security*, the second four to the *creation of challenge*. Security can be established by:

1 Getting to know and to trust each other, and to respect each other as potential resources. Before embarking upon the serious consideration and study of global issues – which will involve students in confronting their own and each other's perspectives and values – it is important that trust, confidence and security are built within the group and that individual self-esteem is promoted. Students need to feel confident that any contribution they make will be treated positively, not destructively. All members of the group need to be able to affirm their commitment to the group.

2 Establishing and acknowledging the knowledge and opinions which students already have. Students do not come to a course as 'completely empty vessels'.[21] They have knowledge, opinions and mental images about the world. What they bring to the class should be acknowledged, accepted, pooled and shared (to be, of course, later challeneged and confronted).

3 Getting a sense of initial self-confidence through the successful completion of simple tasks. The issues to be examined in class are complex and demanding. Confidence needs to be built through simple, easily-accomplished tasks.

4 Getting a sense of the whole. Before beginning a course/course unit, it helps students to have an overall idea of its content and concerns. Simulations and experiential activities, followed by debriefing and discussion, can achieve this, perhaps combined with group discussion work and teacher input.

Challenge can be created by:

5 Stimulating students to address their own ignorance, prejudice, values and limited perspective. Within an affirmed and secure context, it is important that students are stimulated to find out more by being made aware of the present level of their knowledge and understanding the limitations of their perspectives. Stereotypes need to be cracked, horizons widened and easy comfortability challenged by the injection of new ideas, new viewpoints and different worldviews.

6 Realising that the subject-area is controversial. Interest can be whetted by helping students to see that they are being asked to address issues about which there are deep disagreements locally, nationally and globally. The challenge is to identify 'where I stand' on such issues through enquiry, study, reflection and action.

7 Adopting a problem-centred and action-oriented approach to the subject area. It is important that courses on the contemporary world do not come across as 'gloom and doom' laden, thereby creating a depressing, and ultimately disempowering, climate. The challenge should be thrown down that we have 'problems to be solved or managed'. Such a challenge, combined with examples of successful initiatives, local to global, can be motivating and invigorating.

8 Taking a measure of responsibility for designing and managing the rest of the course. Before the introductory phase of a course ends, it is important that students are given space to negotiate between themselves and with the teacher as to what content, concerns and questions will be addressed in subsequent phases. Course negotiation is appropriate to the humane classroom; it also carries important dividends in that it fosters a sense of ownership of and commitment towards what is decided.[22]

As Richardson points out, several of the steps described above can be undertaken simultaneously.[23] It also has to be borne in mind that trust and security can evaporate all too easily if not reaffirmed as and when necessary throughout the course.

The *enquiry* phase (phase 2) of a course has two constituent parts, suggests Richardson: direct experience and study. Direct experience can be obtained from field trips, visits and participation in the world outside the classroom; it can also be obtained from participation in particular kinds of classroom activities such as role plays and simulations. Study involves encountering the concepts, ideas, generalisations, perspectives and theories of others in book or other print form, in audio-visual form or through talks and lectures (by the teacher or visiting speaker). As we suggested in Section 2, study can be very effectively performed in co-operative group contexts as against having individuals working alone.

Collaborative work is also an excellent means whereby students can try to arrive at *general principles* (phase 3) arising out of what they have experienced and studied. In small groups, students can prepare flowcharts and other visual diagrams to express the degree of consensus they have reached and to pinpoint remaining disagreements. Alternatively, they can write joint position statements. 'The arguments, negotiations and reflective discussions created by the task of having to reach consensus are extremely valuable for promoting real learning.'[24] Small group presentations to the class can then provide

a springboard for plenary debate around the issues involved.

The *action* phase can then follow in which students ask themselves what needs to be done – and, particularly, what they individually or collectively might do – given what they have learnt and given their conclusions as to general principles. Action in the classroom might be real, for example students writing about their concerns to interested parties or to the local media, or simulated. Students might also become involved in appropriate social action projects within the community. Any action can be reflected upon and any learning therefrom fed into the outcomes of the climate, enquiry and principle phases as below.[25]

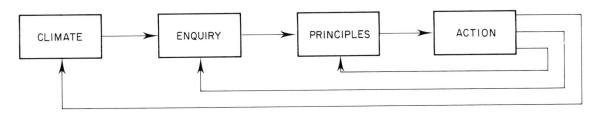

Sections 5 to 12

In this Section so far we have outlined the thinking of three educationalists about the form and rhythm of courses within what we choose to call the global classroom. Whilst recognising that there are significant differences in starting point, emphasis, model and detail between the three, one is struck by what is common in their analysis and recommendations. Each is implicitly or explicitly critical of the left-brain orientation of most classrooms with its emphasis on facts, abstract learning, analysis and deference to expert opinion and its correlative emphasis on frontal top-downwards teaching modes and vertical classroom relationships. Each sees such an orientation as a denial of equality of opportunity in that it favours one particular type of learner against other types of learner. Each is also clear that such an orientation fails to effectively tap and develop human potential and contributes to

schools becoming what we have described as 'human potential dustbins'. All are at one in calling for greater diversity in teaching and learning styles.

The eight Sections that follow offer little guidance on frontal teaching. That is not to suggest that we reject teacher input, in whatever form it takes, but rather that such input needs to relinquish its preponderant position within the classroom and to take its place as one of a range of valid approaches to be applied at the appropriate moment(s) within the rhythm of a course or topic. The eight Sections offer a representative sample of types of activity to redress the hegemony of frontalism within the classroom and to help teachers fuse relevance with diversity. Their emphasis is on co-operation, dialogue, experience, interaction and participation; they are underpinned by the democratic and humane values of fairness, freedom, toleration, respect for truth and respect for reason. They are based upon a profound acceptance and recognition of the untapped potential, uniqueness and richness of experience that each student brings to the classroom.

Openers and Pace-Changers (see Section 5) are activities for beginning a course, topic or lesson, or for introducing into a lesson at other appropriate moments. Mostly brief (5–15 minutes), they serve a number of very important purposes:

- they help students and teachers to quickly get to know each other;

- they help create an enjoyable, secure and supportive classroom climate in which anxieties and tensions are dissolved and in which students feel free to question, opt in or out as they wish, let down their defences and explore their own and each others' attitudes, feelings, perspectives, understanding and values;

- they build trust;

- they encourage and help develop co-operation and interaction;

- they can be introduced as necessary to trigger a change of mood or pace in the classroom process.

They include introductory name games, loosening-up activities, trust building and group co-operation activities. Some also provide an excellent and memorable way of rounding off a lesson.

Activities for Enhancing Self-Esteem (Section 6) are designed to help students value themselves, their viewpoints and experiences. They also promote in each student an awareness of their own talents and strengths. Equally, they confirm to the group that each student has much to offer and provide opportunities for students to express their positive feelings about and regard for each other.

Group Discussion Activities (Section 7) provide frameworks within which a very wide range of issues can be considered and a wide range of skills practised and reinforced. Most, but not all, begin with students working in pairs or small groups before proceeding to large group work and, finally, plenary discussion.

The range of skills promoted include:

- verbal and non-verbal communication skills;

- co-operative and collaborative skills;

- creative, lateral and divergent thinking skills;

- problem-solving skills;

- negotiating, consensus-seeking and decision-making skills;

- values clarification skills;

- empathetic skills;

- evaluation and reflection skills;

- presentation skills.

Group Discussion Activities can often be spread over a number of lessons with enquiry, research and study tasks interspersed between their several stages.

Experiential Activities (Section 8) seek to provide a group-generated and, hence, original experience within an artificially-constructed framework. They often involve a high level of emotional response, learning initially taking place in the affective domain with later reinforcement in the cognitive domain through post-experience discussion and analysis. The 'content' of the activity is not usually of great significance unlike simulation activities (see below), though important concepts may be introduced or developed as a result of the activity and subsequent debriefing. As with simulations, the facilitator's debriefing skills are of paramount importance if real learning is to take place. The debriefing should best take place immediately after the activity when the experience is very fresh; yet, at the same time, students can find it difficult to immediately stand outside an experience which has generated a lot of emotion.

Included in this Section are examples of various forms of imaginal work such as centering exercises, guided (or scripted) fantasy and creative visualisation.

Role Plays (Section 9) are activities in which participants, often working in pairs but sometimes in larger groups, are given prescribed though not necessarily specific roles to act out. Within the limits set by each participant's perception of the role, they provide a rich context for the development of a range of skills including communication, negotiation, decision-making, imaginative and creative thinking skills. They are excellent vehicles for helping students see an issue or problem from a variety of different perspectives; also, for encouraging the exploration of alternative strategies and sol-utions.

Simulation Activities (Section 10) mirror or reconstruct on a small scale events, issues or situations, local to global, so as to enable participants to, as it were, experience them from inside. They usually involve role play and are generally open-ended, i.e. the direction and final outcome is in the hands of the participants. Unlike experiential activities, the 'content' of the simulation is of central importance although it may not be until the debriefing stage that its full implications are established. Of all the types of activity described in this book, simulations re-quire the most careful planning and take up most classroom time.

The **Action** Section (Section 11) offers ex-amples of types of activity that students have been able to pursue in classroom, school or community, either to enhance their understand-ing of global issues or in the light of an individ-ual or collective desire to do something about an issue that has caused them concern. The Section is interspersed with ideas for and reflections upon student action projects.

The **Feedback and Evaluation Techniques** Section (Section 12) suggests ways in which student response to the ongoing classroom pro-gramme can be channelled to the teacher; also means whereby that response can be corporately evaluated. The employment of such open lines of communication is central to the humane, demo-cratic classroom. Techniques for personal evalu-ation are also included.

There is no clear and final dividing line between the various genre of learning activity outlined above. An experiential activity, for example, always contains elements that are simulatory; a simulation inevitably has self-generated expe-riential elements. Openers and pace-changers often enhance self-esteem. There can be role-play elements in some group discussion activities and role play is quite often present in experien-tial activities and almost always present in simulations. One way of coaching action skills, as suggested earlier, is through simulation activ-ity. The eight categories above, nonetheless, offer a coherent and valid means of organising the range of participatory activities available to the process-oriented teacher.

Resource requirements stated are based on a class size of thirty students unless otherwise indicated. The timings given are approximate and refer only to the activity as laid down under 'Procedure'. Teachers should bear in mind that discussion and debriefing are essential aspects of the learning process and sufficient time for these to take place should be allowed. In most cases an age range for the activities is specified but teachers should use their discretion. Many teachers working with us have adapted the activities to suit age groups other than those specified.

The chart that follows suggests how the different types of participatory activity described in this book might be matched to Richardson's four-phase model for the form and rhythm of courses/course units as amended by the present writers.

Course Phases		Appropriate Activities
CLIMATE (A) Establishing Security	(1) Getting to know and trust each other and to respect each other as potential resources	Openers and Pace-changers; Self-Esteem Activities
	(2) Establishing and acknowledging the knowledge and opinions which students already have	Group Discussion Activities
	(3) Getting a sense of initial self-confidence through the successful completion of simple tasks	Self-Esteem Activities; Group Discussion Activities
	(4) Getting a sense of the whole	Teacher Input; Experiential Activities; Simulation Activities; Group Discussion Activities
(B) Creating Challenge	(5) Stimulating students to address their own ignorance, prejudice, values and limited perspective	Experiential Activities (on perspective and stereotypes); Role Plays
	(6) Realising that the subject area is controversial	Group Discussion Activities (e.g. ranking different viewpoints); Role Plays; Simulations
	(7) Adopting a problem-centred and action-oriented approach to the subject area	Group Discussion Activities (Problem Solving); Case studies of success stories (audio/visual, readings, teacher input)
	(8) Taking a measure of responsibility for designing and managing the rest of the course	Brainstorming (see p. 133) followed by group and plenary discussion; Feedback Techniques
ENQUIRY	(1) Direct experience	Field trips; Visits; Action research in school and community
	(2) Study	Teacher/visiting speaker/audio-visual input; study of books, packs, etc.
PRINCIPLES	Working out general principles	Group Discussion Activities; plenary presentations and debate
ACTION	(1) In class	Role Plays; Simulations; Action projects (e.g. letter writing)
	(2) Out of class	Action projects in school/community

FEEDBACK/EVALUATION TECHNIQUES

References

1 Lister, I., *Alternatives and the mainstream and the humanisation of education*, paper presented to the National Organisation for Initiatives in Social Education, 1983, p. 2.

2 Gregorc, A. F., *An Adult's Guide to Style*, Gabriel Systems Inc., Massachusetts, 1982, pp. 5–6.

3 Ibid., pp. 6, 18.

4 Ibid., pp. 19–22.

5 Ibid., pp. 23–7.

6 Ibid., pp. 29–33.

7 Ibid., pp. 35–8.

8 Ibid., pp. 6, 14.

9 Gregorc, A. F., 'An open letter to an educator, part II', *The Razor's Edge*, 1982, p. 40.

10 Kolb, D. A. *et al.*, *Organizational Psychology: an Experiential Approach*, New Jersey, Prentice-Hall, 1979, outlined in McCarthy, *The 4 MAT System*, Excel Inc., 1981, pp. 21–5.

11 McCarthy, B., op, cit., p. 90.

12 Gregorc, A. F., 'An open letter to an educator, part II', *The Razor's Edge*, 1982, p. 40.

13 McCarthy, B., op. cit., pp. 80–3.

14 Ibid., p. 47

15 Ibid.

16 See McCarthy, op. cit., pp. 131–216 and McCarthy, B. and Leflar, S. (eds), *4 MAT in Action*, Excel Inc., 1983.

17 McCarthy, B., op. cit., pp. 185–90.

18 'Learning style across content areas', *Developing the 21st Century Educator*, St Louis Park Public Schools School District, Minneapolis, Vol. 11, No. 1, p. 3.

19 McCarthy, B., op. cit., p. 128.

20 Richardson, R., *Justice and equality in the classroom – the design of lessons and courses*, Global Education Documentation Service, Document No. 7, Centre for Global Education, University of York, p. 2.

21 Ibid., p. 3.

22 Ibid., pp. 3–5.

23 Ibid., p. 5.

24 Ibid., p. 7.

25 Ibid.

5 Openers and pace-changers

Introductory name games

For a group of people who have just met, remembering names is difficult but important. To be addressed by one's name is affirming, to have one's name forgotten can be dispiriting. Here are some activities which help participants learn each other's names, are fun and create a sense of group cohesion. None of them should last for more than a few minutes; try a combination of activities, or repeat an activity at intervals if participants are having difficulty in remembering all the names in a large group.

Angelic Angela

With all participants in a circle, the facilitator begins by introducing herself using her first name and an affirmative or complimentary adjective beginning with the same sound as her name, e.g. 'Hello, I'm super Susan'. Going around the circle, all participants likewise introduce themselves. The alliteration employed is an effective aid to memory, so the facilitator should ensure that only affirmative adjectives are used — 'smelly Simon' might not want to be stuck with that label!

Variation: Instead of an alliterative adjective, participants can use a movement or sound to match the number of syllables in the name, e.g. 'Hello, I'm Benjamin', accompanied by three stamps of the foot or a three-part movement of the hands.

Introducing my Neighbours

Standing in a circle, one participant (Jane) begins by introducing herself to the person on her left (Tony). Tony then introduces himself and Jane to the person on his left (Alice). Alice introduces herself, Tony and Jane, and so on — so that each person is introducing three or four people to the rest of the group in addition to herself. A simple but effective activity, which might be combined with **Angelic Angela** above.

Personal Name Tags

On a large table put out a good supply of paints, crayons, felt tips, paper, scissors, wool or string, pins, etc. As participants come into the room they are encouraged to create their own name tags, being as imaginative as they wish. Alternatively, they can be asked to include a chosen theme, such as 'my favourite season' or 'an animal I would like to be' — these can provide discussion points for follow-up activities.

Catch Name

A fun activity for reinforcing participants' memorising of names. A large circle is formed and the facilitator throws a soft object (such as a rolled-up jumper) to someone (Bill) in the circle, calling out his name just before she throws. The facilitator asks Bill to throw the jumper to someone else, calling out her name, and to remember to whom he threw it. The activity continues similarly until all participants have received the jumper. A second round is played in the same way, keeping to the original sequence but at a much faster pace. On the third round, the facilitator can introduce, at intervals, one or two more soft objects; finally, whilst two or three jumpers are flying around the circle, the facilitator introduces another object to go around the circle in reverse order. Total chaos is guaranteed!

Variation: The jumper is thrown around the circle, with each participant saying their names when they receive it. On the second round, the jumper can be thrown to anyone and the catcher must say the name of the thrower before passing it on.

Sources of these activities

Various
Other name games can be found in: Stephanie Judson (ed.), A Manual on Non-violence and Children; Priscilla Prutzman et al., The Friendly Classroom for a Small Planet;l Donna Brandes and Howard Phillips, Gamesters' Handbook; Matt Weinstein and Joel Goodman, Playfair.

Loosening-up activities

Loosening-up is an important part of self and group affirmation. These activities help to raise energy levels, reduce personal anxiety and group tension through movement and laughter and create a secure environment for the challenges which may follow. Loosening-up need not be confined to the beginning of lessons; many of these activities are ideal for changing the pace or mood. Most of these activities require a large, clear space so that participants can move around freely.

Mathematical Exercises

Participants stand in a circle. Starting with the left hand touching the left toes, the facilitator demonstrates positions from 0–10 (0 = touching toes, 10 = arm raised vertically above head). Participants practise these movements with the facilitator calling out numbers. Both arms are then used in parallel to represent numbers from 11–20 (e.g. 15 = both arms horizontally in front). The facilitator now calls out numbers from 1–20, followed by some simple mathematical calculations (e.g. 7 + 8; 16 − 9; 6 × 3). Finally, more complicated sums can be introduced by means of each participant standing on one leg, thereby doubling the number represented by the arm positions. This activity combines mental and physical exercise in an enjoyable way.

'Mathematical Exercises' in action

Pru-ee

Participants spread out in a large, clear space and close their eyes. The facilitator touches one person on the shoulder – she is now Pru-ee and remains silent and still. Other participants move gently around, trying to make physical contact with each other. When contact is made, one participant enquires 'Pru-ee?'; if the other also responds with 'Pru-ee?', they both move on. When a participant comes across Pru-ee (who, of course, does not respond to the question), she becomes part of Pru-ee by maintaining physical contact and remaining silent. Pru-ee grows and grows until everyone is joined up. Participants then open their eyes, usually to gasps of surprise!

Musical Meetings

Participants walk around briskly in a large clear space with music playing. When the music stops, each participant shakes hands with the nearest person and a mutual exchange of personal information takes place until the music restarts (15–20 seconds). The process is repeated but a new partner must be found each time. Note: because of the level of noise generated by the discussion in a large group, a considerable volume of sound is needed to interrupt the talking.

Sets

Participants stand in the centre of the room. The facilitator calls out a statement and indicates two positions at opposite ends of the room – one for those who strongly agree with the statement, the other for those who strongly disagree. Participants can take up any position on the line between the two places indicated; when in position they discuss the statement with their neighbour. Statements, a mix of the light-hearted and the serious, should be called out at frequent intervals so as to generate plenty of activity and discussion.

Some suggested statements:

I would rather be at school than at home.
I believe in ghosts.
I think smoking should be allowed in school.
I have relatives living abroad (indicate positions in room to represent different continents).
I am optimistic/pessimistic about the future.

Variation: Instead of forming a line after each statement, the facilitator can ask participants to take up alternative physical positions, e.g. 'hands above head' for those who agree, 'hands below feet' for those who don't, 'horizontal position'/'vertical position', etc.

Attribute Linking

An attribute is called out and participants move quickly around the room to join all others with the same attribute. For example, if the facilitator calls 'birthday month', participants call out their birthday month and move around to form a group with others of the same month. When everybody has joined a group, groups call out their month in turn. A new attribute is given, old groups dissolve and new groups are formed. Possible attributes include place of birth, countries or continents visited, favourite hobby, favourite sports team, favourite pop star, zodiac sign.

Variation: Attribute Linking can be carried out non-verbally, or non-lingually (i.e. not in any known language).

Finding Things in Common

Participants take a piece of paper and list the names of all the other students down the left-hand edge. In pairs participants try to find something they share in common – an interest, a skill, a hope or fear, a like or dislike. When they establish a common bond, they talk about it briefly and write it down against the other's name. They immediately move on to another person, repeating the process until they have met up with everybody.

Know Your Potato

Working in groups of six, students choose a potato each. For two minutes each student feels her potato, observes it from all angles, searches for its particular characteristics.

The students then put the potatoes back in the middle of the circle and mix them up. Participants close their eyes in turn and describe their potato to the group. Finally, participants all close their eyes again and search for their potatoes. As well as practising observation and descriptive skills, this activity can be used as a stimulus for considering issues to do with commonality and individuality.

Birthday Line Up

Participants are asked to line up according to the month and date of their birthday, 1 January at one end of the room and 31 December at the other. They should do this without speaking. When each participant has taken up a position a verbal check can be made, either going down the line in turn or by checking with neighbours either side. Participants who end up in the wrong place in the line should be encouraged to change position.

Height Line Up

Participants spread out and find a space in the room. They should make a mental note of their position before closing their eyes. Participants then line up according to height, the tallest at one end of the room, the shortest at the other. When all participants have taken up a place they can open their eyes to check their positions, adjusting them if necessary.

As the solution to the problem requires some physical contact, this exercise generates amusement as well as a feeling of group solidarity. It is helpful to give an occasional commentary during the exercise so that those who find their positions quickly know what is happening.

'Height Line Up' in action

Zoom

Participants stand in a circle. The facilitator makes the sound of a sports car, 'Zoom', passing the sound on to the person on her left or right. The sound is passed quickly around the circle by each participant in turn. At an appropriate point, the facilitator introduces a second sound, 'Eeek!', which represents the squealing of brakes as the car stops and spins round — continuing in reverse direction around the circle. Any participant can then apply the brakes and send the car the other way. A third sound can be introduced: 'Whoosh!', which powers the car across a river to land at the opposite point of the circle, to continue travelling in the same direction around the circle.

This activity generates much laughter and enjoyment. Once the facilitator has introduced the sounds and what they represent, the activity is controlled by the participants who have to make decisions as individuals which directly affect the direction of the group exercise — a common feature of participatory learning which here underlies a simple, but pleasurable group experience.

Sources of these activities

Pru-ee: Stephanie Judson (ed.), A Manual on Non-violence and Children; **Mathematical Exercises**: derived from an idea in Priscilla Prutzman et al., The Friendly Classroom for a Small Planet; **Findings Things in Common**: Nancy Schniedewind and Ellen Davidson, Open Minds to Equality; **Attribute Linking/Height Line-up**: Centre for Global Education; others: Various.

Trust building activities

The success of much co-operative and participatory learning depends upon high levels of trust among participants — and between participants and the facilitator. Many of the activities described in this book require participants to take risks, either physically, mentally or emotionally. They also demand a degree of trust in the facilitator's judgement and integrity, an understanding that — however puzzling or ridiculous the activity may at first appear — the experience does have a worthwhile purpose. Trust building can only be a gradual and continual process; here are some physical activities which can help. The facilitator should join in whenever possible.

Blindfold Trust Walk

Participants divide into pairs. One person leads the other, who is blindfolded or has eyes shut, around a freely chosen 'course' — this can include negotiating doorways, steps, between furniture, etc. The leader can use both physical and oral guidance so as to direct and reassure the blind person. The leader can create a fuller experience, particularly if the walk takes place outside, by directing the blind person to touch, smell or taste trees, flowers, edible plants. When the course has been completed, participants change roles. This activity can provide a memorable experience as well as helping participants to understand the nature of trust, mistrust and dependency. Other issues, such as the relative importance of verbal and non-verbal communication and the effect of loss of sight on participants' sensitivity to the environment, can be explored in discussion after the activity.

Sitting Circle

Participants stand front to back in a fairly tight circle (all with the same shoulder facing inwards) and hold the waist of the person in front of them. At a signal from the facilitator, participants simultaneously bend their knees until everyone is sitting on the lap of the person behind. The circle should now be self-supporting. If it doesn't work first time, it may be that the group has not formed a proper circle, or participants are standing too far apart. When a self-supporting circle has been achieved, participants can try raising their arms in unison, leaning slightly inwards and raising the outer legs or (very difficult) taking alternate steps with left and right feet. This activity, often viewed in disbelief by some participants, can create a wonderful feeling of group harmony and solidarity.

Variation: Sitting circle can also be used as a non-competitive version of musical chairs. Whilst the music is playing participants walk around, in a circle, holding each others' waists; when it stops they all sit down.

'Sitting Circle' in action

Trust Fall

Participants stand in circles of six to eight people. One person stands fairly rigid in the centre of the circle, feet together and hands by her sides, and allows herself to fall backwards, forwards or sideways. Whichever way she falls, the people nearest to her push her gently into an upright position again so that she can fall in another direction. Everyone who wants to should have the opportunity to be in the centre; having one's eyes shut often helps to make this a pleasurable and relaxing experience.

Human Spring

Participants divide into pairs with partners facing each other, about two feet apart, their palms facing outwards at chest level. Both partners lean forward simultaneously allowing their hands to meet in the middle and then to push off again so that they spring back to upright positions without losing their balance. When partners have mastered the technique they might increase the distance between them, or try it with one arm, or standing on one leg.

Blind Explore

Participants close eyes or wear blindfolds. Without talking they move slowly and gently around a room cleared of furniture. The facilitator gives a series of instructions for when participants meet each other. For example, 'gently greet them non-verbally, and move on'; 'stop in front of someone and explore her hands (or face)'; 'find out who has the longer hair (or bigger feet)'; 'express anger (fear, gentleness) with your hands', etc. The activity ends with all participants converging in the centre for a group hug, then opening their eyes.

Sources of these activities

Human Spring: Matt Weinstein and Joel Goodman, Playfair; **Blind Explore**: Donna Brandes and Howard Phillips, Gamesters' Handbook; others: various.

The above books offer a range of other trust building activities. Others can be found in: Priscilla Prutzman et al., The Friendly Classroom for a Small Planet; Jim Wingate, How to be a Peace-full Teacher; Larry Chase, The Other Side of the Report Card; Pax Christi, Winners All.

Group co-operation activities

Many of the activities described elsewhere in the book involve group co-operation to a greater or lesser degree. Here are some more which generate particularly strong feelings of harmony and friendship; some are also excellent for rounding off a lesson in a really positive way.

Massage Circle

Participants stand in a circle, front to back, each person placing their hands on the shoulders of the person in front. Participants gently massage each other's shoulders, neck and upper back, giving and receiving feedback as to what feels good, where there is tension, etc. After a few minutes participants turn around to face the opposite direction, continuing the massage as before.

Group Yell

Participants form three concentric circles in close proximity to each other (see diagram) and put their arms around each other's shoulders. They begin with a very low hum which gradually rises in pitch and increases in sound — the pace is controlled by the group itself. The hum continues until the group collectively decides that it has reached its highest pitch, at which point the hum becomes a tumultuous yell and participants fling their arms into the air.

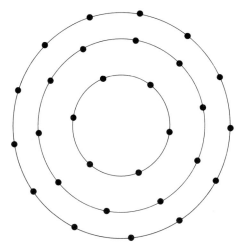

Group Machines

Participants work in groups of 6–8. Each group has to construct a machine with working parts, using all members of the group. The only resources available are their own bodies. Participants have 8–10 minutes to decide upon and rehearse their machines. The groups then come together and each in turn demonstrates its machine. Other participants try to guess what it is.

This exercise demands high levels of co-operation and physical contact, usually accompanied by a great deal of laughter. A good way of helping participants to overcome inhibitions about physical contact.

'Group Machines' in action

Rainstorm

Participants stand in a fairly close circle. The facilitator (who could be a student) rubs her hands together and then makes eye contact with each participant in turn, who imitates and continues the action and sound until the facilitator makes renewed eye contact, thus initiating a new motion. The first action (the wind rustling leaves) is followed by finger snapping (the first drops of rain), hands slapping thighs (steady rainfall) and feet-stamping (the storm's crescendo). The storm then dies down as the stages are followed in reverse order until all participants are still and quiet.

Variation: A less teacher-directed version can be achieved if participants stand front-to-back in a circle. Any participant can start the first motion, but should hold her hands up above shoulder level so that the participant behind her can see and copy. The second motion is performed likewise; the third can be done by each student slapping (gently!) the back of the participant in front of them, and the fourth (feet stamping) is accompanied by participants holding the shoulders of the person in front. The motions continue in reverse order as above.

Spiral

Participants form a circle in a large, clear space (preferably out of doors) and hold hands. The facilitator lets go of the hand of her right-hand neighbour who starts walking around the back of the circle in a clockwise direction, pulling all the other participants behind her. Each participant, with hands holding neighbours tightly, follows the person in front. The facilitator, who has now become the last in a line, holds her ground with feet apart to give more stability. The effect of this is to gradually form a human spiral, wrapped around the facilitator. When the spiral is complete, with all participants forming a very tightly-knit group, the facilitator eases her way down and through the arms and legs of the outer 'layers' of the spiral, pulling other participants with her. The spiral now unwinds; if the facilitator walks in a clockwise direction, the complete circle can be reformed with participants facing outwards.

'Spiral' provides a fitting ending to a lesson or course. The formation of the spiral requires participants to come into close physical proximity to each other; the unwinding is an intriguing and satisfying process, allowing the broken circle to be re-connected. With participants now facing outwards, the activity provides a symbolic representation of the relationship between the journey inwards and the journey outwards in global education.

Sources of these activities

Various
Other group co-operation activities can be found in: Donna Brandes and Howard Phillips, Gamesters' Handbook; *Larry Chase,* The Other Side of the Report Card; *Mildred Masheder,* Let's Co-operate; *Terry Orlick,* The Cooperative Sports and Games Book; *Priscilla Prutzman et al.,* The Friendly Classroom for a Small Planet; *Matt Weinstein and Joel Goodman,* Playfair; *Jim Wingate,* How to be a Peace-full Teacher; *Pax Christi,* Winners All.

Special Numbers

▼ Resources

A number sheet for each student similar to the one below; an open space.

3	9	12	1
7	18	6	40
16	11	5	10
21	100	8	2

▼ Procedure

Each student moves around the room talking to other students and trying to find someone for whom a number on the sheet is in some way special, particular or significant (e.g. house number, birthday, date of a memorable occasion). Having found someone and having listened to the explanation of the number's significance, she crosses the number out. Only one answer can be obtained from a particular individual. She then moves on to talk to others, crossing out further numbers as she meets people for whom the number has some special meaning.

▼ Potential

A good-fun introductory activity enabling students to get to know each other. The activity can also be used to practise listening skills, students sharing what they have found in plenary session.

▼ Variations

1 Students can be given blanks and asked to fill in numbers significant to them before the activity begins.

2 Colours, places, animals, etc. can be used instead of numbers.

Junior/Lower Secondary, 15 minutes.

▼ Source

Various.

Self Portraits

▼ Resources

½A4 sheet of plain paper for each participant; crayons or felt tip pens or paints; a clear classroom space.

▼ Procedure

Students are given 5 minutes in which to represent on the sheet of paper 'things they as individuals like doing'. A graphical representation is encouraged, but words can be used as well. At the end of this time, each student pins her piece of paper to herself, or simply holds it in front of her, and begins to walk around the classroom, meeting and talking with other participants about the activities depicted on the paper. Students are encouraged to meet and share their interests with a number of participants during the time allowed.

▼ Potential

A non-threatening introductory activity which allows personal information about hobbies, leisure pursuits and interests to emerge. Security is provided by allowing participants to have a graphic record of their favourite pursuits — and by sharing them on a one-to-one basis — rather than asking each student to tell the rest of the group. Participants can discover commonalities of interests; students who have minority interests have the opportunity to disclose and explain these. **Self-Portraits** is an effective 'ice-breaker' for use with a group of students who do not know each other, or have only met each other in a 'work' capacity.

Primary/Secondary, 15 minutes.

▼ Source

Various.

People Hunting

▼ Resources

A **People Hunting** handout for each student; open classroom space so that participants can move about freely.

PEOPLE HUNTING

Find someone who:

1 Plays a musical instrument _____

2 Felt proud recently (share what happened) _____

3 Had a scary dream recently _____

4 Had a special day recently _____

5 Had a surprise recently _____

6 Cooked a special meal recently _____

7 Can whistle _____
   (ask her/him to try whistling)

8 Felt left out recently _____
   (ask what happened)

9 Helped someone out recently _____

10 Visited somewhere new recently _____

11 Learnt something new today _____

12 Felt angry lately _____
   (share what happened)

13 Knows a game from another country _____

14 Had some real success recently _____
   (share it)

15 Repaired something that was _____
   broken recently

16 Takes regular physical exercise _____

17 Can say a sentence in a language _____
   that is not English
   (ask her/him to say one)

18 Felt very happy recently _____
   (share what happened)

19 Stuck up for someone who was _____
   'put down' (share what happened)

20 Has learnt a new skill in _____
   the last month

▼ Procedure

Students move around the room hunting for a person who can respond in the affirmative to each of the items on the handout. The person's name is written in the space next to the item and must appear on the sheet only once. Where items refer to feelings, students are encouraged to share the experience at greater length. The activity can continue until everybody's handout is as complete as possible or can be halted after a suitable period. Students then gather in a circle and explore what things they discovered they had in common.

▼ Potential

A lively activity enabling students to find out a great deal about each other very quickly. The activity also provides an excellent opportunity for helping individuals realise that the feelings they experience – and which they believe to be theirs alone – are often shared by many others. Questions to trigger discussion might include: 'What did you learn about someone in the class that surprised you?'; 'Did you realise before that you had so many things in common with other members of the class?'; 'Which feelings did you find others had experienced too?'; 'Were the situations that caused such feelings similar?'; 'Was it hard or easy to talk about feelings?'; 'Why?'

▼ Source

Schniedewind, N., and Davidson, E., Open Minds to Equality, New Jersey, Prentice-Hall, 1983.

Time Lines

▼ Resources

One sheet of sugar paper and a felt tip pen per participant.

▼ Procedure

Participants form groups of six, but work initially on their own. Each participant draws a straight line in the middle of her piece of paper, from one end to the other (vertically or horizontally).

Marking one end of the line as 'birth', the other as 'now', participants indicate significant events and periods in their lives – at home, school and in the community – at appropriate points on the line. Graphics or words can be used to explain the events marked. When completed, explanation of the time lines to the group can be given by each participant in turn, or can be done in pairs first of all, followed by each member of the pair explaining the other member's time line for the benefit of the group.

▼ Potential

This activity allows a small group of students to get to know some interesting details about each other's lives in a secure and non-threatening way. The use of the time line as a vehicle for reflecting on one's life is an encouragement to view it, and describe it, in perspective: seemingly unrelated events may appear to have connections, whilst the significance of long-forgotten incidents can be reassessed. In a well affirmed group, discussion about an individual's particularly difficult or traumatic times can provide helpful new perspectives.

▼ Extension

Once the time lines have been explained to the group, or if there is insufficient time for a full explanation, participants select 'high spots', 'low spots' and 'funny spots'. Each participant describes in some detail three incidents or times in their lives; the first being a time of real success or happiness, the second a time of failure or unhappiness, and the third an amusing incident.

Primary/Secondary, 40 minutes.

▼ Source

Various.

Roadmaps

▼ Resources

One sheet of sugar paper and a felt tip pen per participant.

▼ Procedure

Participants form groups of six. Working initially on her own, each participant draws a road system on the sugar paper to represent her life from birth up to now. The various stages and momentous events of her life, including home, school and community aspects, are represented through appropriate road symbols; these may include long straight roads for trouble-free periods of her life, windy roads for more problematic times, roundabouts and traffic lights to represent indecision or change of direction, etc. The potential for imaginative presentation is enormous; words and other graphical symbols can be added by way of explanation. When all participants in the group have finished their individual roadmaps, they come together to explain, in turn, their maps to the rest of the group. Questions seeking further clarification can be asked by other group members.

▼ Potential

This is a variation of **Time Lines** which allows participants to express the important events and aspects of their lives in a creative and imaginative way. The roadmaps produced by a class make an interesting and visually attractive wall display.

▼ Variation/Extension

Students prepare roadmaps, or extend their existing ones, to represent their predicted lives in the future. The road system can include both personal futures and elements of societal futures which may impinge upon them. A useful stimulus for exploring personal and societal futures and their interrelationship.

Primary/Secondary, 40 minutes.

▼ Source

Centre for Global Education.

Going Dotty

▼ **Resources**

Small, self-adhesive coloured dots, in at least four colours, one for each participant. Open classroom space so that students can move about freely.

▼ **Procedure**

Students form a circle and close their eyes. Each participant has a coloured dot stuck on their forehead. The different colours should be spread amongst the class so that neighbouring students do not have the same colour, but there should be an approximately equal number of each colour. Students then open their eyes and try to form groups of the same-coloured dots without speaking.

▼ **Potential**

A simple exercise with a variety of possible uses. It establishes very quickly the need for co-operation among individuals in order to solve a group task; there is a degree of affirmation in bringing individuals together through a short, enjoyable problem-solving exercise; it heightens the importance of non-verbal communication. At a conceptual level, the exercise provides an illustration of interdependence; at a practical level, it can be used as an enjoyable way of organising students into groups for a further group exercise.

▼ **Variations**

1 Colours can be unevenly distributed, leaving one or two small groups or individuals; some participants may not receive a dot at all. Discussion could then follow concerning students' feelings about finding themselves in a 'majority' or 'minority' group.
2 Students are asked to link arms to form a line using certain rules, e.g.:

> green may join blue or red
> red may join green or yellow
> yellow may join red or white
> white may join yellow or blue
> blue may join white or green

The line is not complete until every participant is correctly linked.

Primary/Secondary, 5 minutes.

▼ **Sources**

Centre for Global Education. Variation 2: Graham Rowland, Feniton Primary School, Devon.

Paired Numbers

▼ **Resources**

None, except a clear space.

▼ **Procedure**

Participants stand in a circle and number themselves, starting at 1 and going around the circle until everyone has a number. (Note: if there is an odd number in the group, the last two participants share one number.) The facilitator mentally adds 1 to the total number in the group and then asks participants to each find a partner with whom their combined score will equal that number. For example, in a group of thirty students, the combined score for each pair will be 31.

▼ **Potential**

A fun way to organise participants into pairs for further work, this activity also provides some practice in basic computation skills.

▼ **Extension**

To create groups of four.
Once in pairs the lower number is subtracted from the higher number giving each pair a positive score; e.g. for participants numbered 1 and 30, their pair score is 29. Pairs then have to seek out other pairs with whom their combined score will equal the total number in the group; i.e. in a group of thirty, the pair with a score of 29 joins up with the pair whose score is 1. (Note: if the total number of participants is not divisible by 4, one pair will be unable to find a matching pair.)

Upper Primary/Secondary, 5 minutes.

▼ **Source**

Centre for Global Education.

I'm Counting on Your Co-operation

▼ **Resources**

For thirty students: thirty self-adhesive dots, each with a different number from the chart below written on it.

80	50	90	60	40	70	60	55	80	75
10	25	5	20	30	15	30	5	5	20
10	25	5	20	30	15	10	40	15	5

Open classroom space so that students can move about freely.

▼ **Procedure**

Students form a circle and close their eyes. Each has a numbered dot stuck on her forehead (the facilitator should as much as possible avoid putting numbers from the same vertical column on neighbouring students). Students then open their eyes and are asked to form groups of three without speaking. They are informed that numbers in each group are to add up to one hundred.

▼ **Potential**

A lively but fairly complex activity providing an illustration of corporate problem-solving and interdependence. The success of the whole group depends upon students being prepared to break up groups they have created (i.e. which add up to 100) to form new partnerships. The activity, which also emphasises the importance of non-verbal communication, helps affirm the group by requiring individuals to co-operate in solving what is a tricky task.

▼ **Variations**

1 If the class numbers less than thirty the necessary number of vertical columns can be left out, i.e. with twenty-four students only eight columns of figures would be used. In cases where the number in the class is not exactly divisible by three, one or two students can be asked to be observers.

2 With younger students, the class can be asked to form groups of three that each add up to ten (teachers devise their own number chart depending on age and ability).

Primary/Secondary, 5–10 minutes.

▼ **Source**

Centre for Global Education.

Machine Making

▼ **Resources**

A large open floor space.

▼ **Procedure**

Students are asked to spread themselves evenly around the open floor space. Each student is to imagine herself as a separate mechanical part making a particular motion and/or sound. The class test their machine parts independently of each other. The students then form into two groups. One group watches whilst the other builds a machine. A volunteer comes to the centre of the floor space and makes a machine sound/movement. A second joins in, attaching herself to and/or co-ordinating her actions with the first person (motions/sounds do not have to be the same as in the first part of the activity). One by one the remainder of the group joins the growing machine. The facilitator should check that all parts are working and can point to one part of the machine instructing it to speed up, slow down or even break down. The second group then makes a machine in a similar manner.

▼ **Potential**

This activity is great fun. It also provides food for thought about the nature of interdependent systems. How did it feel to be a separate machine part? Did it feel different to be part of a mechanical system? Were there any tensions or conflicts? What happened — and how did participants feel — when other parts of the machine speeded up, slowed down or broke down? In which situation did students feel they had greater freedom and responsibility (systems, by definition, limit individual scope for initiative and the impact of any initiative taken)? Was any one part more important than others (in a well-functioning system all parts are essentially equal)? What similarities and differences are there between mechanical and human/environmental systems (predictability and measurablity of former; multi-dimensional and multi-layered complexity and unpredictability of latter with 'effects' looping back to become new 'causes')? Is the global system a 'well-functioning system'?

▼ Variation

Each student is to imagine herself as a separate musical instrument. The volunteer chooses a tune and other instruments join in one by one. A student or the facilitator acts as conductor.

Primary/Secondary, 20 minutes.

▼ Source

Taken from Freeman, R. E. and Karls, A. B., 'Let there be light', Intercom, 79, 1975, p. 14. Variation: Centre for Global Education.

Globingo!

▼ Resources

A **Globingo!** handout for each student; open classroom space so that participants can move freely about.

▼ Procedure

Students spread out and are given copies of the handout (see p. 114). The purpose of the exercise is for each student to fill in as many squares as possible by obtaining information from other students. It should be emphasised that the name of the country and the name of the student should be written in the appropriate square. A particular student's name should only appear once on a sheet so as to encourage the maximum possible interaction amongst the group. Each time a row of four squares — horizontally, vertically or diagonally — has been completed, a student should call out 'Globingo!' She should go on to attempt more rows (ten are possible). It is important to encourage students to actively ask questions of each other rather than passively swapping sheets.

▼ Potential

This is an excellent starter activity for work on global interdependence. Students will probably make some surprising discoveries about their classmates, too! One way into follow-up discussion is to first ask about those surprises. After exploratory discussion, the class can be encouraged to explain and categorise the types of global connection they found during the activity (e.g. trading connections, media connections, connections brought about by the movement of peoples).

▼ Extensions

A useful follow-up exercise is to pin a large world map to a wall board and to ask the students to locate the countries identified during **Globingo!** The squares in each student's handout can be cut up and pinned to the country (repetitive squares being laid aside). The coloured pins are then connected by cotton to a pin identifying the school's location. The final product will show 'the world in our class'. Discussion questions might include: 'do we seem to be particularly connected with certain parts of the world?'; 'if so, can we suggest why?'; 'what would happen to life as we know it if all these connections disappeared?'.

▼ Variations

The **Globingo!** handout offered here, which has been used with 9–15 year olds, can be altered to suit particular circumstances or age groups whilst leaving the basic interactive activity unchanged.

Junior/Secondary, 15–20 minutes.

▼ Source

Derived from Johnson, J. and Benegar, J., Global Issues in the Intermediate Classroom, Boulder, Colorado, Social Science Education Consortium, 1981.

GLOBINGO

Find someone who:

A has travelled to some foreign country

B has a pen pal in another country

C is learning a foreign language

D has a relative in another country

E has helped a visitor from another country

F enjoys a music group from another country

G is wearing something that was made in another country

H enjoys eating foods from other countries

I can name a famous sports star from another country

J has a family car that was made in another country

K has talked to someone who has lived in another country

L lives in a home where more than one language is spoken

M saw a story about another country in the newspaper recently

N learned something about another country on TV recently

O owns a TV or other appliance made in another country

P has a parent or other relative who was born in another country

A	B	C	D
name	name	name	name
country	country	country	country

E	F	G	H
name	name	name	name
country	country	country	country

I	J	K	L
name	name	name	name
country	country	country	country

M	N	O	P
name	name	name	name
country	country	country	country

Lock and Key

▼ Resources

A selection of card locks and keys to match the number of students in the class.

▼ Procedure

Each student chooses a lock or key from the selection and moves around the room trying to find a lock or key that matches. It is explained that the many doors to success will only be opened when each pair has a matching set.

▼ Potential

A very simple activity emphasising the importance of a co-operative approach to work. The class is affirmed by successfully completing a joint task. Questions to be asked include: How did you start? What helped? What was difficult? Did talking help? How did you feel when you matched? Did you then help others to match or did you simply wait for others to finish?

Primary, 10 minutes.

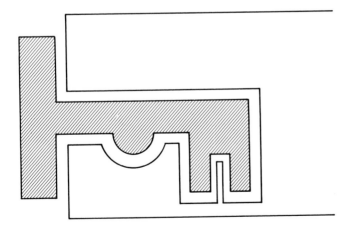

▼ Source

Graham Rowland, Feniton Primary School, Devon.

Colourmatch

▼ Resources

A chart listing a number of colours; an open classroom space.

▼ Procedure

Students are asked to select one colour from the chart without telling anyone else what their choice is. They are then asked to move around the room and to try to find other students who have chosen the same colour. Speaking is not permitted; nor is pointing at or direct staring at objects or clothing of the same colour as that chosen. Miming their own colours, students find a classmate who responds with a mime suggesting that she has chosen the same colour. Together, the pair seek out others until everybody of the same colour seems to be in the same group.

YELLOW
PINK
RED
GREEN
BLUE
PURPLE

▼ Potential

An enjoyable activity that raises a number of questions about non-verbal communication and membership of minority and majority groups. The teacher can begin by asking each group what colour it is. Is each member of the same colour? If not, how did the misunderstanding occur? Are there two or more groups of the same colour? If so, why did they fail to recognise or contact each other? Are there any small groups of isolated individuals? Why? How do they feel? How did students feel when someone could not understand their mime? How did they feel when they could not find someone who had chosen the same colour? How did they feel when they found their first partner? How do the big groups feel?

▼ Follow-up

Students are asked to convey a message to someone who speaks a foreign language using mime, sign language and facial expression, e.g. ordering a particular drink at a café, asking for a hotel room.

▼ Variation

Menumatch. The rules and procedures are the same as **Colourmatch**, students this time choosing from a menu of favourite foods.

Primary, 10–15 minutes.

▼ Source

Graham Rowland, Feniton Primary School, Devon.

Picturematch

▼ Resources

A set of assorted card pictures cut into two, three or four parts (according to age range and degree of difficulty required). Birthday, celebration and festival cards can be used.

▼ Procedure

Stage One   Students are given one picture piece each and are asked to move around the room to find students with the pieces needed to make up the whole picture.

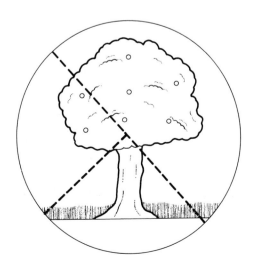

Stage Two   Students are given two minutes to look at their picture piece (new sets are used). Keeping the piece out of sight, they go around describing their part-picture to each other. When students think they have a 'described match', they show their pieces to the teacher who confirms whether or not they have completed a picture. If not, the pieces are given back to the students who try to find new partners.

▼ Potential

An interesting co-operative exercise involving memory, listening and oral description skills.

▼ Variation

The second stage ends with a plenary at which each member of a group describes their picture piece and the group members explain why they think their pieces fit together. Explanations over, they show their pieces to each other and to the rest of the class.

Primary, 25 minutes.

▼ Source

Graham Rowland, Feniton Primary School, Devon.

Setmatch

▼ Resources

Set of objects or pictures of objects (e.g. fruit, things for school work, clothes, things made of wood, toys); an open classroom space.

▼ Procedure

Students are given one object or picture each. By moving around the room and examining what each other has, they try to form sets of the same kind of objects. When they are satisfied that they have found all the members of their set, they sit down in a circle and try to agree upon a set name.

▼ Potential

A co-operative exercise which raises some questions about membership of groups. What gave students an early clue about their set? Did they encounter any difficulties? Of what kind? How did individuals feel when they found someone they felt 'at home' with? How did it feel when the group was complete? Do members have a special feeling towards each other? Did/does anyone feel there is someone in their set who shouldn't be there? Why? Did anyone feel part of two sets? Why? How does it feel?

Primary, 10 minutes.

▼ Source

Graham Rowland, Feniton Primary School, Devon.

Messagematch

▼ Resources

A piece of a message for each student; an open classroom space.

▼ Procedure

Students are asked to move around the room and to join others to make a whole message. The total number of messages is given and it is explained that the group will only be successful when everybody is part of a message. **Messagematch** can be attempted in three stages: **Stage 1** one message duplicated as many times as necessary is used; **Stage 2** more than one message is circulated simultaneously and students seek to join the appropriate group; **Stage 3** students, working in groups of 4–6, devise their own message on blank cards of the same number of words as the number in the group; these are jumbled up and **Stage 2** is repeated.

▼ Potential

An activity emphasising co-operation and interdependence. How did students set about finding what the whole message might be? What made the task difficult? Easy? At what moment did a group feel they had the right answer? Did they then have to accommodate any changes? Did students forget that success involved everybody being part of a message? Who was easiest to find — the first, second or last person? Why? Did anybody refuse to join up with somebody else? How did the rejected person feel?

▼ Variation

The teacher can make the activity easier by saying how many pieces make up a whole message and by writing START and END on the appropriate cards.

Primary, 30 minutes.

▼ Source

Graham Rowland, Feniton Primary School, Devon.

MESSAGEMATCH

| FOR | FIRE | DIAL | 999 |

| FISH | SWIM | IN DEEP | PONDS |

| GLASS | BREAKS | WHEN | DROPPED |

There's More Than One Way...

▼ Resources

Group 1 paper, felt tip pens
Group 2 paints, brushes, paper
Group 3 plasticine or clay
Group 4 musical instruments
Group 5 coloured gummed squares, scissors, paper
Group 6 black and white paper, scissors, glue
Group 7 computer
Group 8 message saying 'use your own bodies'

Several copies of the same message, e.g. 'We want to be your friends and live in peace with you'.

▼ Procedure

Students are asked to form eight groups. Each group is given a different set of resources and a copy of the same written message. They are asked not to let other groups see their message but to devise a way of expressing it using the resources they have available. The use of oral communication, words, letters and numbers is not acceptable. Twenty minutes are given for this task. Each group is then in turn asked to offer their presentation to the rest of the class without saying directly what message they were given. Discussion follows as to what each group's message was (groups withhold explaining their message until asked to do so by the facilitator).

▼ Potential

As the discussion progresses, it will become clear that each group had the same message and that they had been able to express that same message through different media. This is a lively group co-operation exercise which can lead to useful discussion of the effectiveness of different forms of non-verbal communication.

Primary/Secondary, 20 minutes.

▼ Source

Eileen Porter, Manygates Middle School, Wakefield.

6 Activities for enhancing self-esteem

Creating an affirmative environment

The character of the learning environment bears a direct relation to the character of the learning which takes place; in a competitive classroom students will learn to be competitive (though only some will succeed). For a learning process which numbers among its objectives a sense of personal worth, belief in one's own potential, genuineness, appreciation and respect for others, an affirmative environment is crucial: one in which medium and intended message are in harmony. Here are some examples of ideas and activities which can help create an appropriate environment for global learning.

Awards and Certificates

A variety of blank awards and certificate cards are needed. For example, the 'super kid' award, the 'helping hand' award, 'special congratulations' certificates, 'welcome aboard' and 'good luck' certificates, etc. – to cover a variety of occasions and events in school and home life. (See example below.) These cards are then filled in with appropriate words by the teacher or other students and presented to a deserving student as recognition of her as a person and/or of her qualities and achievements. Awards should not be confined to the end-of-year ceremony for the élite group; all students need to be specially congratulated in this way throughout the year.

WELCOME ABOARD!

From _____

Date _____

We're glad you joined us!

Friendly Tree

A large paper cut-out of a tree with lots of branches is affixed to the wall. A number of cards are 'hung' from the branches on short pieces of thread; on each card is printed a friendly act, e.g. 'talk to someone who you don't often talk to', 'help someone out with their work', 'write/draw someone a friendly note/ picture', 'share something with a classmate', etc. At the beginning of each day, a group of students select a card each and are encouraged to carry out the friendly act at some time during the day. The cards are put back on the tree at the end of the day in readiness for another.

Sunflowers

Each student makes a paper sunflower by decorating a paper circle and affixing it to a long stem, to which are attached some leaves. (See example below.) The student's name is

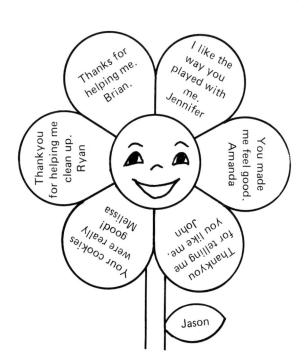

written on a leaf, and all the flowers are affixed to the wall. A supply of paper petals should be readily available in the classroom. Whenever a student wants to make an appreciative comment about another student, she writes the comment on a petal and sticks it onto that person's sunflower. Each student's flower is thus built up over a period of time by a range of affirmative statements.

Interests Collage

From a wide assortment of magazines, students select and cut out pictures which represent their individual interests and hobbies. Working in groups of six, students negotiate how their pictures are to be arranged collectively on a piece of sugar paper. When stuck down, graphics or words can be added with felt pens before all the groups come together to form a collage of the class interests. The collage can be used to encourage individuals to talk about their interests and to promote discussion about similarities and differences between students' interests.

Affirmation Circles

Sharing feelings about themselves and others in a circle can be a regular feature of the affirmative classroom. Students sit or stand, holding hands or linking arms if they wish, in a circle, taking it in turns to speak (either randomly or in order). Topics, chosen by the teacher or students might range from 'something nice that happened to me today/yesterday/at the weekend', or 'right now I feel ...', to sharing of likes/dislikes and attributes: 'I'm happiest/angriest when ...'. Participants should not be under any compulsion to contribute and statements are not discussed, though positive support and encouragement can be given by the group. It is useful for students to have a few minutes 'thinking time' once the topic has been chosen, so that full attention can be given to other people's contributions.

Feelings Thermometer

Each student is given a 'feelings thermometer' — a strip of card onto which the faces opposite are pasted.

*The faces represent happy, sad, silly, mad, scared and proud feelings. During an **Affirmation Circle** time, the thermometers can be used to give a quick gauge as to how students individually and collectively feel about certain ideas or experiences: a paper clip or finger is used to indicate the appropriate feeling.*

Sources of these activities

***Awards and Certificates, Sunflowers, Interests Collage** and **Feelings Thermometer** are based on ideas in Michele and Craig Borba, Self-esteem: a Classroom Affair Volume 2; **Friendly Tree** and **Affirmation Circles** are based on ideas in Self-esteem: a Classroom Affair by the same authors.*

All-about-me activities

At the heart of the theory of affirmation is the belief that 'put-downs', the negative remarks and feelings which permeate our lives and are found in abundance in schools, prevent us from achieving our full potential. To counteract the pervasiveness of put-downs, thoughts and actions are required which reaffirm our sense of worth and belief in our own capacities. Activities which encourage all students to feel good about themselves and to express those feelings in a positive rather than boastful way, play an important part in the global classroom.

Affirmation Notebooks

This is a personal collection of individual self-affirming sheets which are designed and compiled over a period of a term or year. Sheets can include students' drawings of themselves, personal badges and descriptions, likes and dislikes, earliest memories, family trees, affirmative comments or drawings by other students, personal awards and certificates, etc. Many other ideas from this Section can be adapted for inclusion in the notebook.

Silhouettes

Working in small groups students take turns to trace each other's silhouette. This can be done either by drawing around the person as she lies on, or stands against, a large piece of paper, or by projecting her silhouette onto a piece of paper as she stands in front of an overhead projector. Silhouettes are then cut out and pasted up on the wall. As well as highlighting each student's individuality they can be used as props for other affirmation activities, e.g. pasting up affirmative comments about each other, displaying special awards and certificates.

Inexperience

Students in groups are asked to think of real experiences that they have never had which they imagine nearly everyone else has had. They write out these experiences on slips of paper which are collected up and stuck onto a large sheet, with spaces in between each slip. Students then visit each group's sheet and affix sticky dots around the description of any experience which they too have not shared. Discussion that follows might focus on differences and similarities in experience, feelings about 'inexperience' and invited descriptions of relatively uncommon experiences.

People Recipes

Students describe their physical appearance and character in the style of recipe ingredients, e.g.:

 — a large measure of black curly hair
 — two brown eyes
 — one cupful of freckles
 — a generous helping of laughter
 — a dash of wickedness

Personal recipes can be written out and compiled in a class recipe book, illustrating the commonality of separate 'ingredients' yet the uniqueness of each 'recipe'.

A RECIPE FOR JAN

A PINT OF CONFIDENCE
HALF A PINT OF BRAINS
A DASH OF MOODINESS
A PINCH OF RUDENESS AND HUMOUR
A MANGLED TEASPOON OF GOOD LOOKS
A HIDDEN PORTION OF AFFECTION
AMPLE AMOUNTS OF MUM + DAD

METHOD
WHISK THE CONFIDENCE AND BRAINS TO FORM A THICK FOAM. FRY FOR 10 MINS. MEANWHILE, MIX ALL INGREDIENTS APART FROM AFFECTION AND GOOD LOOKS. ADD THE FRIED MIXTURE AND ROLE TO A THICKNESS OF 1 INCH. HIDE THE AFFECTION BY PUTTING IT IN THE MIDDLE AND WRAPPING DOUGH AROUND. SHAPE TO PRODUCE ANY OBJECT. COAT WITH GROUND GOOD LOOKS. BAKE FOR 20 MINS IN A HOT OVEN.

Puppets

Puppets are valuable props for encouraging shy children, in particular, to express their feelings, become more self-aware and confident in a group. Puppets can be easily made using old gloves, socks or a paper bag, with students painting or pasting on the facial features. A number of self-affirmation activities can be carried out using a puppet as the 'alter ego', expressing feelings which the child herself may be unwilling to share. 'Me puppets' – constructed to look like their makers – can encourage discussion about, and appreciation of physical features.

Sources of these activities

Affirmation Notebooks: Priscilla Prutzman et al., The Friendly Classroom for a Small Planet; **People Recipes**: Michele and Craig Borba, Self-esteem: a Classroom Affair; **Inexperience**: adapted from an idea in Larry Chase, The Other Side of the Report Card; **Silhouettes** and **Puppets**: various.

Affirming myself and others

Just as individual rights cannot be safeguarded without a concomitant sense of personal responsibility, so affirmation of oneself is dependent upon a preparedness to affirm others. Many group affirmation activities serve this dual function; here are some examples.

Round Robin Interview

Participants roam around the room for 10–15 minutes interviewing each other to find out personal information such as likes and dislikes, best attributes, favourite television programmes, etc. Students can write notes during the interview. When the group comes together one person comes to the front and says her name. Other students who have met her then venture any information they have, one comment per student, so that a complete description of her character and interests is built up. Another student then comes to the front and the process is repeated until everyone has been introduced.

I'm Going on a Trip...

Participants stand in a circle. One person begins by saying 'I'm going on a trip and I'm bringing a handshake' giving a handshake to the next person. Each person in turn then contributes an additional physical gesture or expression to the list: 'I'm going on a trip and I'm bringing a handshake, a hug, a pat on the back, a smile', etc. so that the last person in the circle receives everything. This activity is affirming through encouraging participants to touch each other and express themselves physically in a structured and amusing way.

This is a Hug. A What?

Participants sit in a circle. The facilitator says to the person on her left (Paul): 'This is a hug,' and hugs him. Paul says, 'A what?' to which the facilitator replies, 'A hug' and again demonstrates. Paul then says to the person on his left (Sarah): 'This is a hug,' hugging Sarah who asks, 'A what?' Paul asks the facilitator, 'A what?' who replies, 'A hug,' and demonstrates. Paul turns to Sarah: 'A hug,' and hugs her. As the message, 'This is a hug' continues clockwise around the circle, each new participant asks, 'A what?' The question is relayed back to the facilitator each time, and the answer (a hug) is sent back around the circle.

In the meantime, *the facilitator says to the person on her right (Amy), 'This is a handshake,' shaking her hand. Amy says, 'A what?'; the facilitator responds, 'A handshake,' and demonstrates. This message continues anti-clockwise around the circle in the same format as above.*

The excitement and laughter builds up as the hugs and handshakes approach each other. An excellent activity for group affirmation through physical contact and fun.

Variation: In a group where physical contact is likely to cause some embarrassment, sounds can be used instead of physical gestures, e.g. 'a bing' and 'a bong'.

Affirmation Posters

Each participant writes her name in attractive or decorative style at the top of a large sheet of paper. Students then circulate around the room writing affirming comments on each other's posters; sufficient time should be allowed for all students to contribute to each poster. Students collect their own poster and read out the written comments to the rest of the group. The posters can then be displayed and added to over a period of time.

Variation: Stocking Fillers: Participants write their comments on slips of paper which are then put into named socks hung up around the room.

Affirmation Video

*The video camera is a useful piece of equipment for self and group affirmation and can be used in a variety of ways. Students can interview each other in front of the camera; **Affirmation Circle** activities or **Round Robin Interviews** can be filmed, as can many of the activities described in other sections of this book; an **Affirmation Video** of class activities might be filmed throughout the year, edited and screened as an end-of-year presentation to parents and others. The facilitator should ensure that whatever is filmed is affirming to the individual student, and that all students are filmed at some point. With a well-affirmed group, video can also be used as a means of developing self-awareness, with students analysing and discussing their 'performances'.*

Sources of these activities

***Round Robin Interview** and **This is a Hug. A What?**: Stephanie Judson (ed.), A Manual on Non-violence and Children; **I'm Going on a Trip**: Priscilla Prutzman et al., The Friendly Classroom for a Small Planet; **Affirmation Posters** and **Affirmation Video**: various.*

The above books offer a range of other self-esteem and group affirmation activities. Others can be found in: Michele and Craig Borba, Self-esteem: a Classroom Affair. Volume 1. 101 Ways to Help Children Like Themselves; Michele and Craig Borba, Self-esteem: a Classroom Affair. Volume 2; Jack Canfield and Harold Wells, 100 Ways to Enhance Self-concept in the Classroom; Larry Chase, The Other Side of the Report Card: a How-to-do-it Program for Affective Education.

7 Group discussion activities

Listening skills

Listening requires a combination of hearing what another person says and active involvement in what she is saying.

EAR

YOU

EYES

UNDIVIDED
ATTENTION

HEART

These characters which make up the verb 'to listen' suggest that the Chinese understand active listening very well.

Teachers in general are not well endowed with the skills of active, effective listening. One of the key qualities in highly facilitative teachers has been shown to be the ability to listen well. One of the crucial dimensions of effective communication, listening has been almost totally neglected by the schooling process. Not only is it important that teachers, who probably spend more time talking to students than listening to them, practise and develop active listening skills but that students themselves have the opportunity to build on a listening facility that is naturally present in their infancy.

The capacity to be a good listener depends upon the appropriate use of certain key skills.

Attending

This requires:

1 adopting a posture of involvement;
2 conscious use of appropriate body language;
3 good eye contact;
4 as non-distracting an environment as possible.

This initial cluster of skills is concerned with establishing the right conditions in which positive interaction can take place. These conditions are very much dependent on the talker sensing that the listener is interested, concerned and available for listening. This is conveyed in the way that she sits in relation to the talker, face to face rather than sideways on, and leaning slightly forward rather than back. Hands and arms should be open rather than folded across the body. Good eye contact with the talker conveys a sense of involvement.

Following

This requires:

1 occasional prompting of the talker — 'Would you like to talk more about that?';
2 some encouragement — head nods and 'I see', 'go on', 'yes';
3 asking limited questions;
4 an attentive silence.

Once the listener has managed to get the other person talking it is important to keep her going so that matters that need to be brought out are done so. This requires good non-verbal communication and some minimal verbal responding. It is difficult to avoid the temptation to intervene and take the agenda away from the *talker. Maintaining an attentive silence is the key skill to cultivate if this is to be avoided.*

Reflecting

This requires:

1 *occasional paraphrasing of what the other person has said;*
2 *reflecting the other's feelings;*
3 *reflecting the other's meanings;*
4 *summarising progress from time to time.*

It is facility with this cluster of skills which marks the difference between active, effective listening and merely hearing. When the talker truly gets the feeling that the listener is really interested, is prepared to stay with the talker's subject and not intervene in a judgemental way, then effective communication can be said to have occurred. Far too often the listener uses time when she should be listening to rehearse in her own mind what she is going to say next. More effective listening involves a capacity to concentrate on the other person's interests and concerns. In conversation, of course, talking and listening are equally important, but in the helping relationship such as that among students working co-operatively and between student and teacher, listening has an altogether more important function, one that can make the difference between healthy growth and development and learning failure.

A listening skills programme

1 *Affirmation/loosening up exercises.*

2 *Students work in pairs; one is A, the other B: A talks to B for one minute on a specific topic (e.g. 'one thing I like about school is …'), B listens. B talks to A for one minute (same topic), A listens.*

3 *Students find another partner and nominate A and B.*

A talks to B for one minute ⎱ *same topic as before, but not mentioning anything said last time.*
B talks to A for one minute ⎰

4 *Students return to first partner (as in 2.)*

A becomes B, recounting what B said ⎱ *using the 'I' (first person) form*
B becomes A, recounting what A said ⎰

5 *The whole group comes together to give feedback on their experiences in activities 2–4.*

6 *Students form new pairs, but work **with eyes closed**:*

A talks to B for one minute ⎱ *new topic*
B talks to A for one minute ⎰

Note: *for activities 6 and 7 it is useful to have one or two students as observers.*

7 *Same pairs as above, but this time students stand or sit side-by-side and look directly in front (eyes open but no eye contact between the pair).*

A talks to B for one minute ⎱ *New topic*
B talks to A for one minute ⎰

8 *Whole group comes together to discuss experiences in activities 6 and 7.*

9 *Input from facilitator on listening skills (based on above text). At the end of the input, students each receive a 'checklist' of the twelve skills for active listening (items 1–4 under 'Attending', 'Following' and 'Reflecting' in the text above).*

10 *Students find new partners. The focus on this activity is on the listener to practise the twelve skills:*

A talks to B for three minutes ⎱ *New topic*
B talks to A for three minutes ⎰

11 In same pairs, students discuss what it feels like to listen actively, and to be actively listened to.

12 Active arguing: students, in same pairs, reject active listening skills and argue for three minutes on any topic, then reflect on the experience.

13 Students form groups of three, nominating A, B and C.
   (i) A talks to B for 3 minutes (topic of A's choice), C to observe B using checklist of active listening skills for reference.
   (ii) C reports back on B's active listening.
   (iii) Students change roles and repeat the procedure so that each participant is talker, listener and observer in turn.

14 Final whole group discussion on the listening skills programme.
   — what was learnt about the place of listening in the communication process?
   — what did I learn about me as a listener?
   — how important is active listening in communication between people at interpersonal to global levels?
   — how often do teachers really listen to me?

15 Group affirmation exercise.

The programme outlined above will take about 1 hour 45 minutes.

▼ Source

Programme based on ideas from Patrick Whitaker, Adviser for Primary Education, Derbyshire. Text adapted from 'The learning process', World Studies Journal Vol. 5, No. 2, 1984.

Conch Discussions

▼ Resources

A shell or other object.

▼ Procedure

Students sit in a circle to discuss a chosen topic with the shell in the centre of the circle. The person who opts to begin the discussion picks up the shell and sits down with it on her lap.

When she has finished speaking, she places it back in the centre of the circle. The next person wishing to speak repeats the procedure.

▼ Potential

A simple technique for promoting self-discipline and co-operative behaviour in discussion work. The act of picking up and returning the shell to the centre of the circle gives time for reflection before the next contribution is made.

▼ Variation

The shell is passed clockwise around the circle. Students can speak or remain silent each time it reaches them.

Primary/Secondary.

▼ Source

Various.

'So you see,' said Ralph, 'we need hunters to get us meat. And another thing.'
He lifted the shell on his knees and looked round the sun-slashed faces.
'There aren't any grown-ups. We shall have to look after ourselves.'
The meeting hummed and was silent.
'And another thing. We can't have everybody talking at once. We'll have to have "Hands up" like at school.'
He held the conch before his face and glanced round the mouth.
'Then I'll give him the conch.'
'Conch?'
'That's what this shell's called. I'll give the conch to the next person to speak. He can hold it when he's speaking.'
'But –'
'Look –'
'And he won't be interrupted. Except by me.'

William Golding, *Lord of the Flies.*

Goldfish Bowl Discussion

▼   Resources

Circle of chairs for each inner group, circle of chairs for each outer group.

▼   Procedure

The class forms into groups of 10–15. Half of each group sits in the inner circle of chairs, the other half in the outer circle. Students in the inner circle are asked to engage in discussion of a controversial topic which is likely to excite a range of strongly-held opinions, e.g. animal rights, nuclear power, a contentious school or local issue (15–20 minutes). Those in the outer circle are asked to remain silent and act as observers. They are to avoid any temptation to break into the discussion.

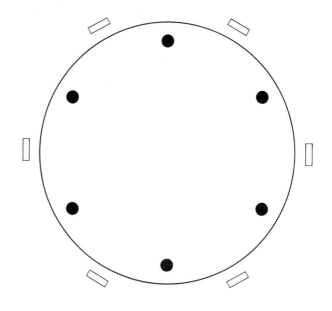

● Discussion group

▭ Observers

'Goldfish Bowl' in action

After the discussion, observers are asked to explain how they perceived the dynamics of the discussion. Their comments should not be so much directed at the respective quality of arguments and ideas advanced but at the performance of the inner group as participants in the discussion process; e.g. the body language employed, the degree to which people were really listening to each other, the extent to which people were reflecting on and responding to each other's contribution or were simply intent on injecting their own ideas, examples of prejudice, obstructive or overbearing behaviours, etc.

The process is then repeated with the discussion and observation groups exchanging places and roles.

▼ Potential

*This activity enables students to identify and practise positive discussion styles. It can be repeated from time to time if the facilitator and the class feel that group and plenary discussion sessions are being inhibited and impeded by the contribution of some class members. It can very usefully be linked with **Discussion Maps** (see below).*

Primary/Secondary, 60 minutes.

▼ Source

Various.

Discussion Maps

▼ Resources

A circle of chairs for each discussion group; a felt tip pen and large sheet of paper for each group observer.

▼ Procedure

The students form into groups of about 10 to discuss a controversial topic. One group member acts as observer. The observer places herself in a position outside the circle where she can clearly see everybody in the group.

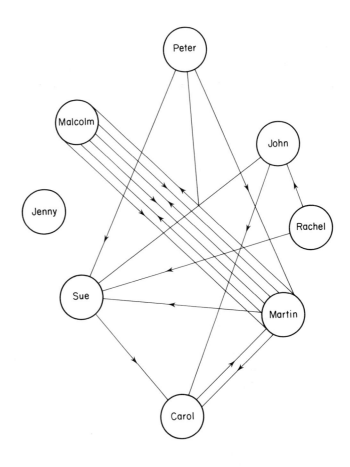

Every time a student makes a contribution, however small, to the discussion, the observer records the fact on the discussion map by drawing a line. If a contribution is directed to a particular person, a line is drawn to that person. If it is directed to the group, a line is drawn to the centre of the circle. If a contribution is interrupted or not completed for whatever reason a short line is drawn. Arrows can be used to indicate the flow of discussion between individuals. A record of contributions made is, thus, built up.

The observer joins the circle and shows the group the discussion map (it is also important that a facilitator joins the group to conduct the debriefing). In the case of the discussion group illustrated, Jenny might be the first to be asked to comment on what the map shows so as to avoid her further exclusion. It can be suggested to her that she is probably in the best position to comment on the discussion in that she chose to observe rather than contribute. Rachel, Peter and John might also be invited to contribute their impressions before the discussion is thrown open.

Students can be asked to reflect on their own and each other's participation in the light of the map and the observer's comments. Why did certain individuals (Malcolm and Martin) dominate the discussion? How did others feel about their domination? On reflection, do Malcolm and Martin feel their contribution helped or hindered the group's task? How could they have acted differently so as to have given space and encouragement to others? What roles did others take up in the discussion? Did some participants respond to some people and not to others? Why? Why were some contributions interrupted? Was gender a factor in determining the level of a participant's contribution? If so, how and why? Would group members behave differently in their next group discussion session? If so, how?

▼ Potential

This is a useful activity for heightening awareness of what is happening within a group. As such, it can encourage students to reflect upon and, if necessary, work at revising the nature of their group and plenary discussions.

▼ Variations/Extensions

1 Each group has a second observer equipped with a stop watch. She records on a chart and then tots up the length of contribution of each participant.
2 A ball of wool is tied around the wrist of the first participant to contribute and is passed around the wrist of each subsequent contributor to the discussion. A very vivid record of the discussion is, thus, created.
3 The facilitator secretly builds up a second discussion map of the debriefing discussion, revealing it at the end of the session.
4 Students are given ten dried peas each. A large container is placed in the centre of the group. Each time a student contributes to the discussion, she throws one pea into the container. Having used up all her peas, she may not participate in the discussion again.

Primary/Secondary, 40 minutes.

▼ Source

Centre for Global Education.

Group Roles

▼ Resources

Set of 'helpful' and 'unhelpful' role cards (such as the examples opposite).

▼ Procedure

Students, in groups of five or six, are each given a different 'unhelpful' role card. They are asked to read it carefully and to avoid showing or reading their card to anyone else. Groups are told that they are shortly to engage in a discussion activity in which individuals will try to make the kind of contribution that is set out on their card. They are then given a topic for discussion. After ten minutes the discussion is stopped and participants try to guess what role each group member had been given. The procedure is then repeated with students working from 'helpful' role cards.

There are countless topics for discussion. One tried and tested task is to ask students to decide on three people, cost being no object, who they would like to invite to speak in school assembly. Another is to ask students to decide upon one invention or initiative which would make the world a better place. Ranking tasks (see pp. 134–5) can also be usefully employed for this activity, e.g. students are given six photographs to rank in order of significance.

▼ Potential

This is a very useful – and often very humorous – activity which helps to make students more conscious of, and sensitive to, the need for a positive approach to discussion work. The following questions can be posed in debriefing:

— how did you feel playing the roles you did?
— how did you recognise the roles that others were playing?
— did you learn anything about yourself in this activity?
— which role or roles do you usually play in group discussion?
— are there other helpful and unhelpful discussion roles?

Helpful roles

Supporter

You try to make others feel good by praising and supporting what they say:

— 'that's a good point'
— 'that's really helpful'
— 'smashing idea'
— 'you've helped me a lot by explaining that'

Organiser

You get the discussion started and try to stop the group from straying off the subject. You encourage everybody to get the job done:

— 'don't forget what we're supposed to be discussing'
— 'come on everyone, don't let's waste time'
— 'let's keep to the point'

Peace-keeper

You try to make peace between people who are arguing and disagreeing:

— 'I think it would be helpful if you both listened to each other'
— 'can we find any common ground between you?'
— 'let's first discuss what you can agree about'

Questioner

You ask others to explain more clearly what they have said and for information to back their opinions:

— 'can you give us an example?'
— 'what precisely do you mean?'
— 'have you any evidence for saying that?'
— 'how do you know that's true?'

Provoker

You try to stir up the discussion so nobody takes anything for granted:

— 'is there another way of looking at this problem?'
— 'this discussion is too comfortable; I think...'
— 'come on, we're forgetting the real world out there!'
— 'are we being really honest in our opinions?'

Ideas-seeker

You ask others to express their ideas and opinions:

— 'I would like to know what Rachel's views are'
— 'Jill, what do you think?'
— 'we can't decide until we've heard everybody's opinion'
— 'how do you feel about that?'

Unhelpful roles

Chatterer

You talk and talk and talk and talk, even when you've nothing really to contribute to the discussion:

— *you tell pointless stories*
— *you repeat, using other words, what you've said already*
— *you interrupt others*
— *you speak as though you have not really listened to the others*

Show-off

You try to show how clever you are by:

— *mentioning books and writers that nobody else has heard of*
— *using long words whenever possible*
— *dropping the names of important thinkers into the conversation*
— *suggesting to people what they should read so they understand the subject better*

Flatterer

You choose one person in the group and praise her/him at every opportunity:

— *'Jane has so many good ideas'*
— *'thanks Jane, I understand the problem now'*
— *'I support Jane's view'*
— *'let's hear more from Jane on this'*

Saboteur

You try to sabotage (destroy) the discussion by:

— *continually pointing out how useless it all is*
— *making fun of other people's ideas*
— *making cynical comments*
— *behaving in an uninterested way, e.g. yawning, leaning back, looking out the window, making paper darts*

Extremist

You take up an extreme position with respect to the subject under discussion. You:

— *put forward one view as the explanation of everything*
— *come back continually to one basic idea*
— *express yourself in extreme terms*
— *refuse to compromise*

Boss

You act as though you know it all by:

— *expressing your views with great force*
— *being strongly critical of anyone disagreeing with you*
— *insisting that people discuss what you think is important*
— *trying to make the discussion revolve around you*

— can you think of situations where helpful roles might be unhelpful and vice versa?
— are there certain circumstances in which people fall more easily into helpful or unhelpful roles?

▼ Variation

The activity can be carried out with a mixture of helpful and unhelpful role cards.

▼ Follow-up

The activity can be repeated - with the same or different cards — whenever the teacher or students think that the quality of group discussion work has deteriorated. The cards can also be put face upwards in subsequent group discussion activities and can be referred to by any participant who thinks that certain group members are adopting unhelpful roles.

▼ Source

From ideas in Richardson, R., Flood, M. and Fisher, S., Debate and Decision, *World Studies Project*, 1980 and Schniedewind, N. and Davidson, E., Open Minds to Equality, *New Jersey, Prentice-Hall, 1983.*

Brainstorming

▼ Resources

Board or large paper chart.

▼ Procedure

Brainstorming involves listing ideas without discussion. The class is given a topic and students are invited to offer their immediate reponses to the topic. The responses are listed on the board or chart. The rules for brainstorming are:

— all ideas are accepted, everything is written down;
— no-one should comment, positively or negatively, on others' ideas;
— participants should feel free to offer any idea even if they feel unsure about it;
— 'piggybacking', i.e. taking somebody else's idea a stage further, is permitted.

The brainstorming is brought to a close when the flow of ideas slows down significantly.

▼ Potential

Brainstorming can be used for a variety of purposes and at many points during a course (some teachers have the rules of brainstorming posted permanently in the classroom). It can be used to help students think creatively and laterally. Equally, it offers a means for focusing upon the intuitive and feelings dimension of a topic or problem. At another level, it can be used as a warm-up activity. Again, it can be used to pool students' images of a topic prior to study/research (subsequent reference back to the brainstormed images thus providing a fertile way into consideration of stereotypes).

Brainstorming has many advantages as a technique. It encourages everyone to take part since the rules protect the individual from criticism, laughter or ridicule. It is democratic in its emphasis upon everybody's right to speak and the value of their contribution. It is confidence-building and encourages openness, open-mindedness and a readiness to be imaginative and speculative. It promotes a lively, co-operative class climate. It can also bring to the surface a wide range of perspectives upon and intellectual and emotional responses to a particular problem.

Brainstorming lists can be used as the basis for class or group discussion, as raw material for ranking activities or for negotiating a course or study agenda. If the brainstorming has been written up on a chart, students can be given 3 coloured dots each to place against what they feel are the best suggestions. The results can be helpful in drawing up an agenda of topics for further exploration.

▼ Sample brainstorming tasks

- brainstorm the names of people who you would like to visit school and talk to you;
- brainstorm things you can do with a paperclip;
- we are going on to study India; brainstorm all the images that come into your mind;
- brainstorm ways in which malnutrition in Africa might be overcome;
- think of occasions when you have been unjustly treated; brainstorm words that describe how you felt;
- let us look at the word 'warmth'; brainstorm images that come into your mind.

▼ Variation

Brainstorming can also be carried out as a small group activity.

Primary/Secondary.

▼ Source

Various.

Diamond Ranking

▼ Resources

Nine brief statements or anecdotes representing a spread of opinion or perspectives for each pair of students. Each statement should be given a short title or number for easy reference. Each set of statements should be cut up and stored in an envelope.

▼ Procedure

Pairs are given an envelope containing the nine statements/anecdotes and are asked to rank the statements in diamond formation, i.e.

```
                1

        2               2

   4          4              4

        7               7

                9
```

A fairly loose criterion for ranking is given such as 'importance', 'significance', 'interest', the teacher resisting any requests for her to be more specific about the criterion. The most 'important', 'significant' or 'interesting' statement/anecdote

is placed at the top of the diamond. The next two are placed in second equal position. The three across the centre are fourth equal. The next two are seventh equal. The statement/ anecdote placed at the foot of the diamond is the one considered by the pair to be the least 'important', 'significant' or 'interesting'. When pairs have completed their task, they form into sixes (the composition of which can have been decided upon before the activity begins using random group formation techniques such as those described on pages 111–2). Each pair explains and seeks to justify its ranking to the other two pairs. The six then try to negotiate a consensus ranking for the group as a whole. Plenary reporting back and discussion can follow.

▼ Potential

This activity helps students in an unthreatening way to clarify what their thoughts and feelings about a particular subject are whilst alerting them to a range of other opinions and perspectives on the subject. Underpinning the activity is the unspoken assumption that everybody has something relevant and valuable to bring to the discussion. The imprecise criterion given is itself likely to be one layer in the discussion. What does 'importance', 'significance' or 'interest' mean? Should we try and pin down what we mean more precisely? Skills used in this activity include discussion, negotiation, accommodation to other perspectives, and consensus-seeking. In the plenary discussion, a group reporting their inability to agree upon a ranking order is as important a discussion point as group reporting that they have achieved consensus.

▼ Variations

Instead of statements, nine pictures, photographs or cartoons can be used alongside a criterion such as 'beautiful', 'funny', 'surprising' or 'unusual'. Other ranking formations can be used such as:

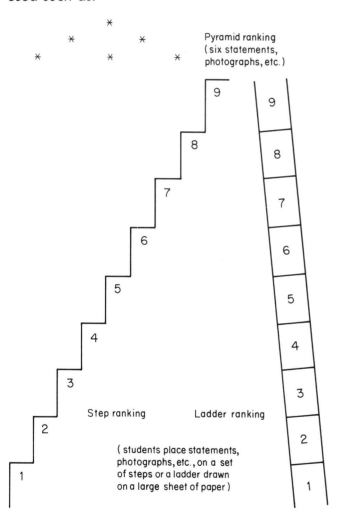

Pyramid ranking
(six statements, photographs, etc.)

Step ranking

Ladder ranking

(students place statements, photographs, etc., on a set of steps or a ladder drawn on a large sheet of paper)

Junior/Secondary, 15 minutes in pairs, 15 minutes in sixes.

▼ Source

Based on an idea in Richardson, R., Flood, M. and Fisher, S., Debate and Decision, World Studies Project, 1980.

Flowcharts

▼ Resources

Written statements on separate slips of paper; four blank slips; sugar paper; glue; felt tip pens.

▼ Procedure

Students work in groups of three on four. Each group has a set (about 20, but possibly fewer with younger students) of statements on slips of paper which they should arrange in any kind of pattern, cluster, sequence or flowchart they wish. When a pattern has been agreed, the slips should be glued to the sugar paper. Lines, arrows, pictures and comments can be added where appropriate. Participants can reject any slips which they do not want or disagree with, and they may write a few more of their own. Groups may need up to 30 minutes for this stage, depending upon the length and complexity of the statements. When they have finished, groups come together as a class in order to explain their flowchart and to report on the main points of discussion.

▼ Potential

This exercise can be used to introduce a range of ideas or perspectives on a particular issue. It encourages discussion and consideration of viewpoints which may not otherwise be heard and can help towards the clarification of an individual's values and attitudes. A flowchart, rather than a linear sequence, allows for greater imagination in exploring the relationships between ideas. In trying to achieve agreement over the formation of the flowchart, it is likely that individuals will need to accommodate, or at least be tolerant of differing viewpoints. Even so, it may be that total group consensus will not be achieved and this point should be represented on the chart and explored in the class discussion.

▼ Extension: Circus

Instead of groups coming together as a class the **Circus** procedure can be adopted: each group should stick their flowchart up on the wall and one member of the group should remain beside it as a 'guide'. Other members then look at the work of the other groups, asking the 'guide' for any explanation or clarification needed. Group members should take turns as 'guide' to give everybody an opportunity to circulate.

▼ Variation

Twenty statements, even if brief, can prove difficult to assimilate in a short time. Cartoons or photographs can be used instead, though the focus of the debate may shift towards the interpretation of the picture, rather than its relationship to others.

Secondary, 45 minutes.

▼ Source

Derived from Richardson, R., Flood, M. and Fisher, S., Debate and Decision: schools in a world of change, World Studies Project, 1980.

Tackling a Question

▼ Resources

Six pieces ('cards') of white paper (approximately 12 cm × 8 cm) per student; a large 'chart' for each group of 5 or 6 students (made by Sellotaping 4 sheets of coloured sugar paper together); felt tip pens; a pot of paste per group; 30 pieces of paper of one colour (6 cm × 8 cm) and 30 similarly sized pieces of another colour; small white adhesive dots (usually no more than 6 per student required); floor or large table top for each group.

▼ Procedure

Stage 1: Writing the 'Cards'
Students form groups of 5 or 6. A question or incomplete statement is written on the board. The range of topics from which to choose is, of course, vast. Two examples might be 'Why is it four times more difficult for a black school leaver than a white school leaver to get a job, when both have equal qualifications?' Commission for Racial Equality figure) and 'Poverty in developing countries is caused by ...' A member of each group writes the question or incomplete statement in the top left-hand corner

of the 'chart'. Group members then each write 4–6 different answers or completed statements on separate 'cards', putting only one idea on each. The answers or completed statements should be brief and boldly written. No discussion takes place during this stage.
10 minutes.

Stage 2: Clustering the 'Cards'
The 'cards' are pooled, read and discussed by the group with a view to identifying and forming clusters of similar responses or explanations put forward. A cluster can be one 'card'. If there is very strong disagreement about which cluster a card belongs to, a duplicate can be written so the 'card' appears in more than one cluster. During this stage the discussion is solely about clustering 'cards' and not about the merit of what each 'card' says.

The clusters are spaced out on the chart and a circle is drawn around each. A heading for each cluster is then decided upon and written in. The cards are stuck down. Students should be advised to leave space within each circle for more material to be included later.
15 minutes.

Stage 3: Clarifications
Discussion now moves on to the meaning of the group's many responses to the question or incomplete statement. Students can ask for clarification if a card seems unclear or ambiguous. It is important to emphasise that the writer of the card should not be singled out to explain; rather the group as a whole should seek to provide clarification. Explanations arrived at should be written up on a coloured piece of paper (the same colour for all clarifications) and stuck across the corner of the white 'cards' concerned.
10–15 minutes.

Stage 4: Objections
At this stage individual students voice their objections to the explanations offered on the 'cards'. In each case the objection is explored by the group and, if sustained by one other group member, is written up and stuck across the corner of the 'card' in question. Pieces of paper of the second colour (see 'Resources') are used for objections.
10–15 minutes.

Stage 5: Ranking the 'Cards'

This stage gives students the opportunity to rank the reasons or explanations suggested, as now represented in the clusters. Each participant is given half as many sticky white dots as there are clusters (just more than half if there are an uneven number of clusters, e.g. 5 dots in the case of 9 clusters). They stick these within the cluster(s) which they consider offer the most important reasons for or explanations of the question at issue.
5 minutes.

Stage 6: Relating the Clusters

Attention now turns to group discussion of the relationship between the several clusters. When a relationship, positive or negative, is identified between two clusters, a two-way arrow is drawn and brief explanation written along the arrow.
10 minutes.

The 6 stages can be followed by class plenary discussion or, perhaps more fruitfully, by a **Circus** examination of the work of each group (see p. 135).

▼ Potential

This sequence of activities has tremendous potential for group exploration of controversial topics in the secondary school and requires students to utilise a wide range of analytical, co-operative, discussion and negotiation skills. The six stages can be attempted one immediately after the other or, alternatively, they can be staggered over a period of time. The latter approach allows for study and research to be undertaken in the intervals. For instance, students, already acquainted with their group's set of cards, could be asked to research the topic in question in preparation for the 'Objections' or 'Relating the Clusters' stages.

▼ Variations

Groups can use the procedure described above to consider in turn two opposite sides of the same issue, e.g. 'What are the advantages of developing nuclear power as an energy source?' and 'What are the disadvantages?'

Another approach is to set a social, economic and/or political problem as a topic, e.g. racism or pollution, and to structure group discussion in three stages. The first is to **define** the topic; the second is to put forward **ideas** to solve the problem and the third is to consider **barriers** that might hinder implementation of the ideas. At each stage a full or slimmed-down version of **Tackling a Question** is used.

The procedure can also be employed to identify students' concerns, needs and wishes at the outset of a course or course component. A trigger question might be something like: 'What would I like to achieve by the time I have finished this course.'

Secondary, 70 minutes.

▼ Source

Centre for Global Education after an idea in Purvis, K., 'The teacher as moderator: a technique for interactional learning', English Language Teaching Journal, Vol. 37, No. 3, 1983.

Tackling a Statement

▼ Resources

Five trays of badges (twenty per tray for a class of thirty) indicating five positions on a continuum of opinion ranging from strong agreement to strong disagreement:

+ + = strongly agree
+ = agree
? = can't decide or don't know
− = disagree
− − = strongly disagree

Open space so that students can move freely about the classroom.

▼ Procedure

A controversial statement, for instance about rights, is written up on the board. The statement should be carefully designed to draw out a wide spectrum of responses, e.g. 'Girls have the right to be taught football' or 'Everyone has the right to private medical care or hospital treatment' or

'An essential right is the right to disobey authority'. Students are asked to reflect upon the statement for 2 minutes and then to choose and wear the badge which most faithfully represents their response to the statement. They next discuss the statement with a person wearing the same badge (3 minutes). Students move on to discuss the statement with someone wearing a badge one position removed from their own badge (3 minutes). They then enter discussion with someone wearing a badge 2 or 3 positions removed (3 minutes). Finally, students are invited to return to the person with whom they originally talked to review what they have heard and learnt. It is important to encourage students to engage in positive, constructive discussion and listening rather than argument. Students should be invited to change badges, if they wish, between stages.

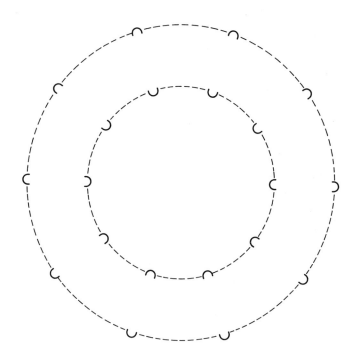

▼ Potential

This peer learning activity can be applied to a wide range of controversial statements and can be used with students of different age levels. It can be used at many stages during the study of a topic. For instance:

— it can be employed as a starter exercise to alert students to the fact that there are perspectives on a topic other than their own;
— it can be used as a 'state of research' exercise during or at the end of a period of study enabling students to share what they have learnt — and their new thinking — with others.

Upper Primary/Secondary, 20 minutes.

▼ Source

Centre for Global Education.

Concentric Circles

▼ Resources

Two circles of chairs, one facing outwards, one facing inwards (see diagram).

▼ Procedure

The class forms two equal groups; one group sits down in the inner circle, one in the outer circle of chairs. In this way everybody sits facing a partner. The students are given a question for discussion. After a short period of time for reflection, they are given a minute or two to discuss the question with their partner. At a given signal, students in the outer circle move one position to the left and discuss the same question with their new partner. Students in the outer circle continue to rotate to new partners as many times as seems appropriate or until they return to their original partner.

▼ Potential

This activity has many uses. It can be used as a peer learning exercise following individual study or project work on a particular topic so that students can share what they have learnt. It offers a means whereby students can be brought face to face with a variety of different perspectives and viewpoints. It can also be employed as a starter activity for, for example, a programme of anti-racist or anti-sexist education by inviting those in the two circles to exchange memories of times when they have felt unjustly treated. As memories are recounted and as feelings engendered by unjust treatment are explored, a fertile climate can be created for consideration of profounder and more widespread forms of injustice.

Alternatively, **Concentric Circles** can be used to enable students to learn more about each other, their fears, frustrations and aspirations. Discussion questions such as 'What makes you feel good?' or 'What worries you most about the future?' or 'When were you last prevented from doing something because of your age/sex?' will trigger off peer learning at a variety of levels.

▼ Variations

In some cases it is advisable to adjust or completely change the topic as students move around the circle.

Concentric Circles can also be used to help students air different positions on controversial topics. For instance, following research, students might be invited to discuss points for and against the operations of transnational companies in the 'Third World'. The outer circle is asked to be critical of the companies, the inner circle to offer a defence. At certain points, students in the two circles exchange seats and take on a different stance.

Secondary.

▼ Source

Derived from Schniedewind, N. and Davidson, E., Open Minds to Equality, New Jersey, Prentice-Hall, 1983.

Reactions

▼ Resources

Four quarter A4 slips of paper per student, some extra slips of paper.

▼ Procedure

Students watch a film, listen to a radio programme or audio tape or listen to a talk by the teacher, a visiting speaker, or another student. They then form groups of five or six. Group members first work separately, writing four different reactions to the stimulus (one reaction per slip of paper). A reaction can be a short paragraph, a sentence or one word. The reactions are collected in by one of the group, shuffled and dealt out as in a game of cards. Everyone looks at their 'hand', discarding into a central pool any reactions they wrote and any with which they are not prepared to identify. They continue to discard and pick up from the pool until they are satisfied with their hand. The aim is for every group member to end up with a final hand of up to three reactions which, to repeat, must be statements (a) they did not write themselves and (b) with which they are prepared to agree. Students then break into twos or threes. They read their final hand to each other, explaining why they chose those particular reactions. They then prepare a composite reaction to the stimulus which may be a consensus statement or an agreement to disagree. The whole group of five or six then joins together, the sub-groups sharing and explaining their composite reactions before writing a final group reaction. Reporting back and discussion in plenary session follows.

▼ Potential

This activity is excellent for achieving a thoroughgoing sharing of reactions to whatever stimulus material is offered. Participants are asked to critically reflect upon and accept or reject other ideas and perspectives, to negotiate a joint agreed position and, if this proves impossible, to at least clarify the nature of the disagreements that emerge and also their own perspectives/values.

▼ Variations

The above procedure can also be followed for a sharing of opinions on a particular topic, e.g. the effectiveness of aid programmes, how to eradicate racism in society, how to stop air pollution.

To prevent the possibility of an individual's statements being completely rejected by other group members, the rules can be altered so that each participant is to have a final hand of four, at least two of which were written by someone else.

Junior/Secondary, 40 minutes.

▼ Source

Derived from Richardson, R., Flood, M. and Fisher, S., Debate and Decision; Schools in a World of Change, World Studies Project, 1980.

What's in a Name?

▼ Resources

Several 'name your baby' books; a card, felt tip pen, pin and blank world map for each student; a large world map (and, possibly, colour-topped pins and wool).

▼ Procedure

The class divides into groups of four and each group is given at least one 'name your baby' book. Students are asked to look up their first names in the books and find out the meaning of the names and the countries or areas of the world from which they originated. Each student is then given a card, felt tip pen and pin. On one side of the card, they write the meaning and place(s) of origin of their first names; on the other side they print their actual names. Larger groups are formed by two groups joining together. Students belonging to a larger group hand their cards to the facilitator without showing them to others. The facilitator lays the group's cards out on a table top with meanings and origins of names face upwards. A 'guessing game' follows in which students try to identify which card belongs to which person in the group on the basis of the meanings of names (the meanings will be positive and the discussion should be entirely about positive characteristics). Partners from the original groups should not reveal what they know about each other's first names. Guessing completed, students pin on their cards displaying the meanings and origins side. They then walk around the room collecting details of the places of origin of each other's first names. The countries or areas concerned are then located and printed in on the blank world maps with arrows connecting them to the location of the school. The large wall map can be used both for reference purposes during indi-vidual map work or for creating a class map of the activity using colour-topped pins, wool (linking places of origin to school location) and students' cards.

▼ Potential

This activity harnesses students' real enjoyment at finding out about their names for the purposes of learning more about the interdependent nature of the world and the myriad influences that have gone to make up 'British' culture. Post-activity discussion can focus upon the influence of other cultures on British life and society and seek to unpick what students have learnt about the nature of 'Britishness'. By emphasising discussion of positive characteristics, the activity can help to reinforce individual and group self-esteem. It also involves practising basic map presentation skills. For classes containing ethnic minority children, it is essential that name books used include some from their families' place of origin.

▼ Follow-up

Students can find out about the first names of other people in their family and add this to their individual maps or the class map. If surname books are available these can be investigated, too, and results added to the maps. A further idea is to brainstorm commonly used words and have groups investigate their place or area of origin (there will be a lot of surprises!). **What's in a name?** *can also usefully lead on to the 'Our Word House' activity in Fisher, S. and Hicks, D., World Studies 8–13, Oliver & Boyd, 1985, pp. 42–7, which examines the global influences on the English language.*

Junior/Lower Secondary, 60 minutes.

▼ Source

Developed from 'What's in a Name?' in Johnson, J. and Benegar, J., Global Issues in the Intermediate Classroom, Boulder, Colorado, Social Science Education Consortium, 1981.

Woolly Thinking

▼ Resources

For a class of thirty students: 10 sheets of sugar paper, 10 sets of labels (3 per set and each set of a different colour), 30 pins, scrap paper and 10 balls of wool of colours to match the labels.

A large open space in the classroom is required so that the following arrangement is possible:

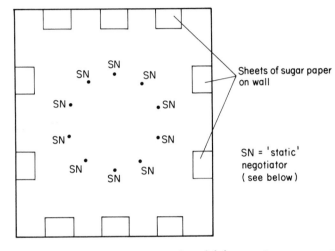

SN = 'static' negotiator (see below)

Sheets of sugar paper on wall

The ten chosen topics should be written up at the top of the sugar paper, one on each sheet. Topics could be: The Arms Race, Environmental Pollution, Unemployment, 'Third World' Underdevelopment, Terrorism/Freedom Fighting, Human Rights Violations, Nationalism, Natural Resource Depletion, Malnutrition, Urbanisation. The topics should also be written on the sets of labels.

▼ Procedure

Students choose one of the ten topics by standing next to a particular sheet of sugar paper. There should be no more than three students per group. Each student should wear a label identifying her as representing that particular topic. Groups first brainstorm the issues surrounding their topic using the scrap paper provided (8 minutes). They then appoint a 'static' negotiator and two 'mobile' negotiators. The 'static' negotiators should take up position in a circle and tie the ends of their balls of wool around their waists. Their role is to stay in one position but to join in negotiations with any of

the 'mobile' negotiators of the 9 other groups. The role of the 'mobile' negotiator is to go out and negotiate connections, links or relationships between topics. Each time a connection between two topics has been discussed and agreed, the two balls of wool are passed across the circle and looped around the waists of the 'static' negotiators of the two groups concerned. It is important that the wool is kept taut and that the ball is brought back to the 'static' negotiator from whom it started each time. It is also very important that the thinking behind each agreement is recorded by 'mobile' negotiators of both groups on their respective sheets of sugar paper. As the activity continues, a spider's web of connections between the 10 issues will be produced; the web will probably be so closely woven that 'mobile' negotiators will have to crawl underneath in pursuit of their task.

▼ Potential

The web of different coloured wools offers a potent visual symbol of the interlocking/systemic nature of contemporary global issues. Throughout the discussion it is helpful to keep the web intact. This can be done by asking 'static' negotiators to sit down where they have been standing. Class members can be encouraged to describe the negotiations in which they were involved and to reflect upon the connections made during the activity. Discussion of the absence of connections can also be very productive. **Woolly Thinking** is an ideal unit for exploring relationships between topics on which students have already undertaken some background work.

▼ Variations

The topics used are, of course, open to considerable variation. Upper primary and lower secondary teachers have used **Woolly Thinking** to illustrate the food web and other types of ecological interdependence. It can also be used to illustrate local community interdependencies (see **Dependency Webs,** p. 8) and the relationships between characters in stories or novels.

Primary/Secondary, 25 minutes.

▼ Source

Centre for Global Education.

'Woolly Thinking' in action

Picture Interpretation

▼ Resources

Eight photographs or pictures, each photo-copied and then cut up into 3 sections (the first to contain one detail from the picture, the second to have more detail and the third to be the whole picture – see example on p. 143); 16 sheets of sugar paper; 8 felt tip pens; 8 pots of glue.

▼ Procedure

Participants form groups of four and are given the first (smallest) section of the picture. They glue this near the top of a sheet of sugar paper and brainstorm a range of ideas, feelings and questions about the image given. These are written on the sugar paper around the picture with arrows or lines to the picture if appropriate.

After about 10 minutes, the second (middle size) picture is given out, pasted below the first picture and the same procedure undertaken. The process is repeated again with the final picture, when the 'whole' image is revealed.

▼ Potential

This activity raises a number of important issues about observation, perception and perspective. The three-stage process often causes participants to reassess and change ideas and feelings that were initially recorded. In a plenary discussion, participants can be asked to reflect upon what factors influence our interpretations of graphical images. Why do some people interpret the same image in a different way? Why is

the 'context' — i.e. what surrounds an image — so important to our understanding? What are the implications of these questions for the way in which we interpret 'reality' through the media? What is 'reality', anyway?

Primary/Secondary, 30 minutes.

▼ Source

Various.

The Rights of the Child

▼ Resources

For a class of thirty students: a supply of 'cards' made by cutting A4 sheets into quarters, a smaller supply of 'summary cards' of another colour, fifteen sheets of sugar paper, six pots of

paste, six felt tip pens, thirty copies of the United Nations Declaration of the Rights of the Child *(see page 144).*

▼ Procedure

Students, working in groups of 5, are briefly introduced to the idea of rights (e.g. 'something to which in all fairness you are or feel entitled') and are offered a few examples of rights children might claim (e.g. the right to your own bedroom, to play space, to pocket money). They are then asked to brainstorm what they consider the rights of children to be. All ideas are to be accepted, each one being written on a separate 'card'. The next stage is for each group to arrange their 'cards' in clusters on one or two sheets of sugar paper. Clusters are to be made up of 'cards' offering similar or overlapping examples of children's rights. A cluster may be one 'card'. When students are satisfied with their arrangement of cards, they paste them down and draw a circle around each cluster. They are then invited to summarise on separate 'cards' what each particular cluster is saying about the rights of a child (no more than a sentence or two

---

U N Declaration on the Rights of the Child (1959)

The right to affection, love and understanding.

The right to adequate nutrition and medical care.

The right to free education.

The right to full opportunity for play and recreation.

The right to a name and nationality.

The right to special care, if handicapped.

The right to be among the first to receive relief in times of disaster.

The right to be a useful member of society and to develop individual abilities.

The right to be brought up in a spirit of peace and universal brotherhood.

The right to enjoy these rights, regardless of race, colour, sex, religion, national or social origin.

---

to be written). The 'summary cards' are pasted at the top of each cluster and, together, form the group's provisional Declaration of the Rights of the Child.

It is then explained that the United Nations Declaration of the Rights of the Child has only ten clauses. Groups are asked to get together with another group to negotiate and write down on sugar paper a joint ten-clause Declaration using their collective 'summary cards' as a starting point. This process may involve omitting some ideas entirely, collapsing 'summary card' ideas together or simply editing two closely approximating 'cards' so they can stand as one statement.

The next stage is for the combined groups to present and reflect upon their ten-point Declar-

ations in plenary. What rights are common to each Declaration? What differences are there between Declarations? Are there any surprises? Are there any disagreements?

Students then return to their combined groups each with a copy of the UN Declaration of the Rights of the Child. They are asked to compare and contrast the UN Declaration with their own work. Are there any important rights that, on reflection, they as a group had overlooked? Are there any important rights which the UN Declaration, now over twenty-five years old, fails to include? Groups are also invited to amend their own Declaration in the light of what they have now read. Finally, students are once again brought together in plenary to discuss their reactions to the UN Declaration and to explain any amendments they have made to their own work.

▼ Potential

This sequence of group activities offers a child-centred introduction to human rights in that it limits itself to children's rights and asks class members to first reflect upon what they perceive the rights of children to be. Typically, group Declarations will tend to lay emphasis upon rights at a materialistic and superficial level. The introduction of the UN Declaration often comes as something of a shock with its emphasis upon rights of a more basic nature. Students will probably want to amend their own Declaration when the realisation dawns that they had been blind to or taken for granted a number of fundamental rights. The ethnocentrism of class perspectives prior to reading the Declaration can be teased out in the final plenary. The final group activity may also bring to the surface the point that we continue to identify new rights as time passes. For instance, the UN Declaration (1959) does not mention environmental rights but there is every chance that the student Declarations will — because of the heightened consciousness of environmental issues in contemporary society and media.

These activities can be attempted in one block of time or spread out over a number of lessons.

Upper Primary/Secondary, 2½ hours.

▼ Source

Centre for Global Education.

'Freedom is a Song People Sing': A World Studies Course for Top Juniors

by **Elaine Hicks**, teacher at Cabot Primary School, St Paul's, Bristol

'Rats'; 'Dilapidated House'; 'Thieves and Vandals'; 'Area too noisy'; 'Divorse'; 'House too small'; 'Shops too far away'; 'A Haunted House'...

These were just some of the suggestions made by my class of 10–11 year olds when brainstorming the question 'Why do people move house?' After a lively discussion – many of their answers were based on the children's own experience of moving or wanting to move house – they wrote about and illustrated their ideas.

The next activity revealed the children's rich variety of family links with countries right across the world. The children drew up graphs showing their country of birth and their parents' country of birth. Although most of the children had been born in Britain quite a few had visited their parents' country of birth for a holiday. A couple of children had some first-hand experience of migration, having come to live in Britain in the last few years.

In order to consider some of the reasons behind the movement of people from country to country the class brainstormed the question 'Why do people migrate?' All children's ideas were written down on large pieces of card which were displayed around the classroom. New ideas, often prompted by news items, were added to the display during the year; for instance, 'Nuclear Disaster' was included after the Chernobyl power station accident.

In any study of migration the geographical language of place is very important. To help the children sort out the relationship that terms such as Street, District, City, County, Country, Continent, Hemisphere, Planet, Solar System, Galaxy and Universe, have to each other, they played the game, *Where do you live?* The object is to see how far the children can answer, using these terms before they make a mistake. Often there is a surprised comment, for instance, 'I didn't realise Avon was bigger than Bristol!'

From thinking about place, the children started to look in greater detail at some of the reasons put forward as to why people migrate. There were many suggestions. People migrate...'for more opportunity', 'for jobs', 'for food', 'because of war', 'because of drought', 'to learn', 'because of prejudice', 'to start a new life', 'to join your family'.

However, one idea became a central theme for in-depth study – that of Freedom. To find out what the children understood by the word 'Freedom', they were given two minutes to complete the phrase 'Freedom is...' Answers varied considerably in sophistication; Freedom is...

'to be out of the house', 'when you can do what you want to do', 'deciding for yourself', 'to be out of prison', 'not to be a slave, to be your own master', 'not to be watched', 'being able to protest', 'not being dominated'.

My favourite answer came from a child struggling to master English. She wrote 'Freedom is a song people sing'.

The next activity involved the children in thinking about freedom and how it affects their own lives. They were given cards to label as follows: Birth, Baby, Child, Teenager, Adult, Pensioner, Death. (See examples on p.147.) Then they had to draw themselves at each stage of their lives adding captions that explained in what ways they were free or not free. A few life-lines showed rather a pessimistic view of life. So some of the children were encouraged by a teacher from the Multicultural Education Centre to interview successful adults in the community who had a more hopeful view of the future. The interviews were recorded on tape and then typed up to make a class book called *Life and Jobs*.

The children next began to think about freedom and other people and the actions people might take if they found that their freedom was restricted in some way. Using large colour pictures of people from all over the world, the children worked in pairs to interpret their picture. The following questions helped them sort out their thoughts:

1 What does the picture show?
2 What is (the person/are the persons) able to do because (s/he is/they are) free?
3 Are there any ways in which (the person is/persons are) not free?
4 If you were the person in the picture and your freedom was taken away from you what would you do?

The children found this activity quite hard, particularly questions 3 and 4. But what surprised me most were the misinterpretations of the actual scenes in the pictures; for example, a man working bullocks at a water wheel was understood by a child as 'milking cows'. While another child thought that a man was 'fishing in mud' when in fact he was brandishing a whip to make his buffaloes work harder!

Nevertheless I am sure these activities did provide a preparation for the study of the Vietnamese migration and the Boat People's search for freedom. But before work could proceed on this topic the children needed to know about some of the historical events that led up to this time in world history. Some knowledge about life in China and Mao Tse-tung was needed in order to understand the background to this subject. So to start, the children brainstormed 'China' individually and then wrote down the questions they would like to ask; they then used reference books to discover some answers.

Then before considering the life of Mao Tse-tung the children considered 'What makes a leader?' and 'How are decisions made?' The children used their own past experience of working in small groups as a focus for their reflections. This revealed that some leaders had been self-appointed, others had been elected, whilst others had emerged during the course of the task. Meanwhile, one group of children had organised themselves around the viewpoint that no one person in the group was the leader – they were all equal (one thought did emerge – leaders tended to be those who could easily put ideas into words). Likewise, the ways in which decisions were made varied. Some decisions were made on the strength of a dominant personality while in other groups every issue was voted on!

Again, before the children could understand the movement of people from Vietnam via Hong Kong to England, they needed some knowledge about Hong Kong. The children made deductions about Western influence on Chinese life in Hong Kong by studying some family photographs given to them by a Chinese nun from Hong Kong who was studying in Bristol. She visited school, talked to the children and gave them a Chinese calligraphy lesson, too!

Against this background of knowledge, the children were shown a video of the programme Settling In from *Tomorrow's People*. This showed the journey from Vietnam via Hong Kong to England of a Vietnamese boy. It showed some of the problems and difficulties he has had to face on his journey and in settling in Britain. The children mapped his route and illustrated the story with captions. They discussed the Vietnam war and other wars. They thought about what images a Vietnamese person might have of Britain and they thought about how things have changed in Britain because of the arrival of Chinese and Vietnamese people. This idea was very aptly illustrated by a child arriving in class one morning brandishing a rather greasy piece of old newspaper that had contained fish and chips the night before to cries of 'Miss, look at this'; a closer inspection revealed print in another language – Chinese calligraphy.

Then, great excitement, a new boy arrived in class. Born in Vietnam he had spent the last seven years in Hong Kong. Although fluent in Cantonese, he spoke very little English. However, on the first afternoon, with the help of an interpreter, the children were able to ask him questions about his life in Hong Kong. This revealed that, although the children knew a lot, there was some misunderstanding about the passage of time. He was asked about the Vietnam war – the children hadn't realised that at the age of 11 years he had been born after the end of the war.

As the term's work on Vietnamese migration came to an end, one of the girls made a request. She wanted to know, 'How did Pakistan become a country?' and, 'Could the class do some work on it?' Therefore during the following term the class began to look at the independence of India, Pakistan and Bangladesh. The work further developed the children's understanding of freedom. It included a topic on Gandhi and his response to conflict. The children thought about times when they wanted to change something and what they did. They then considered what Gandhi had done to change things.

Over the course of the year it was this pattern of approach to introducing new work that was adopted. The children would think and reflect on their own experiences as a preparation for learning about issues and events that were beyond their own immediate knowledge.

Thus, hopefully, the children gained a greater knowledge and understanding of themselves whereby they could, with confidence, tackle more difficult and demanding work; work that in the past I might have considered beyond the ability or interest of top juniors.

Overall, this approach to learning meant there were improvements in the children's ability to listen and communicate but best of all was the lovely response of friendship by the class towards the new lad from Vietnam. The care, warmth and interest they showed towards him was unusual in a class familiar with children leaving or joining in mid-term. Their friendliness was, I believe, a direct result of the world studies work they had undertaken.

hospital. C G

Birth.
When I was a baby I wasn't free because I was so young I could not do any thing.

School C G

12 years old
I am at a seconday school. I have not got much freedom because my parents have control over me I can do some thing like get my own toys at and things like that but if I wanted to go to town and my dad said, no I would not go.

Work C G

When I'm 25
I want to get a job. I will be free to jump skip and things like that.

Married.
When I get married I will have freedom because my husband will let me do what I want.

work C G

30 old
When I'm 30 I want to be a shop keeper I hope I will have freedom. My father has died and my sister is crying.

Me in an old peoples home C G

60 years old
When I'm in an old peoples home I will not have a lot of freedom because I will be week and tierd.

Me and my husband walking down the street C G

Hurry UP!

Sweet Shop

80 years old
I will not have a lot of freedom because I will not be able to skip, run and mess about.

me when I'm dying. C G

When I'm dying
I will not have any freed om because I will not be walking about.

me dead.

Here lies Candy G. died etc. 20.18 of heartattak X X X X X

Jesus

death.
I dont no how I will die but I will not have any freedom because I'll be dead.

The Rights Balloon Game

▼ Resources

Each student requires a Balloon Game form such as the sample shown in Figure 1; extra forms required if the groupwork approach (see 2 below) used; a class chart (Figure 2 or Figure 3).

▼ Procedure

1 Students are asked to imagine that they are on their own gently drifting in a hot-air balloon. On board are ten rights. Each weighs two kilos. Suddenly the balloon begins to lose height. To stop their descent, they must throw a right overboard. The balloon then levels out for a while before beginning to lose height again. Another right must be jettisoned. The process continues until they have only one right left. Students are asked to read the list carefully and think about which rights they are prepared to surrender and which they want to keep as long as possible. They then make their decisions — without discussion — by putting a 1 against the first right to be thrown overboard, a 2 against the second and so on. The right that remains at the end is numbered 10. The teacher then makes a class chart (Figure 2) so that everybody can see the priority given to each right by the class as a whole. Discussion follows.

Figure 1

The right to my own bedroom	
The right to clean air to breathe	
The right to pocket money	
The right to love and affection	
The right not to be bossed around	
The right to be different	
The right to holidays each year	
The right to food and water	
The right to time for play	
The right to be listened to	

Figure 2

	1	2	3	4	5	6	7	8	9	10
Bedroom										
Clean air										
Pocket money										
Love /affection										
Not bossed around										
Be different										
Holidays										
Food/water										
Time for play										
Be listened to										

Figure 3

	Bedroom	Clean air	Pocket money	Love/affection	Not bossed around	Be different	Holidays	Food/water	Time for play	Be listened to
Group 1										
Group 2										
Group 3										
Group 4										
Group 5										

2 Having filled in the Balloon Game form individually and without discussion, students form groups of three or four and discuss each other's decisions. After discussion, each group tries to negotiate a new consensus list using an extra copy of the form. Groups then join with a second group and members of the new large groups proceed to discuss their respective decisions before seeking to negotiate a further consensus list. The class goes into plenary session. Each large group (of 6–8) reports on its prioritisation of the rights and the teacher makes a record on a class chart (Figure 3) before discussion commences.

▼ Potential

This activity can raise some questions surrounding the relative importance of the different rights we claim and the idea of **basic** rights. Which rights do we consider more important than others? Why? Are some rights so important to our well-being and essential humanity that we should never surrender them? Which can – and are – sometimes surrendered? Under what circumstances? Can students suggest any rights which are even more important than the ones on the list – especially those they kept until last? Can students suggest any rights which are even more important than the ones on the list – especially those they kept until last?

▼ Variation

Having made their own decisions (filling in the first column on the Figure 2 chart), students move freely around the room questioning nine others and entering their scores in the other columns. This approach encourages a great deal of interaction and can be less time-consuming and repetitive than attempting to produce a profile of the whole class. Students can then be asked to analyse and reflect upon results they have collected prior to plenary discussion.

Upper Primary/Secondary, (1) 20 minutes; (2) 45 minutes.

▼ Source

Centre for Global Education.

Recalling Injustice

▼ Procedure

Students form groups of six and then divide into pairs. One partner is nominated 'A', the other 'B'. The activity begins with a few minutes' silence in which everybody is asked to recall occasions when they have felt unjustly treated. 'A' students are then asked to recount those incidents they have recalled – and wish to recount – to their partner. 'B' listens actively, contributing only encourager words and prompting questions if need be. After five minutes, 'B' recounts her incidents whilst 'A' listens. The group of six then reforms. The students are asked to take on the story or stories of their partner as their own and retell them, in turn, to the group using the 'I' first person form. When groups have completed the task, the facilitator asks the class to brainstorm the emotions they felt when treated unjustly. These words are recorded on the board or overhead projector.

▼ Potential

This is a powerful introductory activity to work on discrimination, involving the exercise of listening, memory and oral skills. The recounting and sharing of instances of injustice creates a context in which participants tend to respond sensitively and empathetically to injustice done to others. Teachers often follow the activity with film of racial or gender injustice. At points in the ensuing discussion attention can be drawn to the results of the brainstorming. This activity should only be attempted with a well-affirmed group. If the group is particularly well-affirmed, the activity can be repeated with a recounting of occasions when students feel they have treated others unfairly or unjustly.

Secondary, 30 minutes.

▼ Source

Centre for Global Education.

Starting to Think About Rights

▼ Resources

A list of statements (see below) and a sheet of paper for each group of students.

▼ Procedure

Students, working in small groups, read and discuss the statements below. On a sheet of paper, they draw two overlapping circles marked as follows:

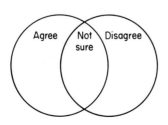

Statements

*We shouldn't be **forced** to come to school.*

*Teachers should be allowed to **hit** us to keep us in order.*

*We should be allowed to choose where we **sit** in class.*

*We should be allowed to **say** and write what we like in class.*

*There should be a school **council**, with representatives elected from each class.*

*The school should provide all the **equipment** we need, like pens, paper, books.*

*People who are good at speaking should be allowed to speak in class **more often**.*

*Really naughty pupils should get **caned** by the Head or Deputy.*

*We should be allowed to **mess about** if we don't want to work.*

*Teachers shouldn't **make fun** of us.*

*There should be **separate** schools for Christians and for those who aren't.*

*The brainiest kids should all be **together** for lessons.*

*Teachers should always **listen** carefully to what pupils say.*

*Teachers should make sure we can work without being **disturbed**.*

*If you need to **leave** the classroom you should be allowed to.*

*Bigger kids should have a **bigger share** of the playground.*

*Girls should have some lessons **by themselves**.*

*Everyone in school should be treated with politeness and **respect**.*

*The school should make sure no one gets **bullied**.*

*The school should be **clean** and comfortable.*

Through negotiation, students decide into which part of the overlapping circles they wish to place each statement, writing in the key word (in bold) in an appropriate position.

Students then discuss how they might rewrite the statements in their 'Not Sure' and 'Disagree' sections so that they can be transferred to the 'Agree' section. They may want to use qualifying words such as 'except', 'unless' or 'usually'. Next, they try to use some of their 'Agree' statements in order to construct five 'Rights' statements, i.e. statements which are acceptable to everyone as being significant for creating a just and peaceful school environment (e.g. 'Everyone in school has a right to be treated with respect').

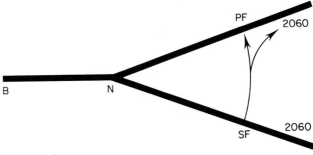

Figure 1

▼ Potential

An activity which encourages students to perceive rights issues as being pertinent to their everyday experience and also introduces them to some of the problems of establishing — and maintaining — rights which are universally acceptable.

Primary/Lower Secondary, 30 minutes.

▼ Source

Devised by Cathie Holden, Bishop Kirk Middle School, Oxford and Hugh Starkey, Westminster College of Education, Oxford.

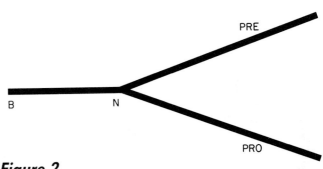

Figure 2

fill in events that they think will happen locally, regionally, nationally and globally in the same timespan. Pairs are then asked to consider the relationships, if any, they perceive between the two future timelines. Will projected societal futures affect projected personal futures and vice versa? One-way arrows in a fourth colour are drawn between the two lines and a brief explanation of the relationship drawn along the arrow. Pairs then share their work using the **Circus** procedure (see p. 135) or through plenary reporting back and discussion.

Futures Time Lines

▼ Resources

Large sheet of sugar paper and three/four felt tip pens of different colours for each pair of students.

▼ Procedure

1 Students, working in pairs, prepare time lines (see Figure 1). Between point B (birth) and point N (now), they fill in key events, personal and societal (local to global), that have so far happened in their lives. Each student uses a different colour for their personal events. From N to PF (personal futures), they indicate projected milestones in their personal lives up to the year 2060, again using their personal colour. From N to SF (societal futures), they

2 Students, working in pairs, prepare time lines (see Figure 2). Between points B and N, they fill in key events, personal and societal, that have so far happened in their lives. Each student uses a different colour for their personal events. From N to PRO (probable futures), they fill in events they consider **are likely to happen** in their lifetimes. From N to PRE (preferred futures), they fill in events that they **would like to see happen** during their lifetimes. Pairs then share their work using the circus procedure or through reporting back and discussion.

'Future Times Lines' in action

▼ Potential

The first exercise provides students with the opportunity to project personal and societal futures but, more importantly, introduces them to thinking about the interactive relationship between futures at different levels. In discussion, students can be asked to explore why they share certain expectations about personal futures and to consider how major developments or events globally might help or hinder the realisation of — or alter the canvas of — those expectations. The exercise can provide a useful springboard for the exploration of future scenarios through the writings of key futurists.

The second exercise again provides a context for the projection of personal and societal futures but, by focusing on preferred futures, offers scope for values clarification work in small group or plenary discussion. A class chart of pairs' choices of preferred futures can provide the basis for work and discussion on how those futures might be realised (see **Decision Trees** and **Alternative Pathways**) and what the repercussions of particular hoped-for futures might be (see **Cross-Impact Matrix**).

Upper Primary/Secondary, 40 minutes.

▼ Sources

The first exercise is developed from an idea in Fitch, R.M. and Svengalis, C.M., Futures Unlimited, Washington DC, National Council for Social Studies, 1979; the second exercise was described by Cathie Holden (Bishop Kirk Middle School, Oxford) in World Studies Journal, *Vol. 6, No. 1.*

Space/Time Grids

▼ Resources

A large space/time grid, such as the example below, for each student; a selection of local and national newspapers or newspaper cuttings.

▼ Procedure

Space/time grids provide a framework for exploring forecasts, projections and ideas about the future at different spatial levels.

Students, working in pairs, discuss what forecasts should be written in each box, using the newspapers/newspaper cuttings as a stimulus for ideas. They are encouraged to write in reasons for their forecasts and also alternative forecasts if they think of them. The task is best approached by completing one horizontal column before going on to the next. Students should also be encouraged to draw in arrows to show how events at different spatial levels can have an impact on each other, e.g. a national event they predict for next week might have an effect on the family in three months' time. Space/time grids having been completed, pairs of students can present their work in small groups, in class plenary or using the **Circus** technique (see p. 135).

Ideally, the space/time grid should be undertaken early in the school year thus allowing for reviews and evaluations of as many forecasts as possible to take place before the school year ends.

TIME ——→

SPACE

	This week	Next week	Next month	Three months' time	Six months' time	One year's time	My lifetime
Myself							
My family							
My school							
My locality							
My country							
The world							

▼ Potential

The initial exercise can help students gain a greater understanding of the ways in which their own lives and futures can both affect and be affected by events at a range of spatial levels. Implicit in the exercise is the view that human action shapes the future. It is not shaped for us. The point of pairs considering alternative forecasts for the future is to encourage students to think about what present action and behaviour is more likely to bring about particular alternatives. Reflection on this point can be made a central feature of post-activity discussion.

Subsequent periodic reviews and evaluations of forecasts allow students to check the accuracy of their predictions (and, of course, encourage them to keep an eye on the news). If forecasts prove incorrect, students can be asked to suggest reasons why events predicted did not happen. The difficulty of predicting the future accurately given the immense number of variables involved will be a lesson learnt.

Upper Primary/Secondary, 45 minutes.

▼ Source

Various.

Futures Wheel

▼ Resources

Large sheet of paper and felt tip pen per three/four students.

▼ Procedure

An event, idea or trend is drawn and circled in the centre of each group's sheet. Groups are then asked to consider possible consequences of that event, idea or trend. Single lines are drawn outwards and the consequences written on and circled. Groups go on to consider the range of possible repercussions emanating from the first-order consequences, this time drawing double lines outwards and writing in and circling second-order consequences. The process is continued for third, fourth and, possibly, fifth-order consequences.

▼ Potential

Groups should be given the opportunity to carefully examine each other's work. Discussion can usefully focus upon differences in group presentations, the problematic nature of forecasting given the unknowns and variables involved and possible interrelationships between the various second, third, fourth and fifth-order consequences. Future wheels offer a linear model of causality and it is not only important to consider the relationship between items not directly linked together on the wheel — an additional exercise can be for students to discuss and draw in links — but also to reflect upon whether the outward-moving causal links could in some cases be reversed.

▼ Variation

A newspaper article describing a likely future development or trend can be used for the centre of a wheel. Students proceed to examine second, third, fourth and fifth-order consequences.

Upper Primary/Secondary, 45 minutes.

▼ Source

From an idea in Fitch, R. M. and Svengalis, C. M., Futures Unlimited, Washington DC, National Council for the Social Studies, 1979.

SAMPLE FUTURES WHEEL

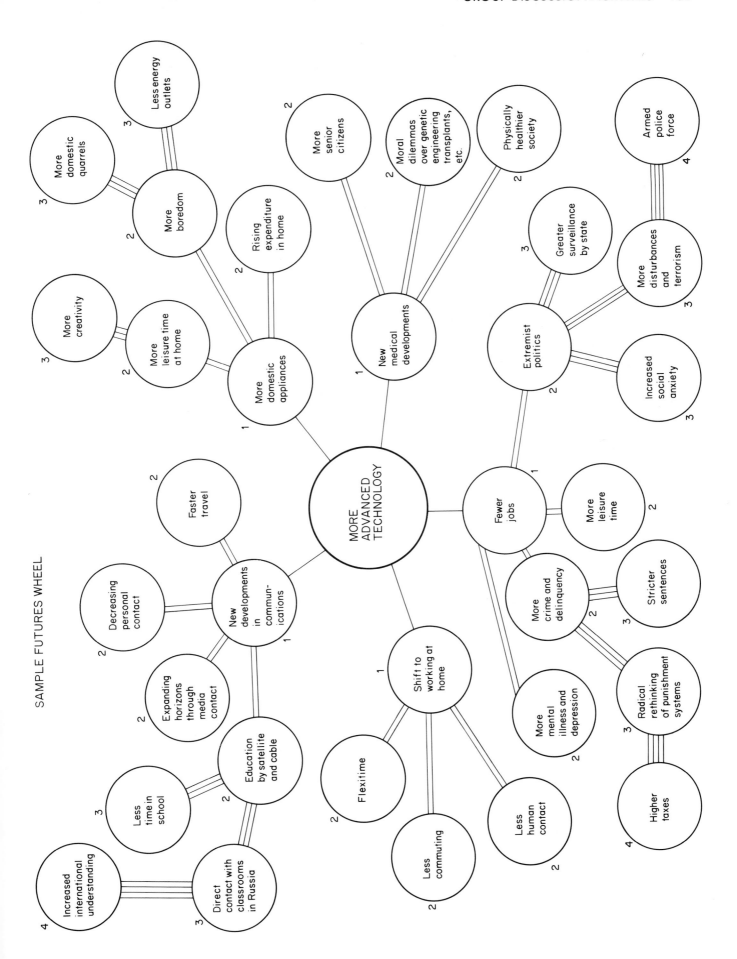

Mini Despair and Empowerment Exercise

▼ Resources

Group seated in circle, well spread out; small pieces of paper or card — 4 per student (12 cm × 7 cm file cards are suitable); pencils; board or flip-chart.

▼ Procedure

1 The sequence and rationale is explained (see below):
Stage A — 'Thinking the unthinkable ...'
Stage B — 'It won't happen because ...'
Stage C — 'A hopeful future ...'
Stage D — 'From ideas to action ...'

2 Four cards and a pencil are given to each student. It is explained that the cards are not to be written on until instructed, and that names should NOT be written on the cards at any stage.

3 **Stage A** Instruction: 'On the first card write down one or two sentences beginning something like:
"The thing what worries me most about the future is ..."
or "What scares me most about the world is ..."
or "What frightens me most is ..."
or "The thing I prefer not to think about happening is ..."'
It is probably best at this stage not to give any examples, but simply to say that the sentences can be about anything the students wish.
Three to four minutes are given for writing. The first cards are collected, shuffled and given out again.
Each student in the circle reads the card she has, without comment. All sentences should be accepted without comment.

4 **Stage B** Instruction: 'On your second card, write several sentences, beginning:
"There won't be a nuclear war because ..."
or "The problems of famine and hunger will be solved because ..."
or etc.'

Some help may be needed by way of suggestion, to encourage the idea that any sentence is acceptable. Humorous sentences should be encouraged, for example:
'There won't be a nuclear war because I'll be the next prime minister and won't let it happen'
or '... because the Easter Bunny will be world ruler'.
As before, three or four minutes are allowed to write, collect, shuffle, give out, and read round, again without comment.

5 **Stage C** Instruction: 'On the third card, complete the sentence:
"The world will be a better place in fifteen years' time because ..."'
As before, three or four minutes are allowed to write, etc.
(It may be helpful each time to collect the previous set of cards whilst the next sentences are being written.)

6 **Stage D** Brainstorming ideas: the group is asked to brainstorm as many ideas as possible about:
'Things I can do to make the world a better and a safer place for ALL human beings.'
As with all brainstorming, any ideas are acceptable; there should be no comments or discussion; as many ideas as possible are gathered. The ideas should be written up on the board or a flip-chart. It may be helpful to have two students doing the writing to keep up with the flow of ideas.

7 In groups of three, the ideas brainstormed are considered, students being asked to identify those which 'YOU could actually do something about'.

▼ Potential

The purpose is to encourage students to share their anxieties about the future, and so to discover that most of their unspoken worries are shared by others. The encouragement of humour in Stages B and C allows for the release from possible despair that is brought about by shared laughter, leading to the development of possible positive and practical strategies, and the empowerment that this can bring.

▼ Possible Follow-up

The investigation of information about the issues raised — especially by Stages A and D.

Linking the possibilities of positive action to our inner perceptions by a creative visualisation (see pp. 189–91).

The following films might be shown: The Global Brain (Awakening Earth) by Peter Russell; Life on Earth Perhaps by Oliver Postgate (both available from Concord Films Council, 201 Felixstowe Road, Ipswich, Suffolk IP3 9BJ).

▼ Variations

Where a group's listening skills are well developed, working in pairs instead of using cards for Stages A, B, and C — but the facilitator should make sure sufficient time is allowed for each partner to complete the sentences in turn.

▼ Development-Consequence Chart

There is no need for the larger group sharing at the end of each of these stages, if this is done.

One hour at least.

▼ Sources

Sandy Parker, Ackworth School, Pontefract, based on ideas from Despair and Personal Power in the Nuclear Age by Joanna Macy, New Society Publishers, 1983, and from Diana Whitmore at the Findhorn Foundation's 'Peace Within' workshop, January 1984.

Considering Consequences

▼ Resources

A Development-Consequence chart (see sample) for each pair of students; a further copy of the chart for each group of six.

Description of the area of the development, e.g. Energy		How likely is the result as a consequence of the development?				Effect of the consequence				
Developments that might occur	Consequence they might result in:	Certain	Probable	Possible	Almost Impossible	Very favourable	Favourable	Little, no impact	Detrimental	Very Detrimental
1 Abolition of civil nuclear power programmes	(A) Research and development of renewable energy sources	√					√			
	(B) Rising electricity costs		√						√	
	(C) No further increase in nuclear waste	√				√				
	(D) Threat of nuclear terrorism removed		√			√				
	(E) Electricity supply insufficient to meet demands of industry		√						√	
2 etc.	(A) etc.									

▼ Procedure

Students form groups of six. Pairs within each six consider and try to reach agreement about the alternatives offered in the Development-Consequence chart, ticking the appropriate columns. The three pairs then join together and each pair explains the choices they have made. The six group members then seek to reach common agreement, filling in a further copy of the Developent-Consequence chart. Plenary discussion follows.

▼ Potential

This is a simple means of getting students to consider possible future developments, to reflect upon the implications of those developments and to share and discuss their perspectives on some aspect of the future. It can usefully be undertaken as both a pre- and post-research project activity. In the former case, the facilitator is probably in the best position to prepare the chart. In the latter, the students can begin by brainstorming both the developments and consequences to be written into the chart.

Upper Primary/Secondary, 30–40 minutes.

▼ Source

After an idea in Fitch, R. M. and Svengalis, C. M., Futures Unlimited, Washington DC, National Council for the Social Studies, 1979.

Cross-Impact Matrix

▼ Resources

A matrix (see p. 159) for each pair of students.

▼ Procedure

The cross-impact matrix provides a framework for considering how a number of aims, developments, events or trends may impact upon each other. Students, in pairs, discuss the relationship between the various items on the matrix and decide how to fill in the boxes. Pairs can then form larger groups to explain and discuss their decisions. Plenary discussion follows.

▼ Potential

Cross-impact matrix analysis reveals the interactive nature of aims, developments, events and trends. It enables students to reflect upon how the short and mid-term future may be shaped by those interactions. The technique can also reveal how new problems are likely to be created when another problem is 'solved'. It can clarify underlying assumptions and reveal to students inconsistencies or flaws in their thinking.

▼ Variations

The matrix used can be varied to suit the age and ability of students; the number of factors in any matrix can be increased or decreased as the facilitator sees fit. When a class has become accustomed to matrix analysis, pairs or groups can be asked to decide what issues they would like to analyse.

Newspaper articles describing likely future developments or trends can be used for matrices, students examining the interrelationships between the forecasts. Matrices can also be used to facilitate reflection on personal goals and futures. In the Personal Goals Matrix (p. 160), each student decides which three things they would most like to achieve or be. Having decided they write in their goals, join with a partner, and discuss the relationship between the goals.

Secondary, 40 minutes.

▼ Source

Derived from idea in Haas, J. D., Future Studies in the K-12 Curriculum, Boulder, Colorado, ERIC Clearinghouse for Social Studies/Social Education, 1980 and in Fitch, R. M. and Svengalis, C. M., Futures Unlimited, Washington DC., National Council for the Social Studies, 1979.

▼ **Figure 1** Sample Cross-Impact
Matrix: How do the factors affect
each other?

	Local Tourism	Employment	Traffic	Quality of Local Life
Local Tourism	X	Seasonal tourism will lead to fluctuations in local employment; pressure to avoid environmentally unfriendly industries.	Heavier in-season traffic; more car parks and pressure for a ring road if tourism increases.	Better shops and public amenities in season; seasonal congestion of amenities and places of interest.
Employment	Use of tourist amenities by local people may fluctuate with employment levels.	X	Use of public and, especially, private transport may fluctuate with employment levels.	High levels of employment can generate greater prosperity and contentment and greater pride in the local area.
Traffic	Well-run local traffic system encourages tourism; traffic jams, etc. act as a discouragement.	Some new jobs from increased traffic, e.g. pump attendants, traffic wardens, police, car park attendants, coach drivers.	X	More traffic means more noise and pollution; road developments can benefit or harm community life (e.g. a bypass can benefit many but harm those close by).
Quality of Local Life	?	Good quality of life breeds confidence and enterprise which can in turn lead to more jobs.	?	X

▼ *Figure 2* Sample Personal Goals Matrix

Personal Goals	Personal Goals		
How Will This Goal → Affect This Goal ↓	Have good friends.	Do well at school.	Have a Saturday job.
Have good friends	X	Good friends makes you confident so you do well; too much time spent with friends affects homework and revision.	Less time for friends but more money to spend with them.
Do well at school.	Studying and homework mean less time for friends but success at school wins admiration.	X	Parents more likely to support you having a job.
Have a Saturday job.	More money for clothes, records and outings. Not available for friends for most of Saturday.	Cuts down homework and revision time; less weekend relaxation so not so fresh on Mondays.	X

Delphi Forecasting

▼ Resources

For a class of thirty students, thirty quarter A4 slips of paper, thirty half A4 sheets, thirty whole A4 sheets.

▼ Procedure

Stage 1 Students are asked to forecast when a future event may take place, stating their reasons, or to give their opinion on possible alternative futures. No discussion takes place. Forecasts/opinions are written on slips of paper (quarter A4 slip per student). The facilitator collates and reproduces all the slips. Contributions are not attributed (indeed, at no point in the four stages are students asked to reveal ownership of any forecast/opinion written).

Stage 2 Copies of the collated contributions are handed out. Students, again working individually, are asked to reflect upon the range of contributions and then to write a longer, more considered, forecast/opinion (half A4 sheet). This can also include searching questions about initial contributions they feel to be extreme or unrealistic. The facilitator again collates and reproduces the forecasts/opinions.

Stage 3 The process is undergone again, students writing a third forecast/opinion (whole A4 sheet each) in the light of Stage 2 contributions and commenting, if necessary, on particular contributions.

Stage 4 Once Stage 3 forecasts/opinions have been distributed, read and reflected upon, plenary discussion follows.

▼ Potential

This is a simple version of the Delphi forecasting technique used in futurology to poll knowledgeable opinion regarding expectations of possible alternative futures. The technique tends to produce a narrowing of the initial spread of opinions. If a broad consensus fails to emerge, the process helps participants clarify their own thinking and identify potential weaknesses in their forecasts.

The four stages described above can be spread over several days or weeks and provide a flexible framework into which a number of additional activities and variations can be injected (see below).

Discussion can profitably begin with the autobiographical. Did participants' ideas change during the several stages of the exercise? If so, how? What ideas did they find particularly attractive or suspect in the forecasts/opinions they read? Were there any ideas which they initially put forward but eventually rejected? Why? Later, students may wish to explore the usefulness of the Delphi forecasting technique and to examine whether the attitude and approach adopted by those taking part can centrally affect the quality of the learning that takes place.

▼ Variations

The class can invite parents, people from the local community and a few representatives of relevant organisations to participate in the exercise, thus widening the number of perspectives pooled. Those invited can also be asked to attend an end-of-exercise class/community 'moot'. It is also possible to inject research stages after Stages 2 and 3 thus giving students periods of time to inquire into questions raised by the forecasts/opinions.

Whilst the Delphi technique is generally used for forecasting, the exercise described above could, of course, be used for collectively examining a contemporary global issue.

Secondary.

▼ Source

Centre for Global Education.

Alternative Pathways

▼ Resources

Large sheet of sugar paper and a felt pen per group of three/four students.

▼ Procedure

Students, working in groups, write down a present situation or problem on one side of their sheet and a desired goal or outcome on the opposite side. Alternative means of reaching the desired goal or outcome are then discussed and written in. Steps along the alternative pathways are linked by arrows. Groups meet to explain and discuss their presentation. Plenary discussion follows.

▼ Potential

Discussion can usefully first revolve around differences in group presentations. In what ways were groups surprised by the work of other groups? Are other presentations felt to be in any way overly idealistic or unrealistic? Having been introduced to the different presentations, would any group like to amend their work? How? Another area for discussion could be the usefulness of goal-oriented forecasting. Can we even take into account all the variables so our forecasting is accurate? Does that matter? Are such approaches nonetheless useful tools for locating constraints and critical decision points in seeking to achieve a desired goal?

Secondary, 40 minutes.

▼ Source

After an idea in Fitch, R. M. and Svengalis, C. M., Futures Unlimited, Washington DC, National Council for the Social Studies, 1979.

ALTERNATIVE PATHWAYS

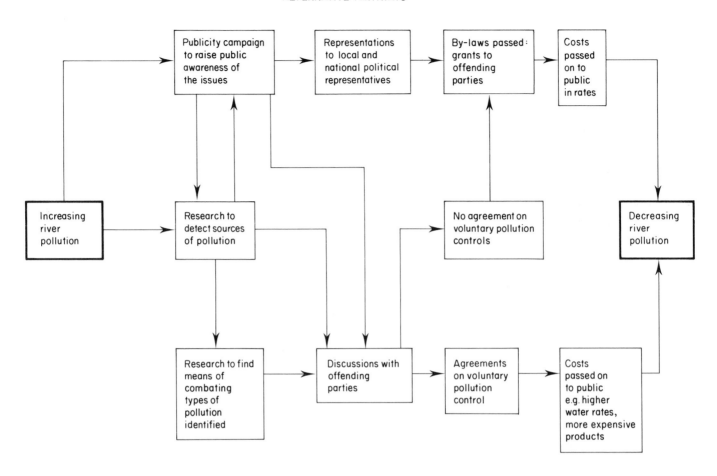

Decision Trees

▼ Resources

One or two large sheets of sugar paper and a felt pen for each group of students.

▼ Procedure

Students form groups of three/four and are asked to consider alternative paths forward with respect to a current problem or with a view to achieving a specific goal. Their decisions are to be expressed pictorially in the form of a tree (see sample). The trunk is the question under consideration. Each branching point represents a decision. A time-scale, if applicable, can be included. Students may wish to undertake research or seek advice from parents, members of the local community, etc. at certain points in their work. In this case, the activity can usefully be spread over a week or two.

▼ Potential

Decision trees offer a helpful framework for planning for the future and for considering alternative futures. This activity is demanding — practice with simple short-range examples is recommended — but it will give students the opportunity to exercise and develop decision-

SAMPLE DECISION TREE : TOWN TRAFFIC

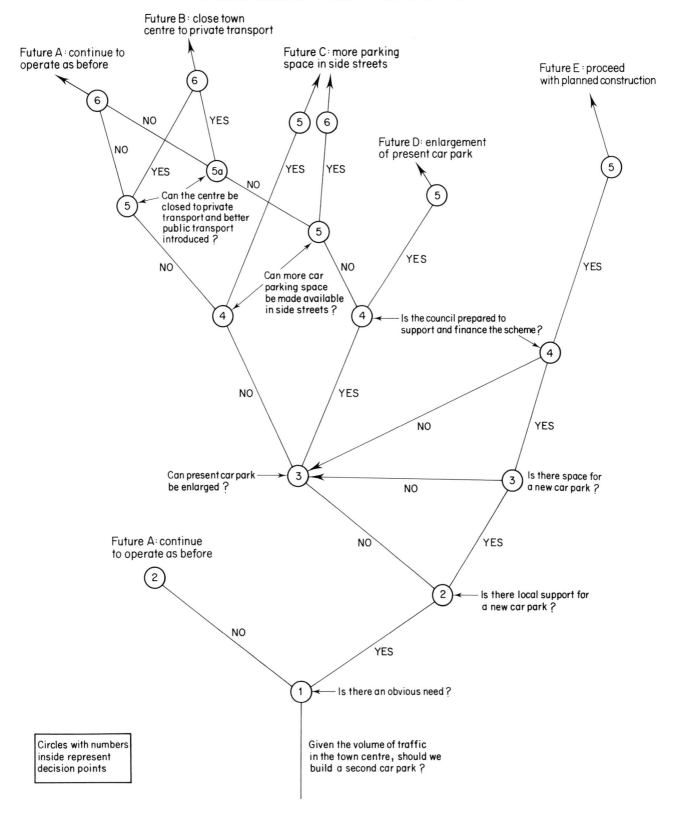

Future A : continue to operate as before

Future B : close town centre to private transport

Future C : more parking space in side streets

Future D : enlargement of present car park

Future E : proceed with planned construction

NO

YES

NO

YES

NO

Can the centre be closed to private transport and better public transport introduced ?

YES

YES

NO

YES

Can more car parking space be made available in side streets ?

NO

YES

Is the council prepared to support and finance the scheme ?

YES

NO

NO

YES

Can present car park be enlarged ?

NO

Is there space for a new car park ?

NO

YES

Future A : continue to operate as before

YES

Is there local support for a new car park ?

YES

Is there an obvious need ?

Given the volume of traffic in the town centre, should we build a second car park ?

Circles with numbers inside represent decision points

making skills and experience the complexities involved in planning and making decisions. The activity has been used with students for planning project work and for dry-run planning of a social/environmental/political campaign in the locality.

Students should be given ample time to inspect each other's presentation — perhaps using the **Circus** procedure (see p. 135) — before plenary discussion. The class might like to reflect upon whether the tree is the most persuasive metaphor for conceptualising the future. Can they suggest other metaphors?

Secondary, 60 minutes.

▼ Source

Various.

8 Experiential activities

Who's Got the Batteries?

▼ Resources

Five identical electric torches each requiring two batteries which can be disassembled into five separate parts (the two batteries count as one part); five paper bags. Before the activity commences, all the batteries are placed in one paper bag, all the bulbs in another bag and so on.

▼ Procedure

Students form five groups. Each group is given a bag of identical torch parts and is asked to inspect its contents making sure that other groups do not see them. The five groups are then told that their task is to 'put together a total system that works'. Groups are to work as a team, making group decisions about strategy and tactics before doing anything.

It will soon dawn on some individuals that bargaining and trading with other groups is necessary to fulfil the task. Some may try stealing. What will not necessarily be realised as quickly or as universally is that for the 'total system' to work, batteries need to be traded in pairs for singles of other parts. Sometimes the battery group will consciously choose to trade only one battery. The activity finishes when each group has a working torch or when it is clear that an impasse has been reached.

▼ Potential

This is a useful starter activity for work on interdependence and the nature of systems; it can also provide some pointers towards the study and discussion of the global energy situation. The debriefing can begin with a pooling of experiences. What did groups make of the instruction, 'to put together a total system that works'? What strategy and tactics did they decide to adopt? Were group members allocated particular roles? How did groups bargain for the resources they needed? Which group drove the hardest bargain? Did any group feel its resource was more valuable than that of other groups? How did this affect strategy? Did any groups feel taken advantage of? As the activity went on, with certain groups unable to put together a torch, did any re-appraisal of the initial instruction occur?

Out of such a pooling of experiences, two areas for more thorough-going consideration may probably emerge:

Systems — In what ways were the five groups interdependent; was the interdependency one between equals; in what ways did the activity mirror the global trading system; what, on reflection, does a 'total system that works' mean; was it achieved; is it achieved in the world today? For older students, the discussion may present a useful opportunity for introducing the concepts of 'closed' and 'open' systems (a 'closed' system is self-sufficient and doesn't interact with other systems). Were the groups 'closed' or 'open' systems? Is a working torch a system? If so, what type of system and how does it differ from human and environmental systems?

World Energy — What do the batteries represent; who owns the 'batteries' in the world today; how does the activity mirror the current global energy situation; what do the groups not possessing batteries represent; what problems do they face?

Primary/secondary, 10–15 minutes.

▼ Variation

Fountain pens can be used instead of torches but some potential is lost in that they only have one cartridge.

▼ Source

Freeman, R. E. and Karls, A. B., 'Let there be light', Intercom, 79, 1975; Johnson, J. and Benegar, J., Global Issues in the Intermediate Classroom, Boulder, Colorado, Social Science Education Consortium, 1981. Variation: Rosemary West, Notre Dame High School for Girls, Plymouth.

Nine-Dot Problem

▼ Resources

A sheet of paper containing nine dots (see illustration) and a pencil for each pair of students.

▼ Procedure

Each pair is asked to work out how the nine dots can be connected using only four straight lines and without removing the pencil from the paper. After several minutes, a member of a pair that has solved the problem is asked to connect a set of dots on the board.

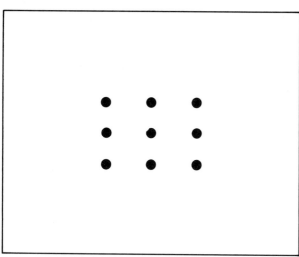

Problem shape

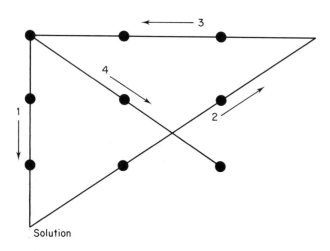

Solution

▼ Potential

An intriguing activity that can be used to raise a number of questions about the limited perspective and framework within which we interpret the world and seek solutions to the problems we face. Why is it that most of us didn't think of going outside the boundaries of the square of dots to solve the problem? Can anybody think of an occasion when, suddenly, a new way of looking at things helped solve a long-standing problem? Might an expanded perspective, gained by listening to and learning from people belonging to a range of other cultures, help us to see new solutions to some of the global problems we face?

Secondary, 10 minutes.

▼ Source

Various.

Co-operative Squares

▼ Resources

Five squares of card or paper, cut up according to the diagram on p.167, for each group of 5 participants. (Measurements should be exact; all lines go either to the corner, the centre or the mid-point of a side.)

Pieces should be put, according to their letter, into one of five envelopes marked A–E.

Each group of five participants should ideally be seated around a table.

▼ Procedure

Each member of a group receives an envelope. The aim of the exercise is for a group to make five squares of equal size. Two rules should be observed by all participants:

– There should be no communication between participants throughout the exercise, neither verbal nor non-verbal (e.g. nods, winks, kicks under the table, gestures).

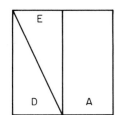 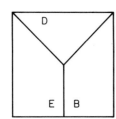 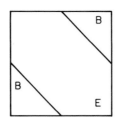 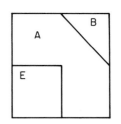 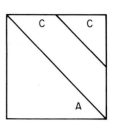

— Participants are not allowed to pass shapes directly to, or take directly from each other; they can, however, put shapes into the middle of the table, and also take from the middle.

Any participant may decline to take further part at any time.

▼ Potential

A classic exercise in group co-operation which can be interpreted at a variety of levels. During the initial stages some individuals often complete squares of the correct size, but in doing so use shapes which are required by other group members. Feelings of frustration, helplessness and inadequacy are common amongst those participants who cannot complete a square, whilst fellow group members can be sitting back with pride and satisfaction. It is only with the recognition that the task demands group collaboration, rather than competition between individuals, that a solution can be found. The exercise can be used to trigger off discussion about co-operation and competition: what were the feelings of those participants who completed squares quickly, and those who didn't? Did participants' perceptions of the task change during the exercise? How did co-operation take place amongst group members? Did some members assume dominant or submissive roles? Why?

The exercise can also generate reflection on rules: were the given rules broken at any time, and for what purpose? Did the rules seem reasonable? What might have been the outcome if verbal communication had been allowed, or if participants could take each other's shapes at any time?

At another level, the exercise can be used to stimulate thinking about the concepts of interdependence and aid: in an interdependent world system, what is the effect of different perceptions of, and different attitudes towards, a common task or problem? Can such differences be overcome? For aid to be worthwhile, does it entail just giving away surplus goods, or does it necessitate an understanding of the aid receiver's particular situation? Can aid alone solve global problems?

Primary/Secondary, 20 minutes.

▼ Variation

Instead of having to put unwanted shapes into the middle of the table, participants can pass shapes directly to other group members. The main effect of this is to focus participants' attention on each other's squares at an earlier stage, so that the co-operative nature of the task is more readily perceived.

▼ Source

Basic format first published in NEA Journal, USA, October 1969.

Co-operative Squares Variations for Younger Children

by **Susan Fountain**, teacher at the International School of Geneva

The following are some more variations on the game of **Co-operative Squares**. They are designed to encourage 3 to 6 year old children to work together co-operatively and develop a sense of group purpose.

Co-operative Faces

The concept of a 'square' may be difficult for young children to understand and visualise. The human face is a far more basic and recognisable unit at this age.

▼ Resources

Six large photographs (approximately A4 size) can be mounted on stiff card. A mixture of races and sexes should be represented. The faces are cut into sections as shown below:

The pieces are distributed among six envelopes so that each envelope contains at least one piece from each face.

▼ Procedure

Six children sit around a table, and each is given an envelope. The children are told that they are to use the pieces in the envelopes to make six faces. The game is not finished until all six faces are made. They may give any of their pieces to a group member who they think might need them, or they may place them in the centre of the table if they do not need them. Children may take pieces from the centre of the table (having a box in which these are placed helps

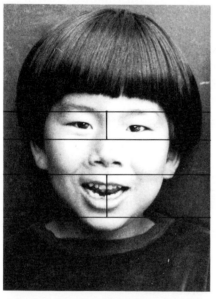
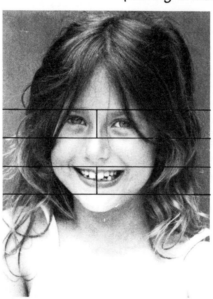
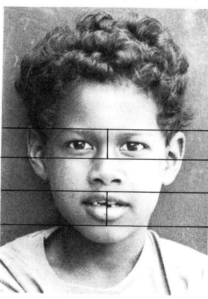
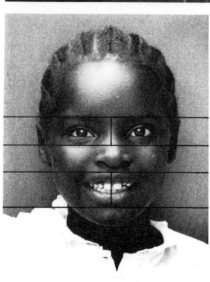
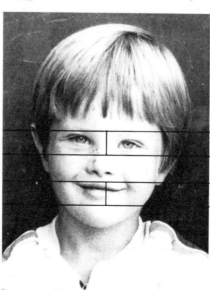
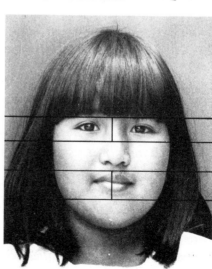

them to realise that these are being 'offered' to the group), but may not take pieces from one another.

While **Co-operative Squares** is usually played with a 'no talking' rule, I find that young children need to reason out loud, and being able to verbalise about the process facilitates their problem-solving abilities.

▼ Potential

It is important to talk first about exactly what happened. Children can be encouraged to talk about feelings they may have had — frustration, jealousy, possessiveness, how it felt to share, to complete the task, etc. In order to bring out the idea of the need for co-operation, I often ask the children what they would say to help others who were playing the game for the first time.

By using photos showing children of different races, children can also discuss how the faces differ, as well as how they are similar. It is interesting to make one list of similarities and one of differences, and to compare them. Which list is longer?

▼ Variations

The children love to play this game with pictures of animals, or animal faces.

Forms of 'Co-operative Squares' in action

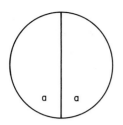 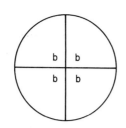 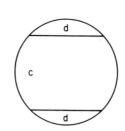 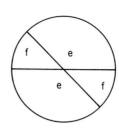 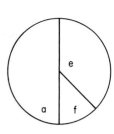

Co-operative Circles

A circle is the easiest of the geometric shapes for young children to understand. This game develops the shape concept while encouraging co-operative work.

▼ Resources

Five cardboard circles, each about 12 cm in diameter, are cut from card according to the patterns shown above:

The pieces are placed in five envelopes:

1 – a, d, f;	a	is a half circle
2 – b, d, a;	b	= ¼
3 – c, b, b, b;	f	= ⅛
4 – e, f, f;	e	= ⅜
5 – a, e, e.		

In addition, five whole circles should be cut from card of a contrasting colour.

▼ Procedure

After a discussion of what a circle is, the game proceeds as with **Co-operative Faces**. Children use the solid circles as guides on which to assemble their pieces. The contrasting colour helps them more easily visualise what shapes they need to complete the circle. Young children sometimes understand the need to work co-operatively more easily if there are more shapes to be made than there are children in the group.

▼ Potential

The children should again be encouraged to reflect on the process of working together and their feelings about it.

Modified Co-operative Squares

This simplified version uses shapes that young children are more apt to recognise as components of a square than those used in the original game. In addition, there is the possibility of more than one solution.

▼ Resources

Five cardboard squares are cut as follows:

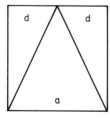 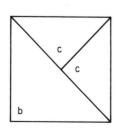 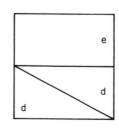 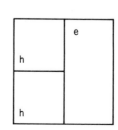 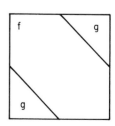

They are sorted into five envelopes in this manner:

1 – b, d, g;
2 – c, h, d;
3 – a, e, d;
4 – c, e, f;
5 – d, h, g.

Five solid squares of a contrasting colour should be provided for the children to assemble their pieces on.

▼ Procedure

As with **Co-operative Circles.**

Square Numbers

by **Arthur Robinson,** teacher of mathematics and computing at the International School of Geneva

Square Numbers is an attempt to convert to numerical form the geometrical **Co-operative Squares.** It offers the possibility of varying the underlying rule of the exercise, so that it can probably be used more often with a given group of people than would be possible with **Co-operative Squares.**

▼ Procedure

Participants are presented with the following situation:

A set of numbers in random order in a central 'pool' area. A participant may move one or many numbers from the pool into her own, private area, or put one or many numbers into the pool from her own area. A participant may not move numbers either to or from the area of another participant. A participant may not communicate with another in any way other than by moving numbers between her own area and the central pool. The objective for all participants is to establish in the private area of each participant a set of numbers which will add up to a perfect square: 1, 4, 9, 16, 25, 36, 49 ...

▼ Notes

Every participant must co-operate in ensuring that all participants fulfil the requirements.

In each activity participants are to use all the numbers given.

It may be necessary for the facilitator of the activity to state at the beginning that 'the squares are equal' or that 'all use the same number of numbers' depending on the sophistication of the participants and the difficulty of the situation.

It is possible to vary the rule for combining the numbers, depending on the numerical ability of the participants. One possibility which I have tried out is to have the 'target' numbers in a particular ratio, say $1:2:4:8$.

The idea has been tried out informally with two groups of students at the International School of Geneva.

▼ Example 1

With four participants and the set of numbers

1 2 2 2 3 3 3 3 4 4 4 5

we expect the result

$\{1 \; 4 \; 4\} \{2 \; 2 \; 5\} \{2 \; 3 \; 4\} \{3 \; 3 \; 3\}$

In this case each participant is expected to get the same square number, 9, each using three of the available numbers.

The group of students involved, mainly 16 year olds, found this to be extremely easy, having been told that the four squares being sought were in fact equal. They each quickly took just as many of the numbers as they needed, having individually decided that 9 was the target number.

▼ Example 2

With four participants and the set of numbers

1 1 1 3 4 4 4 4 5 5 6 6 11 12 13 20

each participant has to get the same square number as target, each using the same number of the available numbers.

The expected result was

$\{1 \; 1 \; 3 \; 20\} \{1 \; 5 \; 6 \; 13\} \{4 \; 4 \; 5 \; 12\} \{4 \; 4 \; 6 \; 11\}$

It is possible to achieve the required total in several ways, but only one of these satisfies the condition that each participant must have the same number of the available numbers.

This was tried on the same group of students as Example 1, with a significantly different outcome. One student quickly decided that 25 was the target to be achieved (or perhaps could recognise only 25 as a square number !), and obstinately refused for a very long time to appreciate that {20 5} is not a permitted way of achieving that total. The other students heroically avoided direct communication and it needed a hint from myself to avoid the deadlock, since they had no way of invading the private area of the one student.

▼ Example 3

With four participants and the set of numbers

10 10 10 10 15 15 20 20 35 55 60 70 70

Each participant to get the same square as target, but not necessarily using the same number of numbers.
  The expected result is

$$\{10\ 10\ 10\ 70\}\qquad\{15\ 15\ 70\}$$
$$\{20\ 20\ 60\}\qquad\{10\ 35\ 55\}$$

After the near-trauma of the previous example, this caused no problem to the group.

▼ Example 4

With four participants and the set of numbers

1 2 2 4 4 4 8 8 8 16 16 32

participants are to collect sets of three numbers so that the totals of the sets are in the ratios 1 : 2 : 4 : 8
  The expected result is

$$\{1\ 2\ 4\}\ \{2\ 4\ 8\}\ \{4\ 8\ 16\}\ \{8\ 16\ 32\}$$

This caused problems of a mathematical nature, since one of the students was not very strong mathematically. However, one of the others 'solved' the problem by annexing all of the numbers which he could, and releasing them to the central area in packets corresponding to the expected solution. It was interesting as a demonstration of how one strong individual can take over a situation, but rather defeated the notion of a co-operative exercise!

  Future implementations might limit movement to only one of the numbers at a time, especially with experienced participants.

Drawing it Together

▼ Resources

16, 24 or 32 squares of unlined paper depending on class size (21 cm × 21 cm squares can easily be made from A4 sheets); crayons or felt tip pens or paints; newspapers spread over an open classroom area.

▼ Procedure

This exercise works best with 16, 24 or 32 squares of paper divided amongst participants working in groups, each group having 4 squares. If any group has less than 4 members, then 1 or 2 participants should have more than one square. A theme is suggested, e.g. peace, health, environment, and each student is asked to draw or paint a picture that comes to mind on their square(s) of paper without discussing the task with others (10 minutes).

  Each group is asked to examine its 4 pictures and to:

— negotiate without verbal communication how they would like to arrange their pictures to form a larger square out of the 4 squares.

— negotiate and draw additions and changes, again without verbal communication, so as to create a more cohesive picture.

Nothing should be added or changed without discussion and agreement (15 minutes).

  The groups then come together — each with their one larger square — and are asked to:

— negotiate, non-verbally, how they would like to arrange them to form an even larger picture (now composed of all the original squares).

— negotiate, non-verbally, and draw additions and changes to create a more cohesive picture.

All additions and changes are to be made by group consent (15 minutes).

▼ Potential

A broad question such as 'What happened?' or 'How did you feel'? is usually enough to trigger off an exchange of experience and feelings. This may well lead naturally into discussion of some of the key issues raised by the activity:

- **Decision-making Processes** – how were decisions made about how to juxtapose the parts and how to create a cohesive whole; were they in fact corporate decisions; if not, what were they; how could the decision-making have been more responsive to individual viewpoints, etc?

- **Co-operation and Non-verbal Communication** – how did individuals and groups co-operate without speaking; was non-verbal communication easier or harder than verbal communication; why; how would the activity and outcome have been different if participants could have spoken; etc?

- **Perceptions** – did others have divergent perceptions of what constituted a cohesive, satisfying picture; can those differences be explained; what different perspectives did others bring to the theme, etc?

▼ Variations

Drawing it Together has a very flexible format. As suggested above, it can be adjusted to class size by giving some students 2 squares. Another approach is to give some students half a square each (in this way 20 students could work with 16 squares). The activity can also be tried using verbal communication, possibly to allow comparisons and contrasts to be made. Two, rather more distinctive, variations are as follows:

On a large sheet of paper, each person in a group of 6–8 makes a spontaneous scribble. The group is then asked to negotiate one cohesive picture out of the scribbles. Alternatively, the group cover the paper with spontaneous colours and shapes. Members pick out and describe the images they see and the group goes on to negotiate and develop a cohesive picture.

Primary/Secondary, 40 minutes.

▼ Source

Idea derived from Marian Liebmann, Art Games and Structures for Groups, Bristol Art Therapy Group, 1982.

Fruitful Co-operation

▼ Resources

Large, clear room with 6 tables around the outside and a space in the centre; 30 role cards (5 of each culture) (see pp. 175–6); 3 large pots of paint – 1 blue, 1 red, 1 yellow; 15 thin brushes; 6 jars of water; 3 empty jars; 9 pairs of scissors; 7 rulers; 25 sheets of white A4 paper; 4 sheets of sugar paper, Sellotaped together on the back; 3 pots of glue; sticky dots in six colours – red, blue, yellow, green, orange, purple – 5 of each colour; poster of 'Market Prices'; OHP or poster of 'Instructions to Participants'; supply of newspaper; waste-paper bin; OHP or poster of 'Urgent Message to All Cultures'.

Distribution of resources to each culture:

Red – Red Culture role cards, red paint, 1 brush, 1 pair of scissors, 1 ruler, 1 sheet of A4 paper, 1 jar of water.

Blue – Blue Culture role cards, blue paint, 1 brush, 1 pair of scissors, 1 ruler, 1 sheet of A4 paper, 1 jar of water.

Yellow – Yellow Culture role cards, yellow paint, 1 brush, 1 pair of scissors, 1 ruler, 1 sheet of A4 paper, 1 jar of water.

Green – Green Culture role cards, 2 pairs of scissors, 6 sheets of A4 paper, 1 ruler, 1 jar of water, 1 empty jar.

Orange – Orange Culture role cards, 6 brushes, 2 pairs of scissors, 6 sheets of A4 paper, 1 ruler, 1 jar of water, 1 empty jar.

Purple – Purple Culture role cards, 6 brushes, 2 pairs of scissors, 6 sheets of A4 paper, 1 ruler, 1 jar of water, 1 empty jar.

▼ *Procedure*

Participants are divided into six groups by means of the **Going Dotty** activity (see p. 111); the colour of their sticky dot indicates the culture to which they belong. In their culture groups, participants, are encouraged to get into their roles – this might be done through some 'Loosening-up Activities' (see pp. 99–102) whilst adhering to their cultural rules and practices. The facilitator introduces the primary aim of each culture – to create wealth through fruit sales – and goes through the Instructions to Participants:

INSTRUCTIONS TO PARTICIPANTS

1 Greet all members of your culture in turn.

2 Elect a work supervisor.

3 Decide upon a work role for each person in fruit production.

4 Begin fruit production; your fruit must be of good quality and of the required size.

5 Before being taken to the market, your fruit must be displayed to all other cultures for their approval. Any fruit considered to be sub-standard can be thrown into the compost bin.

6 Your fruit will only be accepted at the market in kilo bunches. The wholesaler will credit your account with the appropriate number of units.

7 The fruit production season is short – you need to make as much money as possible to buy essential commodities for the rest of the year.

Participants are then left to carry out the instructions and manufacture their fruit. It will be quickly realised that co-operation and negotiation have to take place between different cultures as their own resources are inadequate: green, orange and purple cultures need paint (obtained by mixing two of the three available colours); red, blue and yellow cultures will quickly run out of paper, and so on. The facilitator becomes the market wholesaler and displays the Market Prices list:

MARKET PRICES
One kilo of:

Strawberries = 10   market value = 10 units
(min. width 4 cm)

Blueberries = 20   market value = 15 units
(min. width 2 cm)

Bananas = 5   market value = 5 units
(min. length 8 cm)

Limes = 10   market value = 10 units
(min. width 4 cm)

Oranges = 5   market value = 15 units
(min. width 6 cm)

Plums = 5   market value = 15 units
(min. width 4 cm)

She checks the size of the fruit and keeps an account for each culture of the units they earn from fruit sales. This stage lasts for about fifteen minutes.

At an appropriate moment, the facilitator displays and reads out the following message:

URGENT MESSAGE TO ALL CULTURES
The President of our country has just announced that she will be visiting this area soon to see if we need more money to improve our living conditions. In order to impress the President, the Inter-Cultural Council has asked all cultures to co-operate in mounting a display of our work – an enormous fruit salad! The Council requests that:

– the most successful fruit producing culture should be in overall charge of the design and production of the display;

– the display should be attractively designed and presented;

– each culture's fruit should be equally represented.

The facilitator spreads out the 4 sheets of sugar paper, on which the display is to be mounted, in the centre of the room and announces which culture is to be in charge of the design and production. Participants then have about fifteen minutes to produce the display, using glue to stick the fruit onto the paper.

▼ Potential

A lighthearted, enjoyable activity which does have potential for learning about co-operation, conflict, negotiation and the problems encountered when cultures with different practices, traditions and taboos meet. In the debriefing participants might be asked to reflect upon their feelings about:

— their own cultural rules and practices;
— the other cultures' rules and practices;
— the unequal distribution of resources for fruit production;
— the co-operation and conflict that took place, in their own culture and between cultures;
— the **Going Dotty** activity at the beginning;
— the display that was finally produced.

Upper Primary/Secondary, 45 minutes.

▼ Source

Centre for Global Education.

Yellow Culture

Dominant cultural characteristics:
friendly, easy-going

Sex roles:
women and men equal

Attitudes towards outsiders:
tolerant

Major taboo:
never communicate without touching

Form of greeting:
rub noses

Fruit grown:
Bananas

Culture rules:

1 Always use your form of greeting when meeting outsiders.
2 Always live up to the customs/attitudes outlined above.
3 Only use your culture's colour when working.
4 Stealing is strictly forbidden.
5 Keep your hands clean at all times.

Green Culture

Dominant cultural characteristics:
fun-loving, extroverts

Sex roles:
men dominant: women as 'chattel'

Attitudes towards outsiders:
unconcerned

Major taboo:
never use right hand/arm

Form of greeting:
slap on shoulders

Fruit grown:
Limes

Culture rules:

1 Always use your form of greeting when meeting outsiders.
2 Always live up to the customs/attitudes outlined above.
3 Only use your culture's colour when working.
4 Stealing is strictly forbidden.
5 Keep your hands clean at all times.

Blue Culture

Dominant cultural characteristics:
forward-looking, liberal

Sex roles:
women dominant

Attitudes towards outsiders:
welcoming

Major taboo:
never use left hand/arm

Form of greeting:
link arms

Fruit grown:
Blueberries

Culture rules:

1 Always use your form of greeting when meeting outsiders.
2 Always live up to the customs/ attitudes outlined above.
3 Only use your culture's colour when working.
4 Stealing is strictly forbidden.
5 Keep your hands clean at all times.

Red Culture

Dominant cultural characteristics:
conservative, introverted

Sex roles:
men dominant

Attitudes towards outsiders:
hostile

Major taboo:
never touch other people

Form of greeting:
wink twice

Fruit grown:
Strawberries

Culture rules:

1 Always use your form of greeting when meeting outsiders.
2 Always live up to the customs/ attitudes outlined above.
3 Only use your culture's colour when working.
4 Stealing is strictly forbidden.
5 Keep your hands clean at all times.

Orange Culture

Dominant cultural characteristics:
hard-working, enthusiastic

Sex roles:
women superior in work roles

Attitude towards outsiders:
cautious

Major taboo:
never negotiate with a man

Form of greeting:
right hand shake

Fruit grown:
Oranges

Culture rules:

1 Always use your form of greeting when meeting outsiders.
2 Always live up to the customs/ attitudes outlined above.
3 Only use your culture's colour when working.
4 Stealing is strictly forbidden.
5 Keep your hands clean at all times.

Purple Culture

Dominant cultural characteristics:
cautious, respectful

Sex roles:
women inferior in ideas

Attitudes towards outsiders:
suspicious

Major taboo:
never negotiate with a woman

Form of greeting:
left hand shake

Fruit grown:
Plums

Culture rules:

1 Always use your form of greeting when meeting outsiders.
2 Always live up to the customs/ attitudes outlined above.
3 Only use your culture's colour when working.
4 Stealing is strictly forbidden.
5 Keep your hands clean at all times.

Blockhead!

▼ Resources

For each group of five or six students a set of 'blocks'. Possible 'blocks' are:

35 mm film can;
block of wood 25 × 50 × 100 mm;
block of wood 25 × 25 × 50 mm;
toilet paper tube filled with Polyfilla;
audio-cassette box taped closed;
domino;
school rubber;
hamburger box filled with sand and taped closed;
large hexagonal nut;
small film or tape spool;
50 mm length of 25 mm dowelling;
odd lengths of picture frame moulding;
large wooden bead or small rubber ball (about 25 mm diameter);
25 mm lengths of plastic piping (various diameters);
or whatever else is available — offcuts of perspex, aluminium, etc.

Each set should be identical and placed in a suitable box or bag. A selection of small prizes: tubes of Smarties, packets of fruit gums, etc. are suitable.

▼ Procedure

Students work in groups of 5 or 6. Each group requires a firm flat table, or a suitable space on the floor.

Stage One: After deciding which member of the group is to start, she chooses one of the 'blocks' and, using one hand only, places it in the centre of the table (or space). The next person chooses a 'block' and again using one hand, places the second 'block' on top of the first. This continues in turn until either all the 'blocks' are used up, or when someone placing her block in position causes the construction to fall down.

This person is now a 'character', and a new round of the game is started. If a person causes the 'blocks' to fall over a second time, she becomes a 'square'; if a third time, she is a

'BLOCKHEAD' and is out of the game. If the 'blocks' fall over during the first three 'turns' of a game, the game is restarted without penalty.

The groups are allowed to continue with the game until most groups have at least one 'BLOCKHEAD' in addition to any 'characters' and 'squares'. A small prize is then awarded to each 'BLOCKHEAD'.

Stage Two: It is now explained that the rules of the game are to be changed! The task of the whole group is now to construct as high a stack as possible, using as many of the 'blocks' as they can, and without it falling down. Each player may still only use one hand, and there is to be no talking during the game. When a group considers it has the highest possible stack, it should ask for its height to be measured.

When all groups have finished, and had their stacks measured, the winning group can be announced, and a prize given to the group.

Stage Three: The class reassembles as a whole group to discuss the experience. Questions should centre on students' feelings during the games:

— how did you feel if you were the first to become a blockhead?
— how did you feel if you survived the first game without even becoming a 'character'?
— how did you feel when the 'losers' in the first game unexpectedly found themselves with the prizes? what did you do with your prize?
— what about the differences between the two games, for example, if you made it difficult for the next person to put their 'block' on without the stack falling?
— was it fair to give a prize at the end of the second game, or should all groups have had prizes, or no prizes?
— did one group's design give other groups ideas about how to modify or improve theirs? is this copying or learning from the experience of others?
— how do the two games compare with 'real life' situations (can be taken at whatever level is appropriate to the context — within the class, between groups, between nations, etc.)?

▼ Potential

A simple and enjoyable game is used to focus on our feelings in situations of competition, or of co-operation, and to look at our ability to learn from the experience of others, and at the fairness or unfairness of arbitrarily given rewards.

Upper Primary/Secondary, 60 minutes.

▼ Source

Sandy Parker, Ackworth School, Pontefract, developed from ideas in the Parker Bros. game Blockhead, and the Teaching guide to The Search for Solutions (Phillips Petroleum).

Elephant Game

▼ Resources

Two large rooms or open spaces; in one room, an assortment of 'obstacles', e.g. tables, chairs, boxes, benches; 28 blindfolds (optional); 2 facilitators are required.

▼ Procedure

Participants form two teams in the empty room. Each team appoints or elects one person who acts as 'the eyes' for the team, all other members having their eyes closed. 'The eyes', however, is not allowed to touch or speak to the other team members in any known language. The two teams are advised that they are going to negotiate a maze or obstacle course and that they should formulate and practise an efficient form of communication and mobility as a team. During this practice session, which lasts about ten minutes, participants can speak and have their eyes open; a simple obstacle course might be set up for practice purposes. The facilitators should note how 'the eyes' was selected, how the communication process was developed and the participation levels of team members.

'The eyes' of each team are then taken to look at the obstacle course set out in the other room. This might involve going over, under or round several chairs and tables, up and down steps, etc. They are each shown the 'route' (teams can go one after the other, or in opposite directions) and told of any particular dangers or hazards. They return to their teams, but from then on are only allowed to speak in the form of communication developed with their team. The two teams are then left to their own devices to negotiate the maze as best they can; the facilitators should only intervene when there is danger of physical injury to any participant. On completing the course, teams are allowed to open their eyes and see what they have been through.

▼ Potential

This activity necessarily involves high levels of trust, communication, participation and co-operation. It can be an exhausting experience, physically and emotionally, so participants will need a few minutes to relax or 'let off steam'. They should then be asked to reflect on their experiences, both as an individual and as a team. How was 'the eyes' selected? How were decisions made during the practice stage? Who devised the communication process? How did 'the eyes' feel about their responsibilities to the team? Did other team members totally trust 'the eyes'? Did anything happen to particularly cause distrust? What other feelings did they experience when going through the obstacle course? What did the teams think about the communication process they devised? Facilitators can add any pertinent remarks from their vantage point as observers. Wider questions about leadership, communication and co-operation can also be raised, with participants relating their experiences to real life situations.

▼ Extension

With a well-affirmed group, the facilitators intervene directly in the obstacle course stage by confusing or harrassing some team members, either verbally (perhaps by mimicking their communication code) or physically (by gently pushing or leading participants away). The aim should be to make the task more difficult, to increase tension and stress, but not to make it impossible. The debriefing will need to explore the heightened emotional responses that this action causes in some detail. Facilitators should bear in mind that some temporary lessening of trust in them may result.

Upper Primary/Secondary, 30 minutes.

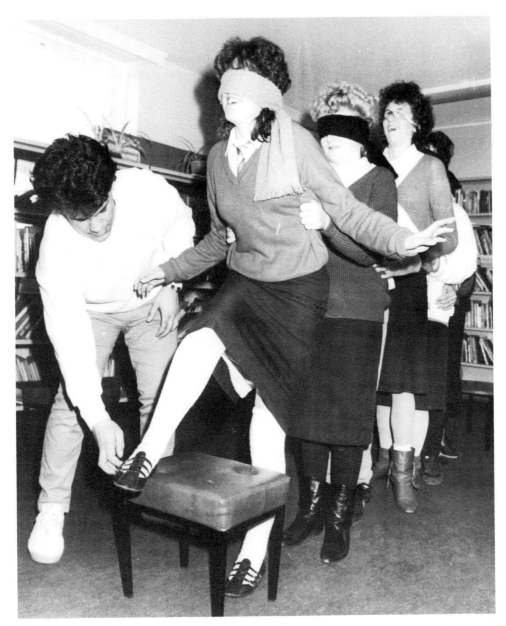

'Elephant Game' in action

▼ Source

Coover, V. et al., Resource Manual for a Living Revolution, Philadelphia, New Society Publishers, 1981.

Peaceful Negotiations

▼ Resources

Four large sheets of sugar paper of different colours, Sellotaped together to form a rectangle. Four thick felt pens of colours to match the four sheets of paper.

▼ Procedure

Students are asked to form four groups of approximately equal size and to spend a short time picking their own Foreign Minister and Road Builder (who is given the felt tip pen). The activity's object and rules are then explained. Each group represents a country and has its own square. The object is for each country to build as many roads as possible from its own territory into the other countries. There are two conditions for building each road: 1 permission to build must be obtained from each country the road is to go through before construction takes place; 2 if it is necessary to cross another country's road outside one's own territory, then permission must, in every case, be sought. All negotiations about permission are to be conducted between Foreign Ministers. Two things are not permitted: (a) building a road through the central point where the four countries touch and (b) allowing a road to fork so as to create two roads (see 1 and 2 on the diagram). Roads

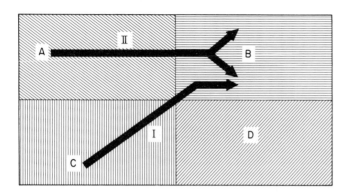

are built by the Road Builder drawing with the felt pen. Nothing is said about the role of other group members save that they are citizens of the country and can exercise what they see a citizen's role to be. Having stated the object and rules twice, the facilitator should refuse to answer questions and avoid intervening in what takes place.

▼ Potential

This exercise normally generates intense activity and feelings may run high. It may be helpful to give time for spontaneous discussion in small groups before beginning a plenary debriefing. The facilitator can begin the plenary by asking members of a particular group to give their account of what has taken place. Other groups can, in turn, be asked to contribute their perspective on events. Versions can differ widely and this can lead to discussion on the accuracy of historical accounts. If there are so many arguments surrounding an event in which one small group participated, what is the likelihood of an 'accurate' account of events in history books? What does 'accurate' mean? Other key areas for discussion are likely to be:

- **Competition, Conflict and Co-operation** Participants can be asked to suggest why they became so involved in such an activity and why (as normally happens), they chose to approach the task in a competitive spirit. Were there, on reflection, co-operative ways of proceeding? Emotional responses within the competitive context can also be explored. What kind of actions tended to generate distrust and trigger conflict? How difficult was it to restore trust when it was broken and to take the heat out of conflict when it occurred?

- **Roles and Relationships** How did the four Foreign Ministers and four Road Builders perceive their role and their relationship with the people they represented (i.e. the rest of their group)? How did the people view their relationship with their Foreign Minister and Road Builder? Were they satisfied with the way the two 'officials' conducted their role? Did the Foreign Minister really represent the people? Were there tensions between Foreign Minister and Road Builder? Did female and male students conduct themselves differently within the activity? To what extent did the roles, relationships and tensions mirror the real political world?

- **Democracy and International Crisis** The Foreign Ministers find themselves caught up in a flurry of activity and decision-making. They have to negotiate with other Foreign Ministers, enter dialogue with their people and carefully instruct and watch the activities of the Road Builder. Is it possible to undertake all these tasks effectively? Which task has each Foreign Minister tended to overlook? It is a safe generalisation to say that a Foreign Minister who negotiates effectively with and meets the pressures coming from other Foreign Ministers will give less time to heeding representations from the people and that a Minister who is scrupulously concerned about the views and wishes of the people will exasperate other Ministers. Is it possible — or reasonable — to expect those conducting foreign affairs to heed the wishes of the people — especially in a crisis? Can government, given the manifold pressures coming from all directions, be anything but reactive however much its actions are portrayed as the result of careful planning?

Sample 1

1 You represent a large powerful country that feels that in these times of 'power politics' it is best to show your power constantly to other countries.

2 You represent a large powerful country that likes to use its power to protect other small countries that you want as allies.

3 You represent a small country that wants to be independent but finds it impossible in a world divided between power blocks. You have to join one or another power block.

4 You represent a small country. The best way for you to keep some independence is to play the big powerful countries off against each other, letting them compete for your friendship.

Sample 2

1 You represent a country which believes that levels of international co-operation should be increased and whose people place great store on participatory democracy of a thoroughgoing kind and environment-friendly policies.

2 You represent a country that believes in free enterprise and continued material and economic growth. Yours is a representative democracy (elections every five years). At the moment, the government is doing badly in the opinion polls because of its economic record.

3 You represent a socialist one-party state believing that lasting peace can only be achieved through the triumph of socialism internationally and the fostering of a collective spirit at home.

4 You represent a developing country with as yet untapped natural resources where there is currently increasing concern about foreign involvement in economic and political life.

Secondary, 25 minutes.

▼ Variations

Interesting – and different – results can be obtained, especially with older students, by giving each country a description of, for example, its strategic policy and position, its ideology or the key elements in its economic/industrial structure. Cards (see samples) are given to Foreign Ministers for showing to the group but not to members of other groups. Time should be allocated for groups to discuss the contents of the card before any activity begins.

▼ Source

Derived from Wolsk, D., An Experience-centered Curriculum, Unesco Educational Studies and Documents, No. 17, 1975. Wolsk's description is based upon Lineham, T.E. and Ellis Long, B., The Road Game, Herder & Herder, 1970.

Identity Auction

Example A	Items for Sale
1	All-round sporting ability
2	Ability to make a few close friends
3	Happy family life
4	Ability to lead others
5	Artistic skills and success
6	Love of learning
7	Good health
8	Chances for adventure
9	Lots of money
10	Ability to do very well in school
11	Success in the job of your choice
12	Good looks
13	Ability to do practical things
14	Feeling important
15	Musical talent
16	Ability to bounce back
17	Ability to give love to others
18	Ability to help other people
19	Ability to make lots of friends
20	Success at changing the world to make it a better place
21	Parents who trust you
22	A secure and safe future
23	The chance to travel wherever you want
24	Real excellence in one sport
25	Feeling really good about yourself
26	Ability to read well
27	Ability to speak out in class or public
28	
29	
30	

Example B	Items for Sale
1	Save the whale
2	Beauty is in the eye of the beholder
3	A woman's place is in the home
4	History is not herstory
5	Arms are for hugging
6	Think global, act local
7	To travel is more important than to arrive
8	Politics is the art of the possible
9	Small is beautiful
10	Silence is golden
11	There's no smoke without fire
12	The future is in our hands
13	War is peace
14	Law and order
15	Co-operation is better than conflict
16	Charity begins at home
17	Wars begin in the minds of men
18	Black is beautiful
19	Truth is rarely pure and never simple
20	Nostalgia is not what is used to be
21	Seeing is believing
22	There is no road to peace; peace is the road
23	Sisters are doing it for themselves
24	Ignorance is bliss
25	Freedom is a state of mind
26	Only one earth
27	There's no place like home
28	
29	
30	

Units of money at start of auction:

Item no.	Price Paid	Balance

Units of money at start of auction:

Item no.	Price Paid	Balance

▼ Resources

A worksheet of items for sale (see p. 182) for each student; a hammer or shoe.

▼ Procedure

Worksheets are handed out and each student is given an imaginary 1,000 units of currency to bid for and buy desired items on the list. Time having been given for everybody to study the list and choose preferred items, the auction begins in a brisk, lively style. Items are sold to the individual bidding the most (the deal is sealed when the hammer or shoe is banged on the table). The auctioneer – teacher or student – takes cues from students as to what item to auction as well as choosing items herself. Students can put up three items of their own choosing for auction (to be written in spaces 28–30). They should keep a careful record of account by filling in the balance sheet provided.

▼ Potential

Before the debriefing it may be advisable to allow students to let off steam by engaging in a pace-changing activity. Discussion can begin by asking students to explain what they bought, why they were keen to buy those items and also to identify items they would have liked but were unable to purchase. Later the discussion can focus upon topics such as:

- **The 'auction effect'** *If something seems to be in demand, why do others start wanting it too? What examples of the 'auction effect' have students noted in everyday life?*

- **Individual differences** *Did the auction help students learn something about themselves and about others taking part? Did it provide a context and opportunity for students to express their own individuality, their hopes and aspirations?*

- **Communication** *Did students find it easier to say certain things about themselves in an auction context which would normally have been difficult to say? Can they think of other kinds of situations which help to make communication easier (e.g. romantic evenings, parties, writing letters rather than telling someone directly)?*

Upper Primary/Secondary, 30 minutes.

▼ Source

Wolsk, D., An Experience-centered Curriculum, draft document, UNESCO, Paris, 1974.

Faces

▼ Resources

A set of nine pictures (colour supplements are an ideal source) each showing a female or male face. The nine faces should reflect the ethnic and multiracial composition of British society. A sheet of paper and pencil for each student.

▼ Procedure

Students make a list of seven different occupations; for example, student, teacher, musician, criminal, policewoman/man, nurse, engineer. They inspect the nine pictures (which are lettered A to I and placed at different points in the room), deciding which face goes with each of the occupations. For the two extra faces, they can suggest possible occupations. Decisions are collated in chart form on the board:

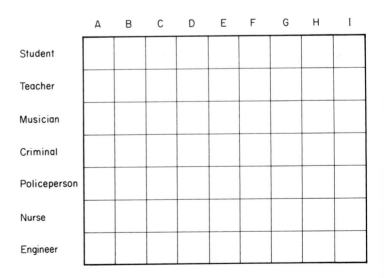

	A	B	C	D	E	F	G	H	I
Student									
Teacher									
Musician									
Criminal									
Policeperson									
Nurse									
Engineer									

▼ Potential

Students can first be asked to identify significant scores (nil scores can be as significant as high scores). In the case of high scores, they can be asked to suggest why they think the particular face and job go together; with nil scores, why, in their view, the face and job do not match. The answers given can provide a very useful springboard for an exploration of stereotyping. What, on reflection, caused so many in the class to link certain faces with certain jobs? In what ways can stereotyping be damaging to ourselves and to those we stereotype? In what ways do stereotypes serve a useful purpose? Are they unavoidable? Do we try to look like a stereotype? If so, why?

Upper Primary/Secondary, 15 minutes.

▼ Source

Wolsk, D., An Experience-centered Curriculum, Unesco Educational Studies and Documents, No. 17.

Imaginal Exercises

by **Sandy Parker**, formerly Head of Religious Education at Ackworth School, Pontefract and now Research Fellow at the Centre for Global Education.

Centering Exercises are a wide range of simple and short techniques that can be used with most age groups, in any subject area, and in almost any situation. Their purpose is to develop a pool of inner stillness, so that body, intellect, and intuition can work in harmony. A typical centering exercise will take only a few minutes, and combines mental and physical relaxation by, for example, encouraging us to relax fully whilst giving attention to our breathing or our pulse. Some examples of centering exercises are given on p. 187.

A Guided Fantasy encourages us to take our intuition seriously, and is like a 'walking dream' in which the individual is encouraged to go along with the images stimulated by the script as it is spoken aloud. The script will encourage her to identify with aspects of her imagination, and to explore her own personal world. The experiences are talked through afterwards in small groups, each person discovering the meaning of her own fantasy for herself. Some typical scripts are given on pp. 187–91 and 194–5. John Stevens, who has given us a wide range of possible scripts, writes:

> In fantasy anything is possible, and even if you start with a particular imagined thing or situation, you create it and its characteristics out of yourself...If you are willing to let your (waking) fantasy develop spontaneously, you can learn a great deal about your existence.[1]

Many people have deeply seated negative expectations about life, and automatically and unconsciously imagine and expect difficulties, problems, and inadequacies. The purpose of **Creative Visualisation** is to create instead positive expectations of what we want in our lives, and to make this a conscious and constructive process.

Creative Visualisation may be very similar to a Guided Fantasy, but will usually be less tightly scripted, and more open to individual development. An example of a Creative Visualisation is given on pp. 189–91. Adelaide Bry and Shakti Gawain have also given us many examples.[2]

Imaginal exercises of this type may be used in a wide variety of contexts, and for many different purposes including:

- introducing or developing new concepts (e.g. in Biology or Physics);

- developing a sense of involvement and empathy with unfamiliar culture (e.g. in History or Religious Studies);

- encouraging more productive brainstorming;

- developing and exploring 'futures scenarios';

- encouraging a positive self-image, and exploring our values and our sense of identity;

- helping the development of new skills and abilities (aesthetic, physical, etc.);

- life-planning and goal-setting;

- encouraging a positive attitude to health and well-being;

- the constructive resolution of conflict;

- the development of positive personal relationships.

Some Guide-Lines for using Guided Fantasy and Creative Visualisation in the Classroom.

1 Any 'script' is a guide, to be used selectively, and adapted to the particular situation and purpose. The focus is on the participants' imaging, and it is important to be explicit that there is no compulsion to take part in any particular way. My experience is that students respond to such opportunities with enthusiasm, and a student who is apparently unwilling to participate and may sit quietly 'reading' during the exercise can still be fully involved in the feedback discussion! (Of course the student must respect the wish of the others to participate, and not in any way disturb or distract them.)

2 The atmosphere should be relaxed and experimental, encouraging participants to 'Try it! Have a go, and see what happens.'

3 The size of groups is relatively unimportant — there should be no difficulty working with a full class or a larger group, providing appropriate arrangements can be made for the feedback that follows.

4 Physical surroundings are also fairly unimportant. Each student should have sufficient space to avoid distraction from others. Most exercises are equally effective with students seated (I suggest arms folded on the table or desk, head resting on arms), or lying down (if this is possible). A group used to such approaches may find light physical contact and closeness helpful for some exercises.

5 Interruptions need to be avoided, and unexpected external noises may be distracting. An effective introductory centering at the start of the fantasy or visualisation will usually enable students to disregard outside noises. Some scripts can effectively integrate wind or traffic noises as part of the experience.

6 It is helpful to make an audio-recording of a script so that you can experience it for yourself before using it with students (or find someone to act as your guide to read through the script for you). In the classroom it is better spoken 'live' in a natural, relaxed, thoughtful, and confident voice, pacing the pauses according to your awareness of the group's response. As far as possible try to take part in the exercise as you guide it (not always easy!).

7 At the end of an extended fantasy or visualisation, it is important to check that all participants have brought their attention back to the classroom and to the people around them, repeating the last section of the script as needed (and even gently waking up someone who has fallen asleep!).

8 Talking through the experience is an essential part of any Guided Fantasy or Creative Visualisation. Along with permission 'to revisit' or return to the experience later, instructions for this should be an integral part of the script. Possible approaches are:
   (a) Talking through the experience in small groups (2 to 4), each person taking it in turn whilst the others listen attentively without comment or judgement. Questions like 'What happened when...?' or 'What did it feel like when...?' may be helpful.
   (b) Individual drawing, using crayons or oil pastels, and then talking in groups about the drawings. The drawings should simply be an expression of the experience, whether abstract, symbolic, or concrete, and are not to be judged for any artistic or aesthetic merit.
   (c) Sentence completion 'telegrams', for larger group feedback.

9 No attempt should be made by the facilitator, or by other students, to 'interpret' or give 'symbolic' meanings to the visualisation or fantasy. Students need to be encouraged to understand that the experience is their own, and they are the only ones who can discover any meaning it may have for them. Open-ended questions may be helpful: 'Do you feel there are any ways in which this helps you to understand how you...'

10 Suitably appropriate and relaxing music may occasionally be helpful as a background for some fantasies or visualisations. It will often be helpful during the feedback in small groups, to encourage a quiet and relaxed atmosphere.

Guided Fantasy and Creative Visualisation: Bibliography, Resources and Useful Addresses

1 **Books:**

Bry, Adelaide, *Visualization: Directing the Movies of Your Mind*, New York, Harper & Row, 1979.
A useful general book about the use of fantasy and visualisation in many different situations.

Gawain, Shakti, *Creative Visualisation*, California, Whatever Publishing, 1978. Also available as a Bantam Paperback.
The classic guide to Creative Visualisation.

Hendricks, Gay and Wills, Russel, *The Centering Book*, New Jersey, Prentice-Hall, 1975.
A valuable guide to a range of centering exercises, and the use of imagery in the classroom.

Hendricks, Gay and Roberts, Thomas, *The Second Centering Book*, New Jersey, Prentice-Hall, 1977.
Has a very useful chapter (pp. 35–50) on the use of fantasy in the classroom.

Oaklander, Violet, *Windows to our Children*, Utah, Real People Press, 1978.
An extended discussion about the use of imaginal work with young people, based on her experience as a Gestalt therapist.

Stevens, John, *Awareness*, Utah, Real People Press, 1971. Also available as a Bantam Paperback, 1973.
Contains an invaluable collection of Fantasy Journey scripts (pp. 38–9 and pp. 136–67) as well as a rationale for the use of Fantasy Journeys.

Whitmore, Diana, *Psychosynthesis in Education*, Wellingborough, Turnstone Press, 1986.
A practical discussion of the psychological aspects of the use of imagery with young people. Also contains many practical classroom units.

2 A useful **audio cassette** of visualisation exercises for young people, aged 8 and over:
Just Imagine, by Anthea Courtenay (Artists Network for a Positive Future).

3 Most teachers will have their own personal preferences as regards **music** suitable for use in conjunction with these approaches.
Recordings I have found helpful include:

Oxygene and *Equinoxe* by Jean Michel Jarre (Polydor)
The Flight of the Condor (BBC)

Salve Regina – Gregorian Chant of the Benedictine Monks of the Abbey of St Maurice and St Maur of Clervaux (Philips)
Zodiac Suite and *Ancient Echoes* by Stephen Halpern (Halpern Sounds, Palo Alto)
Songs of the Japanese Seashore by James Galway (RCA)
Kitaro Silk Road by Kitaro (Canyon Records, Munich)
Ascension by Clifford White (New World Cassettes)
Peace by David Sun (New World Cassettes)
Celtic Harp: Secrets From Stone by Judith Pintar (Sonia Gaia Productions, 2001 HA Haarlem, Holland)

4 **Useful Addresses:**

Artists Network for a Positive Future,
21 Foulser Road
London SW17 8UE
(01 767 1081)

The Inner Bookshop
34 Cowley Road
Oxford
(0865 245301)

Compendium Bookshop
234 Camden High Street
London NW1
(01 485 8344)

New World Cassettes
Strawberry Vale
Twickenham TW1 1BR
(01 755 2828)

The Trading Centre
Findhorn Foundation
The Park
Forres, IV36 0TZ
Scotland
(0309 30110)

Some Centering Exercises

Thought Watching

This activity can be done sitting or lying down.

▼ Facilitator's instructions:

'Settle back and let your body relax, and as your body begins to quieten down and become comfortable, let your eyelids close. Relax a while in the darkness, letting your body become peaceful and comfortable. As you lie there, feel around until you find a place where you can find your pulse, and when you do, rest your fingers lightly on that place and get in touch with the quiet rhythm of your pulse as it moves the blood through your body.'

Pause (thirty seconds).

'And now in the quiet, let's begin watching our thoughts and feelings that come through our minds ...just looking and listening for the pictures and sounds in our heads. Pictures, voices, scenes, music, whatever comes in, just watch and listen...just observe. When you find yourself lost in thought, just return to watching and listening.'

Pause (three to four minutes; work up to about ten minutes as the exercise is repeated).

'Now in the future, when you find yourself angry, sad, or bored, or in any kind of mood, happy or sad, just watch and listen to what is going on inside your head. This will help get you in touch with how you are feeling.

'Let yourself become alert at your own speed. Feel the alertness come into your body, stretching a little to feel more alert. Open your eyes and let the light in, feeling rested and calm.'

Counting Breaths

Sitting cross-legged is a good position for this activity.

▼ Facilitator's instructions:

'Find a spot that feels good to sit on, moving your body around until you feel comfortable and light. This is an activity in which we pay attention to our breath. As you become comfortable, begin paying attention to the way the breath comes in and out of your body. And as you listen to your breath, begin counting each breath, each time you breathe in ...counting to ten, then starting again with one. When your mind wanders, bring it gently back to one and start again.'

Pause (one to two minutes at first, then gradually increase this as the exercise is repeated).

'All of our minds wander, and this exercise helps us know when it's happening. As long as you know it's wandering, you can have more control over where it goes. And now watch your attention come right back here as you get up, feeling comfortable and alert.'

▼ Source

Both of the above exercises, and many others, can be found in Gay Hendricks and Russell Wills, *The Centering Book*. Further useful sources of centering exercises are: Gay Hendricks and Thomas Roberts, *The Second Centering Book*; Gay Hendricks, *The Centered Teacher*.

A Guided Fantasy
Discovering our Own Wisdom:
A Fantasy Journey

Script transcribed from a lesson with a fourth-year secondary group:

'Now then, I want to take about fifteen or twenty minutes for a guided day-dream or fantasy. Can you sit yourselves reasonably comfortably on your chairs...if you're more comfortable with your head resting on your arms on the table in front of you, that's fine...but sitting in a way that you are going to be able to sit without disturbing other people for fifteen or twenty minutes. (Pause whilst people arrange themselves.)...could you four spread yourselves out a bit, please...

'Let your eyelids close, and go into your own world of your own thoughts and imagination ...Just be aware of all the thoughts that are coming into your mind...pictures, thoughts, anxieties, worries, hopes…Imagine that you have beside you a large basket, and into that basket could you put those thoughts as they come to you…The things that you notice around you — the shuffle, the noises from outside…put those into the basket as well…And now put that basket on one side with those thoughts in it…knowing that you can pick up those thoughts later if you wish to — or you can simply discard them…

'Become aware of your own breathing…and as you breathe in, you take in clean fresh air, and a sense of relaxation and calmness…and you breathe out any tensions…

'And now imagine yourselves on a path in the hills at night — it's a full moon…notice your surroundings. Just take time to look at your surroundings whatever they are like…trees if there are any…sky…mountains…You walk along this path in the moonlight, noticing the things around you…As you walk, you come to a small side turning in the path — the side turning goes further up the hill. And you know that this side path goes more steeply up the hill to a cave which is the home of a very old and very wise person…and you turn off, up this path, again noticing your surroundings…

'And as you come near to the cave, there's a small camp fire at the mouth of the cave…And you can see by the light of the flames, someone sitting at the far side of the camp fire near the cave. You can't see very clearly…and you go up to the fire and there's some firewood, and logs, stacked near it…and you pick some up and put them on the fire so that it will burn more brightly …And as it burns more brightly so you can see this person sitting there more clearly. Just notice them…female? or male?…notice their face …their clothes…their eyes…their hands. Just take time to notice all the details of this person who is sitting quietly beside the camp fire, near the entrance to the cave…You realise that this person can answer any question that you wish to ask them…so you ask them some question that is of importance to you…Notice their reaction as you ask the question…their face, any gestures …Do they reply?…they may not…If they do, what answer do they give?…

'And now in your imagination become this wise person who is sitting beside the camp fire …(NOTE: forgot to remind at any stage that our imagination is not constrained by the ordinary rationality — anything can happen!)

'What is your life like? How does it feel? What is it like being there? What is your attitude to your visitor?…How do you feel about the question you've been asked?…What do you say or do in

reply?…

'And now become yourself again, if you wish…and continue the conversation, the dialogue…let your imagination go wherever you wish it to go…you may find my suggestions helpful, but if you don't, whatever direction you let your imagination go is just fine.

(NOTE: I recall realising that I had forgotten to remind of these permissions at the beginning of the fantasy journey.)

'As you continue your conversation with this wise person, do you understand the answer that you've been given to your question?…Do you ask other questions?…How do you feel towards this person sitting on the other side of the fire?…Just for a minute or two, continue to be with them, talk with them, be with them…

'Now as the wise person again…become the wise person sitting beside the camp fire, have you anything else to say to your visitor before they leave you?…And when you are ready, become yourself again, knowing that you will soon have to say goodbye, and leave…

'Have you anything else to say?…And just as you are about to turn and leave, the wise person turns to an old leather bag that's behind them, and reaches into it, and pulls out of it to give you, something very special to give to you…what is it…examine it…how do you feel about this gift that you've been given?…Tell the wise person how you feel, and say goodbye to them…

'And now returning down the path, carrying your gift…notice the path very carefully, so that you can return again at a later time if you wish…Notice your surroundings again…And so you come back down the mountain side and rejoin the main path…And keeping your eyes closed, return, when you are ready, to this room …but you have in front of you, still in your imagination, the gift that you were given by the wise person. Just notice it…identify yourself with it…if it feels right, let yourself become the gift, whatever it is, in your imagination…What is it like being this gift?…What are your qualities?…how are you used?…are you appreciated?…are you valued?…Now become yourself again, and have another look at the gift in front of you…Do you notice anything else about it?….And when you are ready, put the gift away in your imagination, knowing that you can return to it whenever you wish…Say goodbye to that gift for the moment…and when you're ready, bring your attention back to this room, back to the people who are here.

'I want us to take about five minutes, or so, for you in your groups — I would like you in your

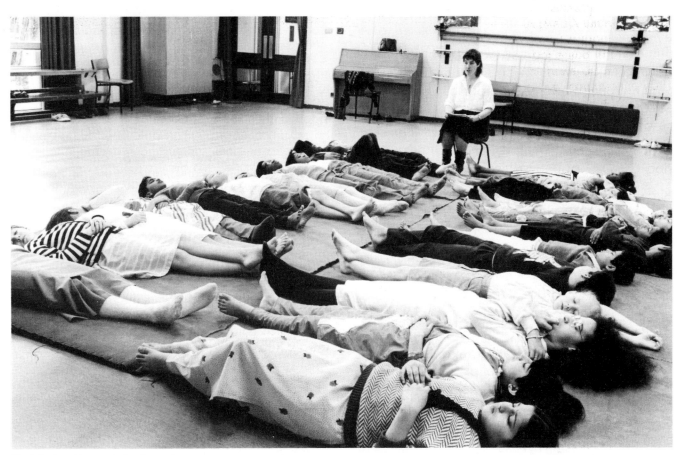

'Settle back and let your body relax . . .'

groups, each to take it in turn to tell the others in your group as much as you choose to of the experience as it's been for you. Whether you've followed along with my instructions as a guide, or whatever it was that you did...

'I want you to talk about it in a particular way. First of all decide what order you're going to do it in...give yourselves numbers 1, 2, 3, 4, or letters A, B, C, D, and just take it in that order. When it's your turn to talk about your experience, I want you to do it in a particular way. The way I want you to do it, is to imagine that it's happening again – talk about it in the first person present tense..."I am walking along this narrow rocky path. There are pine trees on either side. The path is quite steep and difficult to see. I can just make out that there is a full moon. I notice the side turning, it's not very obvious, but it's just noticeable that it's there..." You're doing it in the first person, and present tense.

'When it's not your turn, your task is primarily to listen...You may want to ask questions to help the other people – not simply out of curiosity – but to help the person who's talking.

'Try to talk in the present tense if you can, but don't make too much of a thing of it...So...in

your groups, just go round – we'll give you five minutes or so...

'Listen – on these cards which I've just given out – I don't want you to put your names on them. Rachel...don't put your names on them...this is actually to help us to move into tomorrow's lesson easily and quickly. I would like you, if you can, to write on one or more of these things:
the question or questions you asked;
the answer or answers you got;
the gift, or gifts, you were given.
'One or more of these three things. Don't put your names on them.'

A Future Visualisation

Based on an idea from Guy Dauncey

This script is transcribed from the tape-recording of a lesson, two sessions of about 40 minutes each, with a fourth-year secondary class of average ability.

Students should be in groups of four, each group round a large table or group of desks.

▼ First Session

'The exercise we are about to start has three parts (voice quite quiet, calm, relaxed). I want to get through one part today, and the other two parts tomorrow. Each part has three stages. The first stage is a quiet, thoughtful, reflective stage, where we go off into our own imaginations, and I will be guiding you, directing you in that. The second stage will be five minutes or so when you try to express some of your thoughts on the paper that you have. And the third stage will be talking about it, amongst the three or four of you at the table — you'll be talking about it in a particular way, which I'll explain when we get there.

'So for the first stage — the first part which we will be visualising today — put everything down, and sit reasonably comfortably. Try not to have anything which will disturb other people. Listen for a moment to the sounds you can hear outside the room. Be aware of how you're sitting on the chair. Just let yourself relax. Let the feeling of relaxation spread through your body. Be aware of your toes — let those relax, your ankles, your calves, your knees and thighs. Let the feeling of relaxation spread up through your fingers, up through your arms, your shoulders and your neck. Let the muscles of your face relax. And if you're comfortable with it, let your eyes close.

'I'd like you to imagine yourself in some place that you know well, just be aware of it, notice it, notice the things you like about it, that you dislike. Think of some other place where you really enjoy being, at home, or at school, a warm beach, the top of a mountain, wherever. Somewhere you enjoy being. Think of a town or a city that you know, its traffic, its buildings, shops, factories, factory chimneys, and just for a minute or two explore in your imagination different places around the country, around the world …

'And now imagine yourself leaving the surface of the earth. Perhaps taking off in an aircraft, or in some other way, away from the surface of the earth, seeing more and more of it, seeing the roads, the cars, the towns, the villages, seeing the fields becoming smaller and smaller, and in your imagination you continue to leave the earth until you can no longer distinguish the details. You can see the sea, the clouds, and the land, and the colours of the land, and you continue, in your imagination, to move away from the earth until you begin to see it as a large sphere, filling the whole of your vision, the continents, the oceans, and as you continue to move away from it, the world, the sphere becomes smaller, and you begin to see it as that rather beautiful blue and green, brown and white globe, that we've become familiar with, that the astronauts have so often seen … our planet earth as we view it from space. Just enjoy seeing, and being aware of that beautiful blue, green, brown, white planet … our home …

'And now in your imagination, begin to return slowly towards the planet … it becomes larger … you begin to see more detail again … not just the general outlines and shapes … outlines of the continents, and the islands, and as you come nearer, you begin to realise that, somehow or other, it has … changed … it's not quite the same … it looks the same … but you sense, it isn't. And as you come nearer still, you can see more of the details, the mountains, the hills, the deserts, the towns, the cities … you realise how it has changed, it has become somehow or other the earth of your hopes, of your imagination, the sort of planet, the sort of world that you would always have liked to live in, for yourself. The sort of earth, the sort of planet that you would always hope that your children, your grandchildren, would be able to live in. The world of your hopes, your dreams …

'And so you return to some place that's familiar, yet different, on the surface of the earth. Notice how it's different, notice how it has changed, notice the things that are the same, the things that are familiar, and begin to explore this planet earth, subtly changed. Visit some of the places that you visited in your imagination before you left. Notice how they are different, how they have changed.

'And in a minute I want you to take your sheet of paper, some of the pastels, and in some way — not as a work of art — to represent this earth of your hopes or your dreams. Either as an actual drawing, or by some abstract representation, try to represent, when you're ready, something of this world that you hope to live in. Try to do it without talking, please …'

Allow 10 to 15 minutes for drawing. It may be helpful to use some quiet background music at this time, for example, Oxygene *by Jean Michel Jarre;* Ascension *by Clifford White.*

If the session is to end at this time, the drawings should be named and collected in.

▼ Second Session

'Carrying on with what we were doing yesterday — thinking about what the world is like, and the sort of world we would hope to live in. Yesterday, we got to the stage, with these drawings, where you were trying to express on paper something of what you'd imagined in the visualisation section. What I want to start off by doing, for the first part of this lesson, is for about five minutes — no more than five minutes — for you, in your groups, each to just explain, as best you can to the other people in the group, what your drawing represents, and some of the features of what you were thinking about yesterday.

'One or two things that are important about the way you do it – it's easiest if you take turns, to talk about your own drawings. When you're looking at someone else's drawing and they're explaining it to you, it's OK to ask questions about it, but no judgements or criticisms, no remarks like 'It's rotten', or 'It's lousy', or 'It's weird – or even 'It's terrific' or 'It's great …'

'Questions like 'What does that mean?' or 'Why did you draw that, particularly?' are fine. But no other sorts of questions. So take turns, and … I'll give you about five minutes for this.'

The same music as in the previous session is a useful way of giving an additional link.

'OK. Can you start by putting those drawings from yesterday on one side. Put them together.

'Now I know this is a bit difficult because we haven't been able to go straight on – we had 40 minutes yesterday, and we've had a day's gap before carrying on … I want to try, nevertheless, to return to what we were thinking about yesterday, so can you just stop what you're doing, and sit comfortably …

'Let your thoughts go quietly back, as best you can, to where you left off yesterday. Having been on this journey into space in your imagination, and returning, you find your world different, subtly different, to the world with which you're familiar … being the world, instead, of your hopes, your dreams … the sort of world you would always have liked to live in … that you would like to live in … the sort of world that you might hope for, for your children and for future generations … And just for a moment or two, in your imagination, revisit some of those places that you visited yesterday…. In this world of your hopes and dreams … you have a part … How do you fit in? Perhaps you've helped it to become this way … What is your part in making it this way? However you see it … what is your part in it? How do you relate to other people, how do you treat the animals, nature, how do you fit into the cities or towns … if there are any. And now, in a moment or two I'm going to ask you to take a fresh sheet of paper, and to try to represent on that sheet of paper, something of the way you fit into this world of your hopes … this world that you would like to be in, in the future. As yesterday, it's not meant to be a work of art … just an expression of the way you fit in, of your part in it …

'I'll give out the pastels, and then when you're ready, you can begin …'

Music from the same record or cassette may be helpful. About ten minutes should be allowed for the drawing.

'I'd like you to be finishing off in a couple of minutes … remember, you don't have to produce a finished work of art or anything …

'OK … If you can finish off at whatever stage you've got to … It may well be that you've left things unfinished … that doesn't matter. Just finish off and stop …

'What I'd like you to do now, as with the drawings from yesterday, is just spend five minutes explaining to the other people in your group what it means to you, how you see yourself in this world of your hopes, of the future – that you would like to be able to live in.

'So, again, we'll take about five minutes for that. As before, you can certainly ask questions, but no comments or judgements about the drawings of the other people in your group …'

Music can be switched on again.

'About a minute, then we'll stop and move on to the next stage …

'OK. On each table put your papers together, and put them on one side.

'Sit comfortably again … make yourself comfortable and move back into your imagination again … into the world that you were thinking about, the world that you'd like to live in, and your place in it and how you fit in. And whatever sort of world it is, I wonder what sort of qualities of character like courage, or patience, or strength, or gentleness, … what sort of characteristics, what sort of qualities you feel you need to live in that world, or to help make the world, that we live in now, the sort of world that you would like to live in … perhaps … courage … anger … determination … persistence. Just try and think of one quality … a character that you feel you need, and when you find one, hold that character, that quality, that characteristic in your mind … and just think about it for a moment or two … patience, love, joy, spontaneity, or whatever. When you've got the quality that you need, take a third sheet of paper and try to represent this quality in some way on the paper, using the pastel crayons, whether with an abstract drawing, or by writing the word and decorating it, or …'

Five minutes should be allowed for this drawing.

'OK – finish off in about a minute …

'Once again, in your groups, take turns to explain your drawing, and talk about the quality of character that you've chosen … as with the others, you may ask questions but make no judgements or other comments.'

Inner ecology in the classroom

by **Sandy Parker**

Over the last ten years of my classroom Religious Education I have been using various approaches exploring the inner world of our hopes and fears, of our imagination and dreams. Some I have also found useful in a smaller amount of Science and Maths work.

In the RE context we used short centering exercises, in which focused physical and mental relaxation helped us to integrate mind and body, and to feel balanced, and responsive to our environment. We used simple meditation exercises, and guided fantasies – not just daydreams, but rather, free of intentional control, we are enabled to explore our own inner world, and through this learn more about our identity and experience. With creative visualisation we used our imaginations to discover our hopes for ourselves and our world, and to find ways of beginning to realise them. The stories of Idries Shah[3] picked us up, shook us, and changed our perceptions in ways that rational argument rarely can. Sixth form questioning about extra-sensory perception led us to try experiments in telepathy and clairvoyance.[4] We may not have reached any conclusions, but the results challenged our thinking.

Student feedback was mainly positive, and encouraging. Most enjoyed such opportunities – my classroom became, in the words of one student, a place where anything can happen! Others put it differently:

'It's a good change from other lessons'
'You look forward to it'
'You can think about all the worries you have, and express them all'
and even:
'Crap!'

I became involved with the Centre for Global Education at the University of York, and undertook a research project attempting systematically to evaluate these approaches. I found two analytical models particularly helpful. Satish Kumar[5] reminded me of the interactions between the different levels (personal, local, and global) and the different dimensions of our relationships: with our environment; with other people; and with ourselves. And Magnus Haavelsrud[6] gave a model of our knowledge of the world: it includes future possibilities as well as past experience and knowledge. It looks at the continuum of spatial experience and knowledge from the immediate and personal to the global and cosmic.

I put a number of units together into a term's course with a group of 22 fourth-year secondary students, that I would ordinarily have been taking for a non-examination RE course. They willingly agreed to take part:

A: He gave us the choice.
B: If you didn't want to do it this term, you could have moved into the other group.
C: I'd rather be in this one.

I explained the rationale and purpose of the course to the group, suggesting the following areas:

the range of our human potential and possibilities;
the inner world of our hopes and fears, our fantasies and imagination;
and, our attitudes to the future, whether of despair and denial or of hope and promise.

Possible units for such a course were briefly described, and the group was asked to order them according to their interest and understanding, making any links between them that they could. One student commented: 'It was a bit confusing because people didn't take it seriously – to get the right ideas. As people got used to the course, they took it more seriously.'

We began by considering some of the knowledge about the functioning of our brains, and what it might be like if we were able to use more of our potential:

'I'd be able to understand the thoughts of other people more'
'I'd have a photographic memory'
'I'd like to have the ability to walk on fire and not feel it or burn myself'
'I'd be able to do anything I wanted, just by thinking about it'

This led us to consider the possibility of a 'sixth sense', with some simple experiments.[7] Most found this fun, and thought provoking , if inconclusive!

'I think that telepathy is a skill, just like a person may have a skill to play the piano'
'I didn't find it very useful, but looking at the class – some did'

In another exercise[8] to develop the interaction of our senses, we experienced some music, responding with all our senses. This produced some remarkable scenes – of muscular, sporting, 15 year old boys lying on the floor, totally engrossed, and then producing very sensitive drawings of their 'experience'.

'I felt listening to the music was most interesting ... it worked for me. I drew FREEDOM.'

'I liked this, especially the drawing. I found this was the best way to convey our thoughts, pictures, ideas.'

'It gave me a flash of colour, hence pink and white on piccy (picture) and lots of colour.'

Centering and meditation exercises also produced mainly enthusiastic responses:

'Well that was relaxing. Weird. May do it myself in future.'

'... relaxing and enjoyable. I can well believe that people use this method of relaxing everyday.'

'I couldn't concentrate – thought about reincarnation.'

Next we turned to consider our attitudes to the future, first sharing our anxieties and despair about the present,[9] and then visualising the world of our hopes.[10] Another teacher who was present as an observer, and interviewed some of the students afterwards, commented:

'(the) consensus amongst the group ... was that your lessons made them think beyond the bounds of their own needs and experiences. One girl felt that it shouldn't take RE lessons to make them think of the future.

Initial feelings about the future were pessimistic, but most of the students felt more optimisitc about the future and the part they could play in it because of your lessons.'

The final unit was a guided fantasy,[11] in which students were encouraged to find a question of importance to them, discover their own answers to it, and receive a gift. The similarity of style to the previous visualisation caused some difficulty, and there was not the opportunity to follow this up in the way it deserved. From the brief feedback that there was:

'(the wise person) spoke to me in riddles, and I got mad and hit him, then he just disappeared!'

'The gift was a gift of love, and it was a great feeling.'

'Q. What is the secret of life? A. Self-power, free love and no greed.'

'Q. Where am I? A. You are where you are!'

We ended the course with a celebration of games, music and whiteboard graffiti.

In considering how to evaluate the course, pre-determined questionnaires did not seem appropriate. It was a co-operative venture, with continuous interaction with the students at all stages. Each student kept a diary as a means of personal reflection, and of direct dialogue with the teacher. A small group of students was interviewed each week, outside observers were accepted into the group, and all students completed a written end of course assessment. Follow-up interviews were also arranged three months and six months later.

I've learnt an enormous amount from the students, about myself as a teacher. Possibly it was a mistake to put these units together into one course, rather than using them as naturally integral parts of other work. One of the students was new to the group at the beginning of the term's course, and therefore new to our way of working. Let him have the last word. Early in the term, he wrote: 'This is an absolute waste of time ... All this stuff is so much crap.' Being interviewed at about the same time, with three others, he said: 'We shouldn't talk about ourselves ... everybody knows enough about themselves ... you can find out about yourself by reading a book.' Towards the end of the course, meeting with an observer after the guided fantasy, he commented: 'You find out about yourself – what you were told, what you thought, and what you were given ... tells you what kind of person you are ... It shows you what you really want in life.' A little later in the same interview, commenting about the purpose of the course he said, 'He's all right ... It's good – he's trying to help us so that we can understand life a bit more.'

Our World

▼ Resources

A3 drawing paper, A4 writing paper, felt tip pens, crayons, etc.; a copy of the work-sheet, as described below, for each student; additional stimulus material, for example, posters of people and places, a poster of planet earth from space, poems, lists of useful words.

▼ Procedure

Students should be given a copy of the work-sheet, which includes these instructions, together with a limited quantity of stimulus material:

---

1 Think about the world you know – the places, the people, the animals; its wealth, its poverty; its pleasures and its sufferings.
2 Think about the world you would like to live in, and you would like your children to live in.
3 Think about the world as seen by astronauts from space – that beautiful blue, green, and white planet that we live on – 'Spaceship Earth'.
4 Take several minutes to imagine, to daydream about, to visualise some of these things.

Then either: Draw a model of the world community in the year 2000
(a) working well
(b) working badly
Write an explanation of your drawing(s).

Or: There's this Martian. It has just arrived on planet earth, and you are the first human beings it meets. It is friendly and intelligent but doesn't understand your language. Draw a sketch map of the planet to show the Martian what is going on in the world. Write an explanation of your sketch map.

Students should then have the opportunity to present their maps or drawings to others, either in small groups, or to the whole class. Students should be asked not to make judgements about each other's work, but statements like 'I'm puzzled by that ...' or 'I don't understand why ...' or 'I'm intrigued by ...' are helpful in encouraging another student to talk about her ideas.

▼ Potential

This exercise provides the opportunity for examining our hopes and fears about the world we live in, and for an imaginative visualisation of possible futures. It introduces the idea of creative visualisation through familiar classroom procedures.

▼ Variations

The work can be done individually or in groups of 2 or 3. Appropriate quiet background music may be helpful, for example Equinoxe, by Jean Michel Jarre; The Flight of the Condor, BBC TV.

The whole unit can be completed in one session, or can be divided between several lessons. It could easily lead on to the preparation of a display of alternative maps and models of student perceptions of their world, both present and future.

▼ Source

Sandy Parker, adapted from an exercise in Richardson, R., Learning for Change, World Studies Project, 1976.

Cat and Mouse Fantasy

▼ Resources

A quiet open area, preferably carpeted, so that students can lie comfortably on the floor.

▼ Procedure

Students are asked to lie down, find a comfortable position and close their eyes. The following passage, perhaps embroidered with additional detail, is read slowly, but with animation, and with fairly long pauses between sections and after each question.

'Imagine that you are walking out of this room and down a long sidewalk. You come to an old deserted house. Now you are going up the drive, up the porch steps. You try the door and it creaks open. You step inside and look around a dark empty room.

1 Suddenly you begin to feel a strange sensation in your body. It begins to shudder and tremble. You feel yourself growing smaller and smaller. Now you're only as high as the window sill. You keep shrinking until you look up and see the ceiling very far away, very high. You are only as tall as a book and still growing smaller.

2 Something else begins to happen. You notice you're changing shape. Your nose is getting longer and longer, and hair is covering your whole body. Now you're down on all fours and you realise that you've changed into a mouse.

3 Look around the room from your mouse position. You're sitting on one side of the room. Then you see the door move slightly.

4 In walks a cat. It sits down and looks around very slowly and with great casualness. Then it gets up and calmly begins to wander around the room. You are very, very still. Feel your heart beating. Feel your own breathing. Watch the cat.

5 Now it sees you and begins to stalk you. Ever so slowly, it comes to you. Then it stops right in front of you and crouches. What are you feeling? What does it look like? What choices do you have right now? What do you decide to do?

6 Just as the cat moves to leap on you, both of your bodies begin to tremble and shake. You feel yourself being transformed again. This time you are growing larger again. The cat seems to be getting smaller. And changing shape. You see the cat the same size as you, and now smaller.

7 The cat is turning into a mouse and you have become a cat. How do you feel being bigger and no longer trapped? How does the mouse look to you? Do you know what the mouse is feeling? What are you feeling? Decide what you're going to do and then do it. What do you feel now?

8 It is happening again. The changing. You are getting bigger and bigger. Almost your full size.

And now you are you again. You walk out the door and back to this building and this room. You open your eyes and look around you.'

▼ Potential

Class discussion can first be directed towards **feelings**. *How did it feel, for instance, when the cat entered the room, when it began to stalk you, when the cat got smaller and when you became the cat? It can then move on to* **choices**. *What did you decide to do when the cat crouched in front of you? What course of action did you decide to take after you had become a cat and the cat had become a mouse? The response elicited from questions about feelings and choices can provide a springboard for discussion of dominance/aggression and submission in interpersonal, intergroup and international relationships. Who are the cats and who are the mice (the powerful and the powerless) in various contexts, interpersonal to global? Is might right? What attitudes, feelings, and behaviours do unequal relationships engender in the powerful and powerless? Can students think of occasions in which the cat/mouse metamorphosis has been mirrored in the real world? (Upper secondary students often cite South Africa and Zimbabwe as examples in response to these last two questions.) Or of cases in which a fundamental change in power relationships is likely to occur in the future? What options are open to you, the mouse, when you become the cat? What options are/were open to the once underprivileged or powerless in cases where they assume/have assumed power? How should the once-powerful be treated?*

Junior/Secondary, 15 minutes.

▼ Source

Wolsk, D., An Experience-centered Curriculum, Unesco Educational Studies and Documents, No. 17, p. 45.

References

1 Stevens, J., *Awareness*, Utah, Real People Press, 1971, p. 38.
2 Bry, A., *Visualization*, New York, Harper & Row, 1979; Gawain, S., *Creative Visualization*, California, Whatever Publishing, 1978.
3 Shah, I., *Caravan of Dreams*, Octagon Press, 1968.
4 Hendricks, G., and Roberts, T. B., *The Second Centering Book*, New Jersey, Prentice-Hall, 1977, pp. 157–97.
5 Kumar, S., 'Pilgrims or tourists' in *Resurgence*, No. 102, Jan–Feb 1984, pp. 34–5.
6 Haavelsrud, M., *The Bulletin of Peace Proposals*, No. 2, 1981. For a similar version of the model, see p. 22.
7 See note 4 above.
8 Houston, J., *The Possible Human*, J. P. Tarcher, 1982, p. 478.
9 See p. 156 (**Mini Despair and Empowerment** exercise).
10 See p. 194 (**Our World** exercise).
11 See p. 187 (**Discovering our own Wisdom** fantasy).

9 Role plays

Warm-up exercises

Role play is a natural human activity. Students assume a variety of roles during a normal day – female, male, child, student, friend, enemy, leader, follower, etc. Younger children, in particular, take on a host of imaginary, and often adult, roles during normal play, creating complex characters and scenarios which are acted out with sincerity and commitment. In artificially constructed role play, however, students are asked to take on roles with which they may be unfamiliar or uncomfortable, or to act out situations which they have never experienced, for a particular purpose: perhaps to heighten self-awareness or to develop conflict resolution and problem-solving skills. Students will vary as to the ease with which they can assume different roles, so warm-up exercises are particularly important for those who feel inhibited in any way. A brief warm-up period is useful, however, for all students to facilitate the transfer from the role they are in (a student) to that which they are being asked to take on and to practise the skills required for effective role play. Here are some examples of warm-up exercises; many of them can be used in addition as discussion starters.

Non-verbal Warm-ups

Students work in pairs or small groups. Each participant selects from a pack a card on which is written the outline of a common, but problematic situation. Participants have a minute or two to work out and practise a solution, then take it in turns to demonstrate this non-verbally to their partners or groups. Some suggested situations:

- There's a fly on your nose and your hands are covered in paint.
- Your key won't fit in the lock; the telephone rings.
- Your foot is stuck in a hole.
- You have fruit pips stuck in your teeth.
- Your fishing line is caught up on a distant rock.
- You're at the top of a tree; the branch you are standing on begins to crack.

Persuasion

Students work in pairs. Each partner chooses a different colour and has three minutes to convince the other of the case for choosing her colour rather than her partner's. Any means of verbal persuasion or argument can be used.

Variation: One participant sits on a chair, the other stands up. The standing partner has three minutes to convince the other, through verbal means only, as to why she should give up the chair. If successful, or in any case after three minutes, participants change roles. Both of these exercises can give rise to a range of persuasion techniques such as flattery, bribery, trickery and verbal abuse; they may also result in an entrenchment of original positions.

Traders

Students work in pairs. Each is a trader with some personal qualities or attributes which she wants to exchange, for example, a sense of humour, wisdom, good looks, gentleness, musical ability. The two traders haggle and barter over the relative values of these items, each trying to strike a good deal. A useful exercise for personal clarification of values and attitudes as well as for practising role play and communication skills.

Challenging Roles

In pairs or small groups, students act out brief scenarios in which the role or an attribute of one of the characters is different from what might be expected. Some suggestions:

- a judge who is caught shoplifting;
- a soldier who refuses to fight;
- an English teacher who can't spell;
- a sea captain who is seasick;
- a butcher who is a vegetarian;

From seemingly comic or alarming situations, serious reflection and discussion can develop from the role play concerning stereotypes and assumptions.

Touch Code

Students close their eyes and assume they are also deaf and dumb. They walk around the room to form random pairs and they try to communicate simple ideas or messages to each other through the senses of touch and smell only. Before the exercise begins students reflect on what they might be able to communicate, e.g. asking and telling the time; recognising each other's identity; communicating feelings of friendship, anger, fear; warning each other of danger. A useful activity for exploring the potential of touch and smell in communication and some of the cultural taboos surrounding these senses.

Sources:

Non-verbal Warm-Ups in Michele and Craig Borba, Self-esteem: a Classroom Affair. Volume 2; **Persuasion, Traders, Challenging Roles** and **Touch Code** all derived from ideas in Alex Davison and Peter Gordon, Games and Simulations in Action.

Role play techniques

A range of techniques can be applied to role play situations so as to emphasise and develop different skills. This affords the facilitator considerable flexibility in the management of role plays, enabling her to respond quickly to students' needs and difficulties. Here are some examples:

Role Reversal

Students working in pairs or small groups play prescribed (and often conflicting) roles for a set period of time. At the end of this period and without discussion, participants switch roles so that they now have to represent an opposing view. Discussion then follows, out of role, on what the two roles felt like; whether any alternative solutions were found or new perspectives gained; which role they felt happier in, and why. Role reversal is a particularly useful technique for exploring situations of conflict or dilemma.

Freeze

During a role play situation the facilitator commands participants to 'freeze', at which point the action stops but they stay in role. Questions can then be asked by the teacher, acting as interviewer, such as 'What are your feelings now?', 'What do you think your partner's feelings are?', or 'Have you really listened to and understood what your partner has said?' Questions can be reflected upon individually or answered in the working pairs or groups. The action then continues for a short while before being 'frozen' again and more questions put. The process of stopping and reflecting often lends clarity to the situation in progress by pinpointing actions or attitudes which may be hindering the reaching of an agreement or solution.

Alter Ego

Each participant in a role play has an alter ego – another person beside or behind her. The alter ego's role is to say what her character might be really thinking but not expressing. For example:

A What did you think of that television programme?
(A [alter ego]: I thought it was awful.)
B Oh, not bad, I suppose.
(B [alter ego]: I wonder if she thought it was good or bad?)
A I thought the story was a bit silly.
(A He didn't really like it, did he?)
B Yes, but some of the acting was good.
(B Actually, I thoroughly enjoyed the story.)

After the role play, participants discuss the accuracy of the alter ego's remarks and the part that such secret thoughts play in everyday interaction between people.

Variation: Each participant can have two alter egos, representing conflicting or contradictory thoughts and feelings.

Quick Decision-making

Students working in pairs or small groups are given roles or an outline of a situation. In role, they are then given a problem or conflict to solve and a short period of time (perhaps one or two minutes) in which to come up with a solution. At the end of the allotted time, solutions are announced to the whole group; discussion follows on the processes employed to reach a decision and how participants felt under the pressure of time.

Identity Swap

In this technique each student assumes the role of someone she knows well. Working in pairs, participants spend some time closely observing each other's mannerisms, ways of speaking, writing, walking, etc. Partners then swap identities and, for an agreed period of time, continue the normal lesson in role. As well as assuming physical characteristics, participants should act in accordance with their perception of each other's values, attitudes and expectations. Following the role play, participants discuss the experience, describing any insights or new perspectives gained either about themselves or their partner. To be successful, this technique requires a highly-affirmed group; if the temptation to ridicule or caricature is avoided, participants can develop high levels of empathetic understanding.

'Getting Out of Role' Techniques

After role playing, particularly in extended role plays or simulation games, students may need to physically and mentally 'shake off' their roles so that objective discussion and reflection can take place. Some simple techniques can be used, such as:

- verbal release – shouting loudly, verbally expressing pent-up emotions;
- physical release – jumping, running, dancing;
- emotional release – hugging, or using other physical gestures towards other participants;
- change of scene – going outside or moving into a different room.

In addition, some of the 'pace changer' activities described in Section 5 might be used.

Sources

Identity Swap derived from an idea in Donna Brandes and Paul Ginnis, A Guide to Student-centred Learning; others: various.

Role play situations

'Although role play is normally associated with areas of superficial problem-oriented learning (interview techniques, skill training, social skills, work, etc.), I firmly believe that it can be, if handled correctly, a very effective means of creating learning situations that go far beyond the superficial. There is a very narrow line between playing a role (pretending to be someone else) and a close identification with that role sufficient to stimulate very real responses in the player ...' (From John Carey, 'Peace education through drama – a personal approach', World Studies Journal, *Vol. 3, No. 3, Spring, 1982, p. 21.*) In addition to its usefulness as a tool to develop decision-making and problem-solving skills, role play provides a suitable vehicle for students to develop self-awareness, to acquire new perspectives and to explore a range of global issues and problems such as conflict, rights violations, prejudice and discrimination. The range of pair or group role play situations relevant to the global curriculum is limitless: here are a few suggestions:

1 Student-Student

Bully In the corridor, a student knocks the books out of another student's hand. Then the bully steps on the books and laughs.

Insult A student comes to school in tatty old clothes. Another student insults him consistently about his clothing.

Racism Three students are playing a game. A fourth student, who is black, asks if he can join in. One of the three replies: 'No, we don't want any wogs'. You object to that remark.

Exclusion Two students are playing a game. A third asks to join in; one student doesn't like her, so says 'No'. The second student hesitates.

Cheating Two students are playing chess during break. One accuses the other of cheating and refuses to continue playing.

Repatriation In the corridor a student in your class offers you some National Front leaflets and asks you to sign a 'repatriation for blacks' petition. You are insulted.

2 Student-Teacher

Stealing Money has been stolen from the teacher's purse. One student is suspected, but there is no real evidence.

Disobedience A teacher asks a student to tidy her desk before leaving. She refuses. On being asked again, she swears at the teacher.

Discrimination A female student wants to join in the football training session. The PE teacher refuses her permission on the grounds that 'football is a boys' game'.

Lateness For the third day in a week a student walks in ten minutes late. The teacher has just finished giving directions to everyone else.

Threat A female teacher tells a 15 year old boy that she will report him to the Head for consistent disobedience. He threatens to 'do her in' after school.

Rights A teacher asks a student to write out 100 lines as punishment for rudeness in class. The student refuses, saying that the punishment contravenes Article 5 of the UN Declaration of Human Rights – the right to freedom from degrading punishment.

3 Adult Conflict

Noise Two college students are sharing a room. One wants to listen to his new rock record, the other wants to study for his exams.

Street Hassle You are a young woman walking home. A male friend of your brother's whom you don't like, joins you; you cross the street; so does he.

Theatre You arrange to meet a friend at 7.45 for an 8.00 performance; she has the tickets. She arrives at 8.10, so you can't go in until the second act.

Subway In the subway you see four teenagers bothering an old man. They call him names, tease him and then begin to push him aggressively.

4 Parent-Child

Privacy A parent has found a cigarette in a child's pocket whilst doing the washing. The parent doesn't approve of smoking. The child has just returned home.

Family Meeting A family is trying to share out the chores. The mother usually does them, but then gets angry because no one helps. She doesn't like asking others to help continually.

Responsibility A 13 year old girl wants to take on a baby-sitting job for more pocket money, for two evenings a week. Her parents argue she is not old enough.

Freedom A 15 year old girl wants to go camping with her boyfriend whom the parents don't know very well. The parents express their anxiety; the girl threatens to go with or without their permission.

Rights Role Plays

▼ Resources

Classroom to be laid out so that students, working in pairs, can sit facing each other.

▼ Procedure

Students in pairs, choose to be A or B. They are each given a rights role card to read (see samples) and asked to go into role to argue out the issues surrounding their conflict of rights. From time to time the teacher can ask the students to change seats and reverse roles, picking up the argument where their partner left off. She can also 'freeze' the group, bringing a particular student 'to life' again by tapping her on the shoulder before interviewing her as to her views on the argument she is having. The partner can, in turn, be brought 'to life' and interviewed. It is recommended that at least two sets of role cards are used simultaneously and that students are put into at least two scenarios in the one session. Debriefing should follow each round of role playing.

A During the lunch break you decide to go back to the classroom to finish off the project you had started in the morning. Your friend comes in to remind you of the netball/football practice for the school team (of which you are a member), which is about to begin.

B You are a member of the school netball/football team which is about to begin a practice session in the lunch break. You notice that your friend is missing; on returning to the classroom you find her/him doing some project work.

A You share a bedroom with your sister/brother. One evening you are sitting in your room trying to finish your homework when your sister/brother walks in; she/he wants to play her/his record.

B You share a bedroom with your sister/brother. One evening you return home having just bought a new record which you are dying to play. You go straight up to your room and find your sister/brother in there doing her/his homework.

▼ Potential

This is a lively way of revealing the difficulties involved when the rights claimed by people conflict. It can also be used to give students practice in resolving the kind of rights conflict that can occur. Divergent and lateral thinking skills are very helpful in this kind of exercise! Questions such as 'What was the nature of the rights conflict between you?', 'Which rights claimed were, in your view, the more important and why?', 'Did you find any ways out of the conflict between you?', may prove useful triggers for discussion.

Primary/Secondary, 30 minutes.

▼ Source

Centre for Global Education

Other sources of ideas and suggestions for role play:

Michele and Craig Borba, Self-esteem: a Classroom Affair. Volume 2, pp. 116–17; Donna Brandes and Paul Ginnis, A Guide to Student-centred Learning, pp. 238–40, 248–9; Alec Davison and Peter Gordon Games and Simulations in Action, pp. 38–53; Priscilla Prutzman et al., The Friendly Classroom for a Small Planet, pp. 51–2; John Seely, In Role: Materials for Dramatic Role-play and Discussion for 13–16 year olds, Edward Arnold, 1978.

A Simulation Model

by **Richard Heery** and **Mike Pasternak**, Head of English and Head of Drama respectively at La Châtaigneraie, International School of Geneva

Mr _____ is a very interested parent of a student at our school and a man whose job it is, amongst other things, to send people out into the field in Africa to work and develop projects for the UN. 'I get many young men and women applying for posts as development officers in Africa,' he told us. 'Virtually all of them are highly qualified academically, but alas few of them are adequately qualified in the ability to empathise with the people they will be working with. That is why I'm excited by your work. It teaches the children to empathise; perhaps even more important than being taught the facts.' Mr _____ was, in fact, talking about another of our projects, a semi-improvised play about deforestation in the Himalayas, mostly written by the students themselves, called Nepal: The Limits of Existence, but he might equally well have been referring to the scheme of work described below. This work, which we have rather loosely come to call a 'simulation model' of a community threatened by government, or by private development, is the first of a series of major assignments given to twelve/thirteen year olds in an integrated English/Drama course which demands not only an ability to empathise with others but also the ability to make choices, at first 'pretend' ones, but eventually by the beginning of eighth grade very real ones.

The first stage of the unit is the autobiography cards. The teacher prepares an appropriate number of cards to which he affixes a photograph of a man or woman. There will be as many 'women' as there are girls in the class and as many 'men' as there are boys. Careful choices are essential to obtain as wide a variety as possible of ages, appearances, class, colour, etc. The cards are distributed and redistributed three times. The first time the children note on the card the name, age, marital status, and number of children of the person on their card. The second time, and on a different card, they describe briefly some salient features of the person's character. The third time, and keeping in mind the information already recorded on the card by the other children, the character's most formative experience is invented. The cards are then distributed randomly to the boys and girls, and each child for the remainder of the unit adopts the particular identity which she is dealt.

The next step is to create an environment in which these persona will live. Ideally, for the purposes of the unit, the environment will be a small town of perhaps 5—10,000 inhabitants. (This section of the unit can very profitably be taught in conjunction with the geography department to determine settlement patterns.) The town plan can be drawn on the board, for instance, by the children themselves, each child adding to the work of the previous one. (There are variations on this, for example, the first children develop the core — bridging point, market centre, castle, etc.; the next group the next stage in the town's growth and so on.) Such work demands a degree of co-operation and a readiness on the part of the children to share ideas. As the plan becomes more sophisticated so more suggestions and positive criticisms are stimulated and it will be often necessary for the students to modify an original idea — and that in public too!

We should note at this point that as a consequence of this type of work the teacher should expect spontaneous improvisation. For instance, after the research on place names had been completed with one group and a name for the village having been decided, a petition was presented to the Mayor of the town claiming that the name was undignified, that it ought to be changed and that they had a petition signed by a large proportion of the villagers to support their point of view!

'Portbridge Bugle, Portbridge Bugle. Government Plan Nuclear Power Station Outside Portbridge. Buy your copy now! Read all about it.' The children loved the moment the classroom door was flung open, and a teacher dressed in cloth cap and dirty raincoat delivered to them, completely unexpectedly the local newspaper which describes in an appropriate style plans to introduce some drastic new development to the town. (We have to date tried a nuclear power station and a civil airport.) Invariably such news sparks off arguments, discussion, and dissension amongst the members of the class. Clearly some means of dealing with these problems have to be found, and nearly always the students themselves recognise the urgent need to hold a meeting (sometimes one in which they invite the person responsible to answer questions — outside experts or teachers prepared to role play can be used here). The meeting takes place with all the vocabulary, jargon and structures of a public meeting with the children and the teacher acting the part of their persona. The newspaper itself can lead to some very interesting work on bias in writing. It was an eleven year old who first accused the newspaper of bias and made these teachers very aware of the important work that can be done in this area with alert youngsters. The meeting will be supplemented by letters to the newspaper, further editions written by the students themselves, etc.

An appropriate conclusion to the unit is always difficult. Two possibilities (amongst many others) present themselves. Each student looks ahead and, bearing closely in mind the environment and the characters that have been developed, writes either a short story or a play (both of which should later be 'performed' to the group) describing and enacting what would, in their opinion, probably happen.

How do we assess this work? We were confident that English skills — ranging from the control of indirect speech (in the writing of the minutes of a meeting, for instance) to stream of consciousness thoughts and feelings — and drama skills, were developed very fully and were measurable by testing. But what about the skills of decision-making, sensitivity to environmental issues, the ability to co-operate, negotiate and compromise? These skills were far less easy to assess; perhaps completely objectively they are impossible to assess. What was fairly certain though was that the youngsters enjoyed the work. An enjoyment graph was kept which maintained a consistently high rating for 90% of the students. Comments from some parents recorded a high degree of interest being shown in English homework, spontaneous role playing (the setting up of petitions, for instance) was also evidence of commitment, and 'playground pressure' filtered back in the form of 'why can't we do English like your class?' Even other teachers when some of the work was displayed during the school's Development Education Evening evinced a degree of interest.

But we have yet to discover an objective form of assessment for these (we believe) crucially important skills in the 11 and 12 year old student.

10 Simulations

Destruction of a tropical rain forest; simulations can help students understand why it occurs

Timber!

▼ Resources

A large room, capable of having nine groups around the outside and a clear space in the middle.

A Background Card (pp. 207–11) for each participant (see below for numbers of students in each group); 75 paper/plastic cups, 20 of these marked with a blue cross; 30 name badges/labels; prepared card sign for each group giving their name; whistle; tropical rain forest information sheet (see p. 211).

Resources arranged as follows
Seventy-five upturned cups placed in the centre of the room (not too close together) to represent The Forest; nine circles of chairs arranged around the outside of the room, each circle to contain the group's card sign, the group's background cards (one per participant) and a name badge per participant. The facilitator has the whistle; the rain forest information sheet is for the Forestwatch group.

▼ Procedure

1 Participants are divided into nine groups. Each participant wears a badge with her group name. In a class of thirty students the suggested division is:

Burgerbeef Inc.	3
Forestwatch	4
Government Resettlement Team (each member of this group has an individual role card)	4
Kopano Tribe	4
Medico Ltd	3
National Timber Company	3

2 The facilitator gives some background information about the destruction of tropical rain forests (see Information Sheet, p. 211). She then introduces the nine groups who all live or work in The Forest. Five groups are users of The Forest needing to cut down trees (this is indicated on their Background Cards); four have an interest in The Forest but do not require its timber. The Forest used to be considerably larger in size: all that now remains is represented by the paper cups. It has been rumoured that an international conference to decide what should be done about the destruction of The Forest will take place sometime in the future; nobody knows exactly when, but all groups are advised to prepare their case to put to the conference. Participants then have about ten minutes in their groups to read and discuss the Background Cards. The facilitator should check that all the information has been understood.

3 The facilitator announces that the five minute intervals will be indicated by a blow on the whistle. On hearing the signal those groups with a timber requirement should remove the appropriate number of trees (cups) from The Forest. She then suggests that certain groups might want to find out more about each other's plans, and to negotiate or form alliances. The whistle indicates the start of this period which should last about fifteen minutes (with the whistle being blown at five minute intervals). This stage can be structured more by only allowing one delegate from each group to negotiate with other groups.

4 (Optional) The facilitator announces a 'taking stock' period (of five to ten minutes) when no tree felling or negotiating can take place. Participants discuss in their groups what has happened and what they have learnt, and further develop their case to put before the International Conference.

5 The facilitator announces that the International Conference will take place in 10–20 minutes. The exact timing is dependent upon how the game is proceeding and how much of The Forest remains; if feasible, the conference can be planned to take place at about the same time as the last trees are removed. All groups are asked to have a two-minute (maximum) statement prepared for the conference. A whistle blow announces the resumption of tree felling and negotiation between groups.

6 If all the trees are removed before the Conference is scheduled to begin, an optional ending is to stop the game at this point and go straight into the debriefing.

7 The facilitator assumes the role of an adviser from the United Nations Environmental Programme (UNEP) who has been sent to hear the arguments the groups wish to put forward. She calls all the groups together and chairs the meeting; each group in turn is invited to put its case. After hearing all the groups, the UNEP adviser leaves, promising to send her report 'in due course'.

▼ Potential

This simulation can generate impassioned feelings and action including the protection by some groups of the remaining 'trees' by brute force and, consequently, fervent attempts by other groups to remove them. Some **Getting out of role** exercises (see p. 199) may be needed before debriefing begins. Participants might then be asked to reflect upon the experience in the following ways:

— How did you feel about the role you were asked to play?

— How did the 'local people' (Kopano Tribe, Resettled People, River Basin Regional Council) feel about the 'outsiders' in The Forest?

— What did those working in The Forest think about the people who lived there?

—What were the respective attitudes of the groups towards conservation of The Forest? Was there a similar attitude displayed by all those living there, and by all those working there?

— Did any groups increase their timber requirements during the game, or were any groups persuaded to reduce theirs?

— What do you think would have happened if the game had continued for another 10 (20, 30) minutes?

– Do powerful groups, like wealthy countries and transnational corporations, have a right to cut down large areas of forest? Whose interests are they serving?

– Who should protect the rights of the local people living in such areas, and how?

– What might be the long-term consequences of destruction of the world's forests (a) for people living in the region or country concerned, (b) for the rest of the world?

– What steps need to be/could be taken to halt the destruction of forests?

Notes for facilitator

1 The reforestation process is carried out by simply replacing cups up to the maximum number stated. These cups might be marked in some way to indicate that they have been newly planted.

2 The success of the conservation argument depends to some degree on the abilities of the Forestwatch team to understand and publicise the information they have and to co-ordinate the action of other groups.

3 Copies of information cards, which can be placed underneath some of the cups to provide participants with further information taken from actual case studies of rain forest destruction, can be obtained from the Centre for Global Education. Participants might be encouraged to read these cards (the tree 'roots' that are left after felling during the game); groups trying to conserve The Forest could utilise the information to strengthen their case. Like all available information, however, they may simply be ignored!

Upper Secondary, 60–70 minutes.

▼ Source

Centre for Global Education.

Government Resettlement Team

Individual Role Card
You are the official representative of the Treasury. In a country with rampant inflation, there is considerable anxiety about Government expenditure. Your role is to try to make economies within the resettlement programme, without slowing it down.

Government Resettlement Team

Individual Role Card
You are the official representative from the Foreign Ministry. You are concerned to foster good relations with the Superpower and with the transnational corporations working in The Forest. You are also under pressure from the Ministry to speed up the resettlement programme, so as to improve the image of the cities.

Government Resettlement Team

Individual Role Card
You are the official representative from the Department for Forests and Agriculture. Although your Department originally gave its consent to the resettlement programme, there is now increasing anxiety about the wisdom of such a programme, particularly in the light of mounting international concern about the destruction of The Forest. Your brief is to try to halt the programme pending a thorough review of Government policy.

Government Resettlement Team

Individual Role Card
You are the official representative from the Department of Employment. Although you were in favour of the resettlement programme, the Department is now concerned about the decreasing number of jobs available in The Forest. Your brief is to try to convince the Resettlement Team of the need to look at the employment situation more seriously.

Background Card

Government Resettlement Team

You are responsible for carrying out the resettlement programme in The Forest, which began six years ago. The programme represented one of the principal policies on which the present Government was elected. The cities, particularly the capital, have become grossly over-crowded in recent years as thousands of the rural poor have flocked in to seek work. The outer fringes of the cities have been transformed into notorious shanty towns, whose inhabitants scrabble for food on the cities' rubbish tips. These slum areas are breeding grounds for dysentery and cholera; violence and drug abuse are common. As more of the shanty town dwellers drift into the city centre, pressure on the government to do something about the problem has come from the commercial and financial quarters of the city.

The resettlement programme is, you believe, humane and generous. It provides purpose-built accommodation, in various units to suit the size of families, with mains electricity, drainage and running water. Each unit also has a plot of newly-cleared land on which to grow crops. Employment for men can be found with the logging companies; trades-people have been encouraged to move out into The Forest to provide some of the goods and services found in the city. A main access road has been cut through The Forest, linking the resettlement area to the capital, with other subsidiary roads allowing for communication between communities. The programme is an expensive one, with only a small proportion returning in the form of rent, but it is nonetheless considered to be politically astute, both in terms of relieving the social pressures upon the cities and improving their image, which is beginning to damage the country's economic interests. The programme is therefore regarded as a sound economic use of land, and the Government wants it to be expanded rapidly; there are, however, other claimants to the land.

Timber Requirements

For the resettlement programme to continue, you need to cut down two trees every 5 minutes of the game.

If you wish to speed up the programme, this requirement can be increased by negotiation with, and the agreement of, at least one other group in The Forest. You can voluntarily reduce your requirement at any time.

Background Card

River Basin Regional Council

You represent the 500,000 people who live in the River Basin Region, some 300 miles downstream from The Forest. Until 1970 your people had led uneventful but comfortable lives, growing a high-yield variety of rice as a cash-crop. During particularly heavy rainfall, the area had been prone to flooding, but this had never seriously affected your livelihood until the 1970 monsoon. Then the river burst its banks, destroyed whole village communities and dumped tons of silt into the intricate irrigation systems of the rice fields. 350 people lost their lives. Since that year, serious flooding has occurred on five further occasions. In addition to the actual destruction caused by the flood water, problems have resulted from the fluctuations in streamflows which have left the rice with either too much or too little water for periods of the growing season and have also led to electricity rationing. This has had serious consequences for the livelihood of the River Basin people, many of whom have been forced, through poverty, to look for work in the already overcrowded cities.

It has long been rumoured that the clearing of large areas of The Forest has caused the flooding. The local climate has not changed significantly over the past 20 years; the constant silting up of irrigation channels and smaller river systems is thought to be the result of soil erosion ('runoff') on a massive scale occurring higher up the river. The Regional Council has now been forced, by increasingly militant communities, to find out more about the 'strange goings-on' in The Forest and to find a solution to the current problems of the River Basin. At present, though, the correct course of action has not been agreed upon and time is running out as more and more hectares of forest are cleared.

Background Card

National Timber Company

You are a thriving state-owned company, employing 1500 people, supplying the ever-increasing demand for hardwood from Western Europe and Japan for the manufacturing of quality furniture, window frames and shuttering. Annual turnover has risen by 125% over the past five years, though profits remain low — largely due to the necessary importing of heavy logging equipment from North America.

You have a 'selective logging' policy in The Forest, cutting down only those trees which are of the right quality and maturity to satisfy the stringent quality controls of the market. However, these trees are often closely surrounded by other unwanted trees which therefore have to be cut down in order to get the logging equipment in place and allow the selected trees to be brought out of The Forest. Whenever possible, you employ trained foresters to surpervise the logging operations, but the recent expansion in business has forced you to take on less skilled and experienced men from among the resettled people in order to furnish the lucrative contracts. These include a $100 million investment programme from Japan, which the Government is determined not to lose.

Thinking to the future, you have begun a reforestation policy of planting only the most commercially viable and fast-growing species of trees in some cleared areas. It is in these areas that your foresters need to be particularly vigilant, as there have been instances of 'tree poaching' by members of the Kopano Tribe and by other private logging companies.

Timber Requirements

For your logging operation you need to cut down two trees for every 5 minutes of the game. The best quality trees are those marked with a blue cross.

If you wish to increase your logging operation, this requirement can be increased by negotiation with, and the agreement of, at least one other group in The Forest. You can voluntarily reduce your requirement at any time.

Under the reforestation programme, the maximum you can achieve is the replanting of one tree for every 10 minutes of the game.

Background Card

Medico Ltd

You are a subsidiary of a transnational corporation, based in London and operating in 20 countries. Your company specialises in drugs for use in surgery, many of which are made from substances found only in plants in The Forest. Curare, an extraction from a certain root plant first used by local tribes as a poison for arrow-tips, is an important source of drugs for paralysing the nervous system. Rauwolfia, another inhabitant of The Forest, is used extensively in your medical preparations. One of its constituents, ajmaline, is used to promote a regular heartbeat; another, reserpine or serpentroot, relieves hypertension and schizophrenia and is now one of the main source materials for the tranquillizers manufactured by Medico Ltd.

In addition to extracting these valuable plants from The Forest, you are currently undertaking an extensive research programme, exploring the possible potential of the thousands of flowering plant species of which little is known. Many medical experts believe that the successful treatment of many of the developed world's major ailments, including cancer, heart disorders and respiratory diseases, may be found amongst such plants. The contribution to medical research would be substantial if the source of a new drug was discovered, not to mention the financial benefits to your company in this lucrative industry.

Your research team has become very concerned about the increasing destruction of The Forest, eliminating valuable plant species, both known and unknown, in some areas and upsetting the intricate forest ecosystem in others. Your parent company has given you the financial backing to begin campaigning amongst the other users of The Forest, in order to slow down the rate of destruction until your research has been completed.

Background Card

Resettled People

You are representatives of a group of about 1500 people who moved five years ago from a poverty-stricken slum area of the capital city to a newly-cleared part of The Forest. You have become known locally as 'the resettled people'. You moved voluntarily, because your situation in the city was desperate – living in flimsy shelters made of corrugated iron and cardboard, without running water, drainage or electricity and with little hope of full-time employment. Representatives of the Government Resettlement Department promised new, luxurious homes with all necessary facilities, enough land for growing crops, clean air and open spaces for children to play, and the prospect of work with the National Timber Company. It was to be the start of the new life you had dreamed of.

The promises were initially fulfilled – the homes were indeed relatively comfortable and the allotted piece of land looked sufficient to provide food for the family. Employment was not always available: most of it was casual work when the logging teams were short of labour, often taking the men away from their families. For most families there were long periods with no income, though rent still had to be paid. Many traders had seized the opportunity to make a quick profit by setting up shops in The Forest providing goods and services at inflated prices. During the first two years the crops prospered on the recently cleared forest soil, but since then yield has dropped dramatically so that families are once again entering the cycle of poverty. The joy of the arrival to the promised land has turned to bitterness and anger: your people feel that the Government has simply dumped them in an inaccessible area, with no support services, in order to solve the problems of the overcrowded city. At least there you had the support and companionship of the lively slum community; here, you feel isolated amidst a barren and unfamiliar wilderness.

Some of the resettled people are angry at the continued exploitation of The Forest by various outside interests; others amongst you are arguing that you, too, should also be clearing areas of the The Forest so as to provide some fertile land for crops.

Background Card

Kopano Tribe: 'The Forest People'

Your tribe has been living in The Forest 'since people began', according to the stories handed down through the generations. The tribe's survival is due to the skill of its people to utilise the vast resources of The Forest – for food, shelter and particularly for medicine. The tribe practises a form of shifting agriculture, which produces 85% of your food: good sites are cleared of trees and brush, then plantains, corn, tobacco, cotton and cane are grown for a few years until the soil is exhausted. The site is then abandoned, allowing the jungle to take over again, whilst the tribe moves on. The Forest land can only support farming for a few seasons because the soils are thin and poor: most of the nutrients are stored in the plants and trees whose roots and leaf systems also prevent the heavy rainfall from eroding the thin layer of soil.

You cut down selected trees for constructing shelters and for making weapons and tools. However, your greatest need for timber is for firewood, used for heating and cooking. Because of the Kopano Tribe's rapid population growth over the past 30 years (there are now thought to be 25,000–30,000 members in The Forest) the continual lopping of branches and collecting of brush for firewood is beginning to deplete The Forest's resources in some areas around the larger settlements.

The tribe's peaceful co-existence with nature has been disturbed in recent years by the appearance of foreigners in The Forest who have done a lot of thoughtless damage – either by chopping down the sturdiest trees, or by setting fire to huge areas of The Forest. Some of your people have been killed recently by the foreigners' weapons; the tribe's leaders would like to retaliate, but there is disagreement between those who advocate peaceful protest, in keeping with the Tribe's philosophy, and those who want to use violent means.

Timber Requirements

For your firewood you need to cut down one tree for every 5 minutes of the game.

This requirement can be increased by negotiation with, and the agreement of, at least one other group in The Forest. You can voluntarily reduce your requirement at any time.

Background Card

Superpower Defence Ministry

You are a delegation from the Defence Ministry of the Superpower which exercises considerable political and economic influence within the country where The Forest exists. For a number of years you have wanted to cut a military access route right through the middle of The Forest, from East to West, in order to speed up the transportation of military vehicles to the border with a neighbouring country which has a hostile government. The region is at present inaccessible, except by air, during eight to nine months of the year.

In order to sell the idea, you are promoting the access road as a valuable opportunity to exploit The Forest's natural resources. The road would follow the course of a defunct logging trail, opening up areas of The Forest at no cost to the national government, the bill being paid by the Superpower. Land adjacent to the road could then be sold for timber harvesting, cattle ranching or even for a new resettlement programme, on which you know the national government is very keen.

There has been some strong opposition to the project, from both national and international conservation groups, which has temporarily postponed its commencement. The national government is at present undecided; your own government is anxious that the project should get under way, and wants you to exert more pressure; the resettlement programme is thought to provide the best opportunity.

Timber Requirements

If you succeed in obtaining permission to build the access road, you will need to cut down two trees for every 5 minutes of the game.

If you want the work to proceed at a faster rate, this requirement can be increased by negotiation with, and with the agreement of, at least one other group in The Forest. You can voluntarily reduce your requirement at any time.

Background Card

Burgerbeef Inc.

You are a subsidiary of a large transnational corporation which operates in over 30 countries. Your own company is based in Dallas, Texas. Because of the increased demand for beef products in the North American and European fast-food markets, you have had to search for new ranchland outside the USA. This has brought you into The Forest, where you have now been ranching for six years. It is an expensive operation, burning down the trees and brush and then converting it into quality grazing land – especially as the soil is exhausted after only two or three years and new land has to be found and cleared. However, the land is relatively cheap to buy, and a high price is paid for the lean beef produced, in which the fat content is below the legal limit set by the US Government. The operation does also provide employment for local people – in forestry and ranching – in an area with an expanding population.

Your employees working in The Forest have occasional skirmishes with the Kopano tribe, and rifles are now supplied as standard equipment. There is also increasing competition, from both within the country and internationally, for The Forest's land and resources. You are therefore developing an aggressive puchasing policy, with attractive incentives for the national government in return for unrestricted access to The Forest.

Timber Requirements

For your forest clearing operation you need to cut down three trees for every 5 minutes of the game.

If you wish to speed up your operation, this requirement can be increased by negotiation with, and with the agreement of, at least one other group in The Forest. You can voluntarily reduce your requirement at any time.

P

Background Card

Forestwatch

You are a representative of an international, non-governmental pressure group, financed by public subscription and industry, concerned about the increasing worldwide destruction and exploitation of the tropical rain forests. Your unit has been given the task of trying to persuade the various groups living and working in The Forest to reduce their timber requirements and to promote a reforestation programme.

Your campaigning philosophy is one of non-violent, but persistent lobbying — providing public information and education programmes for people living in The Forest and trying to convince the commerical exploiters of the long-term ramifications of forest destruction. The information given below, available only to your group, can be used in any way you like to facilitate your task.

If you are successful in establishing a reforestation programme, which must be carried out by one or more of the groups that are cutting down trees, the maximum achievable in The Forest is to replace two trees for every 10 minutes of the game (The National Timber Company already has a reforestation programme which should replace one tree for every 10 minutes).

Tropical Rainforest Information Sheet

1   A few thousand years ago a rain forest belt covered 14% of the earth's land surface. Humankind has already destroyed half of that, most of the damage being done in the last 200 years, especially since 1945.

Latin America has 57% of remaining rain forest (Brazil alone has one-third), SE Asia and Pacific islands have 25%, Africa has 18%.

2   Tropical rain forests are being destroyed faster than any other part of the natural world. According to the US National Academy of Sciences Survey (1980), over 50 million acres (the area of England, Scotland and Wales combined) is destroyed or seriously degraded every year. A survey by the Food and Agricultural Organisation of the United Nations in 1981 predicted that, at present rate of destruction, almost one-fifth of the remaining tropical rain forest will be destroyed or severely degraded by the year 2000. There is evidence to show a rapid increase in the rate of destruction: the Brazilian Forestry Development Institute claims that 60% of the area deforested by 1978 had been cut down between 1975 and 1978.

3   The major causes of rain forest destruction are:
— slash and burn clearance for shifting agriculture; the cleared area is then cropped for 2 to 3 seasons before it is abandoned;
— steady clearance for firewood — one-third of the world's population relies on
firewood for heating and cooking. 86% of all wood consumed annually in least developed countries is for fuel;
— organised national/international logging operations for economically useful timber
— logging is selective, only the required trees being felled (particularly SE Asia);
— organised extensive clearing for cattle grazing — the land is cheap (particularly in Latin America) and a high price is paid for lean meat by US hamburger manufacturers, to keep the fat content within legal limits;
— government policies of resettlement — to remove pressure of overcrowding in the cities and to make 'economic' use of the land.

4   Between 40–50% of all types of living things — as many as 5 million species of plants, animals, insects — live in tropical rain forests, though they cover less than 2% of the globe.

These include people; anthropologists estimate that in 1500 the Amazon Basin had a thriving population of 6–9 million. In Brazil today there are less than 200,000 Indians; about half the 230 tribes who lived in Brazil at the turn of the century are now extinct.

▼ *Source*

Allen, R., How to Save the World, Kogan Page, 1980, pp. 53–69; Salati, E. and Vose, P.B., 'Depletion of tropical rain forests', Ambio, Vol. xii, No. 2, 1983, pp. 67–71.

Making Exercise Books

▼ Resources

A room capable of having 6 groups arranged around tables; 1 copy of each of Instruction Sheets 1, 2 and 4; 3 copies of Instruction Sheet 3; 22 sewing needles; 2 staplers; supply of staples; school name stamp and ink pad; 65 sheets white A5 paper; 15 sheets coloured A5 paper; 75 sheets poor quality A4 paper; 20 sheets of good quality A4 paper; 4 pairs of scissors; 3 pens; 3 pencils; 4 reels of cotton.

Resources arranged as follows:

GROUP A – subsidiary of transnational company working outside the country in which the simulation is set
Stapler, containing 20 staples
20 sheets white A5 paper
10 sheets coloured A5 paper
School stamp and ink pad
Pen
Instruction Sheet 1

GROUP B – subsidiary of transnational company working inside the country in which the simulation is set
Stapler, containing 20 staples
30 sheets white A5 paper
Pen
Instruction Sheet 2

GROUPS C, D and E – Local companies producing cheap exercise books

Per Group:

1 needle per person
5–20 sheets of poor quality A4 paper (a different quantity for each group)
Cotton thread
Scissors
Pencil
Instruction Sheet 3

GROUP F – Local company producing high quality exercise books
1 needle per person
10 sheets of good quality A4 paper
Cotton thread
Scissors
Pen
Instruction sheet 4

WHOLESALER
Supply of spare paper and staples

▼ Procedure

The simulation involves groups making exercise books in a developing country using different technologies. There are two categories of company, each category having two types:

(a) Transnational company (Head Office in another country)
    (i) subsidiary working outside the country in which the simulation is set
    (ii) subsidiary working in the country
(b) Local companies
    (i) producing cheap exercise books
    (ii) producing high quality exercise books

A class of 30 is divided into 6 groups as follows:
A & B – 4 people each
C & D – 6 people each
E & F – 5 people each
(The size of the groups can be varied in ratio according to the number of pupils in the class.)

The resources for the 6 groups should be organised before the start of the game. The class is divided into the 6 groups and the following objectives then read out and displayed:

– to make exercise books for sale to the wholesaler;
– to make as much money as possible;
– to make exercise books of as high a quality as possible.

The resources are handed out and groups given five minutes to read their instruction sheets and think of a name for their company. Nobody should start producing exercise books during this period; the facilitator can clarify any points that arise from the instruction sheets.

The groups are given twenty minutes to make as many exercise books as possible. The transnational company subsidiaries will very quickly run out of paper or staples and they can then be encouraged to produce adverts to help sell their products while they are waiting for the next delivery of paper. (Transnational companies in Kenya, for example, spend, on average, 6% of their income on advertising as opposed to 1% by local Kenyan firms.) The facilitator or another person acts as the wholesaler, thereby having some control over production. Supplies of paper, both for the transnational and the local companies, and staples for the transnational subsidiaries, can be bought in exchange for an agreed number of finished products, but there may be occasional shortages because of transport difficulties, foreign exchange problems, etc. The transnational subsidiary working in the developing country may suffer more than its sister subsidiary. The wholesaler keeps a record of materials sold.

Towards the end of the twenty minute production period, groups are warned that production is about to finish and that the wholesaler needs a sample of one of their books to decide on its value. The wholesaler assesses the quality of each sample and gives the exercise book a value between 1p and 10p. The better the quality, the higher the price. Each group then calculates how much they have earned in twenty minutes and therefore how much they would earn in a day. The transnational subsidiaries will almost certainly get higher prices for their exercise books and will produce more than the local companies. The companies' total earnings are then compared.

The finished exercise books can be kept for use as student notebooks or for project work.

▼ Potential

Feelings will be running high as a result of the inequalities in the game so it is important to allow participants to express those feelings. Perhaps the best way to do this is to give each group some questions to consider for five to ten minutes and then to have a class discussion based on those questions.

Possible questions include:
- What did you feel about your job?
- Which job was easiest?
- What problems did you have? Why?
- Which group produced the best quality exercise books?
- What do you think will happen to your job in the future?
- How do you feel about the game as a whole?

The discussion should try to bring out some similarities and differences between the groups and then attempt to focus participants' thoughts onto the role of transnational companies and the possible benefits and disadvantages of their activities in developing countries. At this stage some of the ideas and concepts outlined in the background information (see p. 217) can be introduced.

Some points that may develop from discussion of the game include:
- Local technology is affected by the mass production technology of the transnational company.
- Local technology may require more skill.
- Local technology may be more satisfying but harder work.
- Local technology cannot match transnational technology for quality control and product uniformity.
- Unemployment can result in both parent and host country as a result of transnational company decisions.
- Governments can influence the price of a product.
- Marketing by transnational companies can influence sales.
- Availability of resources hampers production.
- Local companies may use local raw materials while transnational companies import raw materials.
- Foreign goods are often more popular or attractive then home produced goods.

▼ Variation

The game can be played with two or three production rounds, company earnings being calculated between each round. With a longer playing time there can be the scope for some companies to go bankrupt, or to be taken over by others.

Middle and Upper Secondary, 40–60 minutes.

▼ Source

Devised by Paul Weeden, Brislington School, Bristol.

Instruction Sheet 1

Making an exercise book using imported technology

One member of the group is the factory manager. It is her responsibility to organise the other three members of the group into a production line, and to ensure that they maintain the highest quality of production.

The production line is organised as follows:

WORKER 1 – takes 1 coloured and 3 white sheets of paper, folds them in half, with the coloured sheet on the outside.

WORKER 2 – staples the sheets together.

WORKER 3 – stamps the name of the school on the front cover, and writes the name of the company at the bottom of the back cover.

Extra raw materials – paper and staples – have to be imported through the wholesaler.

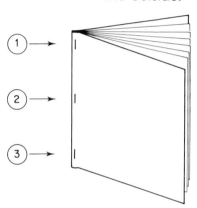

Front view

Back view

Instruction Sheet 2

Making an exercise book using imported technology

One member of the group is the factory manager. It is her responsibility to organise the other three members of the group into a production line, and to ensure that they maintain the highest quality of production.

The production line is organised as follows:

WORKER 1 – takes 4 white sheets of paper, folds them in half and hands them to worker 2.

WORKER 2 – staples the sheets together.

WORKER 3 – writes the name of the school on the front cover, and the name of the company at the bottom of the back cover.

Extra raw materials – paper and staples – have to be imported through the wholesaler.

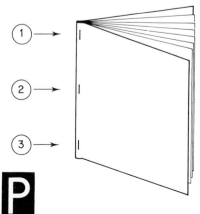

Front view

Back view

P

Instruction Sheet 3

Making an exercise book using local technology

1 Take 2 sheets of paper and fold them into 4.

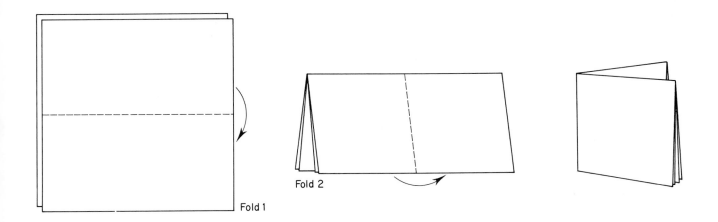

*2 Now take a needle and some thread.
Thread the needle and sew the pages together through the spine in a figure of 8.*

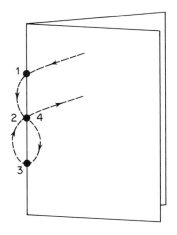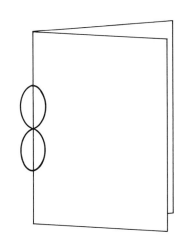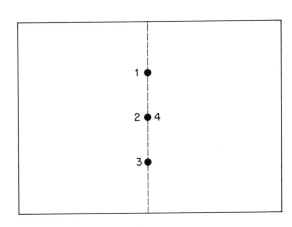

*3 Tie the ends of the thread together.
Cut the ends off.*
*4 Cut through the pages that are joined to-
gether.
You should now have a book of eight pages.*
*5 On the front cover neatly print the name of
your school.*

*6 At the bottom of the back cover print the
name of your company.*
*7 Extra raw materials (paper) have to be
bought through the wholesaler.*

*NB Remember good quality books fetch a
higher price.*

Instruction Sheet 4

Making a high quality exercise book using local technology

1 Take 2 sheets of paper and fold them into 4.

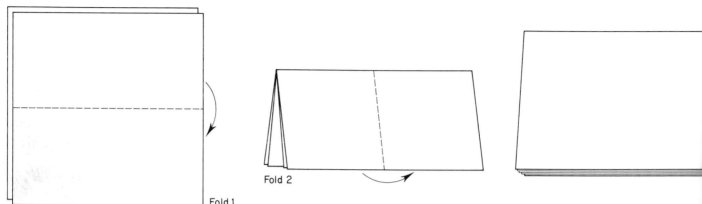

Fold 2

Fold 1

2 Now take a needle and some thread.
Thread the needle and sew the pages together through the spine in a figure of 8.

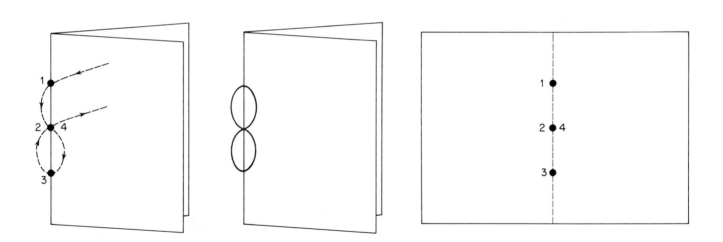

3 Tie the ends of the thread together.
Cut the ends off.
4 Cut through the pages that are joined together.
You should now have a book of eight pages.
5 On the front cover neatly print the name of your school and draw the school badge.

6 At the bottom of the back cover print the name of your company.
7 Extra raw materials (paper) have to be bought through the wholesaler.

NB Remember the best quality books fetch the highest price.

Background Information

Transnational companies that manufacture consumer goods usually develop from companies that have been successful in marketing a product or range of products in their home country and are now looking to expand overseas. They may have developed technology that gives them an initial advantage in the new market.

To sell their product they usually use a strategy that involves exporting to the prospective country first. Having created a market, or a place in an existing market, they may set up a local manufacturing base, if the market is large enough. The easiest way to do this is to take over or merge with an existing company. This has the advantage that the transnational is able to plug into an already existing distribution network and to use local knowledge and exper-

tise coupled with its own management and production expertise. In many countries (e.g. India) it may be forced, by law, into a partnership where it shares ownership with local people. This is because the government is trying to prevent foreign domination in certain industries.

It is difficult to generalise about transnational companies because they are so varied but their argument is that they bring capital, management skills, technology, employment and better quality goods to the countries they operate in. They are creators of wealth. They do not see themselves as distributors of wealth, that being the function of government. They operate within the laws of the country they work in and in some cases they see themselves as being 'moral leaders in countries where corruption is widespread' (British Oxygen Company).

Other games and simulations for the global classroom

Aid Committee Game

A 'limited resources' game. Participants study background information on Brazil, Upper Volta or Haiti and decide which of several schemes they would support if they had the opportunity, but only have enough money to fund some of them. Slides included on loan.

Upper Secondary.

Available from Oxfam.

Bafa Bafa

A classic cross-cultural simulation game in which two groups take on the attitudes and behaviour of two distinct cultures and then begin to meet.

Upper Secondary, 20+ participants. A Junior/ Lower Secondary version, **Rafa Rafa**, is also produced.

Both available from Christian Aid.

Arms Control Game

Intended for higher education students but the basic format could be adapted for sixth forms. A 'conference' type simulation which could be used in many other contexts. Outlined in brief in Simulations in the Study of International Relations (where other 'international crisis' simulations are also described).

Choices

An arms trade simulation with players taking the roles of arms buyers, arms sellers or arms makers.

Upper Secondary, 15–30 participants.

Available from Campaign Against the Arms Trade.

The Closed-system Game

An urban planning simulation involving students in the complexities and consequences of socio-economic and environmental planning and asking the question, 'can we plan for a decent standard of living and still protect the quality of our environment?'

Lower/Upper Secondary.

Described in Intercom, No. 82, 1976, pp. 17–23.

Consejo

Role play exercise based on the city of Cuzco in Peru. Housing is the key problem: the 'Consejo' or City Council have power to arbitrate.

Upper Secondary, 15–30 participants.

Available from Centre for World Development Education and Oxfam.

Crisis in Sandagua

This simulation deals with British press coverage of 'Third World' news, based on Sandagua, a fictitious Central American country. Two versions of the exercise are included.

Upper Secondary.

Available from Manchester Development Education Project, Oxfam and Centre for World Development Education.

Deadlines: Media Bias about the Third World

A simulation for understanding how newspapers cover stories from other countries. Participants are journalists sent to interview people concerned with the failure of the sugar crop in the African country of Batonga.

Lower and Upper Secondary, 10–35 participants.

Available from Centre for World Development Education and Oxfam.

Energy Policy: A Decision-making Simulation

Simple simulation in which students act as advisers to the US President on national and global energy problems. They represent a range of interest groups such as the 'oil and natural gas lobby', the 'nuclear power' lobby, the 'solar lobby' and the Department of Energy.

Lower/Upper Secondary.

Described in Intercom, No. 98, 1980, pp. 24–6; also in Intercom, No. 107, 1985, pp. 9–10, 20–1.

Environmental Decision

A US simulation which intends to help students better understand the working of administrative agencies. Participants working in various interest groups are asked to submit plans to a public hearing concerning the development of an area of land administered by the National Forest Service.

Lower and Upper Secondary.

Described in full in Intercom, No. 107, 1985, pp. 8–9, 18–19.

Farming Game

Participants play roles of subsistence farmers in a savannah region of Africa. They have to decide what food to grow: dice, chance and disease cards to a great extent control their fate.

Upper Secondary, 8–30 participants. A sheet included describes a simpler version of the game for primary students.

Available from Centre for World Development Education and Oxfam.

Grain Drain

A board game based on the politics of food, illustrating the problems facing many 'Third World' countries in buying grain and food on the world market.

Upper Secondary.

Available from Centre for World Development Education.

Gronks and Friends

Concerns the interaction of social groups, how society shapes an individual's identity and what happens when the individual deviates from the norm. Approaches issues such as prejudice, social labelling and stereotyping through fun.

Lower and Upper Secondary, 20–30 participants.

Fully described in Alec Davison and Peter Gordon, Games and Simulations in Action.

Juvenis

A futures simulation in which participants have to decide whether a revolutionary new anti-ageing drug should come on to the market.

Upper Secondary, 20+ participants.

Available from Centre for Global Education.

Limits to Growth

Considers issues surrounding rapid population growth both at local level (a meeting of a city council in a US community) and at global level — developing policies in connection with rising demands for food.

Lower Secondary.

Described in full in Intercom, No. 107, 1985, pp. 12–13, 27–8.

Manomiya

Simulation illustrating the role of women in African farming and how development does not always benefit them. Includes background information for further discussion.

Upper Secondary.

Available from Centre for World Development Education.

The Ocean Resources Game

A simulation which reflects some of the major issues which are at stake in the use of the world's seas. Participants play roles of decision-makers from various nations and explore the potential for co-operation.

Upper Secondary.

Described in full in Intercom, No. 107, 1985, pp. 10–11, 22.

Out of this World

Similar in aim and design to **Terra II** (see p. 220), this simulation is designed to be spread over a number of lessons. In three parts, participants go on a journey to a distant planet where they encounter a range of human and environmental problems. Includes a computer game.

Lower and Upper Secondary.

Available from Devon Educational Television Service.

Panchayat

Participants are villagers in the Indian state of Punjab. They are asked to consider and vote on the government's proposal to buy land for housing the spreading population of a nearby town.

Lower and Upper Secondary, 20–40 participants.

Available from Oxfam.

Paper Bag Game

The aim of this game is to simulate the pressures of trying to survive in an economy like Calcutta's, where there is massive unemployment and no social security, through making paper bags.

Upper Primary/Lower Secondary, 10–35 participants.

Available from Centre for World Development Education and Christian Aid.

The People Grid

A sequence of three simulations ('Growing-up Game', 'Our Word House', 'The Global Cake') which explore the concepts of self, community and whole earth, stressing the interdependence of peoples and how interaction changes and enriches life.

Upper Primary/Lower Secondary.

Fully described in Alec Davison and Peter Gordon, Games and Simulations in Action.

Poultry Game

Participants take the roles of farmers in a 'Third World' country. Each farmer has a certain amount of money to invest in poultry farming and a number of choices to make.

Upper Secondary, 10–18 participants.

Available from Centre for World Development Education and Oxfam.

Raftonbury

Simulation based on the dangers of dust from asbestos to industrial workers and to the community at large. Sub-committee groups of interested parties meet to develop their cases for a series of public meetings.

Upper Secondary, 40–80 participants.

Described in full in Alec Davison and Peter Gordon, Games and Simulations in Action.

Sierra de Cobre

Simulates a crisis in an imaginery South American country caused by a world recession in copper prices and rising costs of key imports (food and oil). Groups take the roles of the Popular United Front cabinet, the board of directors of a mining transnational, the mine workers union and right-wing rebels.

Upper Secondary.

Described in Robert Stradling, Michael Noctor, and Bridget Baines, Teaching Controversial Issues, Edward Arnold, 1984, pp. 85–6.

Spring Green Motorway

Brings out the various reactions of the inhabitants of Spring Green to a proposed motorway route through the village. Leads on from roles established in pairs to a full public meeting.

Upper Secondary.

Available from Community Service Volunteers.

Starpower

The classic 'power' game, in which the relationship between wealth and power in human societies is examined through the formation of a three-tier society.

Upper Secondary, 15–30 participants.

Available from Christian Aid and Oxfam.

Terra II – A Spaceship Earth Simulation

A relatively simple simulation designed to help students see their planet as one environment with limited resources shared by all. Participants assume roles on board a large, experimental spaceship and encounter a variety of problems to do with pollution, shortage of resources, technical failures and human illness.

Upper Primary/Lower Secondary.

Described in full in Intercom No. 107, 1985, pp. 14–17, 29–37.

Trade Game

A simple game in which people play the parts of consumers, traders and retailers of a commodity such as bananas, sugar or coffee.

Upper Secondary, 15–100 participants.

Available from Centre for World Development Education and Oxfam.

The Trading Game

Involves groups, working with inequitably distributed resources, in the manufacture of paper shapes; designed to demonstrate interdependence and the effects of inequalities in the world trading system.

Lower Secondary, 15–30 participants.

Available from Christian Aid, Centre for World Development Education and Oxfam.

World Feast Game

By trading, making a mural and eating the food they've produced, participants are encouraged to question the way the world's food is shared out.

Upper Primary/Lower Secondary, 20–25 participants.

Available from Christian Aid and Centre for World Development Education.

Sources of other simulation games and ideas:

Michael Clarke, Simulations in the Study of International Relations; Alec Davison and Peter Gordon, Games and Simulations in Action; Intercom, Global Perspectives in Education, New York, particularly Nos 82 (1976), 98 (1980), 107 (1985); Ken Jones, Simulations: a Handbook for Teachers; Ken Jones, Designing your own Simulations; Ken Jones, Graded Simulations; John Taylor and Rex Walford, Learning and the Simulation Game.

Addresses

Campaign Against the Arms Trade, 11 Goodwin Street, London, N4 3HQ.
Centre for Global Education, University of York, Heslington, York YO1 5DD. The Centre stocks Intercom.
Centre for World Development Education, Regent's College, Inner Circle, Regent's Park, London NW1 4NS.
Christian Aid, PO Box 1, London, SW9 8BH.
Community Service Volunteers, 237 Pentonville Road, London N1 9NJ.
Devon Educational Television Service, Plymouth Polytechnic, Hoe Centre, Notte Street, Plymouth.
Manchester Development Education Project, c/o Manchester Polytechnic, 801 Wilmslow Road, Didsbury, Manchester M20 8RG.
Oxfam, 274 Banbury Road, Oxford OX2 7DZ.

11 Action

'Member States should promote, at every stage of education, an active civic training which will enable every person to gain a knowledge of the method of operation and the work of public institutions, whether local, national or international, to become acquainted with the procedures for solving fundamental problems; and to participate in the cultural life of the community and in public affairs. Wherever possible, this participation should increasingly link education and action to solve problems at the local, national and international levels.'

UNESCO recommendation concerning education for international understanding, co-operation and peace and education relating to human rights and fundamental freedoms, 1974.

'We would argue that the school should develop "involvement literacy" in each and every emergent adult. By that we mean that the avenues and techniques for involvement and participation in contemporary society should be explored; the limitations confronting us all as individuals when we seek to foster change should be examined and the ramifications of different types of involvement should be opened for consideration and discussion. In addition, the multiplicity of possibilities for involvement need opening up so that pupils leave school with an 'involvement map' enabling them to make mature decisions as to the direction in which they wish to travel as participating members of a dauntingly complex society.'

Europe and the wider world. *Extract from a working party report at the EC/Schools Council 'European Dimension in the 10–16 Curriculum' Conference, Brighton, 1982.*

'...it is a fundamental bias of intellectuals to believe that man thinks first and then unleashes well-considered action. Very often he acts first; if it works he may develop a theory about it.' (Johan Galtung)[1]

Suggested action projects

Teaching language to foreign residents.

Helping to set up integrated youth clubs.

Encouraging kindergartens, playgrounds, parks and play-groups where needed.

Encouraging local radio and TV to provide programmes for foreign residents, old people, children, etc.

Helping in urban renewal and pollution control, e.g. planting trees, documenting and conserving those which exist.

Helping with old people's welfare (painting workshops, 'meals on wheels', reading newspapers, help in shopping, etc.).

Making hospital visits and home visits to sick persons.

Helping with rehabilitation of delinquents.

Analysing and improving local public transportation.

Studying public services (benches on streets, toilet facilities, lighting, maps and time-tables, litter bins, telephones and street signs) and working for improvements.

Helping to develop a new local craft for marketing.

Introducing an anti-smoking campaign.

Making land-use surveys.

Developing new ways in which local charitable organisations could be used.

Safeguarding wildlife.

Helping with the care of children where needed.

Setting up a UN club or information centre.

Conserving and documenting ancient buildings and monuments, historical sites or places of natural beauty.

Writing a town or local area brochure.

From Wolsk, D., An Experience-centered Curriculum, *UNESCO educational studies and documents, No. 17, 1975, p. 49.*

Newcastle Architecture Workshop

The workshop is an environmental education organisation comprising architects, planners, designers and teachers working together 'to help people of all ages to become aware of, and to understand their surroundings, to develop critical response to changes in their environment and to enable them to initiate proposals'.[2]

Workshop staff have collaborated with teachers in a number of schools in Newcastle on projects which meet the above aims. These have included:

• working with a class of 8–9 year olds from Linhope First School on exploring the growth of Newcastle through the Quayside and its bridges;

• working with a class of 6–7 year olds from Hillsview Infant School on the theme of 'movement' in and around the local environment;

• working with two classes, one of 6–7 year olds, the other of 9–10 year olds, from Raby Street Primary School on a study of the history of Byker and the modern Byker development;

• working with a class of 11–12 year olds at Feversham School for maladjusted children on studying the history of the house as a structure and the development of modern housing styles.

The above projects involved taking students into the community, providing them with access to professionals who determine the nature of their physical environment and introducing them to the processes of change in local communities.

Newcastle Architecture Workshop Ltd is at 6 Higham Place, Newcastle upon Tyne, NE1 8AF.

Groby Community College, Leicestershire

The syllabus for the core fourth and fifth-year World Studies course at Groby Community College (first examined in 1980) included the following suggestions for action projects:

• community relations work;

• participation at local, national and international level in the work of an international environmental organisation (e.g. Friends of the Earth);

• participation in the work of IVS, United Nations, Population Concern or a similar body at local or national level;

• money-raising to help fight world poverty, hunger and disease;

• projects connected with the school such as school recycling projects or monitoring the school's use of energy and other resources;

- running a 'globally-conscious' home (conservation, etc.) and 'globally-conscious' shopping;

- local projects involving experimentation with or development of alternative technologies;

- (a) a voice in local
      politics
  (b) a voice in national
      politics
  (c) a voice in European
      politics
  (d) a voice in world
      politics

  students using channels to make known their views on global issues

- a global problems and solutions publicity campaign in the locality.[3]

Projects subsequently attempted included:

- a 'Tools for Self-Reliance' programme (refurbishing old 'tools' collected locally for eventual transportation to Tanzania);

- student swaps with multi-ethnic inner city schools;

- a wheelchair project in which a small group of girls wheeled one of their number into city shops, restaurants, etc. to assess the facilities available from the point of view of a disabled person (a report was sent to the city authorities);

- materials' exchanges with foreign schools;

- a group which attended constituency meetings during the May 1979 General Election and questioned candidates on issues raised in the World Studies course;

- American, Bangladeshi, French and Greek evenings at the school;

- a 24-hour football marathon, two roller skating marathons, a sponsored cycle race, a 72-hour canasta playing session, complete with *Guinness Book of Records* attempt and media coverage, to raise money for international relief organisations, in particular, Action Aid. The college 'adopted' a village in Somalia to which money was sent and links established.[4]

'The ideology of involvement and participation is closer to the rhetoric of Western democracy than it is to the reality. Voting in a secret ballot largely exhausts the repertoire of responsible citizenship — participation is left to the few. Political education in schools is largely geared to this approach. In most schools that offer any explicit political education at all it is far more likely to concentrate on preparation for voting than participation in decision making.' (Chris Brown)[5]

'Education (whether for involvement or for anything else) entails deliberate interventions in the pattern of experience structured and tailored in a way calculated to facilitate and maximise desired learning. A carefully selected and ordered sequence of exercises can vastly improve upon haphazard immersion in experience as a strategy for improving participatory skills.' (Keith Webb)[6]

Anti-sexist work in the middle years: a co-operative and action-oriented approach

by **Cathie Holden**, Bishop Kirk Middle School, Oxford

The type of school I work in is one where the children appear articulate, confident and well-motivated. It is a mainly middle-class, white catchment area with a high proportion of professional families. Just the type of school, you might think, where children would respect each other regardless of gender, and would work in a co-operative manner. Not so. After my first few weeks with a class of 9 year olds I became aware that for all their fluency on paper, the children in this middle school could not work together if they were in mixed groups, and in fact each sex seemed incapable of treating the other as human beings worth talking to. Disdain and indifference were the order of the day.

At first I tried a 'softly-softly' approach, making sure our class readers had leading girls as well as boys, asking both sexes to move furniture, tidy up and care for the hamster. I tried to ensure that neither sex dominated class discussion and that all sports and games were open to everyone. To encourage co-operation at the same time, I began to use many games and activities where the children had to work in mixed groups. One such exercise involved children looking at photographs of activities and having to rank them in order of preference.[7] I selected photographs which related to children's hobbies and pastimes but some of which showed girls in boys' roles (e.g. boxing) and vice versa (e.g. boy playing with a dolls' house). After ranking the activities the children were amazed to discover that they all actually liked the same things: cooking, photography and woodwork. Dolls, soldiers and boxing were unpopular with the majority, and the other activities (fishing, knitting, gardening) were put in the middle by most groups. The comments written around the photographs revealed a great deal of ignorance: 'I thought girls would have put woodwork at the bottom' (Alan), 'I was surprised Nick didn't like boxing' (Philippa), 'Why didn't the girls put dolls top?' (Thomas). I then realised that while it was necessary to provide a non-sexist framework (vis-à-vis books, classroom management, as mentioned earlier), relationships between the sexes would not improve until each learnt more about the other as people, until there was proper dialogue and an understanding of what each other really felt.

Over the next few weeks I followed various routes: I displayed an *ABC of What You Can Be*[8] showing women in non-traditional roles to counter the boys' stereotypes (and to help the girls broaden their horizons), we began work on non-stereotyped Christmas and birthday cards (Mother Christmas, girl on BMX, boy playing house, boy reading, mum playing snooker), and we looked at work in and around the home.

A major focus was toys, which led naturally from the realisation (after the work with the photographs) that many children of both sexes enjoyed the same pastimes. Magazines and mail order catalogues were cut up and groups made Venn diagrams to show toys they thought were aimed at boys, then at girls, and the central overlap included both. The visual result was startling; a predominance of pink in the girls' circle, and black, brown and dark green in the boys'. The things in the middle were mainly board games. The children then wrote comments all around the pictures, and many of the girls drew arrows to the boys' electronic games and construction toys saying they would like to try them and that they would prefer them to their toys. The comments about the so-called girls' toys were that they were 'boring' and you couldn't do much with them. *My Little Pony* was considered 'an insult to ponies' and one wrote: 'Since when have ponies been pink and yellow?'

This led naturally on to looking at advertisements and why certain toys were targeted at either boys or girls. One boy brought in a Lego catalogue and it was quickly pointed out that while pictures of Duplo showed boys *and* girls playing with it, the Lego train set showed only boys and technical Lego was exclusively targeted at boys. The children decided to write to Lego. They stated their case, said they had been looking at advertisements and catalogues and considered Lego's to be sexist, and asked: 'Please could you change this?'

Lego replied that 'the popular misconception that building is a boys' pastime means that the sales (of Duplo and Lego Basic sets) divide 60/40 in favour of boys, much to our dismay . . . As children get older this division of expectation becomes more and more marked so that we are forced to acknowledge it . . . We are quite prepared to be one step ahead of the general public but to swim against the tide of mass opinion … does not make for growth in a company on whose success the livelihood of many employees depends.'

What impressed me hereafter was the reponse of the children. After a class discussion they formed groups to write to Lego. One group suggested Lego 'print a picture of a girl making a structure with a boy also on the packet. The reason for this correspondence is it could improve your income.' Another group sent suggestions for TV advertisements showing Lego being used by both sexes, while two other letters told of incidents where a girl had been teased at school for bringing in technical Lego, and a parent had refused a girl's request for Lego for her birthday saying it was for boys.

The whole issue had obviously touched a raw nerve and another class, hearing of the letters, asked to become involved. One girl whose birthday was coming up, gave her dolls to her younger sister and asked for a technical Lego set. She brought in a helicopter made with the duly acquired kit, which was put on display with a boy's model.

Meanwhile, Lego replied again saying that advertising to both boys and girls would put boys off, as proved by Meccano some years ago. The marketing manager continued:
'Until the day comes when our research shows that at least 25% of these sets are bought for girls we

The photograph in question

Another Lego publicity photograph

must continue to target them to the market that is receptive to them – and that is boys, mainly of 8–10 years.'

Many groups were anxious to write back. A group of boys replied that Meccano's advertising failure took place 'some years ago and people's attitudes have changed a lot since then. Us being four boys writing this letter we would not be put off if you advertised girls and boys on your boxes. Do you believe in equal opportunities for boys and girls. Or is it just your profit you're interested in?'

From being a class composed of pupils who wouldn't co-operate, who wouldn't speak to members of the opposite sex and who held each other in contempt, there had been a noticeable change to a group of children willing to harness their academic abilities for a common cause. The correspondence with Lego became a focus for their energies: the girls were supported by the boys and were given new confidence, and the boys realised that girls had been subject to injustices. Both sexes realised that perhaps those of the other gender were human beings with similar interests after all, and the road to co-operation was thus paved.

'The immediate arena for human rights action is the school itself. All schools subscribe to the general ethos of human rights, the basic respect for individuals and for non-discrimination. However, they do not always support this ethos in their relationships and daily organisation.' (Jeremy Cunningham)[9]

A right to privacy and dignity: or how global education starts in the school toilets

by **Cathie Holden** and **Hugh Starkey** of Bishop Kirk Middle School, Oxford and Westminster College of Education, Oxford, respectively.

The background: summer term 1986 in a 3-form entry 9–13 middle school in North Oxford. Many of the children have university connections though not always academic ones. They bring with them a number of nationalities and languages. The social education programme in the first year (9–10 year olds) consists of one hour per week for each of the three classes. In previous summer terms, the accent has been on looking to the future and thinking about building a better world, using ideas from the World Studies 8–13 project.[10]

The project: Cathie Holden had been responsible for the course in previous years. In 1986 she was first-year co-ordinator for the school. Hugh Starkey, a lecturer at Westminster College of Education, was on a term's secondment to the school. They arranged to team teach each of the three classes and to attempt to add the following elements to the social education programme:

1 to introduce knowledge of and respect for human rights as basic values for life in society;

2 to ensure that the affective dimension, necessary for such values to be owned, was given appropriate weight;

3 to attempt to develop action skills alongside knowledge and attitudes; the skills to be those of living harmoniously in a community and working democratically for change.

The content: During the course of the term the children considered ways of improving their own school community to make it fairer and more accepting of and welcoming towards newcomers and minorities. They looked at what they liked about the school and what could be improved. They shared experiences of bullying, name-calling and racism. These personal concerns were given a wider and international context through literature and case-studies (*Ndidi's Story, The Sidhus come to England, Underground to Canada*, material on travellers and native Americans from the Minority Rights Group and on South Africa from *New Internationalist*).

Human rights were introduced as:

(a) a basis for fair and non-violent communities (equality of rights, dignity, justice, democracy);
(b) strong claims which may be of help when trying to persuade others to effect improvements.

The UN Declaration of the Rights of the Child (see p. 144) was studied and expressed in their own terms with their own examples. An appendix of new rights was also drafted.

Armed with some agreed ideas on how to improve their school environment and the empowering notion of rights (bearing in mind the necessity that improvements be for the benefit of all), the children could prepare to put their case to the Head in as effective a way as possible.

Topics they wished to discuss included more gym equipment, abolition of uniform, provision of drinking fountains and cleaner toilets with soft paper (backed up by their knowledge of their right to a healthy environment), brighter classrooms and improved play facilities.

They learnt much from preparing for the meeting with the Head and from the meeting itself. 'I thought that Mrs Powell could say something and it would happen, and she said she couldn't, that surprised me' (Emma). 'I learnt it is hard to know what the Headteacher was going to say back to us' (Robert).

In fact the Head turned some concerns back to the children (cleaner toilets), agreed to some requests (drinking fountains) and claimed to be prevented by the Council from painting classrooms with any colour except magnolia.

The first-years decided to speak to older children about the toilets, which had become a burning issue of hygiene, comfort, dignity and privacy. A meeting was arranged in the hall where younger pupils worked in small groups with older pupils to agree a code of conduct for the toilets. One of the cleaners came to give her testimony and she was listened to with attention and concern.

A group from one class then wrote to a county councillor who is also a school governor. They asked him to come and speak to them to discuss finance for soft toilet paper and a choice of paint for classrooms.

In this way, when coming to do work on time-lines and other futures work the children had at least some ideas that things can be changed, that there are democratic processes, that people can be influenced, in short that they are not powerless.

Teaching strategies: Each lesson included a short input (a story, a song, a poem, an example, a problem) followed by work in groups to achieve a product such as a list, a statement, a diagram, a picture, a poster. The group work included brainstorming, ranking, illustrating, composing statements. Poster-sized montages of work were displayed in the classrooms and a display was also made for the school.

One class wrote and agreed a class charter to promote more fairness. The classes who met the Head prepared their case (one group per request) and practised putting it confidently in public.

Two units of work:

1 **Starting to Think about Rights** (see activity, p. 150).

2 Having discussed the UN Declaration of the Rights of the Child, one class produced their own list of rights as follows, which they then illustrated and displayed, each group taking a few:

Everyone should have the right:
- to get a job if you are foreign
- to see your friends
- to go to school
- to believe in your own religion
- to live
- to be treated equally
- to make your own decisions
- not to be teased when you say stop
- not to be beaten
- to a decent house
- to go on public land
- to have freedom (unless you have committed a crime)
- to be cared for
- to keep things that are yours
- to have a space to live
- to go to another country
- to hospital care
- to walk down the road safely
- to speak up for yourself
- to a holiday
- to pets

Outcomes: Pupils have displayed a remarkably good understanding of the concept of rights and in particular of the need to be sensitive about and respectful of the rights of others. They have learnt about decisions, political processes and the need to present a good case. Their work on the future and on other countries has been informed by this knowledge and this experience. This is just one small part of what should be a continuous programme of social education for a better planet.

'Another possibility, which might appeal to pupils and students,' suggests John Marks, 'would be the adoption of prisoners of conscience or political prisoners, writing directly to them, or seeking information about them.'[11]

Sources of information about prisoners of conscience include:

- *Amnesty International British Section, 5 Roberts Place, off Bowling Green Lane, London, EC1 0EJ*

- USSR News Brief, *48 Rue de lac, 1050 Brussels*
- Keston College, *Heathfield Road, Keston, Kent, BR2 6BA*

A useful student-eye view on running a school Amnesty International Group is George Webster's 'Three years in the life of a school Amnesty International Group', World Studies Journal, Vol. 6, No. 2, 1986.

'There are quite a range of ways in which the school itself can provide a vehicle for involvement, some of which can be initially structured by a teacher, some of which offer the opportunity for direct participation by students, individually or in groups. Of the teacher-initiated ones, it is interesting to consider the various forms of linking schools. The kind of links that could be considered include those between two schools within the same LEA serving very different catchment areas; between a British school and a school in a "Third World" country, and, a relatively new idea, a link between a British school and a "Third World" school through a teacher, possibly from the local area, who is working in the latter through Voluntary Service Overseas.

There is one other type of British/"Third World" link that offers a very direct involvement which provides a profound experience at first hand, and that is the visit by a group of students to a "Third World" country with a specific task to carry out, alongside students from that country, such as the Tanzania visit by a group from Stantonbury Campus (Milton Keynes). In terms of challenging stereotypes and developing empathy and an awareness of the processes that shape people's lives, this offers a great deal, though clearly there are practical problems, not least of finance, that would make such a project an impossibility for many schools.' (Judy Dyson)[12]

Street theatre offers another way for students to bring their concerns to a wider public

One action suggestion is for students to write letters of criticism to editors, publishers and authors when they find examples of ethnocentrism, racism and sexism in school and library books. At an inner London primary school, one class took exception to a book by 'Althea' on swimming, not because of its content but because in the illustrations some of the figures are coloured grey (in an attempt to reflect the multi-racial nature of British society). The students were upset because they knew that no person is coloured grey. A letter objecting to the illustrations was sent to the publishers, Dinosaur. In their reply, the publishers explained that the grey illustrations were cheaper to produce. The students were, nonetheless, offended and so they went to the local swimming baths and had their teacher take photographs of them. The prints were used by the children to prepare their own book on swimming. The students preferred their book to Althea's in that it showed what black children really looked like. (This story is recounted in *Racism: the 4th R*, 1983, a video available from ALTARF, All London Teachers Against Racism and Fascism, Room 216, Panther House, Mount Pleasant, London WC1.) Other student action possibilities in this area include:

- letters of appreciation to editors, publishers and authors about less biased books;
- discussion with publishers' representatives when they visit school;
- representations to local libraries about books containing pejorative cultural bias;
- the mounting of an exhibition displaying books the students have liked and disliked;
- a student working party on ethnocentrism and bias in books;
- examining newspapers for bias and writing letters to the editor.

(See 'A Note on Classroom Resources', p. 268.)

'In a global age where worldwide interdependence makes itself felt in the daily lives of most human beings, it is critical that individuals learn how they might exercise some measure of control and influence over the public affairs of global society, as well as over the public affairs of their local communities and nations.'(Lee Anderson and James Becker) [13]

'We must encourage and assist our students in identifying their own value and action priorities in light of their concern about particular global issues. We must help them discover their own strengths and learn how they can be most effective. We must help each person find his or her entry point for action.' (David Shirman and David Conrad) [14]

References

1 Cited in Nakhre, A. W., 'Peace action as peace education: an analysis of the impact of satyagraha on participants', *Bulletin of Peace Proposals*, Vol 12, No 2, May 1981, p. 205.
2 Cited in *Walbottle: Houses and Community*, Newcastle Architecture Workshop Ltd, undated.
3 *World Studies syllabus for Groby Community College for first examination in 1980*, Global education documentation service, Centre for Global Education, University of York, Document No. 1, p. 8.
4 Selby, D. E., *World Studies, the participatory school, the open classroom*, Global education documentation service, Centre for Global Education, University of York, Document No. 10, p. 5; Miles, I., *Education for involvement at Groby Community College – examples, problems raised and possible directions*. Paper presented to Education for Involvement Seminar, University of York, April 1984, p. 1.
5 Brown, C., *Education for involvement*. Paper presented to Education for Involvement Seminar, University of York, April 1984, p. 1.
6 Webb, K., *Some tentative steps towards guidelines for world studies teachers*. Paper presented to Education for Involvement Seminar, University of York, April 1984, p. 2.
7 Maidenhead Teachers' Centre, *Doing Things In and About the Home*, Serawood House, 1983.
8 *ABC of what you can be*, distributed by the Letter Box Library, 5 Bradbury Street, London N16.
9 Cunningham, J., *Involvement with human rights – strategies and tactics for schools*. Paper presented to Education for Involvement Seminar, University of York, April 1984, p. 2.
10 Fisher, S. and Hicks, D. W., *World Studies 8–13: A Teacher's Handbook*, Oliver & Boyd, 1985.
11 Marks, J., *'Peace Studies' in our Schools: Propaganda for Defencelessness*, Women and Families for Defence, 1984, p. 60.
12 Dyson, J., *Development education: some possibilities for and problems of student involvement outside the classroom*. Paper presented to Education for Involvement Seminar, University of York, April 1984, p. 2.
13 Anderson, L. and Becker, J., 'Education for involvement', *The New Era*, Vol. 58, No. 2, March/April 1977, pp. 40–3.
14 Shirman, D. and Conrad, D., 'Awareness, understanding and action: a global conscience in the classroom', *The New Era*, Vol. 58, No. 6, December 1977, pp. 163–7.

12 Feedback and evaluation techniques

In the global classroom, with its emphasis upon open communication, interaction, negotiation and horizontal (as against vertical) relationships, it is important that techniques are employed and structures established so that students can feed back to the teacher their feelings, wishes and expectations about the course. It is also important that course evaluation is an ongoing and joint affair (including discussion of teacher and student behaviours). In addition, techniques should be employed which encourage periodic student self-evaluation. A range of feedback and evaluation techniques which have been successfully used in the classroom are described below.

Telegrams

At regular intervals, students can be encouraged to write a telegram stating how they **feel** about the course and/or giving their **feelings** about the topic under study. The telegrams

TELEGRAM

I feel that this classroom lesson has been rather fun. It made me think 'why can't every lesson be like this?'
I felt confident right from the start and L enjoyed it when all the boys and girls in my class came and sat in a ring and talked about our lives.
I believe that sometimes my freinds do not talk enough within their own family and L think they enjoyed it as much as L did.
DATE 23rd July 1987. SIGNED Zoe Dawkes.

should be dated but it is up to students whether they are signed. The telegrams can be 'posted' in a box in the classroom. It is essential that the teacher both takes the telegrams seriously and is seen to take them seriously. Responses to telegrams can include:

- the teacher giving the class an overview of what was written as a stimulus to an evaluation session on the course;

- changing a planned activity as result of suggestions or because the telegrams reveal attitudes to the topic that need exploring (the teacher should make it clear that the change in schedule has been made because of feedback);

- letting the class know that a need expressed in the telegrams will be met later (the teacher should be as specific as possible – 'I hope we can do an activity on that topic in the week after half-term');

- occasionally responding to individuals who have signed their telegrams in writing or by giving them verbal feedback;

- pinning telegrams that encapsulate themes running through the feedback received on the noticeboard prior to class discussion (a signed telegram should not be made public without first obtaining the permission of the author).

A variation on the telegrams approach is the **Reactions and Reflections** sheet, usually half an A4 sheet giving space for a more studied and in-depth response to a lesson or course unit and allowing for rather more self-reflection and self-evaluation.

Mood Messages

The class sits or stands in a circle and, one by one, students convey how they are feeling by reference to a topic, such as the weather, animals, birds, or plants. For example:

- 'There have been a lot of dark clouds around in the last day or two, but the sun is starting to break through'

- 'I feel like a hedgehog, slow and rather prickly'

- 'When I came into class, I was a sparrow, small and unnoticed, but now I feel like a kingfisher'

This activity, in which the teacher should join, can be done at the beginning of the lesson, after a particular task has been completed or just before the class disperses. It gives an outlet for everybody to express their mood and sensitises the teacher and the rest of the class to how others are feeling as the lesson begins and to the effect of the lesson on their emotional well-being.

Thumbs-up/Thumbs-down Circle

At the end of a lesson, the class stands in a circle. The teacher reminds the class of the first part of the lesson. Students give the thumbs-up if enjoyed, the thumbs-down if not enjoyed or waggle their thumb somewhere in between if their response is 'so-so'. The teacher goes on to the second part of the lesson and so on. This technique, which is helpful if the class is reluctant to talk in plenary, can also be used to encourage students to reflect upon what they have learnt in a lesson, e.g. 'Who improved their listening skills?' or 'Who now has a better understanding of interdependence?' Unanimous disapproval of a particular activity or a unanimous feeling that nothing was learnt should subsequently be followed up by the teacher in a small group or one-to-one context.

(**Source**: developed from an idea in Coover, V. et. al., Resource Manual for a Living Revolution, Philadelphia, New Society Publishers, 1981, p. 296)

One-word Circle

At the end of an activity, students form a circle and, in turn, give a one-word summary of their feelings about the activity.

Feelings Graph

A graph (see illustration) is stuck on the class-room wall, each vertical section representing one session in a course unit. At the end of the first session, each student chooses her own number and draws a line from one side to the other side of the first vertical section (the number is written along the line). The line should represent how the student felt at the beginning, during and at the end of the lesson, using the −10 (very negative) to +10 (very positive) scale. In the illustration, person 8 began the first session in a quite negative mood and became very positive whilst person 2 began feeling quite positive and stayed so. At the end of each subsequent session, a further column is filled in, the student beginning her line where it finished at the close of the session before. Individual lines are open to a variety of interpretations but the overall spread and clustering of the lines will give facilitators some idea of how the course is going. The graph can be used as a basis for course evaluation sessions.

(**Source**: Coover, V. et al., Resource Manual for a Living Revolution, Philadelphia, New Society Publishers, 1981, p. 296)

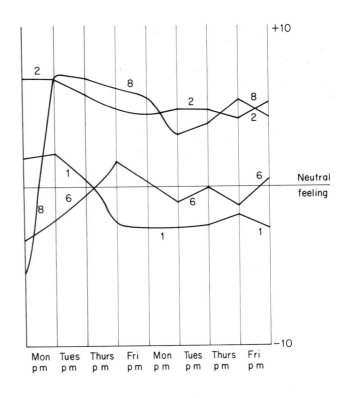

Small Group Evaluations

Students form groups of four to six and are asked to choose a secretary. Groups are asked to address themselves to an evaluation task such as one of the following:

- everyone to identify two or three points in the course unit which were especially important/interesting to them; likewise two or three unimportant/uninteresting points.

- everyone to identify the high point and low point of the course unit;

- the group to examine expectations gathered at the beginning of the course (see p. 276) and to discuss to what degree their expectations have been satisfied or have changed;

- the group to answer the question: 'If the course unit were repeated, what could be changed and improved, and how?';

- the group to ask themselves: 'What have we learnt from this course unit?';

- the group to collect queries they have about the content of the course unit and about the way the unit has been conducted by the facilitator.

Using a felt tip pen and sugar paper, the secretary writes down the points/queries/answers raised by the group. A full class evaluation begins with small groups reporting back.

(**Source**: derived from ideas in Coover, V. et al., Resource Manual for a Living Revolution, Philadelphia, New Society Publishers, 1981, pp. 295–6)

Self-evaluation

Students are given a Self-evaluation sheet after each group activity. The sheet is primarily concerned with social behaviours but can also ask questions about skills development and attitude towards the activities. They file it along with their other Self-evaluation sheets, occasionally being encouraged to compare all their sheets to look for changes and trends, followed, if they wish, by a personal chat with the teacher. A simple Self-evaluation sheet for primary use is illustrated here.

Self-Evaluation

Name _____

Group _____

Activity _____

Date _____

1 How well did you work?	☺ YES	😐 A LITTLE	☹ NO
2 Did you help someone in the group?	☺ YES	😐 A LITTLE	☹ NO
3 Did you help the group?	☺ YES	😐 SOMETIMES	☹ NO
4 Did you listen to what the others were saying ?	☺ WELL	😐 SO-SO	☹ NOT SO WELL
5 Did you like the activity?	☺ YES	😐 SO-SO	☹ NO
6 Did you have enough time?	☺ YES		☹ NO

Source: Borba, M. and C., *Self-esteem: a Classroom Affair.* Vol. 2., Minneapolis, Winton Press, 1982, p. 122–3.

Personal Coat of Arms

A coat of arms (see example) is hung up in the classroom. Students draw their own coats of arms. After some reflection on their week's, term's or year's work, they fill in the sections.

Alternatively, students join together to make a huge coat of arms for the whole class.

(**Source**: Brandes, D. and Phillips, H., Gamesters' Handbook, Hutchinson, 1979, personal development activity, No. 36)

My learning successes this term	Things I shall have to work on
My hopes for next term	My hopes for a year from now
Motto (summing up *me* this term)	Epitaph (how I think others would sum me up)

Part Three
THE GLOBAL CURRICULUM

13 Subject-based approaches to global education

The purpose of this Section is to offer some ideas as to what a global perspective across the curriculum might involve. It is not our intention to be repetitive (what has already been said about aims and objectives, teaching and learning styles and classroom relationships is, we submit, of equal importance for all teachers irrespective of subject specialism). Rather we propose to advance the argument by suggesting some important ways in which global perspectives can be infused into both the content and methodology of the so-called 'traditional' subjects. Such an infusion, we maintain, is a mutually beneficial process; each subject's content and methodology is thereby vivified whilst the concerns of global education are reinforced, as they need to be, across the student's entire school experience.

Language and communications

1 English

The enjoyment and study of literature offers a powerful means of developing self-awareness (including a recognition of the assumptions lying behind our worldview), sensitivity to different perspectives, an appreciation of the rich and dynamic cultural traditions within and beyond our own society and a more vivid understanding of the human implications of global issues. Equally, literature can enable us to take imaginative leaps into the past and future. 'Everyone knows that stories are like spells. They can be magic for children as well as adults, through time and across cultures. Storytime is often when children are most absorbed and intent, spellbound by the power of narrative... Stories give experience of other people's lives, ideas and cultures, both past and present, and allow for fantasising about new worlds and times ahead. They give children access to experiences which in real life they may be denied... Stories can be carriers of cultural traditions and values. Children can be led to assess and confront fundamental messages about human relations and values through stories. This becomes particularly important when a society is changing rapidly, and having to face challenges to its traditional views and attitudes – such as relationships between young and old, attitudes towards women and views held about people of different race, culture and religion.'[1]

A global framework for syllabus construction in first-language courses

by **Anthony Short**, Head of the English and Communication Department, La Grande Boissière, International School of Geneva

Global perspectives mean looking at national, international and universal issues from points of view additional to one's own. We should maintain, as a Bruner-type, working premise, that global perspectives can be presented to children of any age in an appropriate and intellectually respectable form. In a first-language course, the points of view are:

(a) the student's own,
(b) those of the literary work,
(c) those gained by games, role plays, simulations, and
(d) those gained by 'research' and projects appropriately directed.

The 'thrust', of global education has, rightly, been to develop (c) and (d) as an integral part of the curriculum. However, insufficient attention has been paid to (b). The importance of constructing a year's syllabus in a first-language course, especially in English, can be made clear by reference to two extreme forms of curriculum.

One extreme is that of a traditional course in a nearly all-white area. Students seldom if ever participate in classroom improvisation, games and simulations. Studies and library projects are regarded as outside the curriculum. The syllabus is traditional and patriotic, particularly as students move towards external examinations. Unless such a school makes a deliberate effort to internationalise its literary syllabus, its hidden curriculum teaches students that the literature of other English-speaking countries must be inferior or culturally unapproachable, and that this is even more true of literature written in other languages.

The opposite extreme might be an urban multiracial comprehensive in which first-language teachers choose literature that reinforces the social and ethnic cultures of the student population. Humanities schemes, active work and simulations are regarded as basic to a curriculum for global understanding. Yet even here, despite the tremendous opportunities created for students, global perspectives as such remain within the points of view of national and colonial literature.

In an American high school, the same nationalistic pressures include the literature of Hispanic and black minorities within a solidly American choice of authors, apart from the ritual inclusion of Chaucer, Shakespeare and Dickens. As seen from the rootless insecurity of an international school, in which there is no majority culture, almost every national first-language syllabus is embarrassingly national, if not chauvinistic. First-language curricula in French schools are only beginning to recognise the literature of Switzerland, Canada or their ex-colonial African countries. One would like to know how far Spanish schools have started to incorporate the astonishing creativity of South American novelists.

Global perspectives require as a minimum that, in each year, the syllabus includes at least one author from another country in a culturally different form of the same first-language.

The full development of global perspectives also requires that every year's syllabus should include world literature in translation.

A global framework for a year's syllabus construction would thus look something like this:

	First-language national	First-language other nations	World literature in translation
Fiction	X	0	
Poetry	X0		
Drama	0		
Discursive prose	X	0	
Mythology/ religion		X	0

Thus the 'entitlement syllabus' in each year would consist of a minimum of five works or collections that covered both the five genres and the three sources. The noughts and crosses above indicate two of the many possible patterns of choice.

A useful exercise for first-language departments is to fill in the framework with five titles for a particular year, first individually and then collectively. These five works form the core syllabus and should represent between one half and three-quarters of the year's work in reading and reading-related activities. Individual teachers can then be left free to choose whatever they want for the remainder of the year's work. The role of the head of department is to ensure that the choices for each year also provide a coherent foundation, particularly in fourth and fifth year, for 16+ or 18+ studies. Over those years, students should experience a balanced selection from major periods.

As students move towards GCSE, A level (or AP, *baccalaureate*, *maturité* or *abitur*), it becomes more, not less important that the global framework be adhered to. If a particular examining board only offers one non-national or non-native author (the token black in the front office), teachers should either change boards or pressurise the board to accept an individual school syllabus.

Adopting a global framework for syllabus construction is not easy. Any number of arguments can be raised against it. 'Students must know their national literary heritage first' (i.e. exclusively and forever); 'these Galashiel lads are still translating Billy Connolly' (it's all foreign outside); 'poetry in translation isn't' ('I'm an Empsonian Leavisite'); 'mythology isn't relevant' ('I refuse to let them read *Genesis*, for religious reasons; the *Koran*, for political reasons, the *Ramayana*, because I haven't studied it; *Man the Mythmaker*, because it's American').

However, once started, the global framework justifies itself in practice. For British students, for example, *Old Mali and the Boy*, *Walkabout* (especially Roeg's film), *Things Fall Apart*, *Crime and Punishment*, *Life and Times of Michael K*, *The Heart is a Lonely Hunter*, *For Whom the Bell Tolls*, *The Doll's House*, *The Sound of Waves*, *Antigone*, *Pnin*, *One Hundred Years of Solitude*, *The Outsider*, *Siddhartha*, *The Summer of My German Soldier*, *One Day in the Life of Ivan Denisovich* are irresistible doors into other cultures, other mentalities, other ways of living and landscapes in which the students discover their own concerns. Our departmental experience over the years is that such works are also essential for the full development of young people's purely critical abilities.

A broadening of the literary diet offered in the English classroom is therefore called for. There is a place for the autobiographies, plays, poems, stories and novels of a range of countries and cultures where English is spoken (we do well to remember that English as spoken and written by the majority of British people is a minority form of the language). The literature of Africa, the Caribbean and the Indian sub-continent is still conspicuous by its absence from many classrooms. Such literature is not only richly enjoyable in its own right; it also counteracts the notion that non-Europeans have no literary culture, offers sympathetic access to other cultures and, very importantly, offers the perspective of the recipient on Britain's role as a major colonising power, thereby often illuminating 'the schisms of consciousness in individuals caused by the impact of cultural domination'.[2]

For the same reasons, the literature of arrivant ethnic minorities in the United Kingdom demands inclusion in the curriculum. 'The words they bring,' writes Chris Searle, 'are a huge enrichment to our language and cultural resources in Britain, to be welcomed and nourished and added to the language canon of our people.'[3] Nor should we forget the vibrant literature of the many cultures and sub-cultures in English-speaking countries such as Australia, Canada, Ireland, South Africa and the United States. There is also a strong case for the inclusion of world literature in translation in the range of works available in class.

A broadened literary diet will offer ample opportunity for pursuing themes central to global education such as rights, development and the environment and for promoting perspective consciousness. The novels of Nigerian Dan Fulani, for instance, touch upon major global themes in a way which will excite the interest of top primary and lower secondary students. *The Fight for Life* (Hodder and Stoughton, 1982) deals with the advertising and sale of baby milk powders in Nigeria, whilst *The Price of Liberty* (Hodder and Stoughton, 1981) takes up the

Wandering Tribe

Pulled from their homeland,
Like plants from a root.
Driven, beaten into a Strange New World.
Yet they still retained their consciousness
Of who they were.

Their oppression had given birth
To a whole new culture,
Adopted, plagiarised and raped
By their captives.

Years later the world sees how
It has used these influences,
Yet it denies its heritage
And subtly violates it.

Where do we stand now?
Our parentage pulls us one way
Our native land another.
Who do we fight for?
The West Indies? England? Britain?
Or the Atlantic Sea?

Stuck in a Futile Limbo,
With racism on one side
And misunderstanding on the other.

We are truly a Wandering Tribe!

Julie Monica Plenty, *Black Youth Annual Penmanship Award 1981* theme of the sale of dangerous pesticides in the 'Third World' by unscrupulous transnational companies. Higher up the secondary school, *One Hundred Years of Solitude* by Gabriel Garcia Marquez (Picador, 1978), describing the development of a small town in South America, will offer the student a compelling sensory insight into an entirely different perspective on life. Access to the literature of various countries and cultures is easily achieved.[4]

Works by English writers taking up important global themes are also increasingly available. James Watson's *Talking in Whispers* (Gollancz, 1983), a political thriller set in Chile, describes the courageous exploits of three young people in their stand against oppression. Gene Kemp's *The Turbulent Term of Tyke Tiler* (Penguin, 1977) has quickly become a classic means of confronting young students with sex role stereotyping whilst Jay Williams' *The Practical Princess and Other Liberating Fairy Tales* (Chatto, 1979) provides an excellent antidote to the usual image of the folk tale heroine.

'Essentially,' writes Gillian Klein, 'children are looking in literature for aspects of their potential selves.'[5] For this reason stories about children caught up in and responding to major events involving injustice, oppression and war can offer a powerful stimulus for discussion. Anne Holm's *I am David* (Methuen, 1980), a tale of a boy's escape from a prison camp, and Barbara Smucker's *Underground to Canada* (Penguin, 1978), telling of the escape from slavery of two twelve year old black girls, are two such stories.

Some English teachers have sought to link contemporary global themes to their treatment of literature which has long had a place in the classroom. Shakespeare's *Othello*, for instance, has been used as a springboard for discussion of prejudice and racism whilst an examination of sexism and sex roles can follow from the study of *The Taming of the Shrew* and the Wife of Bath's Tale in Chaucer's *Canterbury Tales*.

The study of *language* can also be imbued with a global perspective especially if accompanied by a shift away from the study of grammar towards a 'language awareness' approach. Tracing the etymology of English words can serve to show how interlinked the world has become and that there is no such thing as a 'pure' language. Younger students can play a simulation game entitled 'The Word House' in which words are grouped in 'families' according to their origin. The 'families' represent peoples with whom the English have had contact throughout history and from whom words have been adopted. Students are startled to find that seemingly ordinary English words such as husband, gymnasium, boss, balloon, traffic, shampoo and pyjamas have been 'borrowed' from elsewhere.[6] Similarly, they can go on to discover English words in other languages.

The introduction of elementary linguistics can play a vital part in promoting global-mindedness and consciousness of perspective. 'Human beings do not live in the objective world alone, nor alone in the world of social activity as ordinarily understood, but are very much at the mercy of the particular language which has become the medium of expression for their society. It is quite an illusion to imagine that one adjusts to reality essentially without the use of language and that language is merely an incidental means of solving specific problems of communication and reflection. The fact of the matter is that the "real world" is to a large extent unconsciously built up on the language habits of the group.'[7] What is it about Japanese culture and language, students can be asked, that leads to a corporate as against individual conception of rights? Why do Australian aboriginal languages make it impossible to talk about humanity and the environment as distinct entities? Are there things that people speaking other languages can say and feel that cannot be said and felt through English? Such questions can open up an understanding of the triangular relationship between culture, language and worldview.

Other areas for language awareness work include:

- the exploration of culture-free and culture-bound forms of non-verbal communication (e.g. similarity of all gestures indicating hunger; the different significance of the giggle in English and Japanese);

- body language in different cultures (e.g. eye contact, posture, proximity, gesture, forms of greeting, use of hands in prayer);

- the use of silence in different cultures and different cultural understandings of what silence is;

- an explanation of the basic equality, in terms of communication effectiveness, of all languages/dialects, and of the political reasons why certain languages/dialects – such as Standard English – have come to enjoy prestige and status;

- an examination of the historical development of languages world-wide and of the political, social, economic and cultural influences that have shaped language development;

- an examination of how languages have developed differently according to whether their cultural traditions are oral or written;

- inter-generational changes in language (exploring the differences in language use by parents, grandparents, other older people and the students themselves) and the reasons for these changes (e.g. technological, culture-contact, changes in level of permissiveness);

- gender issues arising from language construction and usage;

- the universality of the need to communicate and elements common to all languages.[8]

Practical ways of introducing such areas into primary and secondary English language work are provided by Audrey Gregory and Norah Woollard in *Looking into Language: Diversity in the Classroom* and by the ILEA English Centre publications, *The Languages Book* and *The English Curriculum: Gender*.[9]

The English classroom is also replete with opportunities for comprehension, written and discussion work around major global themes. English teachers have found the group discussion activities described in Section 7 of this book to provide excellent contexts for language development work. Finally, English teachers have developed highly innovative media studies programmes around global issues.

2 Foreign Languages

by **Hugh Starkey**, Westminster College, Oxford

If there is one area of the curriculum that ought to be central to global education it is languages. If there is one set of skills that the global citizen ought to possess it is the ability to communicate in languages other than one's own. If we are really to empathise with other people we must be prepared to look at the ways in which their language encapsulates and interprets the world.

What a disappointment then to discover that foreign language teaching has been and still largely is one of the most backward and intransigent areas of the curriculum in global terms. An observer of pupils ploughing their weary way through five years of a language course would notice that the foreign language was used essentially as a tool of the consumer. The syllabus has pupils visiting tourist spots, staying in hotels, ordering ice-creams and meals in restaurants. Foreign families are portrayed as classically nuclear and white with fathers in work and mothers in the kitchen. Foreign language textbooks are amongst the most fertile ground for discovering bias, racism and stereotype.

But it does not have to be thus. The content is not fixed and immutable and the new methodology of language teaching based on ability to communicate rather than formal accuracy encourages discussion, exchange of information and opinions perhaps

leading to a personal or collective creative product such as a dramatic sketch, poster, letter or graph.

Two recent changes in language teaching methodology have prepared the way for foreign languages to gain their rightful place as one of the main vehicles for conveying a global perspective. One is the agreement that a language should wherever possible be taught with reference to authentic materials, that is materials produced by and for people who use the language as their main means of communication. This is in opposition to previous traditions where, because the syllabus was constructed following a certain grammatical sequence, material had to be specially written, usually by non-natives. The second innovation is that, with the accent on communication, language learning is no longer perceived as an individual activity but as something collective. Students have to talk to somebody and it cannot always be the teacher. They must therefore work predominantly in pairs and groups. They must be stimulated to talk and they will want to talk if they are able to involve themselves and their feelings. The task set needs to be one that is interesting and worthwhile in itself. The means of achieving it will be through the foreign language. Although the teacher may be primarily concerned with the amount of practice in the foreign language, the learner should be more interested in the content and the nature of the task.

For cautious teachers authentic materials are menus, bus tickets and tourist brochures. For global teachers, authentic materials may be campaign leaflets, advertisements, articles, cartoons or posters about current events, environmental issues, human rights, peace and interdependence. Which materials are likely to produce the better discussion? Which are more likely to involve the learner? Which are likely to achieve better learning? The choice of a content that engages the minds and feelings of the learners, the choice of a task that stimulates them to express themselves are fully justified in purely pragmatic terms. Such an approach gives better results. Global teachers and language teachers have come together in the search for appropriate material and tasks. There is now a two-way flow of influence. Affirmation exercises, group discussion exercises, experiential activities, role plays and simulations are now all part of mainstream foreign language teaching.

The most widely taught foreign language in the world is English. For most people in the world their perceptions of English-speaking society and culture come from television and then what is transmitted in their English lessons. It is to be hoped that the content goes beyond tea and tourism. Foreign language teachers should remain aware of the view of the world they are transmitting. They can also play a useful role in helping their students achieve a better and critical understanding of the media.

In the early stages of learning a foreign language the focus is usually on the individual meeting and talking with others. Affirmation activities have a twofold usefulness here. Speaking a foreign language requires self-confidence (as well as building it). The subject matter of affirmation exercises is personal information; name, likes, shared feelings and concerns. All this can be done in the foreign language at beginner level. So can co-operative games. Language learning too is learning through doing.

The notion of tense in language is the notion of time. A global perspective is also a temporal perspective, building on and learning from the past and looking to the future. Work on time-lines and other future-oriented activites is the ideal way to convey, incidentally, the future tense. Often students have difficulty with tenses because they are taught in a meaningless context. Global education provides an authentic context which facilitates learning.

Foreign language teaching methodology is based on a triptych usually referred to by a formula such as Presentation, Practice, Production. In the first stage the teacher introduces the new linguistic structure or function in a context. For instance, the future and conditional tenses can be presented by reference to wishes for a better world. Comparison can be introduced in the context of national and international statistics. Forbidding can be in the context of an immigration officer and an applicant. Instructions can be about building solar panels or drilling wells. Warnings can be about animals in danger of extinction.

In the Practice phase the teacher lets the students use the language in a controlled way. The control is usually the provision of a game that will rely on formulaic language ('It's your turn') or a role play or structured conversation. Again the teacher chooses the context and devises the roles so that the subject can be anything likely to prove interesting or amusing. Students learn to empathise by playing a role but also by playing it using a foreign language.

The third phase has students using the language to perform a more open-ended and creative task. This may be preparing food or building a model from instructions; it could be writing a letter to a magazine or a politician; it could be making a radio item or video to persuade or inform; it could be making a poster or contributing to an exhibition; it could be discussing an issue and summarising the outcome. The teacher of foreign languages will find much inspiration for such tasks and activities in the major source books on global education. The context will be determined with a view to encouraging a global and multi-ethnic perspective and promoting the central values of justice, peace, solidarity and co-operation.

A textbook* published for students of French in their fourth and fifth years of study has brought together authentic French materials that provides a global rather than Eurocentric perspective. These provide a context for role play, discussion work and a variety of creative activities. Amongst other materials the book includes: a Greenpeace protest about nuclear testing; a leaflet on Tanzanian instant coffee and cartoon strips discussing colonialism and food production; women defending themselves in Chad; an interview with a boutique owner who imports clothes from India; racist incidents in the Paris Metro.

*Aplin R., et al., Orientations, Hodder and Stoughton, 1985.
Also see: Ur, P., Discussions that Work, CUP, 1981; Klippel, F., Keep Talking, CUP, 1984.

Pages from 'Orientations'

Humanities

1 History

The question today is whether, now that we have so evidently become 'one world', the study of our own constitutional and social history in isolation is sufficient. If we have become part of one world must we not concern ourselves with the history of that world, as the only proper approach to understanding it?[10]

So wrote Her Majesty's Inspectors of Schools in 1967. This exhortation to globalise history teaching notwithstanding, traditional school history was still being admonished in 1984 for its élitism, sexism, Eurocentrism and racism: 'One can swing through 300 years of history via Drake, Raleigh, Cromwell, Marlborough, Wolfe, Nelson and Wellington with only passing references to women, non-European peoples and countries.'[11]

The introduction of a global dimension in the history curriculum offers exciting possibilities in terms of content and skills development. It is likely to offer a more accurate picture of the past in that it is not remotely possible to gain a fair picture of the history of a particular nation or region without also examining its many links with the rest of the world.

A first step is, perhaps, to create space for the study of non-European civilisations and countries. Courses on ancient history in the lower secondary school have been very much Greek and Roman-oriented. An input from Indian, Chinese, Arabian, African and Amerindian civilisations is desirable. Likewise, aspects of British and European medieval history can be juxtaposed with material from the history of non-European societies. Tulse Hill School, a pioneer in this field, has developed a series of information booklets and teaching units which aim to help third-year secondary students understand something of the social organisation of African, European, Indian, Chinese, North American, South American and Caribbean societies in the years around 1400 AD. 'The unit on Africa makes reference to the West African Kingdom, the Ethiopian Empire, Great Zimbabwe, the Trans-Saharan and East Coast trading networks

A reconstruction of Great Zimbabwe: a city of some 10,000 people in the fourteenth century.

and Islam. In India we examine both the Moslem Mughal Empire and the Hindu Vijayanagan Empire. China involves the Sung and Ming Dynasties, South America, the Inca Empire, Europe is focused mainly on Britain, the Caribbean on Arawak and Carib histories and North America on the Pueblo and the Kwakiukutl peoples.'[12] The period around 1400 was chosen as the last in which different civilisations could be studied in relative isolation from each other before the age of European expansion. The different societies could therefore be shown to be culturally rich and varied with highly developed life-styles and forms of social organisation.

In the early modern period, the inflated degree of attention given to voyages of exploration/encounter (often inappropriately referred to as 'voyages of discovery') and the deeds of traders and colonists can be remedied by giving greater emphasis to the circumstances, perspectives and responses of those the explorers, traders and colonists encountered.

The last fifteen years have witnessed important developments in the provision of twentieth-century world history courses for external examination. Such courses have provided the opportunity for the study of modern African, Asian and Latin American history, although evidence suggests that most teachers still concentrate on Europe and the USA, giving 'Third World' topics scant or hurried attention.[13]

It is important to recognise that whilst the inclusion of the history of non-European civilisations and countries goes some way towards meeting some of the aims of global education, it is not global history. Rather, it is what we might call 'quasi-global history'[14] in that it compartmentalises the world into separate parts for study. 'Students fail frequently to make important connections. They do not realise, as they concentrate on a particular area of the world, that the events there may be influenced by, or have an important influence upon, what is happening in other parts of the world.'[15] A more thoroughgoing global perspective would involve the historical study of emerging patterns of interdependence and of factors that have contributed towards the world becoming a 'system of lands and peoples'. The history of transnational corporations, the development of the world trading system, the pressure upon natural resources and the world ecology, the growth of organisations and groups sharing transnational loyalties and the emergence of a shared global culture would be amongst the appropriate topics for study.

A thematic approach has much to commend it as a means of putting the global dimension into history. Themes such as self-determination, development, neo-colonialism and migration provide frameworks within which the responses of different peoples and societies to similar issues can be studied. The latitude of real choice within each situation given the increasingly systemic nature of the modern world can be assessed and, with twentieth-century history, case studies of international organisations 'in action' built into each theme.

School history has not been helped by its tendency to think of topics as being 'local', 'national' or 'international'. In studying modern and contemporary history when the world has become gradually, and then dramatically, an interdependent entity, such terms of reference can distort rather than reflect historical reality. Seemingly 'British' topics need to be reappraised to encompass Britain's interactions with the wider world. The Industrial Revolution, for example, is better understood if linked to the study of imperialism and the global search for raw materials, markets and investment possibilities. The burgeoning interest in local history in schools can be enlisted to help students understand the increasing impact that trends, developments and events in the wider world have had upon the lives of ordinary people. Through the collection of oral evidence, local newspaper searches and visits to archives, libraries and museums, they can be asked to plot the stages by which the locality came to be caught up in the global web.[16]

A global dimension to history will necessarily involve introducing a wider range of perspectives into the classroom: Islamic viewpoints on the Crusades; the Jewish experience of English society in the Middle Ages; the experience of black people in Britain since the late-Elizabethan period;[17] native North American perspectives on the white invasion of the American west;[18] women's perspectives.[19] Class evaluation of extracts from school history textbooks from around the world can be an effective means of developing analytical skills and sensitising students to the dramatic differences in interpretation and viewpoint that can exist between one country and another.

In advocating a global dimension in history teaching/learning, one is not asking history teachers to do other than be historians – to present a wide range of evidence offering different perspectives and viewpoints, to bring to students' attention the spread of factors impinging upon any particular occurrence, to encourage interpretation and evaluation of evidence, to develop students' empathetic skills and to provide research opportunities within a limited context. One is also reminding history teachers of the inescapable connection between past, present and future. History teaching tends to be exclusively past-oriented or, at best, asks students to consider the past in the light of the present and the present in the light of the past. A global dimension must also involve the future and address questions such as: 'Given what has gone before how do we see the years that lie ahead?', 'Can we/how do we avoid such things happening again?' and 'Knowing what people in the past have or have not done to influence their future, what should we be doing to influence ours in the way we want it to be?'

2 Geography

'It is generally agreed that geography is about places and is legitimately concerned with anything that is mappable.... There can be no question that a map showing spatial variations in the levels of human welfare is as important a document for geographical education as, say, maps of rainfall, relief or political boundaries.'[20] It seems, however, that many geographers were, until recently, resistant to the possibilities offered by their subject. 'The idea that geography might concern itself with matters of social relevance is still often a new one,' wrote David Hicks in 1979.[21]

A global dimension in school geography takes the teacher far beyond the descriptive survey of lands and peoples that has characterised much of what has taken place in the classroom. New priorities emerge which include helping students understand the systemic nature of today's world, promoting awareness of the global condition (human and environmental), *explaining* as well as *mapping* and *describing* the spatial distribution of wealth, exploring different meanings and models of development, listening to the voices of the marginalised and oppressed, treating a range of contemporary themes that are of global concern and exploring future geographies.

To achieve these ends, there needs to be less emphasis on the geography of Europe and the West and a re-appraisal of how the geography of the 'Third World' is taught. Geography teachers need to ask themselves questions such as:

- Am I encouraging the study of other countries in terms of what 'they' provide for 'us'?

- Do the case studies I offer students (e.g. plantations) remain at a largely descriptive level thereby neglecting issues such as exploitation, injustice and environmental degradation?

- Do I focus on people and *their* problems thereby individualising failure and neglecting economic and political aspects of those problems, local to global?

- Do I allow consideration of the symptoms of poverty (which, on its own, can reinforce negative images of peoples) to deflect from an analysis of its causes, local to global?

- Do I focus on the crucial role of women in development?

- Do I offer countervailing arguments and evidence to set against the prevailing Western orthodoxy that 'overpopulation' is the principal cause of poverty, hunger and malnutrition?

- Is the Western model of development explicitly or implicitly conveyed to students as the only model of development?

- Do I allow those we study to 'speak for themselves', especially peoples and groups who have neither power nor ready access to the media?

- Is classroom time given over to studying a range of proposals for achieving greater fairness in the spatial distribution of wealth?

- Are students encouraged to develop and share their own proposals and to calculate the viability and implications of those proposals?[22]

Developing students' understanding of the global system – and of the factors within the system operating to the disadvantage of certain countries and certain groups within these countries – necessarily involves classroom study of important political and economic topics such as colonialism, neo-colonialism, aid, protectionism, the operation of transnational corporations, transfer pricing and international finance. It also requires that the relationship between different aspects of the world system is explored. What, for instance, is the impact on the environment of the present world economy and vice versa? What are the implications for the environment of various models of development? What are the rights implications of different models?

Global themes to be woven into the fabric of the geography curriculum include gender, peace and war, and human rights. It is so patently the case that gender makes a difference to life experience. A geography curriculum ignoring those differences is failing to reflect the diversity of human experience and the fact that 'development depends on women'.[23] Geography's basic concern with location and spatial patterns means that 'an obvious way to integrate women and gender is to ask where the women are. Where are they in relation to men? What are the implications of these distributions?'[24] Such questions are, for instance, of critical relevance for understanding global trends in the location of industry as transnational corporations seek out low-cost female labour.[25] The theme of peace and war can be taken up by the geography teacher in a variety of ways. The exploration of spatial patterns and social processes can be extended to contexts such as armaments, security and defence. The environmental impact of military activity, military-related industry and actual armed conflict can be studied, as can aspects of global geopolitics (spheres of influence, buffer zones, foreign bases, nuclear-free zones proposals) and the geography of nuclear confrontation.[26] Another approach is to apply the concept of 'positive peace' (societies/relationships evincing high levels of justice) to topics/areas studied. Civil and political and social, economic and cultural rights provide important yardsticks which students can use in case study work, in evaluating levels of human well-being in different societies and in interpreting the workings and effects of the global system. Is the right to life being enjoyed (the geography of life expectancy and infant mortality)? If not, what are the reasons? Are people able to enjoy their right to work (the geography of employment)? If not, what are the local/global factors creating unemployment? Geographical topics are, by definition, replete with rights issues.[27]

Important sources for dealing with global themes in the geography classroom are now readily available. Amongst the most attractive and most useful are *The State of the World Atlas* (1981), *The New State of the World Atlas* (1984), *The War Atlas* (1983), *The Gaia Atlas of Planet Management* (1985), the *Third World Atlas* (1983) and *World View, an Economic and Geopolitical Yearbook*.[28] These provide overviews of the world system and are excellent stimulus material for classroom group work and research. Maps such as 'Bullets and Blackboards' (showing the ratio of teachers to soldiers), 'Scourges of the State' (on political prisoners, torture and use of capital punishment) and 'Women Workers' (on sex discrimination in jobs) offer ways into a more relevant, issues-based geography. Advice on classroom activities using such maps is available.[29]

Such maps also provide a useful antidote to the traditionally-used Mercator Projection which, by distorting land area in favour of accuracy of direction and distance, exaggerates the size of countries in the 'Rich North'. It is helpful to have in class a copy of a map which shows land area accurately so that students gain a more accurate picture of the smallness of Europe relative to, say, Africa or South America.[30]

Imaginary maps of the future (see overleaf) are one way of providing a future orientation in the geography classroom. Others include extrapolative work in which students are asked to project present trends forward in time, techniques to seek a consensus of opinion about geographical futures (e.g. 'the world map in fifty years' time') such as **Delphi Forecasting** (see p. 160) and imaginative work in which students try to anticipate the surprises of the future.[31]

3 Religious Education

A global dimension in Religious Education can be achieved through:

- the study of the beliefs, practices and customs of world religions;

- the study of and reflection upon global issues and the general global condition in the light of the teachings of world religions.

Whilst the multi-ethnic classroom provides the greatest opportunities for the study of world religions and religious cultures, there is now an increasing range of attractive textual and audio-visual resources for use in all schools. In the multi-ethnic classroom, the starting point can be the students and their own experiences. Such a 'grounded' approach can and should also involve input by parents, community groups and local religious leaders.[32] In the case of junior and lower secondary classes, topics can usefully include festivals (e.g. Christmas, Divali, Eid, Ramadam), holy places and places of pilgrimage (e.g. Amritsar, Jerusalem, Mecca), significant women and men in the development of each faith, a basic understanding of the main articles of belief, religious signs and symbols and their significance (e.g. Cross, Crescent, Star of David), sacred writings, significant events in the history of each faith and religious traditions, ceremonies and rituals. In the upper secondary school, the list can be extended to include, amongst others, the following activities: the

PROJECT IF: INVENTING THE FUTURE WORKSHEET SERIES

TOPIC   ANTARCTICA

INPUT   Below is the latest travel poster from 21st Century Tours

SHEET 1 of 1

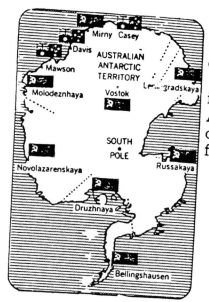

It's just three hours away. and has more natural beauty than just about any country on earth.

You will find a range of hotels from top international standard to budget priced. And they are ideally located to suit your choice of outdoor activity, be it skiing, fishing, golfing, trekking or whatever

For further details, see your travel agent

Antarctica
the all-year paradise.

OUTPUT

1   What does this poster tell you about changes that have taken place since the present?

2   List possible reasons for the changes in Antarctica

    Try to find current evidence that suggests how these changes could be brought about

3   In the 21st century, what other places in the world might be very different from the way they are today? Design a travel poster for one of these changed places and describe your holiday there

4   Consider the place where you now live (suburb, town, city. etc). What changes would you like to have take place in fifty years time? Describe how these changes might be brought about

5   Many people are concerned that the world is losing its wilderness areas because humans want or need more places to be used for mining, hydro-electricity, timber, sport, tourism. etc

    What reasons can you suggest for conserving the "uselessness" of the world's wilderness areas?

PROJECT IF: RUSDEN CENTRE FOR STUDIES IN THE CURRICULUM
Inquiries to Noel Gough Victoria College Rusden Campus Blackburn Road Clayton Vic 3168

interpretation of religious expression in various artistic, literary and musical forms, the use and interpretation of primary religious sources, study of the lives and work of contemporary religious figures and an exploration of what insights faiths have to offer on the nature and purpose of life, suffering, death and god.[33] Visits to places of worship are important in 'the support they provide for pupils of particular faiths, in links they establish with the local community in the demonstration of religion as a living thing and in the insight they afford into beliefs and practices'.[34]

The exploration of world religions will alert students to both what is different in and what is common to those religions. It will also highlight the universal need of humankind to find meaning in life. For that reason, the beliefs of those who profess no religion should also find a place in the RE curriculum.

Religions of the world 'teem with issues of justice, equality and dignity'.[35] It follows that Religious Education has a distinctive contribu-

tion to make to global education by examining global issues in the light of the teachings of different faiths. Such a process is of two-way benefit. It will serve to sharpen students' understanding of cultural and religious perspectives (the World Wildlife Fund's *Worlds of Difference* pack, for example, introduces students to how the environment and environmental matters are perceived by different faiths).[36] It will also help develop heightened awareness of the ethical dimensions of the issues themselves. The exercise should not stop at 'what a religion teaches in theory' but should also include 'how its members behave in practice'.[37]

Another way of approaching global issues in the Religious Education classroom is through studying the lives of outstanding religious figures who have worked to ameliorate injustice, poverty, oppression and persecution in the modern world. A list would include Gandhi, Martin Luther King, Mother Theresa, Helder Camera and Desmond Tutu. An advantage of this approach is that it 'highlights in concrete terms the necessity of action'[38] and the relationship between action and values.

4 Economics

'The "one country" bias of many economics courses has been under attack for over a decade,' writes Steve Hurd, 'and yet still the majority of students in school are exposed to the problems of the UK economy to the virtual exclusion of socialist, Third World and even other Western economies.'[39] There has also been a tendency, particularly at advanced level, to emphasise economic theory at the expense of 'applied economics in general, and of topical real world issues in particular'.[40]

The potential for a global dimension in school economics is huge. Studies of the local or national economy can be used as a springboard for the exploration of the international economy including aspects of the international market and financial systems (e.g. protectionism, transnational corporations, primary product price instability, international financial institutions, aid, the international debt crisis). Another important area for study is that of development/underdevelopment. A range of explanations for underdevelopment can be explored including those which emphasise the characteristics of the

Chola bronze of Dancing Shiva

underdeveloped countries/regions themselves (e.g. poor physical environment, corruption, military spending) and those which emphasise the malign influence of 'the North' (e.g. adverse terms of trade, imposition of inappropriate technologies, interest charges). Likewise, students can be introduced to alternative development strategies – autarky versus dependency/interdependency, high-tech/capital intensive versus low-tech/labour intensive, urban-based versus rural-based and so on.

Work on the world economic system and development/underdevelopment can be underpinned by comparative work on national economies. Students can be introduced to indicators of economic well-being such as Gross National Product per capita, health and literacy rates, and, bearing in mind the limitations of such indicators, they can conduct a comparative study of a representative sample of countries. The economic structure of the countries can,

likewise, be investigated (e.g. production methods and type of control exercised over the economy). Students' research findings will inevitably give rise to discussion about different development strategies and about economic relationships globally.

A further approach is to address the economic effects and implications of world problems, such as the arms race, systematic rights denials (e.g. in Chile and South Africa), resource depletion and environmental degradation.

The economics classroom also offers scope for forecasting, speculation about and reflection upon the future. Given present economic trends what does the world's economic future look like? What would be the characteristics of a future economic system designed to reduce global disparities in wealth? What will the economy of a 'post-industrial society' look like?

Resources to support the globalisation of the economics curriculum are readily available.[41]

Mathematics and the sciences

1 Mathematics

by **Brian Hudson**, formerly Head of Mathematics, Greenlands High School for Girls, Blackpool, and now Senior Lecturer in Mathematics, Sheffield City Polytechnic

The mathematics classroom offers exciting opportunities for the consideration of global issues since mathematics itself is central to much of the communication that takes place daily in all our lives. Most of the information continually being fed to us provides opportunities for meaningful mathematical activity. This is particularly true since the advent of the calculator and its subsequent acceptance by teachers and legitimisation through the examination boards.

For instance, it is possible to give consideration to such information as unemployment figures, inflation rates, population growth, infant mortality rates, life expectancy levels, adult literacy rates, energy consumption and levels of social and military spending. The mathematical activity arising from dealing with data of this kind would allow for the development of statistical skills and understanding and also skills in graphical interpretation and representation, to identify just two relevant areas of the mathematics curriculum. Such an approach, being open-ended and entailing a range of concepts and skills to be developed and applied, contrasts with the traditional approach which is based upon the con-

sideration of a narrow range of skills or concepts, often divorced from any meaningful context.

The classroom examples which follow are drawn from a package of classroom materials which was developed as part of a project carried out at the Centre for Global Education during 1984/85. This package consists of a computer data base of statistics relating to demographic, social, military and economic factors, and supporting classroom materials focusing upon related issues at a local, national and international level.

World population figures can, for example, be used to develop skills in graphical representation and interpretation. Skills in calculation may also be developed and applied as in the example below.

▼ Population growth

Two thousand years ago the world population was approximately 250 million. By 1830 it had reached 1000 million or 1 billion. The figures in the table below show the significant stages in population growth since that time.

YEAR	TOTAL WORLD POPULATION (billions)
1850	1
1930	2
1960	3
1970	3.5
1983	4.6

(Table compiled from: Jonathon Porrit, *Seeing Green*, Basil Blackwell, 1984, p. 26; *Information Please Almanac, Atlas and Yearbook*, New York, Simon & Schuster, 1972; *The World Almanac and Book of Facts* 1986; *Whitaker's Almanac*, 1986)

1 Show these figures clearly on a graph using suitable axes.
2 Use your graph to work out the expected world population in the year 2000
3 When was the world population half of that given in your answer to 2?
4 Using your previous answer, work out how long it will have taken for the world population to double itself up to the year 2000.

▼ Infant Mortality

Having started by considering the levels of world population it would then be appropriate to examine the levels of infant mortality at a global level. The table below is a print out from the computer data base of the infant mortality rates for the years 1960 and 1981. The figures represent the number of infants failing to survive beyond the age of one year per thousand live births. INFMORT 1 represents figures for 1960 and INFMORT 2 figures for 1981.

The data in the table above has been selected on the basis of the figures for 1981. The level set for this figure was 13 or less and in the following table the corresponding figure was 140 or more. Both of these tables serve to demonstrate how information may be selected using the associated information retrieval programme.

COUNTRY	INFMORT 1	INFMORT 2
UNITED STATES	26	12
CANADA	27	10
BELGIUM	31	12
DENMARK	22	8
FRANCE	27	10
WEST GERMANY	34	12
NETHERLANDS	18	8
NORWAY	19	8
UNITED KINGDOM	23	11
EAST GERMANY	39	12
FINLAND	21	7
SPAIN	50	10
IRELAND	29	11
SWEDEN	17	7
SWITZERLAND	21	8
JAPAN	30	7
SINGAPORE	36	11
AUSTRALIA	20	10
NEW ZEALAND	23	12

127 records searched
19 records matched

COUNTRY	INFMORT 1	INFMORT 2
YEMEN, ARAB REPUBLIC	210	190
YEMEN, PEOPLES DEM. REP.	210	140
AFGHANISTAN	230	200
NEPAL	200	150
ANGOLA	210	150
BENIN	210	150
CENTRAL AFRICAN REP.	200	150
CHAD	200	150
CONGO	200	150
ETHIOPIA	180	150
GUINEA	210	160
LIBERIA	190	150
MALAWI	210	170
MALI	200	150
MAURITANIA	190	140
NIGER	190	140
RWANDA	150	140
SENEGAL	180	140
SIERRA LEONE	230	200
SOMALIA	180	150
UPPER VOLTA	250	210
KAMPUCHEA	150	190

127 records searched
22 records matched

A further development would be to investigate other items of data in order to identify any correlations. For example, the table on p. 250 gives information on both life expectancy and access to safe water and the activity has been designed to enable an investigation of these figures to take place.

▼ Water and Health

The following table shows two things about several countries.

LIFEXPEC: is the average age which people reach.
WATER: shows the percentage of people who can get good drinking water without germs and disease.

COUNTRY	LIFEXPEC	WATER
ARGENTINA	71	60%
BOLIVIA	51	39%
BRAZIL	64	63%
CHILE	68	76%
COLUMBIA	63	64%
CUBA	73	62%
DOMINICAN REP.	62	57%
ECUADOR	62	51%
EL SALVADOR	63	48%
GUATEMALA	59	42%
HAITI	54	12%
HONDURAS	59	55%
MEXICO	66	59%
NICARAGUA	57	46%
PARAGUAY	65	28%
PERU	58	49%
URUGUAY	71	78%
TURKEY	62	69%
BULGARIA	73	
CZECHOSLOVAKIA	72	78%
HUNGARY	71	44%
POLAND	73	55%
ROMANIA	71	
USSR	72	
ALBANIA	70	72%
SPAIN	74	78%
IRELAND	73	73%
YUGOSLAVIA	71	58%
IRAN	58	51%
IRAQ	57	76%
JORDAN	62	66%
OMAN	49	52%
SAUDI ARABIA	55	64%
SYRIA	65	71%
YEMEN, ARAB REPUBLIC	43	4%
YEMEN, PEOPLES DEM. REP.	46	37%
AFGHANISTAN	37	10%
BANGLADESH	48	68%
INDIA	52	41%
NEPAL	45	11%
PAKISTAN	50	29%

1 Find the ten countries which have the lowest life expectancy. Work out, for these ten countries, the mean (average) life expectancy *and* the mean percentage of people who can get safe water.
2 Find the ten countries with the highest life expectancy. Do the same calculations.
3 What do you notice? Can you explain your results?
4 Draw up a *scatter diagram* for all of these results. Put *life expectancy* on the x-axis, and *water* on the y-axis.

There will undoubtedly be resistance on the part of many mathematics teachers to handling potentially controversial issues of such a wide-ranging nature. However, my own experience in trialling the classroom materials is that such an approach has elicited some very positive responses from students. The following comment from a class teacher in an inner city multiracial comprehensive school is typical of this response:

It offered an original and interesting approach to statistics and aided the pupils' personal development in their awareness of world problems. I received many comments from them regarding their astonishment at the differences between rich and poor.

Robert, a member of the class, made a particularly poignant comment which said a great deal about his own previous educational experience:

I found the disk easy to work with, enjoyable and interesting. It tells you things you thought you would never know.

With some older pupils in particular I observed a greater tendency to resist the consideration of the underlying issues and to concentrate solely on the 'mathematics'. Comments typical of this attitude were:

What has this got to do with maths?
I dropped geography in the third year.

I would argue that examples of such compartmentalised thinking need to be challenged, as does the whole subject-based curriculum of which it is a product.

One outcome from working in this way in the mathematics classroom is a reduction in the control of the teacher over the content and direction of lessons. The role of the teacher will become more that of a facilitator directing students to sources of further information as a result of their own paths of enquiry. This process will entail the teacher dealing far more with the student's mathematical development at an individual level.

If the opportunities for dealing with global issues in the mathematics classroom are taken up, I believe that they will lead to challenging and worthwhile experiences for both students and teachers alike. An awareness of the places of the United Kingdom in the world has become an important educational aim in recent years and should contribute to a growing awareness of the place of the United Kingdom in Such an awareness is undoubtedly central to the lives of many young people, concerned as they are with the threat of war and famine on a world scale.

In relating mathematics to such real issues not only is it possible to develop greater global understanding and awareness but it also provides a context and, hence, the motivation on the part of students for their mathematical development to take place.

Sources for data:

The State of the World's Children, UNICEF, 1984; Sivard, R.L., *World Military and Social Expenditures*, Washington, D.C., World Publishers, 1983.
Brian Hudson's computer software package, *Global Statistics*, is available from the Centre for Global Education.

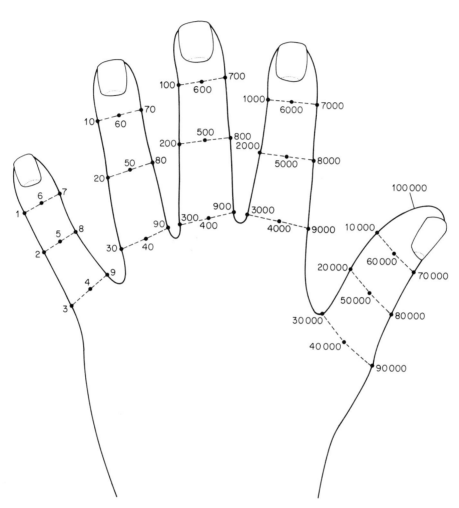

A finger counting system developed in China, using three faces of each finger

Mathematics also presents rich opportunities for the exploration of cultural achievement and diversity globally. Primary and secondary students can be introduced to non-denary counting systems such as the Mayan whilst practising basic mathematical skills. Through such work, including some introduction to Mayan history and culture, students can learn to recognise that important mathematical breakthroughs and efficient mathematical systems are by no means an exclusively European preserve.[42] Another approach is to study the way in which different societies have used geometrical patterns as a form of cultural and religious expression. Islamic art forms, based on the geometry of the circle and stressing tesselation, can provide a means of introducing geometrical shapes and exploring pattern, symmetry and the properties of circles.[43] Whilst such activities can promote an understanding of cultural diversity, they also help students appreciate the universality of humankind's need for numerical forms of expression.

Some other mathematical activities with a global dimension

Apartheid (percentages/ratio)
adapted by **Brian Hudson** from an activity devised by the Centre for Teaching International Relations, University of Denver

In South Africa 13% of the territory has been set aside as homelands for 18 million blacks, while the remaining 87% is for the country's 4 million whites.

(a) What is the total population of South Africa?

(b) What percentage of the people are black?

(c) What percentage are white?

(d) How many people are in your class?

(e) What number in your class is equivalent to the percentage of blacks in South Africa? Use the percentage that you calculated in (b).

(f) What number in your class is equivalent to the number of whites? Round off your answer to (e) and (f) to the nearest whole number. The whites occupy 87% of the land and the blacks occupy 13%.

(g) Measure the length and width of your classroom and hence calculate its area.

(h) Work out 13% of the area and divide this off from the rest. Choose the required number of people in your class to represent the blacks and to occupy the 13% of the room which has been divided off, leaving the whites in the remainder.

Finally, whilst remaining in your positions discuss the activity and your thoughts about it.

Military and social expenditure (drawings, percentages, addition)
developed by **Brian Hudson**

The following table gives details of military and social spending by government during the period 1975 to 1980.

Sector	Expenditure (£ billions)			
	1975	1977	1979	1980
Military	5.2	6.9	9.0	11.4
NHS	5.1	6.8	8.8	11.5
Education	6.6	7.8	9.6	11.9
Social Security	8.9	13.2	18.5	22.2
Housing	4.5	5.1	6.1	7.2
Debt Interest	4.2	6.4	9.0	11.3
Other	17.1	15.7	23.9	28.2
Total				

(Source: Central Statistics Office, National Income and Expenditure, 1981, HMSO)

(a) Show this information graphically using a key for each area of expenditure (i.e. a colour code or dotted, dashed lines etc.).

(b) Work out the total expenditure for each of the years shown in the table.

(c) Work out the military expenditure as a percentage of the total in (i) 1975 and (ii) 1980. Give your answers correct to one decimal place.

(d) Work out the expenditures upon health, education, social security and housing in (i) 1975 and (ii) 1980. Give these answers correct to one decimal place. Which sectors showed a percentage increase in spending during this period and which showed a decrease?

2 Biology

by **Reg Unitt**, Head of Biology at La Grande Boissière, International School of Geneva

Traditional biology courses in secondary schools have centred around studies of the anatomy and physiology of animals and plants 'with special reference to man'; extending into mechanisms of heredity and genetics; with accounts of 'evolution' and a nod in the direction of 'ecology'. During the last twenty years or so, this material has been amplified with some of the discoveries and insights provided by modern cytology and molecular biology.

Clearly, these studies have value in equipping students with a better understanding of their own bodies, basic physiological mechanisms at both cellular and organismal levels, genetic expression, variation, inheritance and the interaction and interdependence of living things. As such, they are of direct relevance to human beings everywhere and clearly fit in with some of the aims of global education.

In addition, they form the basic grounding for careers in many professions and thus must remain a major part of introductory biology syllabuses.

Yet modern courses of biology should aim to do more. Young people need to be better equipped to understand human development as individuals and as members of societies; their relationships with each other and the world around them. A great deal of information is becoming available concerning applications of new biological knowledge in agriculture, public health, environmental matters and biotechnology, to select but a few areas from a wide field. The applications of this knowledge will have an increasing impact on the lives of people throughout the entire world. Biologists need to incorporate an additional emphasis on human beings in relation to such matters and in relation to each other as a complement to the programmes summarised above. Our students need to be able to explore attitudes and values and to develop an informed awareness of the global consequences of many human activities. To take an example, many 'basic' biology courses stop accounts of human development at 'birth'. Childhood, puberty, adolescence, adulthood, parenthood, social relationships, senescence, are ignored (or largely so). This is wrong. These topics are ones that young people are particularly interested in, are certain to be *involved* in and are yet least informed about.

Biology teachers are in a position to contribute extensively to meeting these needs. But the syllabuses they teach have to allow them to do so. I suggest that this could be done by reducing the time spent on lengthy accounts (often out of date by the time they filter down to teachers in schools) of the biochemistry of cell respiration, photosynthesis, details of the carriage of respiratory gases in the blood, and so on.

We might then not only have courses in biology that are more relevant to the lives of human beings, but which begin to build links with and underpin the traditional 'humanities'.

A suggested biology syllabus

Studies of various biology syllabuses as presently taught in several different national systems, indicate that there is a large degree of mutual agreement on the aims and content of these courses.

This recognises that certain, identifiable concepts and skills are directly relevant to human beings everywhere and so should be included in 'international' syllabuses.

Such syllabuses can be built around a number of 'themes' or approaches. These are not separate, distinct compartments of a body of knowledge, however, but each one impinges on and is complementary to the others. Similar interrelationships can also be recognised between biology programmes and other subject areas such as geography, sociology, possibly economics, chemistry, physics, etc. They are often complex and difficult to show

in a topic-by-topic syllabus list, without a great deal of redundancy, but it is in stressing and evaluating the consequences of them that provision is made for seeing 'human beings' as human beings, i.e. whole organisms with their own behaviour patterns and their own ecology. Again, understanding these interrelationships is essential to an understanding of the issues involved in a global approach to environmental matters and how we should try to cope with them.

The basic themes can be indicated briefly as follows:

1 *The structure and function of the human body*, leading to a better understanding of ourselves and how we 'work'. Although the emphasis here is on the human body, reference will need to be made to the structure and function of other animals. Topics under this theme would include:

- nutrition, food and diet: to incorporate health problems associated with unbalanced diets, dietary requirements in pregnancy, world food supplies;
- reproduction and growth: to incorporate such areas as parent-child relationships; the importance of affection, diet and stimulation in child development; puberty, developmental change and hormonal control, adolescence, adulthood, menopause, senescense, growth in human populations and causes for concern, methods of spacing births, family and community attitudes.

2 *Microbiology — an introduction to the world of microscopic organisms.* This is fundamental to an understanding of disease, good hygiene, the importance of a supply of clean water, vector control, soil fertility, natural cycles, etc.

3 *Cell and molecular biology* — the nuts and bolts that relate the variety of living organisms to a central pattern and how they may be modified.

4 *Plant science — structure and function of green plants.* Almost all forms of life depend on green plants, the needs of which must therefore be appreciated. Topics under this theme would include:
- problems associated with the use of inorganic fertilisers;
- examples of crop husbandry, plant disease and control;
- poor agricultural practices;
- non-conservation of forests;
- desertification.

5 *Genetics and evolution.* The basis of inherited variation, selection, the appearance and relationships of different forms of life.

6 *Ecology* — the part and place of living organisms in the ecosphere. The impact of human activities. Topics would include:
- ecosystems, habitats, environmental factors;
- energy flow, food chains, webs, cycles.

This list of 'themes', is not meant to indicate an order of importance or, indeed, a teaching sequence. Because of their interconnections any of them would make a convenient starting point from which to lead to any of the others.

3 Chemistry

by **Patrick Hazlewood**, Head of Science, Queen's School, Wisbech

In this section, Patrick Hazlewood reflects upon the third, fourth and fifth-year chemistry courses with a global perspective that he carried out when teaching at Pilton School and Community College, Barnstaple, Devon.

Rather than viewing a global perspective in the teaching of science as an unusual strategy, it could be better regarded as the obvious approach. The demands of teaching science to secondary students and the needs of those students which education generally should meet, necessitate a far broader view of science education than something which only generates a knowledge of science and the processes of science.

Science education represents the interface between science and society and as such is far more

Using wave power to produce electricity: a futuristic application of electromagnetism in conjunction with wave motion

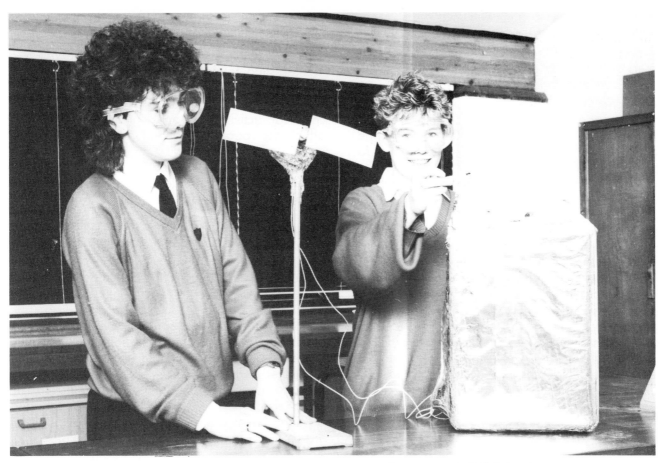

Development of a methane generator (right) and an aerogenerator as a practical answer to future energy needs (global physics)

relevant to the students and their personal needs. Their need is to understand how science relates and interrelates with the world around them. The increasing importance placed on breadth and balance in science is a vital step on the way towards meeting these needs, and yet skills and processes still form the basic science experience. The introduction to the classroom of problem solving, encouraging students to *think* about the science they have learnt, about its applications and potential, all form part of an exciting framework.

There is a further and more important facet to the construction of any science course and that is teaching the science with a global perspective. The global perspective is 'global' in two senses. First, students are given the opportunity to explore science topics from the viewpoint of the real world. Exploitation of the world by science and science by the world, for whatever justification, is an intricate web totally interwoven within the fabric of civilisation. An understanding of the background to scientific advance, development and application is a fundamental cornerstone to educating students. Issues which affect the inhabitants of the earth, as well as the earth itself, can be better understood by integrating them within the science curriculum framework.

Secondly, integration of science with other curriculum subjects offers students more balance and coherence which can be utilised for rational thought and effective decision-making.

The development of courses introducing global perspectives into the third to fifth-year chemistry curriculum have been documented elsewhere.[44] However, restatement of some of the underlying philosophical guidelines behind the course development will help to add context to this account.

The first premise was that if all students were to study chemistry then chemistry should be relevant to *all* students; secondly, there should be no assumption that examination constraints were the main structural principle; thirdly, chemistry, like any other subject, is concerned with the world and therefore it should help students understand the key issues of the world today and of the future; fourthly, chemistry is a science and essentially an experimental one and the course must reflect this; fifthly, the world is made up of living things and chemistry has an important role in the dynamic equilibrium of life on planet earth; finally, the course should encourage all students to understand chemistry in its broadest context, socially, politically, geographically, industrially, philosophically, historically, economically and culturally.

The introduction of a global perspective in chemistry is not as daunting as one might imagine. For the students it is in fact quite natural; at year three level, having probably studied an integrated science course for the first two years, most students have no prior expectation of what chemistry (or any other science) 'should' really entail. Rather, the problem is with the teacher who may have to radically rethink her views not only on science education and social issues but also on teaching strategy.

In considering the practical context of such a course, it is a natural progression to consider the world as a collection of resources which are tapped to supply humankind's 'needs'. Energy, the air and metals form basic resources; specific areas relating to these resources such as nitrogen and the world food problem and the recycling of waste complete a broad content outline. However, many more issues emerge from this basic view of the world. Extraction of metals in impoverished countries has extreme effects on the rights of the individual, for example, tin mining in Bolivia or gold mining in South Africa; energy is an apparently straightforward concept but it means different things to different people. Oil, coal and natural gas are accepted as a way of life to Western peoples but do they mean the same to the people of Peru or Chad or India? Then there is the nuclear issue. Is it clear cut? Is there a right or wrong perspective? What about unilateral and multilateral disarmament? In a course of this type no question can be avoided, no issue ignored because a real understanding of chemistry (science) demands a real understanding of issues. If science and scientists had been more aware of the implications of innovation, development and progress, would the world be more secure?

Taking this last point, it is one which frequently arises during the third year course. The main teaching strategies try to evolve the chemistry from the issues. For example, one unit involves atmospheric pollution. Until recently it has been alluded to in chemistry courses which tend to treat pollution as an unfortunate, but probably necessary, by-product of industrial chemistry. The chemistry of pollution has much to offer both in terms of chemical principles and in terms of global awareness. Students are introduced to acid rain pollution by a video tape showing devastation of the Black Forest and parts of Scandinavia. They are encouraged to discuss the effects in chemical terms. What is acid rain? How is it made? What processes are involved? How does mineral leaching occur? What biochemical effects are likely? On the basis of their findings they devise laboratory experiments which illustrate the effects of acid rain on trays of grass, etc. The practice of neutralisation by aircraft dropping tonnes of alkali is clearly a matter of concern for everybody. It is interesting to note how seriously most students take lessons like this.

Gradually they acquire an awareness that the chemical activities of one country can seriously affect the people and natural environment of another. They also realise that a straightforward chemical process is nowhere near as straightforward as they, and indeed most people, would imagine. Incidents like Seveso (the Dioxin incident in Italy, 1976) are considered, as is the current high incidence of unexplained livestock deaths in certain parts of Scotland and Ireland. In the latter case, the suspected role of dioxin pollution from incineration of waste has proved difficult to demonstrate legally; the students are encouraged to think of the effects of such disasters on individual people. Inevitably the political, economic, industrial link emerges. Bhopal can now be discussed in more meaningful terms! It is probably important to note that this course is integrated as it develops; for example, the 'recycling as a resource' section has much to offer to the 'pollution' section.

Mineral mining is another area in which pollution rears an ugly face. In considering the existence of 'tin' cans students are guided through extraction processes linked to tin; for example, froth flotation (which they do practically) and some of the metal chemistry. In addition to considering the appalling life of miners in Bolivia and the poor living conditions that they endure in order to keep tin a viable competitor in world markets, waste features strongly. In the development of the course a parallel is drawn between mineral pollution in a country like Bolivia and the proposed tungsten mining development at Hemerdon in South-West England. This is later extended to a consideration of the Amazonian rain forests and the state of Himachal Pradesh in North-West India. At Mussoree, a limestone quarry (limestone, CaC, is investigated practically!) has caused local rivers to become choked causing desert-type conditions further downstream which dramatically affects rice-growing. Shortsightedly, quarrying in this area has not contemplated the role of the rain forests in soil and water replenishment. The River Ganges is also silting up at an alarming rate. Solving the problem was clearly urgent but government agencies did not seem inclined to help. The fight against the destruction of the local habitat was led by the Chipko women of Mussoree — illiterate women whose main concern was the families that their husbands had had to leave to find work. Their existence was made increasingly precarious by deforestation: by sheer persistence these women won their battle against commercial exploitation.

Besides being an example of women fighting for the environment, this scenario reinforces the fundamental right of the individual to be able to live on an unpolluted earth, a right that industrial civilisation often appears to have usurped from individual citizens.

In this brief outline, it should be made clear that every effort is made by the teacher to present as balanced a view as possible of each issue. Student responses to this course are very positive. All students seem to enjoy the high practical content (75%) and feel that they are gaining an awareness of more than just chemistry.

In 1978 31 students (5 girls, 26 boys, 13.25% of the year) opted for chemistry based on traditional syllabuses. After the introduction of this approach in 1981 this number had increased in 1985 to 217 students (106 girls, 111 boys, 71% of the year). A research study investigating this phenomenon[45] found that both boys and girls rated chemistry their most interesting subject out of 16 studied. The highly-motivated students produced highly-motivated staff (and vice versa!). One important finding from this research was that students (girls especially) saw the teacher as a major positive influence. On analysis, however, it appeared that the perception of sensitivity and patience attributed to the teacher may have been a function of the course. Integral issues in the course like gold mining in South Africa, apartheid, the Ethiopian famine or children dying through avoidable pollution demand sensitivity in the teaching of the subject. It seems that if girls are to be attracted to the physical sciences then the pathway of 'issue to scientific concept' is likely to be a far more attractive and educative possibility. An early criticism of this global perspective approach by colleagues suggested that exam results would suffer. In 1985 144 students entered external chemistry examinations. 46 out of 47 passed GCE O level, 94 out of 98 passed CSE (17 grade 1).

4 Physics

by **Patrick Hazlewood**, Head of Science, Queen's School, Wisbech

Physics has been the focus of much concern in recent years. The concern emanates from the observation that many students do not find the subject either appealing or relevant to them personally. This is particularly so for girls who tend to opt out of the subject at the earliest opportunity. Various strategies have been employed to overcome this problem with varying degrees of success. Many of these attempts have rested on a continuing assumption that the content of physics syllabuses is basically correct, i.e. what is currently taught needs to remain in the syllabus.

The degree of sexual discrimination alone is cause for tremendous concern. Two recent surveys by the Equal Opportunities Commission and the Assessment of Performance Unit[46] yield the following data:

	Students Taking Physics Nationally		
	Mixed Schools		Single-Sex Schools
	EOC	APU	EOC
Boys:	55%	61%	57%
Girls:	16%	22%	37%

Comparison of the data for single-sex and mixed schools appears to suggest that factors are operating at a social level to deter girls from studying physics when it becomes optional. This conclusion must however be regarded with extreme caution. Strategies, such as sexual segregation, based on this type of information are missing a vital point. The attitude of the teacher is also a highly significant factor.[47]

There can be little doubt that physics has a lot to offer to the education of every child. Hirst[48] considers the physical sciences to be one of seven fundamental forms of knowledge vital to any person acquiring a complete education. Despite this importance many parents, students and even teachers regard physics as an awesome, mysterious subject riddled with mathematical and mechanical difficulty. There is also an almost tangible division between physics (science in general) and the arts in schools and yet cultural development binds the two inextricably together. Jacob Bronowski's *The Ascent of Man*[49] illuminates the interaction of science and culture in an inspirational way but how often do students in school see those links? Physics is taught in isolation; it may make concessions to social relevance and focus on applications in the 'real world', but they are transient excursions into an obscure relevance without ever meeting, or needing to meet, the essential, interlocking role that physics plays in the future of life on earth.

Rethinking the teaching of physics in schools, certainly in the 14–16 age range, raises two main themes. The first relates to how the subject is taught, how the concepts are approached and how the students assimilate necessary information. The second centres on the perception of the teacher of the role of physics in the educative process and in the future of the world. Certain conditions are essential if the demands of physics understanding are to be met and external requirements are to be fulfilled:

- a number of concepts are vital to understanding physics — these concepts form a framework on which the fabric of physics hangs; appreciation of physics depends on an appreciation of the framework — any course must accede to this principle;

- coherent development of principles is essential;

- essential practice in problem-solving activities must be built into the course;

- applications and possibilities within the field of physics need to be clarified for all students;

- social relevance must be an integral part of the course rather than an addendum;

- important issues concerning physics in the world must not be circumvented but should be confronted and investigated as they arise;

- ethical considerations should be given equal weighting with the theoretical and practical aspects of the course.

Most physics courses are based on an energy-type theme — physics is almost a study of energy! The diagram below suggests a partial framework for developing a course which extends physics beyond the boundaries of science into all aspects of the curriculum and into a global view of the world.

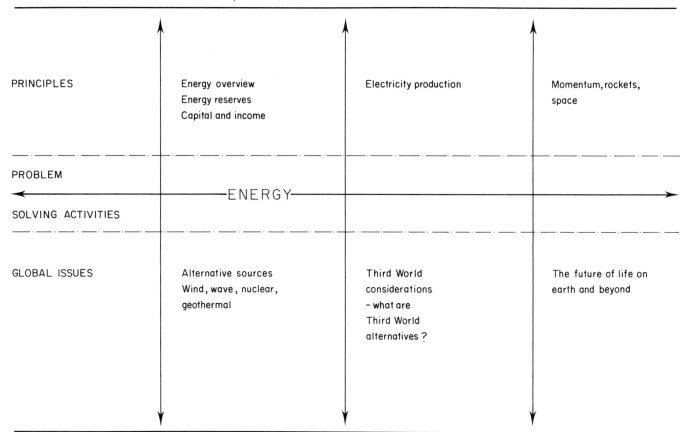

PRINCIPLES	Energy overview Energy reserves Capital and income	Electricity production	Momentum, rockets, space
PROBLEM		ENERGY	
SOLVING ACTIVITIES			
GLOBAL ISSUES	Alternative sources Wind, wave, nuclear, geothermal	Third World considerations – what are Third World alternatives?	The future of life on earth and beyond

The approach, in common with chemistry outlined elsewhere,[50] extracts the concepts from the issue. The principles almost emerge on a 'need to know' principle. For example, the world's energy resources are rapidly being depleted; the implications for civilisation are potentially catastrophic so what are the alternatives? What can physics offer to humankind to maintain progress, to enhance the future? This is where problem-solving can be introduced — making machines which use wind or wave power — converting that movement energy into electrical energy. Links with CDT are an obvious attraction!

Interdependency webs also start to develop. Where nuclear power arises as a distinct alternative, the pros and cons of a nuclear future can be discussed not in the realm of poorly-informed ignorance but in the context of the physical science of nuclear reactions. There is real potential for small groups to work towards a greater understanding of the nuclear issue, bringing in study skills, discussion techniques, debate, role play and learning to view situations from a multitude of perspectives. The diagram opposite illustrates the beginning of a web.

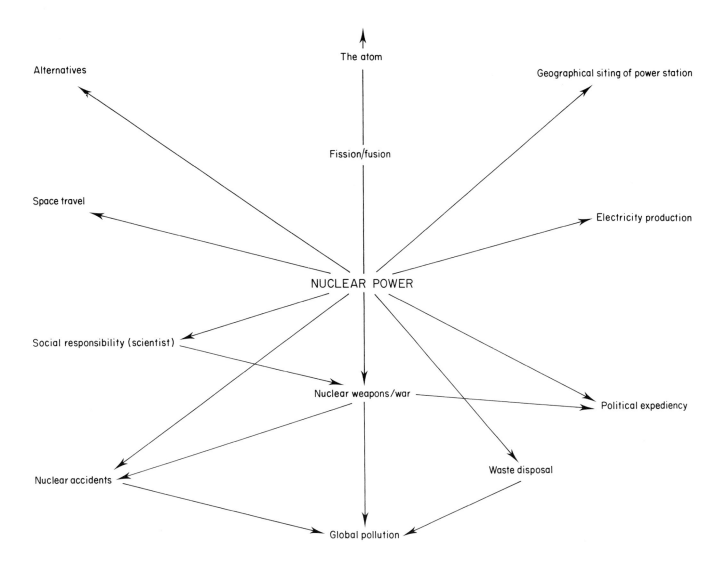

The globality of the nuclear issue is such that a complete understanding of nuclear power and the implications that it has require a multidisciplinary approach. Hard work for the teacher, but well worth it! Ethics is also an unavoidable area – is a scientist restricted by national loyalty or a loyalty to humankind? Where does her conscience take over or become submerged? Already the role of the physics teacher has changed from being subject-oriented to being a teacher in the true sense of the word. The indications are that such a teacher is far more highly regarded than the subject entrenched 'specialist'.[51]

All aspects of current GCSE syllabuses lend themselves to similar developments. Momentum, for example, leads to a discussion of planetary exploration. Why is planetary exploration important? Pollution, exhaustion of resources, population explosions, the nature of woman/man, all flood to the surface. Time is important but time can be made to discuss

issues of such vital importance to tomorrow's citizen. A view of the future through the eyes of physics illustrating its benefits to humankind in human terms rather than abstract perspectives, can only be educationally beneficial.

Whilst I have outlined in the briefest terms the development of physics and, earlier, chemistry as individual subjects into more meaningful and exciting subjects, the case for integrated science extrudes as an almost irresistible step in secondary education. The exploration of human experience through science will help create individuals who can recognise the reality of the world around them, make decisions in an informed and sensitive way and who are aware of the delicate balance between all areas of life. Teaching integrated science with a global perspective is the logical extension of the ideas developed hitherto.

Design and the arts

1 Art and Design

A global dimension in art and design inevitably involves the acknowledgment of the value and achievements of non-Western cultures. This is not simply achieved by introducing examples of ethnic minority and Third World art into the curriculum. An awareness of the 'arts-cultural socialisation' that has deeply influenced European perspectives on art needs to be fostered in the classroom as does an understanding of the fact that 'non-European art tends to stem from societies where in many cases art serves a markedly different cultural function and offers a stronger everyday life statement than we are usually accustomed to.'[52] Historically, European art – 'high art' or 'fine art' – has been the sponsored and sophisticated domain of the rich and powerful to be differentiated from 'folk art', 'crafts', 'primitive art' and, latterly 'ethnic' and 'community arts'.[53] The global art classroom can offer a context for the historical, social, economic, political and aesthetic unpicking of such norms and for the enrichment of students' perceptions by exploring alternative definitions and functions of art.[54]

Illustrations from the World Studies Journal

In the multi-ethnic school, 'Western European art and design forms are the equivalent of a foreign language to a substantial proportion of the school's population'. As Ann Taber has pointed out, Western art is 'involved with notions of innovation, creativity and originality' and is, thus, 'essentially concerned with change'.[55] The tendency in many non-Western societies (though, in some cultures, very much only a tendency) is for the artist to work 'within hallowed tradition, keeping to rules and set forms which ... are learnt gradually from a master and skill ... achieved through constant study and practice. Personal feelings are subordinated to the traditional art learnt. The artist's individual expression merges with that of others and becomes the manifestation of the group's philosophy. For this reason the individual's identity as an artist is unimportant.'[56] The exploration of such issues, which go straight to the heart of global education's concern with perspective consciousness, is an important task for all schools. Resources for introducing students to different artistic traditions are now readily available and there are a growing number of ethnic minority arts groups prepared to visit schools and work with students.[57] Below, Debbie Sander describes the facilities offered by the Commonwealth Institute in introducing students to a range of art forms from different cultures. The Minority Arts Advisory Service publishes a resource guide identifying individuals and groups working within ethnic arts and offering a regional ethnic arts contact list.[58]

A fertile area for exploration is the hybridisation of art forms when cultures meet. Cultural contact often brings vitality and innovation to artistic expression; new ways of perceiving and depicting things are often the result. The 'high art' of Picasso, Braque and Modigliani, which owe so much to 'Third World' influences, are cases in point.[59] The vibrance and originality of various forms of artistic expression in modern-day multicultural Britain is another, more immediate, example.

A sense of place

by **Deborah Sander**, Education Officer at the Commonwealth Institute in charge of the extramural services

African pottery used to teach physics! Does that sound incredible? It is exactly what was done with a group of 11 year olds in Avon. A Nigerian potter, Dominic Effiom, showed the children several techniques used to make pots in West Africa and then set them to making their own examples. In order to decide on the shape of the pot they had to think of its function. A water pot must be light because it may be carried a long way and it needs to be porous to keep the water cool. Just in case you've forgotten your own physics, I'll explain that a porous pot allows water to evaporate and in the process it takes up latent heat of evaporation thus cooling the remaining water. The lack of running water and electric refrigerators leads into teaching about development. Storing the water in its pot returns us to physics. The woman (a lesson on sex roles) who has carried the water, won't be pleased if a playing child knocks the pot over. The storage pot must be stable which means a low centre of balance, in other words it should be comparatively wide at the base and narrow at the top. Biology is the next lesson. Malaria is the scourge of West Africa and the mosquitoes breed in still water. A lid for the pot is the obvious precaution.

Other pots lead to further teaching points. Cooking and eating pots must be easy to clean in a society where water for washing is at a premium. Grain storage pots must keep the grain from rotting or being eaten by rodents and insects. Decorations on pots may be influenced by religion as in Northern Nigeria where Islam dictates that the designs are abstract.

The secondary school system in the UK encourages teachers to see each subject in isolation. The 'Arts' are seen as the province of their specific teachers. Many teachers of Music, Art and Drama are aware that ours is a multicultural society (even if a particular school is monocultural) and that the world is getting smaller every day. They have made great efforts to draw on examples from other cultures in their teaching. The Commonwealth Institute offers considerable support to them. The Library at the Institute offers a postal loan service and can supply records and tapes of music from most parts of the Commonwealth. Teachers of art can borrow these horribly expensive 'coffee table' books with lavish illustrations of paintings, sculpture and craft work, that few schools could afford to buy. Drama teachers will find only a tiny collection of plays but plenty of stories which can be used as a base for their own writing and the same 'coffee table' books will give ideas for costumes, especially masks.

The permanent exhibition at the Institute includes many fine examples of costume and design and art work. The India exhibit even includes a music section in which a tape provides a commentary and musical examples next to an extensive collection of instruments.

The Commonwealth Arts Centre mounts regular art exhibitions, performances and film seasons which would be of interest to teachers. Sometimes these include workshops which children may attend. Occasionally exhibitions are held of children's art from all over the Commonwealth. Last time the show was stolen by the sculpture submitted by children in Zimbabwe.

The most important resources available from the Institute are people. School groups can book for lessons which vary week to week but regularly include music and dance and may sometimes include other art forms ranging from Kenyan pottery to Alpana floor decorations from Bangladesh. The lessons are free but must be booked in writing with the Schools' Liaison Officer.

Like Mohammed and the mountain, the Institute sends people out to work in schools that can't get into London. All the team members come from Commonwealth countries and the majority are performers. The current team comprises a poet from Guyana, a drummer from Ghana, musicians from India and a potter from Singapore. The Institute has to charge for these programmes and they are normally booked for a week at a time through the local education authority. If you haven't come across the service please make enquiries at your education office first.

The Institute believes that the 'Arts' can be used as a tool in the teaching of other subjects as well as a worthwhile end in themselves. Primary schools are used to this idea. A project on India would commonly include making a collage of a tiger, learning the handkerchief dance, acting out the story of Rama and Sita and tackling some simple calligraphy. In the vast majority of secondary schools, India would be taught in Geography or perhaps RE. In some schools it is rare for teachers of physical and regional Geography to collaborate on their work let alone for teachers of 'academic' subjects to get together with those in 'practical' subjects. Sometimes it is easier for an outsider to point out the potential links as in Dominic Effiom's pottery lesson where I, with my science training, provided the link.

In one school it emerged that an English teacher had made a hobby of calligraphy which could be used by the RE and art departments for work on Islam and Islamic art. On a residential course Geography teachers were stimulated by Indian cellist, Anup Biswas; and by the linking of the Motswana drummer, Molefe Pheto with Guyanese poet John Agard, in creative writing on the theme of a Sense of Place.

What is Geography or World Studies but a 'Sense of Other Places', since the sense should be part of that learning process? A lesson about the slave trade is more likely to be remembered if it includes listening to or even singing a song from that period. A smell of incense will reinforce a lesson on Indian religions. How much harder is it to forget that yams are a staple diet in much of West Africa if you've pounded and eaten the yams yourself.

World Studies, like multicultural education, should go right across the curriculum and the arts subjects should be an integral part.

The Commonwealth Institute is at High Street, Kensington, London W8 6NQ. Telephone 01-603 4535.
For Library loans ask for extension 243.
For school visits to the Institute ask for extension 283.
For extramural visits ask for extension 251.
Schools in Scotland should contact: Commonwealth Institute, Scotland, 8 Rutland Square, Edinburgh EH1 2AS. Telephone 031-229-6688

This piece first appeared in *World Studies Journal*, Vol. 5, No. 1, 'Arts in Action', 1984, pp. 34–5.

The art/design classroom also offers rich opportunities for creative work and self-expression around global themes. Students can, for instance, be asked to interpret an environmental or rights or peace/conflict theme using the medium or media of their choice. Work on images of the future has also proved a fertile area for highly imaginative art work.

2 Music

Most music education in schools is Eurocentric in nature and content; it also concentrates on music of a particular type within a limited historical period. A student's experience of music within her wider education outside school is likely to be replete with cultural influences from around the world. That experience will be in marked contrast with her classroom experience.[60]

A globally-oriented music curriculum will introduce students, through creating, listening to and performing music, to the musical forms and styles of different cultures. It will also give students the opportunity to learn about the importance and role of music within each culture and so enable them to obtain a more coherent understanding of that culture.

Entry-points for music from non-Western cultures abound. For instance, the study of technical aspects of the music curriculum such as rhythm, pitch and timbre can be extended to include African, Asian or South American examples. Study of notation can be based upon songs from non-Western composers with whom students will find some common ground; the songs, for instance, of Bob Marley.[61] Non-Western instruments – often cheaper than Western instruments – can be employed for creative music-making by groups of students. Records and tapes of non-Western music are readily available for musical appreciation and critical listening work. 'With critical listening will come equally critical questions. By listening to blue grass, Chinese opera, the choir of King's College, and Bhutanese chanting, pupils will experience many different styles of singing. Instead of a model voice they will discover as many "natural" voices as cultural situations and styles of music.'[62] The learning that takes place through listening will enrich both the creation and performance of music. Wherever possible this process should be enlivened by the students having the opportunity to at least occasionally make music alongside local representatives of non-Western cultures.[63]

Music can also provide a powerful stimulus for student reflection upon current social, political and economic issues. A people's response to injustice and oppression often takes the form of song; for instance, the songs of the Chilean New Song Movement and of those involved in the freedom struggles in Namibia and South Africa. In the 1980s, the women's, environmental and peace movements have created a wealth of song reflecting their particular and joint concerns. The 1980s have also witnessed a renaissance of 'concerned' pop music with which many students identify.

Young children trying West African shakers at the Commonwealth Institute

Message from Mother Earth

I am the soil that harbours the seed
I am the crops the good soil yields.
Remember, I give you birth,
Remember Mother Earth.

I am the woods, the forest, the trees,
I give the buds, take back the leaves.
Remember, I give you birth,
Remember Mother Earth.

I am the rains, the rivers, the seas,
All creatures born must drink of me.
Remember, I give you birth,
Remember Mother Earth.

I have been here since time was new
But now I fear what your time may do.
Remember, I give you birth,
Remember Mother Earth.

You plunder me for coal and for oil
Leaving me scarred, leaving me spoiled.
Remember, I give you birth,
Remember Mother Earth.

You clear the forests, uproot the trees,
Poison the air, pollute the seas.
Remember, I give you birth,
Remember Mother Earth.

Pure air, pure rain, for millions of years
Now on the wind come acid tears.
Remember, I give you birth,
Remember Mother Earth.

Why can't you hear, why can't you see?
You kill yourselves if you kill me.
Remember, I give you birth,
Remember Mother Earth.

Words and music by Frankie Armstrong. © Frankie Armstrong. Recorded by Frankie Armstrong on a single, available from her at 8 Abbeville Road, London SW4.

Another approach is for students to be given stimulus material on a particular theme prior to forming into groups to corporately compose and practise a song responding to the theme. Such group work combines both the practice and reinforcement of musical skills and of skills such as co-operation, negotiation and problem-solving.

Finally, a word on the relationship between music and holistic (whole-brain) learning. Music offers the listener an often powerful emotional statement inviting her to exercise her imagination, look into her inner self and reach new levels of awareness. 'It touches our innermost being and in that way produces new life.'[64] As such, music has an important contribution to make to the learning process as we have described it: 'the journey inwards, the journey outwards'. We particularly recommend the use of appropriate pieces of music in experiential learning contexts such as guided fantasy, imaging and visualisation work.

3 Home Economics

Home economics – the study of the household group, its organisation and management of resources – provides an invaluable context for exploring aspects of global interdependence, gender roles and cultural similarities and differences.

The home is composed of and continually receives fresh inputs of raw materials from all over the world. The study of clothes, fabrics, food, furniture and other personal or household items can usefully include survey work on the point of origin of things found in the home (see **Ideas for Teaching/Learning about Spatial Globality/Interdependence**, pp. 8–12). Such work can provide a basis for the subsequent exploration of aspects of world trade, food/wealth distribution and world health. What are the causes of malnutrition in underdeveloped countries? Why are cash crops exported from such countries, leaving people who have insufficient buying power to purchase on the world market with insufficient home-produced food? What is the relationship between the beefburgers in the freezer and the cutting down of the tropical rain forests? What are the causes – and effects – of overnutrition in the developed world?

Home economics – traditionally the enclave in the curriculum preparing girls for the role of wife and mother – is an appropriate area for exploring sex-role stereotyping and the changing role of women and men within the family and within society at large. An excellent photopack for stimulating class discussion of sex roles in the top junior and lower secondary school is *Doing Things – In and About the Home*.[65] The home economics classroom also needs to recognise and reflect the fact that the 'cereal-packet norm' family is but a minority genre of household group nationally and globally. In cross-cultural studies of aspects of the home, the teacher, it has been suggested, should 'build on the similarities to introduce the differences'.[66] Human beings share a need for food, clothing and shelter. They also feed, clothe and house themselves often using a similar range of materials. The diversity of cultural responses to these needs and materials reflects an interplay between factors such as climate, agriculture, economic conditions, raw materials, religion, social structures, social

Gender roles in the home – an important issue in home economics

customs and tradition. It is important that an understanding of cultural diversity, locally, nationally and globally does not remain at a purely descriptive level but explains cultural expression as a response to those factors. 'It is not the fact that tortillas are a feature of Mexican diets or rice of Chinese cuisine that is important, but why.'[67]

Home economics topics inviting exploration of cross-cultural variations include cookery and food; clothes, fabrics and textiles; housing styles; interior design; health and hygiene practices and, very importantly, family life, child rearing and development. The Birmingham Development Education Centre's book, *Values, Cultures and Kids* has pointed the way forward in offering active, student-centred learning strategies and resources for home economics that reflect the multicultural and pluralistic character of British society and the interdependent nature of the modern world.[68]

References

1 *Stories in the multilingual primary classroom*, ILEA Learning Materials Service, cited in Newman, C., 'World studies, language and literature in the primary school', *World Studies Journal*, Vol. 5, No. 3, 1984/5, p. 18.

2 Bleach, J., 'English' in Craft, A. and Bardell, G. (eds), *Curriculum Opportunities in a Multicultural Society*, New York, Harper & Row, 1984, p. 80.

3 Searle, C., 'All our words', *World Studies Journal*, Vol. 5, No. 3, 1984/5, p. 4.

4 See, for instance, the catalogue of Third World Books, 151 Stratford Road, Birmingham B11 1RD; Klein, G., *Resources for Multicultural Education, an Introduction*, York, Longmans Resource Unit for Schools Council, 1984; Klein, G., 'The world in young hands: the world of books', *World Studies Journal*, Vol. 5, No. 3, 1984/5, pp. 20–2; Ballin, R., Bleach, J. and Levine, J., *A Wider Heritage: a selection of books for children and young people in multicultural Britain*, National Book League, 1980; Elkins, J., *Books for the Multi-racial Classroom: a select list of children's books, showing the backgrounds of India, Pakistan and the West Indies*, Library Association Youth Libraries Group, pamphlet No. 10, 1971; Twitchin, J. and Demuth, C., *Multi-cultural Education*, BBC, 1985, pp. 67–9; Gunner, E., *A Handbook for African Literatures*, Heinemann, 1984. Contractor, C., 'Introducing Indo-British literature into the secondary school in Britain', *World Studies Journal*, Vol. 5, No. 3, 1984/5, pp. 34–8.

5 Klein, G., 'The world in young hands: the world of books', *World Studies Journal*, Vol. 5, No. 3, 1984/5, p. 20.

6 'The Word House' is one of three simulations in *The People GRID* available from the Cockpit Theatre, Gateforth Street, London NW8 8EH.

7 Sapir, E., *Culture, Language and Personality*, cited in Postman N. and Weingartner, C., *Teaching as a Subversive Activity*, Penguin, 1971, p. 125.

8 These ideas are taken from Grinter, R. and Lashley, H., *Report of multicultural and antiracial permeation of the subject curriculum in teacher education workshop held at Greystoke Hall, Manchester Polytechnic, 12–14 July 1985*, pp. 50–8 and Bleach, J., op. cit., pp. 73–8.

9 Gregory, A. and Woollard, N., *Looking into languages: diversity in the classroom*, Support Service for Language and Intercultural Education (Lydford Road, Reading, Berkshire RG4 5QH), 1984; Raleigh, M., *The Languages Book*, ILEA English Centre, 1981; *The English Curriculum: Gender*, ILEA English Centre, undated. See, also, Newman, C., op. cit., pp. 18–19; Woollard, N., 'Language for development', *World Studies Journal*, Vol. 5, No. 3, 1984/5, pp. 28–31; Gregory, A., 'Water', ibid., pp. 32–3.

10 HMI, *Towards World History*, DES Education Pamphlet No. 52, cited in File, N., 'History', in Craft, A. and Bardell, G. (eds), op. cit., p. 4.

11 File, N. and Hinds, D., 'World History at Tulse Hill School', in Straker-Welds, M. (ed.), *Education for a Multicultural Society*, Bell & Hyman, 1984, p. 84.

12 Ibid., p. 88.

13 Shah, S., *The Contribution of History to Development Education*, The Historical Association Teaching of History Discussion Paper, No. 3, 1982, p. 8.

14 Ibid., p. 6.

15 Ibid., p. 9.

16 The Humanities Faculty at Carlton Bolling School, Bradford, have used field trips to Piece and Shibden Hall, Halifax, and to the Saltaire industrial village site as a means of exploring the growth of West Yorkshire's connections with the wider world over the last five hundred years; see Burgess, P., *A review of the changes in teaching methods adopted by the Humanities Faculty at Carlton Bolling School*, University of York Diploma in Applied Educational Studies, 1985.

17 See, for instance, File, N. and Power, C., *Black Settlers in Britain 1555–1958*, Heinemann, 1981.

18 See, for instance, Brown, D., *Bury my Heart at Wounded Knee*, Picador, 1972.

19 The *Women in World Cultures* series by Marjorie Bingham & Susan Gross (GEM publications, 411 Mallalieu Drive, Hudson, Wisconsin 54016, USA) offers excellent material on the history of women in different countries and cultures.

20 Storm, M., 'Geography and development' in Fyson, N. L., *The Development Puzzle*, CWDE/Hodder & Stoughton, 1984, p. 87.

21 Hicks, D. W., 'Global perspectives in the curriculum: a geographical contribution', *Geography*, Vol. 64, part 2, April 1979, p. 108.

22 Some of ideas in this list of questions were taken from Gill, D., 'Geographical education in a multicultural society' in Straker-Welds, M. (ed.), op. cit., pp. 58–9.

23 *North-South: a Programme for Survival*, Pan, 1980, p. 60.

24 Monk, J. and Williamson-Fien, J. 'Stereoscopic visions: perspectives on gender – challenges for the geography classroom' in Fien, J. and Gerber, R. (eds), *Teaching Geography for a Better World*, Australian Geography Teachers Association/Jacaranda Press, 1986, p. 191.

25 Ibid.

26 Hicks, D. W., 'The geography of war and peace' in Fien, J. and Gerber, R. (eds), op. cit., p. 222.

27 See Burnley, J. and Pettmann, R., 'Teaching about human rights in geography' in Fien, J. and Gerber, R. (eds), op. cit., pp. 57–89.

28 Kidron, M. and Segal, R., *The State of the World Atlas*, Pan, 1981; Kidron, M., and Segal, R., *The New State of the World Atlas*, Pan, 1984; Kidron, M. and Smith, D., *The War Atlas*, Pan, 1983; Myers, N. (ed.), *The Gaia Atlas of Planet Management*, Pan, 1985; Crow, B. and Thomas, A., *Third World Atlas*, Open University, 1983; *World View. An Economic and Geopolitical Yearbook*,

published annually by Pluto Press.

29 See Hursh, H. and Prevedel, M., *Activities Using 'The State of the World Atlas'*, Denver, Center for Teaching International Relations, 1983; also Burnley, J. and Pettmann, R., 'Teaching about human rights in geography' and Hicks, D. W., 'The geography of war and peace' in Fien, J. and Gerber, R. (eds), op. cit., pp. 57–89, pp. 221–38.

30 The *North and South Map* portraying Arno Peter's 'equal area' projection is available, with notes, from Christian Aid, PO Box No. 1, London SW9 8BH.

31 See Gough, N., 'Alternative futures in geographical education' in Fien, J. and Gerber, R. (eds), op. cit., pp. 268–83; Gough, N., 'Teacher education for the future', *World Studies Journal*, Vol. 6, No. 1, pp. 26–31.

32 Hassall, D., 'Religious education in the multi-racial school' in Lynch, J. (ed.), *Teaching in the Multi-cultural School*, Ward Lock, 1981, pp. 41–3.

33 These ideas are taken from the *Agreed Syllabus for Religious Education*, Bradford Metropolitan District Council, 1983, pp. 9–16.

34 Hassall, D., op. cit., p. 45.

35 Wood, A., 'Religious education' in Craft, A. and Bardell, G. (eds), op. cit., p. 59.

36 Palmer, M., *Worlds of Difference*, Blackie, 1985.

37 Davies, B. *et al.*, *The Changing World and RE*, Centre for World Development Education, 1979, p. 12. On the relationship between Religious Education and global issues, see also Wood, A., op. cit., pp. 58–61 and Richardson, R., 'World studies and world religions' in Jackson, R., *Approaching World Religions*, John Murray, 1982, pp. 182–91.

38 Ibid., p. 13.

39 Hurd, S., 'Economics and development education' in Fyson, N. L., op. cit., p. 93.

40 Guratsky, S., 'The adequacy of "A" level syllabi', *Economics*, Summer 1984, p. 67.

41 See, especially, the catalogue of the Centre for World Development Education (Regent's College, Inner Circle, Regent's Park, London NW1 4NS). A very useful source for activities introducing the complex links between personal and global economics is Koranski, B., *Teaching about the Consumer and the Global Market Place*, Denver, Center for Teaching International Relations, 1981.

42 Gilbert, D., 'Multicultural mathematics' in Straker-Welds, M. (ed.), op. cit., pp. 97–107.

43 Hemmings, R., 'Mathematics' in Craft, A. and Bardell, G. (ed.), op. cit., pp. 117–24.

44 Hazlewood, P. K., 'Teaching third year chemistry with a world studies perspective', *School Science Review*, Vol. 65, No. 231, 1983, pp. 380–2; Hazlewood, P. K. and Yeo, G., 'More about third year chemistry with a world studies perspective', *School Science Review*, Vol. 66, No. 236, pp. 539–43; Hazlewood, P. K.,

'Developments in teaching chemistry with a world studies perspective', *World Studies Journal*, Vol. 5, No. 4, 1985, pp. 44–7; Hazlewood, P. K., 'Chemistry with a world studies perspective: lesson "pen-portraits"', *World Studies Journal*, Vol. 5, No. 4, 1985, pp. 47–50.

45 Hazlewood, P. K., *Attracting girls to the study of chemistry*, unpublished MEd dissertation, University of Exeter, 1986.

46 Pratt, J., *et al.*, *Option Choice: a Question of Equal Opportunity*, Windsor, NFER-Nelson, 1984; Assessment of Performance Unit, *Science in Schools: Age 15, Report No. 1*, DES/HMSO, 1982.

47 Hazlewood, P. K., *Attracting girls to the study of chemistry*, op. cit.

48 Hirst, P. H., *Knowledge and the Curriculum*, Routledge and Kegan Paul, 1974.

49 Bronowski, J., *The Ascent of Man*, BBC, 1973.

50 Hazlewood, P. K., 'Teaching third year chemistry with a world studies perspective', *School Science Review*, Vol. 65, No. 231, 1983, pp. 380–2.

51 Hazlewood, P. K., *Attracting girls to the study of chemistry*, op. cit.

52 McKenzie, A., 'The visual arts – a response from development education', *World Studies Journal*, Vol. 5, No. 1, 1984, p. 6.

53 Ibid.

54 Ibid., p. 8.

55 Cited in Leary, A., 'Art education' in Craft, A. and Bardell G. (eds), op. cit., p. 204.

56 Taber, A., 'Art in a multicultural school', *New Approaches in Multiracial Education*, Vol. 7, No. 1, Autumn 1978 cited by Leary, A., op. cit., p. 203.

57 See *World Studies Journal*, Vol. 5, No. 1, 1984, various articles and, especially, pp. 44–7.

58 The *Minority Arts Advisory Service Register*, available from MAAS, Beauchamp Lodge, 2 Warwick Crescent, London W2.

59 Leary, A., op. cit., pp 203–4.

60 Floyd, L., 'Relevance in music education', *World Studies Journal*, Vol. 5, No. 1, 1984, p. 39; Dobbs, J. and Shepherd, F., 'Music' in Craft, A. and Bardell, G. (eds), op. cit., p. 180.

61 Floyd, L., op. cit., p. 40.

62 Dobbs, J. and Shepherd, F., op. cit., p. 184.

63 See note 58. The *MAAS Register* covers ethnic music.

64 Floyd, L., op. cit., p. 39.

65 *Doing Things – in and about the home*, Maidenhead Teachers Centre, 1983.

66 Twitchin, J. and Demuth, C., *Multi-cultural Education*, BBC, 1985, p. 76.

67 Grinter, R. and Lashley, H., op. cit., p. 38.

68 Birmingham Development Education Centre, *Values, Cultures and Kids – approaches and resources for teaching child development and about the family*, 1983.

14 A note on classroom resources

The implementation of a global dimension across the curriculum also requires that both teachers and students become sensitised to the ethnocentrism and racist and sexist bias, explicit or implicit, in many of the texts and resources used in the classroom. Checklists such as that offered here can be used by teachers, working individually or in departmental/faculty teams, to assess class texts and resources. Such checklists can also be usefully employed when worksheets and booklets prepared by teachers themselves are at the draft stage. In the case of materials already in use in the classroom, the question arises as to whether those found to be biased, and to contain negative images, be withdrawn. The question is a complex one, the age of the students being a major determining factor. With younger, more impressionable, children, who have not reached the age or stage where textual/media discernment skills can be nurtured, there is a stronger case for withdrawal. With older age groups, offending passages in texts can provide opportunities for sensitising students to bias, ethnocentrism and negative/ stereotypical images and for practising textual/ media discernment skills. Students themselves can use checklists such as the one here or they can be encouraged to compile their own. In answering her own question, 'sanitise or sensitise?', Gillian Klein states that: 'A totally sanitised collection of resources would be so out of touch with reality as to be of little use to pupils. Prejudice is a reality of their lives and cannot be wholly expunged from their literature. The most effective and lasting strategy for combating racism and sexism and other damaging bias in books is to teach children to challenge everything they read. They need to learn to doubt the messages of the media and to develop and ultimately to trust their own judgement. This cannot be taught in a single lesson, nor even in a term. A healthy scepticism for the apparent authority of print and a real respect for the children's own experience so that it is brought to bear on their learning, has to be a powerful and continuing dimension of the visible and hidden curriculum.'[1]

Ethnocentrism and bias are to be found in texts and resources used in every area of the school curriculum.[2] A *sine qua non* of the global curriculum is that teachers of all subjects critically examine the materials they use and ensure that examples of bias to which students are exposed do not pass unchallenged.

Images in textbooks
A Checklist of Questions

1 Top nation
Does the book suggest or state that 'our' country or power-bloc is more civilised, inventive, peace-loving, sensible, tolerant, etc. than others?

2 Foreign devils
Does the book suggest or state that a certain other country or power-bloc is completely evil, is scheming destruction, trying to dominate the world, etc?

3 Acts of God
Does the book refer to so-called natural disasters (floods, earthquakes, drought, etc.) without mentioning that it is normally the poor who suffer from them, not the rich?

4 Sexism
Does the book imply that men are superior to women, or that traditional sex roles (breadwinner, homemaker) are unchangeable? And is the word 'man' used to mean all human beings rather than just males?

5 Self-interest
Does the book look at world affairs – for example, the system of world trade – from the point of view of just one country or type of country?

6 Ignoring the background
Does the book refer to 'problems' such as poverty and pollution without referring to the social and economic background?

7 *Ignoring human nature*
Does the book criticise certain social systems (e.g. capitalism or communism) without referring to the attitudes and behaviour of individuals?

8 *Catching up*
Does the book imply that all countries should try to get richer and richer, e.g. try to 'catch up' with the United States? And does it imply that this is not only desirable but also actually possible?

9 *Happy savage*
Does the book imply that 'primitive' or 'backward' people have happy carefree lives free from the problems of 'civilisation'?

10 *Between the lines*
Does the book suggest, though perhaps not state, certain assumptions which would definitely not be shared by people in other countries?

11 *Ignorance*
Does the book state things which few if any knowledgeable people would agree with, regardless of their political views? For example, that poverty and hunger are caused mainly by the population explosion?

12 *Problems, problems, problems*
Does the book describe problems (poverty, war, pollution etc.) without referring to what can be done, and has been done, to tackle the problems; and the background to them?

13 *Leaders*
Does the book imply that world events are caused by 'leaders' – 'great' men and women, who wage war, make treaties, pass laws, etc., apparently regardless of the millions of 'ordinary' people?

14 *All or some?*
Does the book speak of, for example, 'the French' when it really means, 'the French government', or 'many French people' or 'some French people', etc? Does it similarly make a blanket use of terms such as 'rich countries', 'developing countries', 'Third World countries'?

15 *Misprints*
Does the book contain misprints which perhaps reveal the assumptions and bias of the printer and proofreader?

16 *Own bias*
Does the book admit that it is itself biased? Does it say what its bias is? Does it at least admit that its subject matter is controversial?

17 *Challenge*
Does the book challenge you to re-examine your own assumptions – for example, those which are present in questions such as these?

18 *Excellence everywhere*
Does the book draw example of excellence from all parts of world society? Given the present maldistribution of power and wealth in world society, does the book in particular draw attention to excellence in non-Western cultures and societies?

Robin Richardson, *Learning for Change in World Society*, World Studies Project, 1979.

References

1 Klein, G., *Reading into Racism. Bias in Children's Literature and Learning Materials*, Routledge & Kegan Paul, 1985, p. 113.
2 See, for instance, Hicks, D. W., *Bias in Geography Texts*, Centre for Multicultural Education, London Institute of Education, 1981, and Hudson, B., 'Social division or adding up to equality? Militarist, sexist and ethnocentric bias in mathematics textbooks and computer software', *World Studies Journal*, Vol. 5, No. 4, 1985, pp. 24–9.

15 Interdisciplinary courses

Some secondary schools have responded to the call for a global perspective in the curriculum by establishing courses in 'World Studies' usually but not always exclusively taught by humanities teachers. There has been considerable variation in the type and pattern, of course. In some schools, a first and second-year world studies course is followed by separate geography and history courses in third, fourth and fifth years. In others, a core O/CSE World Studies course appeared in the fourth and fifth years whilst in at least one school World Studies is an unexamined core course for fourth and fifth-year students. Again, some schools have World Studies as an option set against history and geography on the timetable.

The first interdisciplinary core O/CSE World Studies course in England and Wales was established at Groby Community College, Leicestershire, in 1979.[1] The Groby course provided an example which a number of secondary schools in other parts of the country followed, particularly in Devon where teachers from ten schools developed a Mode III CSE in World Studies for first examination in 1985. The syllabus was designed to be used in conjunction with the then Joint Matriculation Board's O level in Integrated Humanities (the O level also used at Groby College).[2] Interest in core world studies in Devon continued to grow and, with the introduction of the General Certificate in Secondary Education timetabled for September 1986, a group of teachers from Devon (joined by colleagues from Cornwall) began planning a GCSE in World Studies in mid-1985. The syllabus, as accepted by the Southern Examining Group (see Appendix) has since been taken up by schools in other parts of the country.

An interdisciplinary core, examined course has some attractions as a strategy for implementing the aims and objectives of global education. As recognised in Section 3, great store is set by parents, employers and others upon examin-

ation qualifications and there is the danger that a global dimension in the curriculum will be squeezed out in the years closest to external examinations unless it is legitimised by alliance with a specific examination. A second advantage is that a team of teachers working together on an interdisciplinary core course are more likely to collectively develop the commitment and expertise to successfully implement a global dimension.

An alternative approach is the cross-curricular – sometimes referred to as the 'diffusionist' or 'permeationist' approach. A weakness is that it assumes commitment on the part of hard-pressed subject teachers and a preparedness on their part to invest time and effort in yet another educational initiative. The reality is that some will be persuaded to commit themselves to such an investment whilst others will not.

On the other hand, a timetable slot called 'World Studies' may have a negative effect on student attitudes and on their perceptions of the importance of the issues raised in the course. However important the insights offered, they may well be devalued in students' eyes if not reinforced in other parts of their school experience. The fact that 'World Studies' is examined can compound this problem. In the first place, teaching staff may be tempted to accentuate those (principally cognitive) aspects of the course that feature in the assessment scheme at the expense of holistic learning. In the second place, examinations may lead students to relegate the knowledge acquired in the course to the level of significance of most other knowledge acquired for examinations, i.e. noted down, held in abeyance, used if necessary for assessment purposes, then fairly lightly discarded. There can thus be a critical disharmony between the message of holistic learning and the medium of one-off assessment.

The World Studies GCSE (see Appendix) is a thoroughly enterprising and professional attempt to face up to such considerations, involving as it does some very innovative criteria for, and forms of, assessment. It remains the case, however, that the assessment is preponderantly in the cognitive domain and that teachers following the course will need to be on their guard against pushing to the periphery those (principally affective) objectives of global education which are not and, in some cases, cannot or should not be assessed.

One interim answer to the dilemmas raised in this Section is for the secondary school to marry a timetable-slot approach with the 'diffusionist' model. This gives some guarantee that serious and often complex issues will be thoroughly explored in at least one part of the curriculum and also provides the school with a team possessing the experience and expertise to support the implementation of a global dimension across the curriculum. The latter approach – a dimension across the curriculum and the whole school experience of each student – must remain the ultimate objective if we are to succeed in achieving the 'irreducible global perspective' outlined in Section 1.

References

1 See Selby, D. E., 'World studies and the core curriculum' in Hicks, D. W. and Townley, C., *Teaching World Studies*, Longman, 1982, pp. 55–71.
2 *South-West Mode III CSE World Studies syllabus*, Global education documentation service, Centre for Global Education, Document No. 15. For the early history of world studies in Devon, see Stephenson, B., 'The growth of world studies in Devon', *World Studies Journal*, Vol, 4, No. 3, Spring 1983, pp. 5–17.

Part Four

THE GLOBAL TEACHER

16 The global teacher: a profile

There are leaders the people FEAR.
There are leaders the people HATE.
There are leaders the people LOVE.
But when the best leaders of all
Have finished their work
The people say,
"We did it ourselves"

Lao Tzu
Chinese Philosopher.

Running through the pages of this book – at some points quite explicitly, at others fairly implicitly – has been a statement about the characteristics of the global teacher. It is now time to pull the threads together and to profile what we conceive to be the type of teacher required if schools are to respond effectively to the task of preparing students for a constructive role in a fast-changing, interdependent world. What, in short, is the global teacher?

- **The global teacher is globalcentric rather than ethnocentric or nationcentric.** She applies her understanding of systems to the modern world and, thus, avoids propagating simple, unhelpful dualities such as cause and effect, local and global. She facilitates student enquiry into current global conditions, trends and developments and their interlocking nature. She promotes discussion of and reflection upon current global issues and the arguments surrounding them.

- **The global teacher is concerned about culture and perspective.** She seeks to develop awareness and understanding of cultures within and beyond the students' own community, her aim being to promote a *coherent* understanding of the cultures studied. The exotic, romantic and stereotypical is avoided. Cultures are portrayed as neither monolithic nor unchanging. Learning opportunities are chosen which enable people of the cultures concerned to speak for themselves. Human commonalities as well as dissimilarities are highlighted. The in-depth study of cultures is seen as the most important means whereby students learn to respect diversity and become sensitised and receptive to other perspectives and worldviews. Questions of prejudice and discrimination are dealt with thoroughly and comprehensively in the classroom.

- **The global teacher is future-oriented**. Whilst recognising that present conditions, developments and trends need to be set within their historical context, she holds it to be crucially important that students are given the opportunity to reflect upon possible, probable and preferred futures. It is equally crucial, she believes, that they learn that human beings, individually and collectively, can consciously influence a future that is not pre-determined. Central to her classroom will be the development of the skills and capacities needed for participation in democratic, social and political processes and for coping with and handling an accelerating rate of social change.

- **The global teacher is a facilitator.** Her role is not primarily to impart knowledge (which, more often than not, quickly becomes redundant in a fast-changing world) but to facilitate students in their learning and in their learning how to learn. She recognises that there are certain personal qualities which the effective facilitator must possess such as a healthy level of self-esteem, the ability to trust in the capacity of others to think and learn for themselves, a preparedness to let go, a lack of defensiveness, the confidence to be seen to be wrong and for it not to matter and to be seen to be learning from her mistakes. She sees an essential pre-requisite of successful facilitation and, hence, of successful learning as the nurturing of individual self-esteem within a warm, affirmative, relaxed and friendly classroom. She enjoys genuine, self-disclosing relationships with students; she is responsive to their feelings and ideas; she gives a lot of praise; she tries hard to view the world through each student's eyes.

- **The global teacher has a profound belief in human potential.** She recognises that students do not come to class as empty vessels but with some knowledge, some experience and a range of opinions and perspectives to share with others. She knows that students who are put in contact with what they perceive to be real issues and problems are intrinsically motivated; they are curious; relish a challenge; are eager to discover, to learn, to grow, to solve problems; they learn to exercise individual and collective self-discipline. She has a respect for each student as a separate person with a uniquely special mix of potential.

- **The global teacher is concerned with the development of the whole person.** She accepts as a basic premise of her work inside and outside the classroom that there are diverse and synergistic dimensions to human learning including the abstract, the concrete, the experiential, the analytical, the rational, the intuitive and the emotional. She, likewise, accepts that learning is as much an inward as an outward journey and that the two journeys are complementary. Obversely, she understands that the heavy emphasis on cognitive learning in the traditional classroom is distortive of personality and an impediment to the full development of personhood.

- **The global teacher employs a range of teaching/learning styles in the classroom.** She recognises that each student has a predisposition to one or more particular learning styles and that students are either left-brain, right-brain or whole-brain dominant. Given her belief in providing real equality of opportunity for each and every student, she ensures that all students have an equal share of comfortability in working through their preferred style(s) but also that they are encouraged to 'stretch' to other styles. It follows that her students are regularly offered a varied diet of teaching/learning approaches including affirmation and self-esteem activities, group discussion work, experiential units, role plays, simulation games, direct and 'hands-on' experience, action research, individual study and teacher input.

- **The global teacher sees learning as a process that is lifelong.** She views learning as a journey with no fixed or final destination; her priority is to encourage students to ask good questions rather than offer 'right' answers. She recognises and helps students to see that the answers we give, the solutions we arrive at, the decisions and judgements we reach, are, by their nature, impermanent. That is why the global teacher is also the global learner. The global teacher accepts that she has not finished learning and that she often has much to learn from her students and from what takes place in the classroom. In the final analysis, she is a 'facilitative learner among learners'.[1]

- **The global teacher tries to be congruent.** She is alert to the dangers of structural hypocrisy in both classroom and school and of how teachers and institutions professing aims such as 'education for democracy' and 'respect for human rights' can rapidly lose credibility if there is a critical disharmony between medium (environment, processes and quality of relationships) and message. She is concerned, too, to avoid dissonance between her professional and personal life (for instance, emphasising to students the value and importance of participation in global society at all levels whilst being complacent and uncaring herself outside of school).

- **The global teacher is rights-respectful and seeks to shift the focus and locus of power and decision-making in the classroom.** She is egalitarian. As students acquire confidence, self-esteem and individual and collective self-discipline, she gradually devolves power and control to the group (which includes herself as facilitator-learner). Her goal is the autonomy and empowerment of the individual within an affirmed, democratic and participatory environment. One important means of achieving that goal is through establishing procedures for student feedback and contexts for joint student/teacher evaluation of the course. She believes, too, in the 'human rights school' and the establishment of school wide democratic decision-making and open procedures through which students, teachers and others can complain about and seek redress for perceived rights' denials.

- **The global teacher seeks 'functional interdependence'[2] across the curriculum**. She holds that 'no classroom is an island'[3] and that congruence in aims, objectives, teaching/ learning strategies and methods of assessment across the curriculum is required in the global school. A prerequisite of such congruence is a preparedness on the part of teachers to share ideas, to enter open professional discourse, to seek the widest possible areas of consensus and, finally, to achieve 'the negotiated integration of individual teacher contributions'.[4] Congruence, she maintains, is required horizontally across each year group and vertically through the infant, junior and secondary years. She, therefore, places a premium on inter-school liaison.

- **The global teacher is a community teacher.** She believes that whole-person, whole-brain learning is impossible if the school raises the drawbridge on the local community. She would accept Marilyn Ferguson's assertion that 'only a community can offer holistic education and only a whole person can take it'.[5] She recognises that no teacher – or group of teachers – can afford not to draw upon the opportunities offered by the local area (in which there will be much that is global) or the rich and diverse seams of experience and expertise within the community. They should, therefore, share responsibility for the learning process with parents and community members. Parental rights also demand that teachers are in ongoing consultation with parents about school policies and practice. Finally, the recognition of learning as a lifelong process places a responsibility on the school to offer opportunities for continuing education for those above the age of compulsory schooling.

Learning is finding out what you already know.
Doing is demonstrating that you know it.
Teaching is reminding others that they know just as well as you.

You are all learners, doers, teachers.

Richard Bach, *Illusions*, Pan, 1978.

References

1 Rogers, C., *Freedom to Learn for the 80s*, Charles E. Merrill, 1983, p. 139.
2 Elliot-Kemp, J., 'Toward more effective teaching: a managerial perspective' in Elliot-Kemp, J. and Rogers, C., *The Effective Teacher*, Pavic Publications, Guidelines in Education & Management Series, No. 10, Sheffield City Polytechnic, p. 17.
3 Ibid., p. 15.
4 Ibid., p. 17.
5 Ferguson, M., *The Aquarian Conspiracy*, Granada, 1982, p. 349.

17 Teacher education

'How many teachers are real persons in the classroom? We know that the number is very small. Nearly always the teacher puts on a professional mask at the beginning of each day, and takes it off only when the instruction is finished. It is much safer to hide behind the role of the teacher than to meet the students as a genuine, human person, with feelings as well as thoughts, with faults as well as virtues. It seems very risky to be fully human with students. How many teachers exhibit a respect and caring for the student as a separate person? We tend so often to lump students into categories, to treat them as an undifferentiated mass. Or even worse, to look down on them as incompetents. In our country, our educational institutions probably are the most significant factor in reducing the self-esteem of our children. Pupils very often do not feel respected at school. Rather they are made to feel inferior and inadequate. As to the degree of empathy shown by teachers, I know of one investigator who planned to study this topic, but gave up because he could find so few instances in which teachers displayed a careful listening, a sensitive understanding. So it would take a drastic change in our mode of training teachers, and in the basic attitudes of the instructor, in order for our classrooms to become centres for the facilitation of learning. Such changes are always threatening.'[1]

'The creation and implementation of a teacher education program modeled after the person-centered approach is harrowing, draining and painful. To respect students as persons, to believe in giving power and control to individuals, to convey an unconditional respect, to stop and truly listen to another's deeper feelings and to be aware, genuine and sharing of one's own ongoing experience often are met with suspicion and incomprehension. The basic stance of simply respecting a student as a person is for many a frightening heresy, so new that it muddles and confuses. These are not the rantings and ravings from brief and superficial encounters with the system.'[2]

The above two statements bear ample testimony to the fact that the creation on any scale of what we call global teachers is going to be an uphill task. There are, however, grounds for optimism. In the first place, it has been shown that teachers can improve the level of facilitative conditions they offer in the classroom with 'as little as fifteen hours of carefully-planned intensive training, involving both cognitive and experiential learning'. The *sine qua non* of such rapid development is that the trainers themselves exhibit a high level of these facilitative conditions.[3] Secondly, a facilitative, experiential model for teacher education with a strong global dimension has been provided in the United Kingdom by recent in-service work in world studies and global education.[4] This model, which is now being taken up in a growing number of teacher training institutions,[5] is characterised by

- an emphasis on the development of inter-personal skills;

- the use of co-counselling techniques;

- a concern to develop listening and other non-verbal communication skills;

- the exploration, experientially, of a rationale for co-operative, interactive, experiential and participatory learning;

- facilitative course leadership (thus providing a role model for teachers/trainee teachers and ensuring a harmonisation of medium and message);

- an exploration of non-didactic learning activities in which teachers/trainee teachers are invited to experience what the trainers are suggesting school students should experience (in the debriefing participants are asked to try and comment on the activities from the students' viewpoint);

- an exploration of learning style theories through input, questionnaire and group work on implementation strategies;

- an emphasis on the 'permeability of boundaries'[6] by bringing together infant, primary and secondary teachers of various disciplines on the same course;

- the use of units which 'shock' teachers/trainee teachers into a realisation of the limitations of and assumptions behind their perspective/worldview (culture shock has been identified by at least two writers as the trigger leading to personal and professional transformation in teachers).[7]

In the pages that follow, some teacher education activities are described and an in-service course offered by the Centre for Global Education is outlined. Two teachers then offer their reflections upon in-service training and staff development.

Introductions and Expectations

▼ Resources

An open space with chairs; a large sheet of sugar paper and felt tip pen for each group of four/six.

▼ Procedure

Participants find a partner. For four to five minutes one member of each pair talks to the other about 'who am I and what are my fears and expectations of this course'. The other partner listens carefully without interrupting. The process is then reversed. Pairs then join with one or two other pairs to form groups of four or six. Each member of the newly-formed group introduces their original partner to the others. Another member acts as secretary recording all the hopes, fears and expectations expressed. The various sheets are put on the wall to serve as a focus for evaluation and reflection during the remainder of the course.

Opposite, above and right; Dorset teachers involved in, and debriefing 'Woolly Thinking'. Activity description p. 141; Dorset Programme pp. 283–6.

▼ Potential

A useful confidence-building technique which helps small goups of participants to get to know each other and which alerts the facilitators to participants' expectations. It is important that participants work with as wide a range of course members as possible. The group formed by this activity should not, therefore, be kept together for too long before fresh groups are formed, perhaps using random grouping exercises (see p. 111).

20 minutes

▼ Source

Various

Diamond Ranking Activity

Participants, following the sequence of steps described on page 134, rank nine statements about some aspect of global education. A set of statements used by the Centre for Global Education (on education for a multicultural society) is given on p. 278.

NO PROBLEMS HERE
Yes, it's all very well, but we simply do not have a multicultural school here. We have no racial conflict. We should serve the community for what it is, that is overwhelmingly white. That is the cultural background for this school. Admittedly the problems are there in London, Birmingham and so on — that is where the real anti-racist work must go on. Here we do not have such problems and children and parents would not see the sense in our dealing with race issues.

BRINGING CONCEPTS ALIVE
Certainly it seems idle to promote 'a world community' or 'a democratic and participatory multi-racial society' without seeking to bring these concepts alive — these concepts of community, democracy, participation, equality — in each classroom, and without enhancing teachers' images and expectations of their pupils.

DIVERSITY
Education can be an affirmation and celebration of diversity. We aim on this Campus to impart a sensitivity to others, and a pleasure in the variety of individuals. The natural extension of this mood is to incorporate, or go out to meet, a vast range of different cultures. We should affirm the value of individuals and their beliefs, the value of cultures in Britain — their language, dialect and traditions, the value of cultures in the world.

A FOCUS FOR ATTENTION
If we were to select just one focus for our immediate attention, we might well choose the re-education of schools in areas of the country where the school population is largely white. It is rare indeed to find white schools which are consciously trying to adjust to a new ethos or to rethink their activities and beliefs to the end of a multi-racial society. The real skill in such schools lies in providing day-to-day situations which present a culturally-diverse society as the norm to the children, without stereotyping.

BALANCE
I support the treatment of contemporary and controversial issues in the classroom as long as teachers ensure that every viewpoint is given equal weight and emphasis.

FORGET IT
Once I chaired a debate on race. After the debate, a West Indian boy said to me, 'if some well-intentioned teachers would only shut up about race, the kids themselves would forget it'. I claim that the race industry bears a grave responsibility as one of the major factors in promoting race consciousness in our adolescent population, thereby stimulating racial violence in and out of school.

MUSLIM SCHOOLS
Multicultural education has failed. It has failed to tackle black underachievement; it has failed to meet the religious, linguistic and cultural needs of a large minority community. This is why Muslims wish to run their own schools. If British society is not divided when Bradford Muslims buy and inhabit street after street of sub-standard slum homes and do all the dirty jobs, then it should not be divided when they venture into the schooling of their own children.

EQUALITY
Simply valuing cultural differences is mischievously apolitical; almost certainly biased towards white and Western norms and insensitive towards black people since it ignores the issues which they themselves consider to be most important, institutionalised racism. We have to move away from 'multi-culch'. Our concern should be instead with equality.

NATIONAL VALUES
One of the aims of studying history is to understand the development of shared values which are a distinctive feature of British society and culture and which continue to shape private attitudes and public policy. Schools should impress on pupils the primacy of Parliament, respect for individual rights, equality before the law and traditions of liberty, tolerance and decency. Pupils should learn how these features have determined the contemporary social and political system.

*The criterion used for ranking is '**significance for education in a multicultural society**'.*

Objectives Exercise

Using the flowchart formula described on page 135, participants in groups of four prepare a graphical presentation of a range of possible global education objectives. A specimen set of objectives is given below and on pp. 280–1. Participants are at liberty to reject certain objec-

tives and to write new ones (blanks should be provided). Flowchart production will take up to 45 minutes. It can be followed by a plenary session involving group presentations and debriefing or by a **Circus** (see p. 135).

▼ Source

Centre for Global Education.

Limited Perspectives An objective is to help students become aware that their view of the world is shaped and limited by their own experience and by the culture, class, nationality, race, gender and generation to which they belong.	**Participation** An objective is to help students develop and practise the skills necessary for active and democratic participation in school, local, national and global communities.
As Others See Us An objective is to help students learn about their own lifestyle through study of how other peoples view it.	**Changing the World** An objective is to help students understand the concept of change and the means and channels through which change can be effected.
Facts An objective is to help students learn about basic world geographical, political, social and economic facts.	**Communication** An objective is to help students develop the skills of effective communication including listening, verbal and non-verbal skills.
Issues An objective is to help students understand current global issues, trends and developments.	**Cultural Enrichment** An objective is to help students appreciate and value the riches offered by different cultures within and beyond our own society.
Interdependence An objective is to help students grasp the interdependent and systemic nature of the contemporary world.	**Respect** An objective is to help students develop respect for the rights, feelings and essential worth and dignity of other human beings and living things.

Empathy

An objective is to help students sense the thoughts and feelings of others especially those who belong to a different culture, class, nationality, race, gender and generation.

Relationships

An objective is to help students develop the insights and skills necessary for establishing and maintaining meaningful personal relationships.

Critical Skills

An objective is to help students develop the skills of critical analysis so they can detect bias and form their own judgement about what they learn from information media and what they hear in class.

Co-operation

An objective is to help students experience and understand the importance of co-operation and to develop apposite skills including conflict avoidance and conflict resolution.

Self-awareness

An objective is to help students become aware of their own strengths and weaknesses, biases and prejudices, and to help them achieve a positive self-image.

Equality

An objective is to help students appreciate that relationships between individuals, groups and societies should be based on principles of equality.

Feeling Concerned

An objective is to help students develop a concern for and solidarity with the poor, the disadvantaged and oppressed in their own society and in the world.

Structures

An objective is to help students understand that social, political and economic structures impede the chances of life fulfilment for many and that these structures are controlled by the powerful.

Commonality

An objective is to help students understand the commonality of needs, talents and aspirations shared by humankind.

Justice

An objective is to help students understand that the principle of justice entails a commitment to defending the rights of others.

Futures

An objective is to help students imagine and reflect upon possible futures, personal, local, national and global, and to help them develop the skills needed to achieve their desired future.

Alternative Visions

An objective is to introduce students to alternative versions and visions of reality and to alternative strategies for achieving personal and social transformation.

Shock Avoidance

An objective is to help students cope with and achieve some meaningful control over their own destiny within an increasingly rapidly changing world.

Study Skills

An objective is to help students develop appropriate study skills including planning, organising and pursuing independent enquiry, drawing and evaluating conclusions.

Snap Groups

At various points throughout the course, participants move into 'snap groups' of 4–5 members. Groups are given four minutes to discuss the problem outlined on a 'snap group' card (see examples on this page). Each group notes down suggested strategies for dealing with the problem. A plenary debriefing can follow straight away; alternatively, discussion can be held over until a 'snap group' debriefing session held at an appropriate moment towards the end of the course.

▼ Source

Centre for Global Education.

You teach in a multi-ethnic comprehensive school. As you walk into class, you see two white students reading National Front literature. They tell you that it is being distributed by a group of white students in the class, some of whom have parents and relatives in the National Front. What action, if any, do you take?	You teach at an 'all white' school which has its own multicultural education across the curriculum statement. At parents' evening, two parents of a student in your tutor group object to the policy on the grounds that it highlights a problem that doesn't exist in the school and community. How do you respond?
You have tried to make your classroom more 'processive' by using role plays, rankings, simulations and some conflict-resolution activities. Some students and a couple of parents complain, saying: 'When are you going to do some real work?' What should you do?	The elections have just taken place for next year's head boy and head girl. In the staffroom you are sitting near the head of sixth form and his deputy who are counting votes for head boy. You, a probationary teacher, notice that they are tearing up and discarding some of the votes of the only black candidate, saying 'he could never do the job'. What action, if any, do you take?
The one black student in your class bursts into tears a couple of weeks after you have started a 'Third World' project. When you take him aside he says to you: 'Miss, I don't think you should be teaching this stuff, because the other kids say I'm like them kids in the Oxfam posters.' What do you do?	A colleague complains bitterly to you that a student who had recently attended your human rights lesson had refused to do the 100 lines punishment set for the lunch break. The student had argued that the punishment contravened two articles of the UN Declaration of Human Rights – Article 5, freedom from degrading punishment and Article 24, the right to rest and leisure. What do you say and do?

Brantub

▼ Resources

A number of statements offering a wide range of viewpoints on a chosen issue, e.g. gender, rights, teaching/learning styles, each statement written on a separate card. The cards are put in a 'brantub' and thoroughly mixed.

▼ Procedure

Participants are invited, one by one, to come to the 'brantub', to pick out a statement and read it out to the group. The statements can be factual or can offer opinions. After each statement is read out, participants form 'buzz groups' of two or three people and discuss its meaning, implications and (if appropriate) whether or not they concur with the point(s) it makes. New 'buzz groups' are formed after each statement so participants have the chance to talk with as many others as possible. Plenary discussion follows.

▼ Potential

A lively way of introducing participants to information about, and major arguments surrounding, an issue. 'Buzz groups' encourage a sharing of viewpoints across the group and give individuals the time and space in which to reassess and, perhaps, adjust their own ideas in the light of what others say.

▼ Source

Centre for Global Education.

Creating a Curriculum Programme

▼ Resources

A short (5–15 minutes) film or videotape; 10 sheets of sugar paper; assorted felt tip pens; Blu-tack.

▼ Procedure

Participants are told that the aim of the activity is to create a two-hour curriculum programme, using the film or video as stimulus material at some point in the programme. Participants can decide for themselves for what age range and ability levels the programme is intended, and how the two-hour period is to be used (i.e. either as a single block, or divided into separate lessons). They are asked, however, to be sensitive to the range of preferred learning styles likely to be found amongst any group of students in drawing up their programme. Participants then watch the film/video, taking notes if they wish. Tried and tested films and videos for this activity are:

- The Big If, a cartoon film which fantasises about the prospect of arms and military equipment turning into food and clothing for those in need (available from Christian Aid or Concord Films Council);
- The Party or The Job, two parts of the video from the Starting Points pack exploring issues of interpersonal conflict amongst teenagers (available from Concord Films Council).

Working, if feasible, in mixed primary and secondary groups of five or six, participants have 45–60 minutes to discuss and devise the content and methodology of the two-hour programme, giving details and timings of each activity or stage. The final negotiated programme is written up on the sheets of sugar paper and stuck on the wall. Participants then look at each other's programmes using the **Circus** technique (see p. 135).

▼ Potential

Coming, as it should, towards the end of a course which has explored and demonstrated global education theory and practice, this activity provides a much-needed outlet for the creative potential of individuals and groups. The mix of primary and secondary teachers in each group, although initially providing some difficulties over the choice of target age range, encourages the cross-fertilisation of ideas and experiences from the two levels of schooling. Through this activity participants are asked to establish a definite context and framework in which to place some of the ideas and activities introduced on the course, thereby exploring their practical potential and seeing their appropriateness in terms of the overall form and rhythm of the two-hour programme (see page

96). *The resulting programmes are often innovative and of high quality, giving participants a well-deserved sense of achievement.*

▼ Variation

Other stimulus material can be used, such as a photoposter set, a series of photographs or slides, or a set of artefacts.

70–90 minutes

▼ Source

Centre for Global Education.

Programme for the Devon/Dorset DES Joint Regional Course in World Studies, 1985/6

A course for about thirty teachers (primary and secondary) involving two three-day 'long-weekend' meetings (October 1985 and January 1986) and a one-day review meeting (April 1986). In-between meetings, participants were involved in developing and trialling techniques and course units in the classroom.

Weekend One (October 1985)

Day One

10.15	Registration/Coffee/Making Personal Nametags (see page 98)	
	Session I: Making Acquaintances	
11.00	**Musical Meetings** (see page 100)	Whole Group
11.15	**Attribute Linking** (see page 100)	Whole Group
11.25	**Self-Portraits** (see page 107)	Whole Group
11.45	**Roadmaps** (see page 109)	Small Groups
12.20	**Sets** (see page 100)	Whole Group
12.40	**Rainstorm** (see page 106)	Whole Group
12.45	Lunch	
	Session II: World Studies: Aims and Areas	
14.00	**Zoom** (see page 102)	Whole Group
14.05	House business	Facilitators
14.15	Input: what is world studies?	Facilitators
14.40	**Objectives Flow Chart** (see pages 135 and 279)	Small Groups
15.40	**Birthday Line-up** (see page 101)	Whole Group
15.45	Tea	
	Session III: Teaching and Learning about Interdependence	
16.15	**Globingo!** (see page 113)	Whole Group
16.30	**Day in My Life**, part one (see page 287)	Facilitators
16.35	Input: world interdependence	Facilitators
16.50	**Woolly Thinking** (see page 141)	Small Groups/ Whole Group
17.35	**Day in My Life**, part two (see page 287)	Facilitators
17.40	Description of range of activities for introducing students to the concept of interdependence (see pages 8–12)	Facilitators

17.55	**Day in My Life**, part three (see page 287)	Facilitators
18.00	**Sitting Circle** (see page 103)	Whole Group
18.05	Break/Dinner	

Session IV: World Studies: the Learning Process (1)

20.00	Guided fantasy (see page 187)	Whole Group
20.25	**Elephant Game** (see page 178)	Whole Group
20.55	Brainstorming of thoughts and reflections, so far, on the implications of the day for the learning process (see page 135)	Small Groups
21.05	**Circus** – for sharing of thoughts and reflections (see page 135)	Whole Group
21.15	**Four Hands on Clay** (see page 46)	Pairs
21.45	Close	

Day Two

Session V: World Studies: the Learning Process (2)

9.00	**Mathematical Exercises** (see page 99)	Whole Group
9.05	Input on the learning process (1)	Facilitators
9.15	**Co-operative Squares** (see page 166)	Small Groups
9.45	Input on the learning process (2)	Facilitators
9.50	**My Son, My Son** and debriefing (see page 52)	Pairs/ Whole Group
10.00	**Nine-dot Problem** and debriefing (see page 166)	Pairs/ Whole Group
10.10	Input on the learning process (3)	Facilitators
10.15	**Linking Pictures** (see page 71)	Small Groups
10.40	Input on the learning process (4)	Facilitators
10.45	Coffee	

Session VI: World Studies at Southway School, Plymouth

11.15	Members of the World Studies team at Southway School (see pages 79 and 290) describe their fourth and fifth-year interdisciplinary core course	Facilitators/ Whole Group/ Small Groups
13.00	Lunch/Break	

Session VII: World Studies 8–13

16.00	Elaine Hicks of Cabot Primary School, Bristol (see page 145), describes her world studies work with primary children	Facilitator/ Whole Group
18.00	Dinner/Break	

Session VIII: Simulation

20.00	Simulation game, **Timber!** (see page 204)	Small Groups/ Whole Group
21.30	Close	

Day Three

Session IX: Creating a Curriculum Programme

9.00	**Creating a Curriculum Programme** (see page 282)	Small Groups/ Whole Group
10.45	Coffee	

Session X: Thinking Forwards, Thinking Backwards

11.15	Regional groups (Dorset, North and South Devon) discuss plans for period until second weekend)	Small Groups

12.00	Reflection on/evaluation of the weekend	Individuals/ Whole Group
12.40	**Spiral** (see page 106)	Whole Group
13.00	Lunch and Departure	

Weekend Two (January 1986)

Day One

10.15   Registration/Coffee

Session I: Renewing Acquaintances

11.00	**People Hunting** (see page 108)	Whole Group
11.15	**Group Machines** (see page 105)	Small Groups
11.30	**Roadmaps** (see page 109)	
12.05	Regional Groups prepare and perform presentations about their activities since first weekend	
12.45	Lunch	

Session II: Education for a Just World (1)

14.00	**Trust Fall** (see page 104)	Small Groups
14.10	**Recalling Injustice** (see page 149)	Small Groups
14.40	**The Rights of the Child?** (see page 143)	Small Groups/ Whole Group
15.10	Video montage: implication of race issues for education	Facilitators
15.30	Discussion	
15.45	Tea	

Session III: Education for a Just World (2)

16.15	Input: the nature of rights	Facilitators
16.30	**Human Rights Sets** (see page 100)	Whole Group
16.45	**Brantub** (see page 282)	Whole Group
16.55	**Tackling a Question** (see page 136) The question was 'Why is it that when 77% of all primary teachers are female, 56.7% of all primary headteachers are male?'	Small Groups
17.45	Input: gender and rights	Facilitators
18.00	Break/Dinner	

Session IV: Education for a Just World (3)

20.15	**Identity Auction** (see page 182)	Whole Group
20.50	Simulation, **Starpower** (see page 221)	Whole Group
21.30	Close	

Day Two

Session V: Education for a Just World (4)

9.15	**Musical meetings** (see page 100)	Whole Group
9.20	Input: Education for a multicultural society (1) assimilation/ education for diversity	Facilitators
9.30	Video (on racism)	
9.45	**Concentric Circles** (see page 138)	Whole Group
10.00	Input: Education for a multicultural society (2) anti-racist education	Facilitators

| 10.15 | Plenary discussion | Whole Group |
| 10.45 | Coffee | |

Session VI: Controversial Issues in the Classroom

11.15	**Tackling a Statement** (see page 137) The statement was: 'LEAs should practise a policy of positive discrimination to encourage the appointment of black teachers in all schools.'	Whole Group
11.35	Group discussion, 'What makes an issue controversial?'	Small Groups
11.45	Input: tackling controversial issues in the classroom	Facilitators
12.00	Further group discussion	Small Groups
12.15	Reporting back/discussion	Whole Group
12.45	**Group Yell** (see page 105)	Whole Group
12.50	Lunch/Break	

Session VII: Creating a Curriculum Programme

16.15	**I'm Counting on Your Co-operation** (see page 112)	Whole Group
16.25	**Creating a Curriculum Programme** (see page 282): photographs/artefacts to raise gender issues used	Whole Group
17.45	Dinner/Break	

Session VIII: Simulation

| 20.15 | Simulation game, **Bafa Bafa** (see page 217) | Whole Group |
| 21.30 | Close | |

Day Three

Session IX: Open Session

| 9.15 | Participants, having been previously advised that nothing was planned for this session, decided how it was to be used. In the event, a whole-group discussion took place. | Whole Group |

Session X: Thinking Forwards, Thinking Backwards

11.15	Regional groups to discuss plans for period until final one-day course meeting in April	Small Groups
12.00	Reflection on/Evaluation of the weekend	
12.35	**Affirmation Posters** (see page 124)	
12.50	Lunch and departure	

Note – an exhibition of world studies resources was available at both weekends. Participants filled in a **Feelings Graph** (see page 233) and wrote a **Reactions and Reflections** sheet (see page 232) after each of the twenty sessions.

Below are a selection of responses to the course as recorded on **Reactions and Reflections** sheets.

'This weekend has got me to think about issues that I had previously taken for granted. It has been a good chance to discuss and think in some depth about values, feelings and prejudices.'

'Some 'mind blowing' thoughts on racial prejudice. One's own deep-rooted prejudice is frightening.'

'Sustained and deepened interest. What fun!'

'The weekend has made me aware of the need to get junior children to think about world issues.'

'Varied, stimulating on the whole, ideas abounding, good balance between listening and doing; impressive organisation and excellent presentation and management.'

'It would seem at present that although I have enjoyed both weekend courses I may have to wait until I leave my present school to introduce the world studies programme into the curriculum. The frustration is increased when working with the people on the course — then looking back into the educational wasteland of my school.'

'A drink would have broken the ice much quicker. If making acquaintances is what is intended, why not have proper party games accompanied by free beer and wine? Important time was being wasted when we could have been told what world studies is.'

'Good ice-breaker. Lifted 'formal' atmosphere.'

'One of the most effective things about the first weekend was the way our own assumptions were shaken. I didn't think that sort of attack could be sustained but it was.'

'Enjoyed very much. Almost too much to handle — the problem is now going back for longer reflection about all the ideas buzzing and finding the time once back at school to enable them to gel enough to start producing concrete plans of action.'

A Day In My Life

▼ Resources

A set of cards similar to those given on pp. 288–9. Two facilitators are required for this activity.

▼ Procedure

One facilitator reads out the 'story card', prefacing the reading with the remark, 'This is an account of a typical day in my life'. When he has completed the last sentence, the other facilitator interrupts by suggesting that he has detected a number of global influences already in the story and asking for the story to be repeated. On the second reading the facilitator with the 'global detector cards' interrupts, at the points indicated with an asterisk, by reading out the appropriate 'global detector card'.

▼ Story Card

I awoke at 7.00 to the ringing of an alarm clock.*... pulled on a tracksuit and went out of the house for a run along local country lanes.*
On returning home, I showered and shaved.*
I then ironed my favourite shirt, which I had forgotten to do last night.*
As time was running short, I dressed hurriedly.*
Whilst eating breakfast I glanced at the newspaper report of riots in London.*
My daughter was trying to finish her maths homework at the table.*
Shortly before 8.30 I left home and drove to a nearby petrol station.*
Whilst driving to work I noticed a distant plume of smoke from the coal-fired power station.*
On arriving at my office I received a phone call from Minnesota.*

Global Detector Cards

1

I awoke at 7.00 to the ringing of an alarm clock. Stop! You have encountered the global. Your clock is a product of the Sony Corporation, based in Japan. The clock was assembled in a Sony plant in Brazil from component parts produced in Japan, Mexico and West Germany. It was shipped from Brazil to the UK in a Greek-owned ship manufactured in Sweden, licensed in Liberia and staffed by a Portuguese crew.

2

...pulled on a tracksuit and went out of the house for a run along local country lanes. Stop! Not only are you wearing the global – your tracksuit was made in the Philippines by women working in factories which directly contravene Article 23 of the UN Declaration of Human Rights, the right to just and favourable conditions of work – you are also participating in a widespread trend towards physical fitness as a measure of precaution against the health problems associated with stress, lack of exercise and an unbalanced diet.

3

On returning home, I showered and shaved. Stop! Now you are putting on the global. The soap you used was made from palm oil grown in Zaire by Unilever, a transnational corporation owned jointly in the Netherlands and the UK. The razor was made by Gillette and the aftershave lotion by the British-American Tobacco Company; the former is a US-based transnational, the latter is based in the UK.

4

I then ironed my favourite shirt, which I had forgotten to do last night. Stop! You are participating in a global movement towards a re-definition of women's and men's roles in the family and home, triggered by the increasing number of married women in full-time employment. Incidently, the shirt you ironed was bought at Marks & Spencers, a UK-based company which now has branches in five countries overseas.

5

As time was running short, I dressed hurriedly. Stop! You are, of course, wearing the global. Your shirt was made from cotton grown in the United States, your underpants were made in Israel and your socks manufactured in Taiwan from wool grown in Australia. The raw materials used to make your clothes are subject to the Multi-Fibre Agreement, which now covers 80% of the world's textile trade. This Agreement limits the import of textiles from certain countries, such as Hong Kong and Taiwan, into the EEC whilst allowing export growth by other countries like Sri Lanka and the Philippines.

6

Whilst eating breakfast I glanced at the newspaper report of riots in London. Stop! You are really steeped in the global. As well as reports from correspondents in all parts of the world, the newspaper you are reading obtains much of its news from United Press International, Associated Press International, Reuters and Tass, all transnational information agencies. The paper on which the news is printed comes from Finland. The report suggests various underlying causes of the riots, including rising levels of unemployment – a global problem. The riots took place in an area whose population typifies the increasing global trend towards the development of multi-ethnic and multicultural communities.

7

My daughter was trying to finish her maths homework at the table. Stop! Your daughter is learning maths, but what else besides? The text book she is using is replete with cartoon and photographic images conditioning her to accept a woman's role as home-oriented, passive and subservient. In the majority of illustrations, boys and men have active, responsible roles usually outside the home whilst girls and women are engaged in domestic play and work. Significantly, too, the book fails to reflect the multi-ethnic composition of British society in its illustrations and examples.

8

Shortly before 8.30 I left home and drove to a nearby petrol station. Stop! Now you are driving the global. Your car is a Renault, a product of the third largest French-based transnational corporation. The various raw materials going into your car came from more than 70 nations. You buy your petrol from Shell, an Anglo-Dutch transnational which is the world's second largest. The price you pay for that petrol is largely influenced by the decisions of the oil-producing countries belonging to OPEC, who have played a significant role in the development of a global economic system.

9

Whilst driving to work I noticed a distant plume of smoke from the coal-fired power station. Stop! You are part of the global environment. The burning of fossil fuels is contributing significantly to the pollution of the earth's atmosphere. In the prevailing south-westerly wind, that smoke may fall as acid rain in a forest in Scandinavia or Northern Europe, thereby adding to the serious problem of deforestation. The ever-increasing demand for energy by our consumer society is causing a serious depletion of the earth's non-renewable resources, such as coal and oil.

10

On arrival at the office I received a phone call from Minnesota. Stop! You are now employing a global communication system. The caller dialled your number direct thanks to the use of space satellites hovering several hundred miles over the Atlantic and put there by an international consortium of governments and business firms.

11

So, in just a few hours of your life you have consumed raw materials from most parts of the world, used products sold by many of the world's major transnational corporations, benefited from global communication and information systems and contributed to prevailing political, economic, social and environmental trends and developments in the world.

The role of INSET: a personal perspective

by **Jim Christophers**, Head of Humanities at Southway School, Plymouth

Have you, like me, sat in a large hall listening to a trained teacher lecturing at you for an hour or more as your eyelids, heavy with drowsiness, seek to release you from the feelings of inadequacy and incompetence which seem to grow with every new overhead projector transparency? Have you wondered, amidst the daydreams of your mind, why such an apparently accomplished teacher, when placed in the role of external expert, seems to forego all the attributes of good presentation which makes her successful in the first place? Have you subsequently felt the frustration arising from your lack of success at convincing your colleagues that your freshly acquired but secondhand ideas are worthwhile?

To a greater or lesser extent all of us in the teaching profession will be able to answer 'Yes' to one or more of the questions posed above. Certainly the picture I hold in my mind as I pose these questions is a fair reflection of the approach to INSET I have encountered for much of my career. In fact I became totally convinced that the most profitable part of any INSET course was most likely to be encountered during the informal conversations I had with other participants during coffee, tea and lunch breaks.

It is with relief then that a different model is now gaining favour in the presentation of INSET; one which places an emphasis on the education rather than the training of teachers and, in consequence, one which encourages a careful consideration of the process employed as well as the material and/or ideas to be presented. My first and most dramatic experience of this change of emphasis came as a participant on a course considering the nature of world studies.

The typed programme, received prior to the course, gave an indication of what was to come in that the whole weekend was divided into a series of 'Activity Sessions' and 'Workshops', including one on 'Interpersonal Skills'! We found that for much of the time we were invited to work as small groups, not simply for the purposes of discussion but in order that we could take part in activities which, while simple in nature, encouraged us to consider directly our understanding of and attitudes towards a whole variety of issues relating to the nature of the learning process and world studies. I was introduced to terms like 'experiential learning' and 'medium and message' in such a way that the whole experience had a fundamental and enduring impact. In other words, I

had experienced an educational process of the most valuable kind.

Of direct significance for my approach to my world studies teaching was the appreciation that the attitudes and values dimension of the issues could be handled sensitively without indoctrination and given the level of emphasis it requires. In the process young people could be given the scope to grow intellectually while at the same time developing the social skills of value for a pluralistic society.

It was shortly after this experience that I was invited by the school Parent/Teachers Association to give a talk as part of a programme in which heads of departments had attempted to make parents more familiar with the courses they offered. We had recently initiated a core upper school World Studies course and they were particularly interested to 'hear about' this course. I had given talks before, at great length and with many carefully prepared overhead projector transparencies and had received compliments for my efforts. Dare I change the tried, tested and successful format and adopt a more participatory approach, I wondered; an approach that would provide the opportunity for the parents to appreciate some of the fundamental principles underpinning our course?

With some reticence, inspired by comments about how much they enjoyed 'the talks already provided by Heads of Departments', I decided to grasp the nettle and stand by my convictions. And so it was that I found myself reading fables, making rain storms and playing 'Globingo' with a 'class' of parents one evening in the school library. And so it was that I found myself delegated to make the coffee while they grappled with their picture sequencing; they were sorry but 'would I mind as I did not seem to be as busy as they were and we could hear what the groups have to say while we have our coffee then, couldn't we?'

The results of the experience were twofold. Firstly, a group of interested parents had enjoyed an evening together while acquiring a depth of understanding of a part of the school curriculum which they certainly would not have achieved from the lecture format. Secondly, I had demonstrated to myself that I could successfully use the approach and that my belief in its value was well-founded.

Since then, circumstances have been such that I have made contributions to pre-service and in-service courses in a variety of situations. On each occasion, as an individual or as part of a team, I have been anxious to present myself as a facilitator rather than a trainer and have sought to structure my contribution around a set of small group activities designed to involve the members of the course as active participants rather than passive receivers. I feel that it is important not to present oneself as the 'visiting expert' and to be aware of the potentially negative value of emphasising the 'experiential' approach to the exclusion of others. I define a 'processive classroom' as one in which the emphasis is explicitly on the learning process and one must appreciate that learning takes place within a variety of situations; indeed a variety of approaches may enhance the process of learning in its own right. A summary of a programme recently used with a group of teachers may serve to illustrate some of these points while raising others. The programme occupied one day of a three-day course and was designed to consider how world studies could be implemented in schools. Many of the teachers had some knowledge of the school and its world studies course.

Session 1 9.00–10.30 Implementation in the Whole Curriculum

Activity	Comment
Picture sequencing	Used as an affirmation exercise – the group had already been together for a day. The pictures offered scope to consider some gender-related issues and to introduce the idea of 'perspective consciousness'.
Reading	Extract from *Larkrise to Candleford*. The dichotomy between the limited personal experience of children and their global awareness was considered.
Globingo	The placing of dots on a world map outline enhanced this exercise which, together with group consideration of interdependence, seemed to reveal our potentially Eurocentric perspective of the world.
Comment	Issues arising from the introductory activities relating to our understanding of world studies and to the activities employed were discussed in an open forum.
Bob Geldof statement, 'Band Aid' video	Bringing our consideration 'down to earth.' Real people are involved, some of the issues are unpleasant. How ought we present this to children?
Input	Short OHP presentation outlining the school's curriculum policy and the place occupied by world studies.

Session 2 11.00–12.30 Implementation in the Classroom 1

Activity	Comment
Picture interpretation	This enabled groups to consider how they react to information and was extended into the area of 'media bias'. The choice of Apartheid as a theme proved to be controversial. The general discussion provided an unanticipated link with the next activity.
Anticipating difficulties	A statement ranking exercise. The statements were negative in their content but by clearly focusing discussion the outcome was entirely positive and generated much confidence.
Input	Short OHP presentation considering the ways in which 'activities' are integrated into our course programme alongside more traditional approaches.

Session 3   14.00–16.00   Implementation in the Classroom 2

Activity	Comment
Simulation	The use of role play to promote empathy and enhance appreciation. The simulation used was developed within school.
Input	Short OHP presentation considering the nature of the learning process and the implications of this for our work with young people especially within the affective domain.
Group picture drawing Tower building	Two activities taken from the more aesthetic areas of our course. How relevant are activities such as this to our work? How successfully can we expect to explore these areas?

Session 4   17.00–18.30   Preparation of Materials

Activity	Comment
Reviewing school-produced materials	A small group activity in which participants could review booklets issued to students as 'core' materials for sections of our course. This is important in that it represents an explicitly pragmatic input.
Selecting and developing activities	Even smaller groups selected activities within published materials and considered their use in their own situation. This proved remarkably useful and the participants were very creative. This kind of reinforcement proved of value in that most felt that they had already taken the first step.

You will appreciate that the course participants were directly involved in the programme throughout the whole day. They have gained a good understanding of one school's approach to world studies. For those who have a clear desire to take the approach further there is a selection of activities which they have already experienced and that can be readily adopted for use in their situation. Those who are unsure will be making future decisions based on firsthand rather than secondhand experience of this approach. All the members of the course have been challenged to reassess their understanding of the nature of the learning process and of their role within it. For this reason, if for no other, I would suggest that a programme such as this offers in-service education for teachers of the very highest order, and in doing so has an effective potential far in excess of that associated with the more traditional in-service training model.

The format proposed above is ideally suited to programmes such as those focusing on world studies where one has to acknowledge and service the vitally important but personal areas relating to attitudes, values and their manifestations as perspectives. The technique of using small group activities and related exercises has proved of value in situations as diverse as considering the implications of making adjustments to the school day and providing INSET for the school Social Studies department in preparation for GCSE. Using the same approach as part of our primary/secondary liaison work has also proved to be successful though it also brought the personal realisation that some primary school teachers have been working to an extent in this way for a number of years. Is nothing ever quite new?

Crisis of confidence: turning departments into teams

By **Richard Hedge**, teacher in charge of World Studies at Southway School, Plymouth

Any curriculum innovation is likely to be more readily accepted by some people than by others. Perhaps because of its greater novelty in terms of aims, content and methodology, world studies appears more prone to this selective welcome than many other developments. This is certainly true of those watching events from the 'outside': parents, governors, management teams, etc. but also, I suspect, usually applies to some of the teachers who will be involved in working directly with the students.

At Southway School, Plymouth, where we have been offering World Studies courses in years three, four and five for four years, we have a team of eleven teachers presenting the course to three hundred students in each year group. This team was drawn in 1982 from three separate departments (Geography, History and Business Studies) which had absolutely no tradition of working together. Initially the stimulus for change came from a new headteacher and, perhaps predictably, was greeted with more enthusiasm in some quarters than others.

A selection from the doubts expressed by some of our more hesitant colleagues will make familiar reading to some:

— 'Will the course still have enough Geography/History/Commerce in it?'
— 'Will students really learn from all these processive activities?'
— 'How will we cope with the assessment?'
— 'Where will the resources come from?'
— 'Why do we need to do this?'
— 'I'm not familiar enough with the subject material'
— 'What will the results be like?'
— 'How much time will it take?'
— 'Who will be in charge?'

Four years on (1986), it would be dishonest to suggest that all these questions have been answered to the complete satisfaction of all concerned. It might perhaps be true to say that through a variety of experiences — some more enjoyable than others — we are beginning to arrive at some sort of common understanding. This has not always been a painless process and it might help other colleagues to be aware of at least three of the pits into which we have fallen at different times.

1 *The Outside Expert Syndrome.* Once a few members of the team had been infected with a real enthusiasm for some of the developments which were taking place in world studies in other parts of the country, the natural inclination was to invite into the school people whom we felt were best qualified to spread the 'gospel'. Staff from the Centre for Global Education duly arrived and within minutes we were all actively involved in picture sequencing, clay handling and the rest. All this produced a very enjoyable day but in the long-term added little to our course and in the case of one or two members of the team actually increased their sense of alienation from what was going on. This may simply have reflected inadequate follow-up but I suspect there is a more important lesson to be learnt: that real innovation and development must be promoted and nurtured within departmental teams. This is not to say that outside contributors have no role to play but rather to stress that INSET time is so rare and precious that it must be used to encourage a sense of confidence in what the whole team has to offer rather than to impose frightening and unfamiliar ideas on those whom the INSET programme is most designed to help.

2 *Hedge's Autocracy Syndrome.* This is clearly a related complaint and differs from the first only in the source from which unfamiliar and threatening ideas are imposed. To facilitate the easier and cheaper handling of resources, our course is in the process of being produced as a series of booklets — a development which most staff warmly welcome. The danger in this process is, however, that as most booklet writing and, therefore, course development takes place in the school holidays — particularly the summer holidays — there is a tendency for teachers to return to school in September to be presented with a set of lessons for the next term. Understandably this has tended to reduce the extent to which teachers feel an ownership of and involvement in the courses and has been counter-productive in that classrooms have become less of a source of innovatory practice than in the past. The tension between achieving a clarity of understanding and purpose on the one hand and encouraging

individual interpretation on the other is not always easy to live with but its successful resolution is in the evolution of a healthy and creative teaching team.

3 *The Modular Disease.* In some areas this appears to be reaching epidemic proportions. Because of its historical origins, World Studies at Southway was initially offered on a modular basis with students rotating on a carousel through three courses largely based on History, Geography and Commerce each year. In this situation any attempt to produce a coherent learning experience was almost inevitably doomed to failure. The first lesson any world studies teacher has to learn is that they are no longer an historian or a geographer or whatever it may be but a world studies teacher pure and simple (if either of those words really apply in this context!).

Although I know of no school which offers a course along this early model, there are a number who now think in terms of a course of five or six modules based on more recognisable world studies concepts such as war and peace or development. While this is clearly a massive improvement on our early subject-based efforts, I feel it still involves some of the problems we experienced. Not only does a modular course make the idea of the interrelationships between issues less obvious but it also works against the aim of achieving a well-integrated and thoroughly involved team. This objective requires all teachers to participate fully in all areas of the course.

It is my hope that at Southway we are slowly beginning to learn from our mistakes. Certainly the programme at the recent GCSE INSET planning day benefited from some of the lessons I have described above. Some of the activities which were found to be most helpful are set out below in the hope that they may provide pointers in more positive directions.

Title	Activity	Comments
Where Are We Now?	Each working group (2–3 people) was given a copy of the aims of the GCSE course printed on the lefthand side of a sheet of A3 paper. Groups had to identify activities or areas of the course practised at present which went some way towards fulfilling these aims.	This exercise played an important role in building confidence in our course and our common understanding of it. It could equally well be used as a framework for brainstorming within a department new to world studies
The COW chart	Each working group was given strips of paper on which the assessment objectives of the GCSE were written. These were then stuck on to large sheets of paper in three columns indicating whether we were Confident, Optimistic or Worried about devising strategies to assess them. Any strategies suggested were written on the sheet next to the objectives.	Again it is the framework rather than our particular application of it which is important. While much of the discussion following this activity was positive, it did allow people to express fears and doubts in a non-threatening and non-vulnerable way.
Worries in a Hat	Larger working groups (5–6 people) were formed. Each person wrote down their single greatest concern about the course. These were then placed in a large container and removed in turn. Each one was stuck onto a large sheet of paper and possible solutions discussed and written next to each worry.	Again the great value of this exercise is that although the discussion is cast in a positive framework, it takes real fears and doubts as its starting point. It also gives all members of the team a clearly recognised problem-solving role.

See Appendix for the GCSE syllabus referred to above and page 270 for a discussion of world studies in Devon.

References

1 Rogers, C., 'Education – a personal activity' in Elliot Kemp, J. and Rogers, C., *The Effective Teacher*, Pavic Publications, 1982, p. 11.

2 Cited in Rogers, C., *Freedom to Learn for the 80's*, Charles E. Merrill, 1983, p. 173.

3 Rogers, C., 'Education – a personal activity' in Elliot-Kemp, J. and Rogers, C., op. cit., p. 8.

4 See, for example, Richardson, R., Flood, M. and Fisher, S., *Debate and Decision*, World Studies Project, 1980; Fisher, S. and Hicks, D. W., *World Studies 8–13. A Teacher's Handbook*, Oliver & Boyd, 1985, pp. 162–81.

5 See Selby, D.E., 'Truly a breath of fresh air – teacher training in world studies', *Multicultural Teaching*, Vol. 11, No. 2, 1984, pp. 23–9. From October 1986 the York University Postgraduate Certificate in Education course has included a core Global and Multicultural Education course for all students. Those facilitating the course (staff from the Centre for Global Education) also contribute to the PGCE induction week and advise tutors on the means whereby a global and multicultural dimension can be infused into their subjects. The University of Exeter PGCE course has a world studies option.

6 Elliot-Kemp, J., 'Toward more effective teaching: a managerial perspective' in Elliot-Kemp, J. and Rogers, C., op. cit., p. 16.

7 Ferguson, M., *The Aquarian Conspiracy*, Granada, 1982, p. 338; Cogan, J., 'Educating teachers for a global perspective', *World Studies Journal*, Vol. 4, No. 1, Autumn 1982, pp. 20–3.

Appendix — World Studies Syllabus

Southern Examining Group

The South-East Regional Examinations Board (SEREB)	The Associated Examining Board (AEB)	The Southern Regional Examinations Board (SREB)	The Oxford Delegacy of Local Examinations (OLE)	The South Western Examinations Board (SWEB)

World Studies

A GCSE Group Mode III Scheme for first examination in 1988

1.0 Introduction

1.1 This scheme is a response by teachers, advisers and teachers trainers to:
(a) curriculum statements by the Department of Education and Science and a number of statements and initiatives by Local Education Authorities.[i]
(b) the need to promote an understanding of a range of important issues that face us at the personal, local, national and global levels.

1.2 World studies encompasses a recognition that on our earth we all have a future which is dependent on a common natural environment, humanity, economy and spirituality. Changes in any one locality, at whatever level (personal to global), can affect the whole; processes and factors that bring about change operate within an interrelated and interdependent system.

1.3 A more comprehensive understanding of the reality which students experience within and beyond the school can be encouraged if students have the opportunity to integrate concepts, ideas and perspectives derived from within and beyond the established disciplines and to draw from these disciplines the rigorous procedures for the appraisal of evidence from a variety of sources and points of view.

1.4 World studies is concerned to develop an enhanced awareness and understanding of perspective and of the limitations of relying upon personal perspective as the sole yardstick for judgement. A student's exploration of the wider world can lead to a greater self-awareness, just as heightened self-awareness can aid and enlarge understanding of global issues. This two-way process can be facilitated by the use of experiential and interactive learning techniques.

1.5 It is important that recognition be given to the value of students exploring their own attitudes and feelings as a starting point for – and subsequently throughout – their work in world studies.

2.0 Aims

The aims[ii] of this course are to develop:

2.1 An understanding of the systemic nature of the world:
(a) in the spatial dimension: on a range of scales including personal, local, national and global;
(b) in the temporal dimension: the relationship between past, present and future.

2.2 A range of skills leading to both an understanding of, and a concern for, the issues raised (see separate skills list).

2.3 Consciousness of personal perspective and of how all perspectives are influenced by a range of factors such as age, class, creed, culture, ethnicity, gender, ideology, language, nationality and race.

The three aims above inform the further aims of promoting:

2.4 An awareness and appreciation of a range of cultures and their diversity and of what humanity holds in common.

2.5 Empathy with other people whatever their age, class, creed ethnicity, gender, ideology, language, nationality and race.

---

i The DES statements referred to here include *Education in Schools: A Consultative Document* (1977); *Aspects of Secondary Education* (1979) and *A Framework for the School Curriculum* (1980). Devon Schools Sub-Committee approved recommendations for schools on 'World Studies and Multicultural Education' in March 1983 and world studies initiatives are in evidence in some forty-five other local education authorities.

ii It is not intended that all the above aims will be translated into Assessment Objectives (see 3.0).

2.6 A concern for justice, human rights and responsibilities.

2.7 An understanding of the dynamics of conflict and co-operation from the personal to global levels.

2.8 An understanding of the sources, distribution and exercise of power.

2.9 An understanding of and an enhanced capacity to participate in political and other decision-making processes.

2.10 An awareness and understanding of the complex interrelationships within environmental systems and the place of the human species within those systems.

2.11 An awareness and understanding of development and of the various processes, types and meanings of development.

2.12 An awareness that there is a range of choices open to humanity leading to reflection upon possible, probable and personally preferred futures.

2.13 Heightened levels of self-awareness and selfesteem.

2.14 An appreciation of the holistic concept of health as being the fusion of the bodily, emotional, intellectual and spiritual dimensions of a person living in harmonious relationship with the planet.

In pursuance of the above aims, the development of the skills set out in the chart that follows will be fostered.

3.0   Assessment Objectives
       Candidates will be expected to demonstrate

3.1   An **Understanding** of:

3.1.1 the terms, concepts and ideas relevant to a particular Key Idea as identified in the Content Model (see 8.4);

3.1.2 the web of relationships between processes, in time and space, which influence events and developments in the contemporary world;

3.1.3 a range of perspectives on key world trends and

Skills List

Recall Knowledge of Dimensions, Key Concepts and Key Ideas drawn from the Content Model
Communication Verbal Communication Processes (including Listening) Non-Verbal Communication Processes (including Observing)
Inquiry Formulation of Questions and Hypotheses Data Collection
Evaluation Extraction of Relevant Data Analysis and Interpretation Distinguishing between Opinion and Evidence Recognition of Bias Identifying Perspective
Judgement Deduction Induction Decision Making Reflection
Creative Thinking Application Lateral Thinking Problem Solving Projection Extrapolation Perception of Relationships Holistic Thinking

Interpersonal

Co-operation

Negotiation

Participation

Action

issues and of how these perspectives may have been shaped.

3.2　An Ability to:

3.2.1　select relevant evidence and distinguish between evidence and opinion;

3.2.2　present information and ideas clearly and coherently in an appropriate form;

3.2.3　evaluate evidence and critically examine arguments in relation to issues and ideas identified in the Content Model;

3.2.4　make reasoned judgements;

3.2.5　make projections based upon a consideration of events, evidence and trends.

3.3　A Capacity for:

3.3.1　self-reflection in order to appreciate the relationship of personal experiences and processes to the wider world;

3.3.2　the use of personal experience and imagination in an attempt to understand the attitudes, feelings and actions of others;

3.3.3　self-awareness through personal reflection upon processes involving group co-operation, collaboration and negotiation.

4.0　Assessment Pattern

The assessment pattern for the syllabus is common to all candidates on the principle that the objectives which world studies is seeking to assess can be demonstrated to some degree by all candidates, although clearly at different levels.

The examination of candidates will consist of the following components:

4.1　Periodic Testing – Assessment Units　　　　　　　45% of Total Marks (15% per unit)

Three assessment units to be completed by all students each of which will be used to examine particular assessment objectives. Each unit will comprise approximately two weeks' work and will be based upon work carried out during the course. Units will be presented to pupils at prescribed points during the course. In designing assessment units centres will be expected to take due account of the assessment objectives and of the appropriate part of the Content Model. All assessment units must be approved in advance by the adviser/moderator (see section 6).

	Assessment objectives to be tested
4.1 i　Assessment Unit 1 (Evidence) This unit will be completed by students working on their own and will require them to employ a range of skills relating to evidence from a variety of sources. This unit will be undertaken in the Spring term of the first year of the course.	3.2.1, 3.2.2, 3.2.3, 3.2.4
4.1 ii　Assessment Unit 2 (Groupwork) This unit will be completed by a group of 4–6 students working together on a common task but with each student producing an individual piece of work which should demonstrate her/his contribution to the work of the whole group. This unit will be undertaken in the Autumn term of the second year of the course.	3.3.1, 3.2.5, 3.3.3
4.1 iii　Assessment Unit 3 (Issues) This unit will be completed by students working on their own to employ a range of skills relating to the study of an issue. This unit will be undertaken in the Spring term of the second year of the course.	3.1.2, 3.1.3, 3.2.5, 3.2.4

4.2　Continuous Assessment – Student Profile　　　　　　30% of Total Marks

A student profile is to be developed over the two years of the course requiring discussion and negotiation between the teacher and the student. This will be based in part upon students carrying out one of the following activities for a period of at least one term.

Assessment objectives to be tested

4.2 i　A diary kept by the student of activities of particular interest to her/him resulting from work done during the course.

4.2 ii　A folder consisting of a structured selection of media items with an accompanying commentary relating to events and issues relevant to the course and to the student.

4.2 iii　Practical activity carried out by the student such as participation in community relations work, environmental conservation projects and projects to raise awareness of global issues.

3.3.1, 3.3.2,
3.2.4, 3.2.5

4.3 Terminal Assessment – Oral

25% of Total Marks

Each student will undertake a terminal oral examination of between ten and fifteen minutes' duration in a personal interview with a teacher. In this interview, the student will be expected to respond to questions, develop arguments and express reasoned opinions on issues.

Assessment objectives to be tested 3.1.1, 3.1.2, 3.1.3, 3.2.3

4.4 The interview will have the following structure:
  (a) a talk of up to five minutes by the student on a topic selected from an approved list of four (one from within each Dimension in the Content Model).
  (b) five to ten minutes of question and answer in which the interviewer seeks to explore the student's broader understanding of the chosen topic and its relationship to relevant Key Concepts and Key Ideas within all four Dimensions of the Content Model.

Each centre will be responsible for compiling a list of four topics from which candidates will select one for their talk. Each centre will also compile a list of twenty-five questions for each topic which will satisfy the test of candidates' deeper understanding of the topic and its relationship to relevant Key Concepts and Key Ideas. Questions of increasing difficulty should be varied enough to permit permutations responsive to the student's talk. The Board will provide centres with a list of questions as exemplars.

Each interviewer at a centre will be required to tape an anticipated representative sample of oral examinations, the recording to include pre-and post-statements by the interviewer anticipating and reflecting upon the candidate's performance.

4.5 Mark Allocation

		Assessment Unit 1	Assessment Unit 2	Assessment Unit 3	Student Profile	Terminal Oral	Total marks for each assessment objective	Total marks for each group of assessment objectives
Understanding	3.1.1					10	10	
	3.1.2			5		5	10	30%
	3.1.3			5		5	10	
Ability	3.2.1	5					5	
	3.2.2	5					5	
	3.2.3	3				5	8	34%
	3.2.4	2		3	6		11	
	3.2.5		3	2			5	
Capacity	3.3.1		4		8		12	
	3.3.2				10		10	36%
	3.3.3		8		6		14	
Total marks for each assessment unit		15%	15%	15%	30%	25%	100%	100%

5.0 Differentiation

5.1 Differentiation will be achieved by using a variety of assessment techniques which provide ample opportunity for pupils to demonstrate positively their knowledge and abilities in a range of situations. Wherever possible questions will not be content specific, allowing students to select examples from their own experience and from the particular course they have followed. Where students are asked to handle evidence this will be presented in a variety of forms and derived from various sources.

5.2 In the oral assessment differentiation will be achieved by providing lists of questions of ascending difficulty. Interviewers will pose questions either for a maximum of ten minutes or until they are satisfied that the candidate has achieved her/his optimum performance.

5.3 The assessment units must be designed in terms of resources and tasks so as to allow a range of responses at different levels of skill and conceptual understanding. All assessment units will seek to emphasise positive achievement by pupils.

6.0 Examination Board Adviser/Moderators

6.1 Each centre will be allocated an adviser/moderator appointed by the Board who will be responsible for a group of schools. This person, who should be an experienced world studies teacher, will be responsible for maintaining regular contact with each centre for the

6.1 i approval of course outline designed by the schools as reflecting the aims of the syllabus within the context of the Content Model.

ii approval of assessment units, submitted in advance, by schools to examine the periodic assessment element of the course.

iii approval in advance, of topic titles and question lists for terminal orals' assessment.

iv moderation of assessment units and terminal orals for centres in the group.

6.2 The purpose of the adviser/moderator is to ensure compatability between centres and the effective moderation of assessment units and terminal orals. A second important function of the adviser/moderator is to encourage schools and teachers to undertake a continuing review and development of their courses in relation to content and teaching/learning styles.

7.0 Grade Descriptions

7.1 Grade descriptions are provided to give a general indication of the standards of achievement likely to have been shown by candidates awarded particular grades. The grade awarded will depend on the extent to which the candidate has met the Assessment Objectives overall and it might conceal weakness in one aspect of the examination which is balanced by above average performance in some other.

7.2 Grade F

The candidate shows:
1 A basic understanding of world issues and some of the relationships between them and an awareness that they may be viewed from different perspectives.
2 The ability to handle simple evidence in a way which shows some degree of selection, interpretation, evaluation and judgement.
3 A capacity for some level of:
(a) awareness of relationships between individuals and wider issues.
(b) imagination in making future projections out of familiar situations and in understanding others' actions, attitudes and feelings.
(c) reflection on personal and group behaviour.

7.3 Grade C

The candidate shows:
1 A broad understanding of world issues (including the ability to handle relevant terms, concepts and ideas); an appreciation of a variety of ways in which these issues are related; an understanding of the nature and basis of some different perspectives from which they may be viewed.

2 The ability to distinguish between evidence and opinion and to select from, interpret and evaluate evidence from a variety of sources in order to produce reasoned judgements presented clearly and in a variety of forms.
3 A capacity for:
(a) reflection on a variety of relationships between individuals and the wider world.
(b) an empathetic use of personal experience and imagination.
(c) reflection on processes of negotiation and co-operation.

8.0 Content Model

8.1 The Content Model below (8.4) illustrates the content at three tiers – Dimensions, Key Concepts and Key Ideas – within a fundamental framework of interrelatedness of issues and world interdependence.

8.2 Centres will be required to submit course exemplars demonstrating adequate coverage of the Key Ideas.

8.3 These exemplars should include:
(a) an exploration of each Dimension at various points on a spatial scale, personal to global;
(b) an exploration of each Dimension at various points on a temporal scale, past to future;
(c) an exploration of the relationship of the Dimension to the three other Dimensions;
(d) an exploration of each Dimension from the vantage point of a range of perspectives (age, class, credal, cultural, ethnic, gender, ideological, linguistic, national and racial).
(e) some reflection upon the relationship of each Dimension to the holistic concept of health as defined in 2.14.

8.4 Content Model (see opposite)

8.5 Centres should submit course outlines to the adviser/ moderator for approval. An examplar is appended to this syllabus as a guide. It is emphasised that this is *for guidance only*.

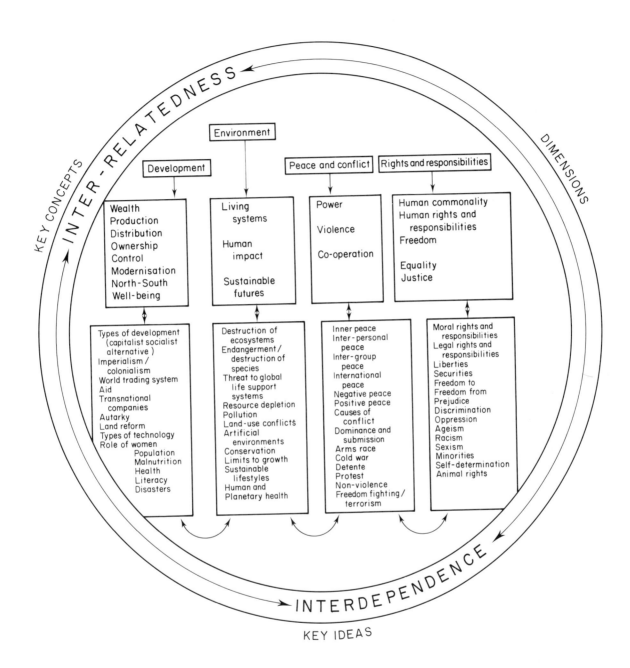

WORLD STUDIES
STUDENT PROFILE

Name of Student _____ Tutor Group _____
Name of School _____
Date Record Started _____

Student's Choice of Activity	
(a) Diary based on coursework	
(b) Collection of media items with commentary	
(c) Practical activity with commentary	

Student Profile Record Sheet

Student's Comment

Agreed Comment by Student and Teacher

Assessment Objective	Agreed Comment	Mark
3.2.4		
3.3.1		
3.3.2		
3.3.3		

Date _____ Signed by Teacher _____
Student _____

Guidance on the Completion of Student Profile

1 This profile should be developed over the period of the course.

2 Entries should be made on at least four occasions.

3 Each occasion requires

i   a comment by the student relating to her/his performance on the course since the beginning or the previous entry. This comment should include reference to developments in knowledge, understanding, skills and attitudes;

ii   discussion between student and teacher based upon work done as part of coursework and/or student's own chosen activity leading to an agreed comment;

iii   a written comment in relation to one of the assessment objectives and a mark. This should also be based upon work done as coursework or student's own chosen activity;

iv   that over the whole period of negotiation of the profile the teacher must ensure that attention is given to all four of the assessment objectives at some time.

4 During the final meeting between student and teacher to complete the profile, a summative agreed comment upon the student's progress over the course must be produced together with a final mark for each assessment objective.

WORLD STUDIES GCSE EXEMPLAR DEVELOPMENT

Key ideas	Content	Activity/Output	Resources
RICH NORTH/POOR SOUTH	(a) comparison of statistics on GNP, population, land area, location and consumption of natural resources	(a) 'If there were 100 people in the world' exercises as in Richardson, R., *Learning for Change* and Weeden, P., 'Numbers in an Unequal World', *World Studies Journal* 5/4	(a) Kidron & Segal, *New State of the World Atlas*, UNICEF *State of the World's Children*
	(b) location of 'rich north' and 'poor south'; comparison of Mercator and Peters map projections	(b) Exercises comparing maps	(b) Lunn, P., *Peacemaking in Practice*
	(c) interdependence of 'rich north' and 'poor south'	(c) 'World in the Classroom' and 'World in our Town' activities; 'World in the Larder'/World in the Supermarket'; 'Globingo'	(c) CWDE, *Change and Choice*; Birmingham DEC, *The World in Birmingham* photopack; Pike & Selby, *Global Teacher, Global Learner*
DEVELOPMENT/ UNDERDEVELOPMENT	(a) Models of development: capitalist, state socialist, self-managing and alternative	(a) experiential unit to enable students to arrive at different models of development, e.g. 'Apples'	(a) CTIR, University of Denver, *Teaching about Food and Hunger*
	(b) case studies (e.g. UK, GDR, Cuba, Taiwan)	(b) teacher input/student research	(b) various CWDE materials
	(c) comparative study of individuals living in developed and underdeveloped contexts: e.g. suburban housewife, shanty-town dweller, aboriginal Australian; a range of perspectives on development	(c) student reading/research; small group leading to plenary discusson of what is development, and which path to development is preferable	(c) film/chart/literary evidence
WORLD INEQUALITY	(a) history of colonialism; positive and negative effects	(a) research and production of project	(a) film/video material; J. Stuart, *The Unequal Third*; Indian or African literature
	(b) imbalances caused by world trading system: tariffs, quotas, the role of multinational companies	(b) experiential unit, e.g. *Slicing the banana* (Christian Aid); filmstrip 'Banana Split' on banana production in the Dominican Republic (Christian Aid); slide set *Our cup of tea* on Sri Lankan tea workers *(CWDE)*	b) J. Turner, *World Inequality*; Christian Aid, *It's not fair*; tape/slide set 'The shy giants' (CWDE)

Select Bibliography

1 General Reading

Briggs, J.P. and Peat, D. *Looking Glass Universe. The Emerging Science of Wholeness*, Fontana, 1985. Fascinating exploration of how several prominent scientists have developed a holistic worldview as a result of their research.

Capra, F. *The Tao of Physics*, Flamingo, 1976. Explores the parallels between the emergent holistic paradigm in modern physics and Eastern mysticism.

Capra, F. *The Turning Point. Science, Society and the Rising Culture*, Flamingo, 1983. A brilliant book; a turning point for many who read it. Explores how the mechanistic worldview of Newton and Descartes has led to the current global crisis and identifies an ongoing shift towards a holistic/systemic worldview.

Dammann, E. *The Future in our Hands*, Pergamon, 1979. Critical analysis of the unequal relationship between rich and poor countries and the responsibility of those with power to lead the movement towards global justice.

Elgin, D. *Voluntary Simplicity*, New York, William Morrow & Co. Inc., 1981. Maps out a way of life 'that is outwardly simple, inwardly rich' in its emphasis on frugal consumption, ecological awareness and personal growth.

Feather, F. (ed.) *Through the '80s. Thinking Globally, Acting Locally*, Washington, World Future Society, 1980. Valuable collection of essays by leading futurists and globalists.

Ferguson, M. *The Aquarian Conspiracy. Personal and Social Transformation in the 1980s*, Granada, 1982. An account, painstaking in its detailed research, of the emergence of a vastly enlarged concept of human potential amongst people in all walks of life which, the author argues, will eventually reach a critical point and lead to a radical change in Western culture.

Fromm, E. *To Have or to Be?*, Abacus, 1979. A clear, philosophical exposition of the distinction between the 'having' mode of existence (the materialistic mode dominant in modern industrial society) and the 'being' mode (the ascendency of human over material values). Some important insights for the global educator.

Handy, C. *The Future of Work*, Basil Blackwell, 1984. An important book for those struggling to reconcile the aims of education and the future needs of the workforce. His realistic forecast of the future of work leads to some sharp criticisms of current educational practice.

Higgins, R. *The Seventh Enemy. The Human Factor in the Global Crisis*, Pan, 1980. Indentifies seven main threats to human survival of which moral blindness coupled with political inertia is the greatest.

Houston, J. *The Possible Human: a Course in Enhancing your Physical, Mental and Creative Abilities*, Los Angeles, J.P. Tarcher, 1982. A literally mind-blowing journey into the enormity of one's own potential. Inspirational in style and authoritative in its scope, this book clearly charts the parallel pathways of personal and planetary development.

Lovelock, J.E. *Gaia. A New Look at Life on Earth*, Oxford University Press, 1982. Investigates the hypothesis that Earth's living matter forms a single complex system which defines and maintains conditions necessary for its survival.

Muller, R. *New Genesis. Shaping a Global Spirtuality*, New York, Image, 1984. Challenging, optimistic statement of the author's vision of the transition to global harmony. Chapter on 'The need for global education'.

Naisbitt, J. *Megatrends*, New York, Warner, 1984. Bestseller offering a 'road map to the 21st Century' through the exploration of ten key trends in US society.

Porritt, J. *Seeing Green. The Politics of Ecology Explained*, Basil Blackwell, 1984. A delightfully lucid survey of contemporary ecological thinking.

Rifkin, J. *Entropy. A New World View*, Paladin, 1985. A critique of the mechanistic and materialist worldview. Offers an alternative worldview grounded in the Entropy Law (which states that available energy is decreasing) and asks us to consider its social, political, economic and personal implications.

Robertson, J. *The Sane Alternative*, James Robertson, Spring Cottage, 9 New Road, Ironbridge, Shropshire TF8 7AU. Explores alternative futures and, in particular Robertson's conception of a Sane, Humane and Ecological future.

Roszak, T. *Person/Planet*, Granada, 1981. A brilliant and inspirational work linking together two powerful contemporary movements – the exploration of human potential and emergent planetary awareness.

Roszak, T. *Unfinished Animal. The Aquarian Frontier and the Evolution of Consciousness*, Faber & Faber, 1976. Explores the contemporary search to attain the fullness of human potential and to so rediscover elements of personality repressed by prevailing mechanistic culture.

Slaughter, R.A. 'Towards a critical futurism', *World Future Society Bulletin*, July/August 1984, pp. 19–25. 'Towards a critical futurism. Part two: revising and refining a futurist perspective', *World Future Society Bulletin*, September/October 1984, pp. 11–16. 'Towards a critical futurism. Part three: an outline of critical futurism', *World Future Society Bulletin*, September/October 1984, 17–21. A three-part survey of the futures field.

Sterling, S.R. 'Culture, ethics, and the environment – towards the new synthesis', *The Environmentalist*, Vol. 5, No. 3, 1985, pp. 197–206. Lucid outline of the mechanistic and holistic/systemic worldviews. Global ecological crisis attributed to the former.

Toffler, A. *Future Shock*, Pan, 1971. An influential bestseller when first published, the thrust of this book still deserves attention though its facts – and its forecasts – may be outdated.

Toffler, A. *The Third Wave*, Pan, 1981. An analysis of the new revolution – 'the high speed revolution' – now underway in global society and its social, political and personal implications.

Toffler, A. *Previews and Premises*, Pan, 1984. Toffler offers further reflections on the ideas elaborated in *Future Shock* and *The Third Wave*.

Wilber, K. (ed.) *The Holographic Paradigm and other Paradoxes*, Boulder, New Science Library, 1982. Essays by prominent scientists exploring the holistic nature of reality.

2 Global Education: General

Anderson, L. *Schooling and Citizenship in a Global Age: an Exploration of the Meaning and Significance of Global Education*, Bloomington, Indiana, Mid-America Program for Global Perspectives in Education, 1979. Seminal work analysing the ongoing transition to a global age and exploring the educational implications.

Aucott, J., Cox, H., Dodds, A. and Selby, D.E. 'World Studies on the runway – one year's progress towards a core curriculum', *The New Era*, Vol. 60, No. 6, November/December 1979, pp. 212–29. A detailed account of how a core World Studies course at a Leicestershire secondary school was planned.

Bridges, D. 'World studies in a multicultural society: some questions', *World Studies Journal*, Vol. 4, No. 1, Autumn 1982, pp. 7–9. Asks some fundamental questions about the weight that should be given to world studies in the curriculum and about the extent to which teachers have the right to shape students' choice in their construction of the world.

Brown, C. 'National identity and world studies', *Educational Review*, Vol. 36, No. 2, June 1984, pp. 149–56. Argues that world studies has failed to adequately address the fact that schools were set up to foster nationalism, national interest and cohesion.

Burtonwood, N. *The Culture Concept in Educational Studies*, NFER-Nelson, 1986. A challenging work asking teachers to place themselves and their students in a position to learn from other cultures. The message is particularly addressed to teachers in 'all-white' schools.

Cogan, J. (ed.) *The Global Classroom. An Annotated Bibliography for Elementary and Secondary Teachers*, University of Minnesota, 1984. A guide to reading, teaching resources, organisations and research in global education in the United States.

Collins, H.T. and Zakariya, S.B. (eds) *Getting Started in Global Education. A Primer for Principals and Teachers*, National Association of Elementary School Principals (1801 North Moore Street, Arlington, Virginia 22209), 1982. Useful collection of introductory essays on global education.

Corlett, J. and Parry, G. (eds) *Anthropology and the Teacher*, Association for the Teaching of Social Sciences, 1985. Collection of essays calling for anthropology in schools and exploring the relationship between anthropology and multicultural/anti-racist education.

Davey, A. *Learning to be Prejudiced*, Edward Arnold, 1983. Interesting research into the development and maintenance of prejudiced attitudes amongst young children; its conclusions about the organisation of learning in the school are important for global education.

Department of Education and Science *Education for All. The Report of the Committee of Inquiry into the Education of Children from Ethnic Minority Groups* (The Swann Report), HMSO, 1985. Its recommendations have attracted criticism from all quarters, but this Report does provide a comprehensive summary of a large body of research in the field of multicultural education.

Drake, P. (ed.) *World Studies Resource Guide*, Council for Education in World Citizenship, 1987. Comprehensive guide to resources, organisations and some publications in world studies and related fields.

Evans, A. and Rowe, J. (eds) 'Wider horizons', *Primary Education Review*, No. 15, Autumn 1982. Special number on world studies, peace and human rights education.

Fitch, R.M. and Svengalis, C.M. *Futures Unlimited: Teaching about Worlds to Come*, Washington, National Council for the Social Studies, Bulletin 59, 1979. Surveys the field of futurism and its application to the classroom. Useful chapter on innovative methods for teaching about the future.

Greig, S., Pike, G. and Selby, D.E. *Earthrights. Education as if the Planet Really Mattered*, Kogan Page/World Wildlife Fund UK, 1987. Offers an overview of current global problems and trends and explores the implications of the person/planet relationship for schools.

Haas, J.D. *Future Studies in the K-12 Curriculum*, Boulder, ERIC Clearinghouse for Social Studies/Social Education, 1980. A survey of futurist thinking and of the potential for future studies within the primary and secondary school.

Hanvey, R.G. *An Attainable Global Perspective*, New York, Global Perspectives in Education (218 East 18th Street, New York, NY 10003), 1982. Seminal pamphlet laying out five dimensions to a global perspective in education. The starting point for the development of our 'irreducible global perspective'.

Hatcher, R. 'The construction of world studies', *Multiracial Education*, Vol. 11, No. 1, Winter 1983, pp. 23–6. Argues that the world studies classroom excludes radical critiques of world capitalism.

Heater, D. *World Studies. Education for International Understanding in Britain*, Harrap, 1980. Interesting historical account and analysis of the development of the movement for the promotion of a global perspective in British education.

Hicks, D.W. and Slaughter, R.A. (eds) 'Future studies', *World Studies Journal*, Vol. 6, No. 1, 1985. Collection of mainly practical articles on the injection of a futures dimension into the primary, secondary and tertiary curriculum.

Hicks, D.W. and Townley, C. (eds) *Teaching World Studies. An Introduction to Global Perspectives in the Curriculum*, Longman, 1982. Offers a useful overview of world studies as it appeared to a number of key practitioners and proponents in the late 1970s.

Lamy, S.L. (ed.) 'Global perspectives education', *Educational Research Quarterly*, University of Southern California School of Education (Philips Hall, University Park, Los Angeles, California 90089-0031), Vol. 8, No. 1, 1983. Special issue exploring the theory and practice of global education.

Lister, I. *Teaching and Learning about Human Rights*, Strasbourg, Council of Europe, 1984. A useful overview of aims, content, methods and evaluation of human rights education.

Mehlinger, H.D., Hutson, H., Smith, B. and Wright, B. *Global Studies for American Schools*, Washington, National Education Association, undated. Offers a rationale for global studies across the curriculum plus practical approaches and teaching strategies.

Mullard, C. 'The problem of world studies in a multicultural society', *World Studies Journal*, Vol. 4, No. 1, Autumn 1982, pp. 13–17. Argues that world studies fails to give adequate consideration to issues of power and inequality in British society.

Pike, G. and Selby, D.E. *Scrutinizing Scruton. An Analysis of Roger Scruton's Attack on World Studies*, Centre for Global Education, Global Education Documentation Service No. 17. A response to Scruton's *World Studies: Education or Indoctrination?* (see below).

Remy, R.C. (ed.) 'Global education', *Theory into Practice*, College of Education, Ohio State University (149 Arps Hall, 1945 N. High Street, Columbus, Ohio 43210). Special issue offering a theoretical basis for global education and a range of articles on classroom practice and teacher education courses.

Scruton, R. *World Studies: Education or Indoctrination?*, Institute for European Defence and Strategic Studies, 1985. Scruton accuses world studies of limiting the range of classroom conclusions to those falling within the 'radical consensus' and of employing teaching techniques that manipulate feelings to the exclusion of rational thought.

Selby, D.E. 'World studies: towards a global perspective in the school curriculum', *Briefings*, No. 37, *The Social Science Teacher*, Vol. 13, No. 2, Spring 1984. Develops the argument for a global perspective and explores some relevant teaching/learning approaches and implementation strategies.

Slaughter, R.A. *Futures Education: Why we Need to Teach for Tomorrow*, Centre for Peace Studies Occasional Paper No. 5, undated. Theoretical overview of futurism and futures education combined with some ideas on the translation of theory into practice.

Smith, C. and Beck, J. (eds.) 'Multicultural education', *Cambridge Journal of Education*, Vol. 12, No. 2, Easter Term 1982. Special issue which includes an extremely useful contribution by Robin Richardson on the importance of group discussion activities in multicultural education.

Spender, D. *Invisible Women: the Schooling Scandal*, Writers and Readers, 1982. Illustrates the historical influence of dominant patriarchal values on education and the many ways in which schools continue to perpetuate these, despite the equal opportunities movement.

Twitchin, J. and Demuth, C. *Multi-cultural Education*, BBC, 1985. Perhaps the best overview of multicultural/anti-racist education in the United Kingdom. Strong practical emphasis.

Weiner, G. (ed.) *Just a Bunch of Girls*, Open University Press, 1985. Useful collection of articles on issues of sexism and racism in the education of girls.

Wellington, J.J. (ed.) *Controversial Issues in the Curriculum*, Basil Blackwell, 1986. Chapters on gender, peace and race issues, global education, religious education, education for employment and unemployment.

3 Global Education: Learning Process

Carpenter, S. *A Repertoire of Peacemaking Skills*, Peace Education Network of the Consortium on Peace Research, Education and Development, 1977. A useful annotated list of skills relevant to peace-making and examples of how they can be developed.

Cell, E. *Learning to Learn from Experience*, New York, State University Press, 1984. A thorough and clear exploration of the concept of experiential learning and the various ways in which people learn. A philosophical, rather than practical work.

Chase, L. *The Other Side of the Report Card: a How-to-do-it Programme for Affective Education*, Illinois, Scott, Foresman & Company, 1975. Some interesting ideas and techniques for realising affective goals in the classroom.

Elliot-Kemp, J. and Rogers, C. *The Effective Teacher: a Person-centred Development Guide*, PAVIC publications (Department of Education Services, Sheffield City Polytechnic), 1982. A theoretical examination of a person-centred approach to teaching.

Gregorc, A.F. *An Adult's Guide to Style*, Massachusetts, Gabriel Systems Inc., 1982. A guide to identifying preferred learning style.

Johnson, D.W. and Johnson, R.T. *Learning Together and Alone: Cooperation, Competition and Individualization*, New Jersey, Prentice-Hall, 1975. A readable and practically-oriented exploration of co-operative learning and its place alongside competitive and individualised learning. Research findings and guidelines for the classroom are included.

Johnson, D.W., Johnson, R.T., Holubec, E.J. and Roy, P. *Circles of Learning. Cooperation in the Classroom*, Alexandria, Association for Supervision and Curriculum Development (225 North Washington Street, Alexandria, Virginia 22314, USA), 1984. Useful summary of much of the Johnson brothers' research into co-operative learning.

Kurfman, D.G. (ed.) *Developing Decision-making Skills*, Virginia, National Council for the Social Studies (1515 Wilson Boulevard, Suite 101, Arlington, Virginia 22209, USA), 47th Yearbook, 1977. Some useful chapters analysing a range of skills necessary for informed decision-making and how they might be developed in schools.

McCarthy, B. *The 4 Mat System. Teaching to Learning Styles with Right/Left Mode Techniques*, Barrington, Illinois, Excel Inc., 1981. Offers teachers an easy-to-read and highly practical application of brain and learning style research. Highly recommended.

McCarthy, B. and Leflar, S. (eds) *4 Mat in Action. Creative Lesson Plans for Teaching to Learning Styles with Right/Left Mode Techniques*, Excel Inc., 1983. A collection of lesson plans based on the 4 Mat system covering all the key areas of the primary/secondary curriculum.

Parekh, B. 'The gifts of diversity', *Times Educational Supplement*, 29.3.1985, pp. 22–3. Important article suggesting that multicultural education is an indispensible component in the development of the imagination and of critical and divergent thinking skills.

Postman, N. and Weingartner, C. *Teaching as a Subversive Activity*, Penguin, 1971. Not a new book, but their ideas – and their forthright style of writing – are as refreshing and as relevant as ever. A 'must' for the global teacher!

Rogers, C. *Freedom to Learn for the 80s*, Ohio, Charles E. Merrill, 1983. A seminal book for the global teacher. Carl Rogers' writing continues to dominate person-centred education and to inspire its adherents. Contains an important chapter on research findings, including the monumental research programme of Aspy and Roebuck.

Whitaker, P. *Education as if People Really Mattered*, Centre for Peace Studies, Occasional Paper No. 3, 1983. Useful summary of some principal arguments for person-centred education.

Whitaker, P. 'The learning process', *World Studies Journal*, Vol. 5, No. 2, 1984. A succinct and practically-oriented introduction to person-centred approaches to teaching and learning; lots of ideas for the classroom.

Williams, L.V. *Teaching for the Two-sided Mind*, New Jersey, Prentice-Hall, 1983. An exploration of the relevance of split-brain theory for teaching and learning and some examples of classroom approaches which stimulate whole-brain learning.

4 Practical Handbooks

Borba, M. and C. *Self-esteem: A Classroom Affair*, Minneapolis, Winston Press, 1978. A treasure chest of ideas and activities for enhancing self-esteem, particularly suitable for the primary classroom.

Borba, M. and C. *Self-esteem: A Classroom Affair. Volume 2*, Minneapolis, Winston Press, 1982. More imaginative image-building ideas from the Borbas.

Brandes, D. and Ginnis, P. *A Guide to Student-centred Learning*, Basil Blackwell, 1986. A useful handbook for teachers wishing to develop person-centred approaches in their teaching. Some interesting classroom activities and cross-curricular ideas.

Brandes, D. and Phillips, H. *Gamesters' Handbook. 140 Games for Teachers and Group Leaders*, Hutchinson, 1979. A valuable source of interactive and participatory activities for the classroom, clearly and concisely described.

Canfield, J. and Wells, H.C. *100 Ways to Enhance Self-concept in the Classroom*, New Jersey, Prentice-Hall, 1976. Excellent ideas and techniques for image building in a beautifully presented book.

Coover, V., Esser, C., Deacon, E. and Moore, C. *Resource Manual for a Living Revolution*, Philadelphia, New Society Publishers, 1977. A manual designed for non-violent direct action training, it contains some interesting ideas on group work and some activities for the secondary classroom.

Fisher, S. and Hicks, D.W. *World Studies 8–13. A Teacher's Handbook*, Oliver & Boyd, 1985. Attractively presented and deservedly popular handbook of activities for top junior and lower secondary students. Contains a teacher education section.

Fisher, S., Magee, F. and Wetz, J. *Ideas into Action: Curriculum for a Changing World*, World Studies Project, 1980. Some interesting case studies of global education activities and courses at a range of educational levels.

Fyson, N.L. *The Development Puzzle*, Centre for World Development Education/Hodder & Stoughton, 1984. A best-selling source of information, resources and ideas for teaching about world development.

Gabelko, N.H. and Michaelis, J.U. *Reducing Adolescent Prejudice*, New York, Teachers College, Columbia University, 1981. Handbook which explores some theories of prejudice and discrimination through a range of case study-based exercises, suitable for secondary students.

Gregory, A. and Woollard, N. (eds) *Looking into Language: Diversity in the Classroom*, Support Service for Language and Intercultural Education (Lydford Road, Reading RG4 5QH), 1984. A collection of case studies, articles and practical ideas for exploring and utilising linguistic diversity in the classroom.

Hendricks, G. *The Centered Teacher*, New Jersey, Prentice-Hall, 1981. Centering activities, and the philosophy underpinning them, specifically designed for teachers and their students.

Hendricks, G. and Roberts, T.B. *The Second Centering Book*, New Jersey, Prentice-Hall, 1977. More centring activities for children, parents and teachers.

Hendricks, G. and Wills, R. *The Centering Book*, New Jersey, Prentice-Hall, 1975. Clear explanation of the need for centering and many practical ideas and activities to help children and adults become centered.

Hicks, D.W. *Minorities. A Teacher's Resource Book for the Multi-ethnic Curriculum*, Heinemann, 1981. Offers guidance to teachers on thinking about majority/minority issues plus teaching ideas/resources.

Hopson, B. and Scally, M. *Lifeskills Teaching*, McGraw-Hill, 1981. Comprehensive resource book for the promotion of personal skills development at all levels of education.

Jones, K. *Designing Your Own Simulations*, Methuen, 1985. Useful do-it-yourself guide to the construction and playing of simulation games, using some well-known games as case studies.

Judson, S. (ed.) *A Manual on Non-violence and Children*, Philadelphia Yearly Meeting of the Religious Society of Friends – Peace Committee/New Society Publishers, 1984. Excellent handbook of co-operative approaches and activities for the classroom, interspersed with the theory of non-violent action and case study examples.

Kinghorn, J.R. and Shaw, W.P. *Handbook for Global Education. A Working Manual*, Dayton, Charles F. Kettering Foundation, 1977. Designed to help facilitators conduct in-service 'We Agree' workshops in global education.

Liebmann, M. *Art Therapy for Groups: a Handbook of Themes, Games and Exercises*, Croom Helm, 1986. Some excellent ideas and co-operative activities for small groups involving art as a means of communication and self-expression.

Masheder, M. *Let's Co-operate. Activities and Ideas for Teachers and Parents of Children Aged 3–11*, Peace Education Project, 1986. Good collection of ideas and activities fostering co-operation, conflict resolution and positive self-esteem.

Orlick, T. *The Co-operative Sports and Games Book*, Writers and Readers, 1982. Co-operative activities for the classroom, the gymnasium and the sports field; some interesting versions of traditionally competitive games.

Pax Christi *Winners All*, Pax Christi (St Francis of Assisi Centre, Pottery Lane, London W11 4NG), 1980. Booklet outlining some affirmative and cooperative activities developed by the Non-Violence and Children Program (see Judson, S., ed., 1984).

Pepper, B., Myers, K. and Coyle/Dawkins, R. (eds) *Sex Equality and the Pastoral Curriculum*, ILEA Spencer Park Teachers' Centre (Trinity Road, London SW18), 1984. Handbook of activities designed to stimulate awareness of gender roles, assumptions and expectations.

Prutzman, P., Burger, M.L., Bodenhamer, G. and Stern, L. *The Friendly Classroom for a Small Planet*, New Jersey, Avery, 1978. A classic handbook for the co-operative classroom, full of imaginative ideas, activities and their underlying philosophy.

Richardson, R. *Learning for Change in World Society: Reflections, Activities and Resources*, World Studies Project, 1979. A goldmine of ideas, activities and readings which has inspired global teachers for ten years since its first edition.

Richardson, R., Flood, M. and Fisher, S. *Debate and Decision, Schools in a World of Change*, World Studies Project, 1980. An in-service handbook designed to raise teacher awareness of global issues and of their implications for school and classroom.

Schniedewind, N. and Davidson, E. *Open Minds to Equality. A Sourcebook of Learning Activities to Promote Race, Sex, Class, and Age Equity*, New Jersey, Prentice-Hall, 1983. Excellent collection of activities for primary or secondary use, organised to offer a year's curriculum or for use on a 'shopping basket' basis.

Slaughter, R.A. *Futures Across the Curriculum. A Handbook of Tools and Techniques*, Department of Educational Research, University of Lancaster, 1986. A practical workbook for introducing future studies into the upper secondary school.

Stevens, J.O. *Awareness*, New York, Bantam, 1973. Offers a range of awareness and imaginal activities for possible classroom use including guided fantasies and creative visualisations.

Stradling, R. Noctor, M. and Baines, B. *Teaching Controversial Issues*, Edward Arnold, 1984. Offers practical strategies for teachers of the 14–19 age range on handling controversial issues such as sexism, the nuclear debate and 'Third World' issues.

Taylor, N. and Bloodworth, J. *Living with Posters*, United Society for the Propagation of the Gospel, 1980. Offers a range of classroom activities based around posters.

Vitale, B.M. *Unicorns are Real: a Right-brained Approach to Learning*, California, Jalmar Press, 1982. Outlines in simple terms the theory of hemispheric specialisation and describes learning strategies designed to stimulate right-brained learning.

Weinstein, M. and Goodman, J. *Playfair. Everybody's Guide to Noncompetitive Play*, California, Impact Publishers, 1980. Co-operative games for all occasions described and evaluated.

Wilkinson, A. *It's not Fair!*, Christian Aid, 1985. Handbook containing information and activities on world development issues.

Wingate, J. *How to be a Peace-full Teacher*, Waterford, Friendly Press (61 Newtown Road, Newtown, Waterford, Ireland), 1985. Trust games, awareness exercises and action-oriented activities for the classroom.

Wolsk, D. *An Experience-centered Curriculum*, Unesco Educational Studies and Documents, No. 17, 1975. A collection of experiential units for the classroom with suggestions for their application to different school subjects.

5 Global Education Across The Curriculum

Allinson, B. *Art Education and Teaching about the Art of Asia, Africa, and Latin America*, Voluntary Committee on Overseas Aid and Development, 1972. Guidance on using 'Third World' art in the classroom.

Craft, A. and Bardell, G. (eds) *Curriculum Opportunities in a Multicultural Society*, Harper & Row, 1984. Sections on introducing a multicultural dimension into humanities, language and literature, mathematics and science, the arts and physical education.

Davies, B. (ed.) *The Changing World and RE*, Centre for World Development Education, 1979. Suggests topics and resources for introducing development issues into the RE curriculum.

Fien, J. and Gerber, R. (eds) *Teaching Geography for a Better World*, Brisbane, Australian Geography Teachers Association/Jacaranda Press, 1986. Lively collection of essays recommending the injection into the geography curriculum of issues such as human rights, gender, war and peace and unemployment.

Gill, D. (ed.) *Racist Society. Geography Curriculum*, Association for Curriculum Development in Geography, 1983. Collection of conference papers exploring the political context and ideological content of geography teaching in schools.

Hicks, D.W. 'Global perspectives in the curriculum: a geographical contribution', *Geography*, Vol. 64, Pt. 2, April 1979, pp. 104–14. A useful exploration of the important contribution geography can make towards promoting a global perspective in schools.

Klein, G. *Reading into Racism*, Routledge & Kegan Paul, 1985. Provides guidelines on how to identify and combat racist and ethnocentric bias in the materials used in classrooms and school libraries.

Lindsay, L. *Racism, Science Education and the Politics of Food*, All London Teachers Against Racism and Fascism (Room 216, Panther House, 38 Mount Pleasant, London, WC1 0AP), Occasional Paper No. 1, 1985. Discussion of anti-racist science and of an anti-racist approach to nutrition within the biology curriculum.

Lynch, J. (ed.) *Teaching in the Multicultural School*, Ward Lock, 1981. The main part of the book is comprised of eleven essays on how to introduce a multicultural dimension into different school subjects.

McKenzie, A. and Pike, G. (eds) 'Art in action: music, drama, visual arts', *World Studies Journal*, Vol. 5, No. 1, 1984. Articles on promoting a global perspective through the expressive and dramatic arts in the primary and secondary school.

Pike, G. and Starkey, H. (eds) 'World studies. Language and literature for understanding and transforming the world', *World Studies Journal*, Vol. 5, No. 3, 1984/5. Collection of articles describing how global, multicultural and anti-racist perspectives can be injected into primary and secondary language and literature classes.

Selby, D.E. (ed.) 'Global pi: world studies in the science and maths classroom', *World Studies Journal*, Vol. 5, No. 4, 1985. Collection of very practical articles describing how a global dimension can be injected into science and maths teaching.

Shah, S. (ed.) *The Contribution of History to Development Education*, The Historical Association Teaching of History Discussion Paper, No. 3, 1982. Explores the relationship between history and development education and offers two course descriptions.

Straker-Welds, M. (ed.) *Education for a Multicultural Society*, Bell & Hyman, 1984. Case studies from the Inner London Education Authority of attempts to develop a multicultural dimension across the curriculum at primary and secondary level.

General Index

Activities Index

(Entries in bold denote types of activities; numbers in bold refer to photographs)